Fresh from the Word

Rosalind Brown

CANTERBURY
PRESS

© Rosalind Brown, 2016

This collection first published in 2016 by the Canterbury Press Norwich
Editorial office
3rd Floor, Invicta House,
108–114 Golden Lane,
London EC1Y 0TG

Canterbury Press is an imprint of
Hymns Ancient & Modern Ltd (a registered charity)
13A Hellesdon Park Road, Norwich,
Norfolk, NR6 5DR, UK

www.canterburypress.co.uk

Scripture quotations are from the New Revised Standard Version
of the Bible, Anglicized Edition, copyright © 1989, 1995
by the Division of Christian Education of the National Council
of the Churches of Christ in the USA. Used by permission.
All rights reserved.

British Library Cataloguing in Publication data

A catalogue record for this book is available
from the British Library

ISBN 978 1 84825 853 2

Typeset by Mary Matthews
Printed and bound in Great Britain by

CPI Group (UK) Ltd, Croydon

Contents

CONTENTS

YEAR C

CONTENTS

In memory of my mother, Monica Brown, who read most of these reflections when they were first published, and of my father, Roy Brown, who did not but would have been both delighted and surprised that his daughter wrote a book like this

Introduction

The invitation to write the weekly column in the *Church Times* on the week's lectionary readings came out of the blue in an email. My immediate reaction was to say 'no' because I had more than enough deadlines and commitments to meet already. However, I was going on retreat the next day and, by the time I returned, I had prayed and thought my way round to being more open to the idea.

And so began three years of submitting 750 words each week, although I found it easier to work in batches covering a season – Advent, Lent – or a few weeks at a time so that I could see each weekly column in the context of what went before and after. In some ways it was like preparing a sermon, but there were significant differences. I was immersing myself in scripture on behalf of other people I did not know, who would read what I wrote rather than hear what I said, and would do so on their own at home or in their study rather than with others in the context of worship. I quickly found that while some sermons might contract down into a column, I could not simply expand the column to create my own sermon because the congregation at Durham Cathedral, or wherever I was preaching, required something specific for that occasion whereas the column was more generic. Sometimes people commented that they recognized the column they read on Friday in the sermon they heard on Sunday; at other times they were surprised that it was completely different.

When I accepted the invitation to write the columns, I asked that the Collect for the week should be printed because I believe the Collects are under-valued, both as prayers that all Christians can use during the week and as lenses or filters for the biblical readings. However, I was building in a problem for myself when it came to editing the columns into this book. Some explanation is needed if readers are not to be confused. The problem derives from the way the calendar for the church year works. From Advent Sunday to Candlemas (also known as the Presentation of Christ, the end of the Christmas season) and then from Ash Wednesday to Trinity Sunday there are fixed numbers of Sundays so the Collect and the readings match consistently year after year. But the use of the lunar calendar to set the date of Easter means that the number of Sundays in Ordinary Time, the periods between Candlemas and Ash Wednesday and then after Trinity, varies from year to year. The lectionary's provision of readings for Propers 1–25 are dated so that, for example, Proper 8 always provides the readings for the Sunday that falls between 26 June and 2 July. However, because of the changing date of Easter, this Proper 8 calendar week was the sixth Sunday after Trinity in 2013, the third Sunday after Trinity in 2014, and will be other Sundays after Trinity in other years. The same variation applies to the number of Sundays before Lent – the earlier Easter is the fewer there are of them, and unused Propers can be transferred to the end of the Sundays after Trinity if needed. While this has the advantage that we hear different combinations of readings and the Collect from year to year, it complicates the process of editing columns written for three specific years into a book for future use.

I wrote these columns between Advent Sunday 2011 and the Sunday before Advent 2014; Year A readings were written in 2013–14, Year B in 2011–12 and Year C in 2012–13. The particular combination of Propers and Sundays before Lent or after Trinity therefore reflects those three specific years. I have chosen to use the church year to set the shape of Ordinary Time, so the reflections are listed as Sundays after Trinity. The changing date of Easter means that the particular matching of Collect and Proper for which I wrote will not always apply, so if this book is being used as an aid to sermon preparation, preachers should not assume the same Collect for the Propers. I have added reflections for the Propers that were not used in 2011–2014 and have paired them with the Collect for the Sundays before Lent or the First Sunday after Trinity. If the Sunday between 24 and 28 May follows Trinity Sunday, Proper 3 is used.

The experience of writing the columns for three years was a privilege for which, both at the time and with hindsight, I was (mostly!) grateful, not least because it was good for my own spiritual life. The many letters and emails that arrived over the three years expressing appreciation for what I had written were an encouragement and bonus.

I would like to express my thanks to my clergy colleagues at Durham Cathedral for their support and consistent example of fine preaching that is deeply rooted in scripture and daily life. The same thanks go to the worshipping community who are invariably both demanding and encouraging of those of us who preach. They listen hard and respond actively with insight and honesty, and are generous with their appreciation. They have, perhaps unknowingly to them, influenced what lies within these pages. I hope that this book will continue to inspire and encourage all people to engage with scripture for themselves.

Rosalind Brown
Durham Cathedral,
Feast of the Blessed Virgin Mary, 15 August 2015

Year A

Advent Sunday

Isaiah 2.1–5; Romans 13.11–14; Matthew 24.36–44

ADVENT: STEADY AS WE GO

Almighty God, give us grace to cast away the works of darkness and to put on the armour of light, now in the time of this mortal life, in which your Son Jesus Christ came to us in great humility; that on the last day, when he shall come again in his glorious majesty to judge the living and the dead, we may rise to the life immortal; through him who is alive and reigns with you, in the unity of the Holy Spirit, one God, now and for ever. Amen.

The readings in Advent have a different flavour in each of the three liturgical years. Last year, with Luke as the controlling Gospel, we entered Advent with hope and joy as promises are realized. The first reading began, 'The days are surely coming when I will fulfil the promise I made.' Next year, Advent opens with Isaiah's cry, 'O that you would tear open the heavens and come down,' as Mark roars on to the scene like the lion that is his Gospel symbol, disrupting any complacency about the status quo. This year, anticipating a year in Matthew's company, the first spoken words we hear come from Isaiah, 'Come, let us go up to the mountain of the Lord, that he may teach us his paths and that we may walk in his paths.'

There is a determined steadiness about this compared to the other two openings to Advent. To be walking, by definition, we have to have at least one foot on the ground at all times. Otherwise we are not walking but running, which we will come to next week (and, the following week, to being unable to do either). Walking involves keeping on keeping on, covering the ground steadily and rhythmically, staying in touch with the world. No wonder it functions as a metaphor for discipleship.

Advent this year will keep taking us back to our discipleship, drawing us to be attentive first to God and then to the way we live. We begin with Isaiah asking his hearers to come to the Lord, to learn from him, to walk with him. Then Paul exhorts Roman Christians, living at the heart of the pagan empire and thus very conscious of their vulnerability, to wake from sleep, lay aside the works of darkness, put on the armour of light and live honourably. Jesus, speaking to his disciples of cataclysmic and cosmic events when the Son of Man comes, couched his warning in very domestic terms – working in the field, grinding meal, securing the house against a thief. This is down-to-earth stuff.

In all three readings the cosmic and the ordinary belong in the same sentence. On the one hand, God is at work on the large scale, sending instruction out of Zion, judging the nations, arbitrating for many peoples – not just the people of Israel. The bottom line is that salvation is nearer than at any time in the past. The Son of Man is coming and life as we know it will be swept away.

On the other hand, we are part of this story too. It matters that we learn God's ways and walk in his paths, that we live honourably, not gratifying the desires of the flesh, keeping awake and being ready for the Lord's coming. Abandoning weapons of war and turning them into farm implements for food production is a vivid image: in war the opposite usually happens but, under God's sway, nations will stop learning war and we will live peacefully with one another.

Just what do we do day by day to live as people of Advent hope? Our task is to work out how to live as though the Lord is coming soon. There are nearly 100 references in the Bible to what is to be 'put on', many of them referring to the clothing of Aaron and the priests which was the public expression of their vocation, others to the people of God putting on the garments of salvation or sackcloth for repentance. What we put on signifies our purpose in life. This week, as people of Advent hope, we are told to put on two things, the armour of light (hints of Ephesians 6) and the Lord Jesus.

The Collect is an essential prayer with which to begin Advent. We need God's grace to cast away the works of darkness and put on the armour of light. There is no escaping the connection between glorious Advent hope and how we live day by day. Walking steadily in the ways of the Lord, one foot on the ground, appropriately dressed and equipped for our vocation, is the way to begin.

Second Sunday of Advent

Isaiah 11.1–10; Romans 15.4–13; Matthew 3.1–12

IT'S TIME TO RUN THE RACE

> *O Lord, raise up, we pray, your power and come among us, and with great might succour us; that whereas, through our sins and wickedness we are grievously hindered in running the race that is set before us, your bountiful grace and mercy may speedily help and deliver us; through Jesus Christ your Son our Lord, to whom with you and the Holy Spirit, be honour and glory, now and for ever. Amen.*

This Advent the readings focus on discipleship. John the Baptist's words are straight to the point, but only Matthew gives the reason for his call to repent: the Kingdom of heaven has come near, bringing with it a new citizenship, a distinctive way of life.

Before we duck the outburst against the brood of vipers by saying that we are not Pharisees and Sadducees, we might ponder if we are their equivalent today, since John rooted their problems in their presumption on God's good will towards them. We come unstuck with the acknowledgement in the Collect that we are grievously hindered by our sins and wickedness (note the 'grievously') in running the race that is set before us. That is familiar territory even for the most faithful Christian; and Paul had already despaired that did not understand his own actions, doing what he hated rather than what he wanted (Romans 7.15).

The Collect alludes to our presumption on God's good will towards us. Like last week, we predicate our petition on God's grace. However, everything is more urgent as new, vivid words enter our vocabulary: having walked in God's ways last week, now we are running and want God to come speedily. There is no waiting for the rescue service to come to our aid when we break down; like Habakkuk and Job from whom we heard in the Sundays before Advent, we want God to come as soon as we cry. Are we being as presumptuous as the Pharisees or faithful in taking our troubles to God?

In response, all three readings steer us in the direction of God's nature and actions. God is righteous; all else flows from that. So God judges the poor with righteousness and the meek with equity. However, God's righteousness cuts both ways and, confronted by it, the world experiences judgement because God will strike the earth with the rod of his mouth and will kill the wicked with the breath of his lips. Recalling that Jesus said we are to live by every word from God's mouth (Matthew 4.4), we are back to discipleship.

There are at least two consequences to this. First, in Isaiah, as part of God's righteousness breaking into our world, nature is healed: wolves and lambs get on with each other, cows and bears share grazing land without incident, and toddlers play with poisonous snakes. That is a miracle in itself but there is more because, second, the way we live is to be transformed. We are to welcome one another as Christ has welcomed us, to bear fruit worthy of repentance. What is that fruit? Paul describes it in more detail when writing to the Galatians; here it is expressed as we live in harmony with one another, welcoming each another. That thought leads Paul to recall words of rejoicing and praise because as a result all sorts of unlikely people – in his case, the Gentiles – will glorify God.

Benedict, who, like Paul, was strong on living in harmony and welcoming people, also had something to say about running. For 'monastic life' we can substitute 'Christian life':

> But if, for good reason, for the amendment of evil habit or the preservation of charity, there be some strictness of discipline, do not be at once dismayed and run away from the way of salvation, of which the entrance must needs be narrow. But, as we progress in our monastic life and in faith, our hearts shall be enlarged, and we shall run with unspeakable sweetness of love into the way of God's commandments; so that, never abandoning his rule but persevering in his teaching in the monastery until death, we shall share by patience in the sufferings of Christ, that we may deserve to be partakers also of his kingdom. (*The Rule of St Benedict*, Prologue)

Advent's promise is that God will enlarge our hearts so that, more and more, we can delight to run in the way of God's commandments. As we run, we will find that God's righteousness fills us with joy and peace in believing so that we abound in hope. Repentance, hope and rejoicing belong together.

Rejoice! Rejoice! Emmanuel shall come to thee!

Third Sunday of Advent

Isaiah 35.1–10; James 5.7–10; Matthew 11.2–11

PREPARATION'S UNSEEN FRUITS

O Lord Jesus Christ, who at your first coming sent your messenger to prepare the way before you: grant that the ministers and stewards of your mysteries may likewise so prepare and make ready your way by turning the hearts of the disobedient to the wisdom of the just, that at your second coming to judge the world we may be found an acceptable people in your sight; for you are alive and reign with the Father in the unity of the Holy Spirit, one God, now and for ever. Amen.

If the first Sunday of Advent was about walking in the Lord's paths and the second Sunday was about running the race set before us, then the third Sunday comes as something of a jolt. The readings take us into a world where we are not determinants of our actions but have to learn to wait.

James introduces the farmer who has to be patient with his precious crop. Watering, weeding and fertilizing it, yes; digging it up to see what is happening, no. Rain, beyond his control, will come in due season. The lesson James draws from this? To be patient we must strengthen our hearts, knowing that waiting is not wasted time. Then James strings together some seemingly disjointed thoughts about not grumbling, being judged, enduring suffering and speaking in the name of the Lord. There is a sermon about patience waiting to be unpacked in those verses.

The Gospel is also about patience, but approaches it from a different angle. Last week we heard John the Baptist in full flow, unafraid to call religious leaders a brood of vipers. Now we find him, in prison for crossing Herod, voicing his doubts. He was learning patience the hard way because, for someone used to the wide open spaces, solitude and freedom of the wilderness, being shackled in a dungeon must have been dreadful.

Having proclaimed Jesus as the One who is to come, he was hearing reports of what Jesus was doing. He needed to hear from Jesus himself if he really was the Messiah or if he, John, had based his life on a ghastly mistake. Jesus's response is fascinating. Refusing to answer 'yes' or 'no', he challenged John by sending his disciples back with stories of what they saw and heard.

Jesus couched his reply using the language of Isaiah's vision which we hear this week and in Isaiah 61.1 where there is the significant addition of the proclamation of liberty for the captives and release to the prisoners. By adding 'And blessed is he who takes no offence at me' to the end of this litany of salvation, Jesus's implicit challenge to John was: 'You hear of me doing the things the Messiah will do, but I have not mentioned release for prisoners and I have not secured your release. Do you nevertheless believe I am the one who is to come?'

Could John, forced to do nothing in uncongenial surroundings, learn the farmer's patience of which James wrote? Having sown the seed when he was a free man, he had to wait in prison while it grew. Can we, facing whatever feels like unanswered prayer, learn similar patience?

Perversely, Jesus waited until John's disciples left before affirming John's vocation and ministry to the crowds. John never heard those words which would have been so comforting to him. Instead, he only heard the challenge to believe despite Jesus not doing, for him, the very thing the Messiah was supposed to do.

If we live faithfully, much of our ministry involves sowing seeds, the fruit of which we never see. That is a particular ministry of cathedrals with anonymous visitors but it is also true of the smallest parish church and of each of us personally. We have to learn to wait patiently for the gospel to bear fruit. At Durham Cathedral we encourage ourselves by collecting the stories we hear of the fruit of seeds sown years earlier. I think, for example, of the chaplain who met someone who once prayed in the Cathedral for the gift of a baby when, apparently, conception was not possible. The family was in the Cathedral to celebrate that prayed-for child's graduation from the University. Their comment? 'We are here to say thank you to God.'

What is the key phrase in this week's readings? 'Strengthen' must be a strong contender. It is hard, but possible, to piece together the bigger picture when our own circumstances challenge the faithfulness of God. Then we can strengthen ourselves and one another – whether it is hands, knees (Isaiah) or hearts (James) that are failing. Advent is about learning to wait strongly.

Fourth Sunday of Advent

Isaiah 7.10–16; Romans 1.1–7; Matthew 1.18–25

EMMANUEL, GOD IS WITH US

God our redeemer, who prepared the Blessed Virgin Mary to be the mother of your Son: grant that, as she looked for his coming as our saviour, so we may be ready to greet him when he comes again as our judge; who is alive and reigns with you, in the unity of the Holy Spirit, one God, now and for ever. Amen.

Ahaz and Joseph were both up against the inscrutability of God. One was a rebellious king who exhausted God and stood on the brink of disaster, the other a righteous man, soon to be married, whose carpentry business was all the excitement he expected in life. Both were thrown into turmoil when God came to them.

Ahaz's reign was marked by political and military insecurity. He had declined to join a military alliance of smaller nations who were in the way of the Assyrians' march to conquer Egypt. In retaliation, the other kings threatened to invade Judah. Ahaz and his people were terrified as God faced him with a crisis of trust.

The story of Ahaz's reign has no redeeming moment, just rebellious disobedience and God's resulting anger: simple cause and effect, it seems. But Isaiah's account throws a spanner into the works because God offered Ahaz the opportunity to ask for a sign to test God's faithfulness, a down payment on God's intervention in the situation. Given the number of times the people of Israel had been rebuked for testing God Ahaz's refusal sounds wise, but it masks a failure to distinguish between faithful and rebellious testing of God. His pious answer was a rebellious refusal to risk belief in God, a refusal to experience the love God longed to lavish.

The invitation to Ahaz to ask for a sign was double-edged; he was invited to test God, to prove God true, but was himself being tested by God's word (Psalm 105.19). In a mystery novel, clues are scattered throughout the book. God does that with Ahaz: a clue here, 'ask me for a sign'; a clue there, 'a child's name'. But Ahaz, conditioned by a lifetime of rebelliously ignoring God, could not or would not seize this moment of grace. God asked Ahaz to pay attention to children's names; if he could not hear the subtext of Isaiah's son's name, 'A remnant shall return', God spelled it out more clearly through another child's name: 'God is with us'. The king's actions tell us he did not believe this, but an unnamed young woman in his troubled kingdom could and did.

Ahaz's life was marked by rebellion against God. So, given his refractory history, why was Ahaz offered a sign of God's presence and power while Joseph was not? Joseph was righteous and it would be so easy for the angels, visiting several people in the Nazareth and Bethlehem area, to put in an appearance to him as well and make it all clear from the beginning. Instead Joseph faced the dilemma of what to do when his uprightness was rewarded with seeming disaster.

Being righteous, Joseph tried to piece his jigsaw puzzle together using the template of what he knew of the law of God and his compassion for Mary. But God was doing something new and Joseph was working with the wrong picture for his jigsaw. God was putting the finishing touches to a new one. The God who in last week's Old Testament reading was a highway engineer making new ways through the wilderness, a gardener turning deserts into flower gardens, was now the artist painting a new perspective of the age-old promise of the Messiah. Joseph had to catch up with God.

The initial silence of God to Joseph was just as demanding for him as was the clarity of God's word to Ahaz. God was testing both. 'Are you going to act faithfully? Rebellious Ahaz, can you live with my clear word? Righteous Joseph, can you live with my silence?'

Joseph's fidelity reminds us that times of silence or awkward questions can be the prelude to new works of God in our lives. Advent is a time of preparation for the coming of God, a time to pay attention to the clues that God is active, to notice the meaning of things we might take for granted, a time to practise the scales of fidelity that will enable us to play the new music when God puts it in front of us, when suddenly our night sky is torn apart by angels singing 'Glory to God in the highest and peace to his people on earth.'

Emmanuel, God is with us. Thanks be to God.

Christmas Day

Isaiah 52.7–10; Hebrews 1.1–12; John 1.1–14

A GLIMPSE OF HEAVENLY BLISS

Almighty God, you have given us your only-begotten Son to take our nature upon him and as at this time to be born of a pure virgin: grant that we, who have been born again and made your children by adoption and grace, may daily be renewed by your Holy Spirit; through Jesus Christ our Lord. Amen.

Unlike Matthew and Luke, John's Gospel does not begin with narrative stories of Nazareth and Bethlehem told from human perspectives, but sets a theological context, what we might say is God's-eye view.

We hear John's words this Christmas alongside Isaiah's affirmation to the exiled people that God reigns, that God is a God of salvation and comfort, and alongside the bold assertion in the epistle that God has spoken to us through a Son, through whom he created the world. Hebrews, like John's Gospel, opens with its gaze firmly on heavenly things. So it stresses the divinity of the Son; that he sits at the right hand of the majesty on high; that he is God enthroned for ever and ever. Taken on its own, this reading suggests little need for this heavenly way of life to engage with the world. In one sense, it appears self-sufficient.

Except, and this is the big exception, 'In these last days God has spoken to us through a Son.' That changes everything. That is why we celebrate Christmas. There is an impulse in the Godhead to embrace the world in love, despite human rejection of God's previous reaching out through the prophets. A Hasidic tale explores this theme. It tells how the grandson of Rabbi Baruch, Yechiel, was playing hide-and-seek with a friend. He hid and waited for his friend to search for him. After some time, during which nothing happened, he came out of his hiding place and could not find his friend. It dawned on him that his friend had not bothered to look for him. Distraught, he ran to his grandfather, sobbing about his heartless friend. Rabbi Baruch wept too as he said, 'O, Yechiel. That's exactly what the Almighty Himself says: "I hide myself but nobody wants to look for me."'

The whole point of hide-and-seek is that we are found. Christmas is the moment when we celebrate the mutual joy, with God, that God has looked for us and we are found through the incarnation of the Son.

Jaroslav Vajda, one of the great hymn-writers of recent years, wrote a lovely, imaginative hymn ('Before the marvel of this night') which explores, poetically, God's motivation in sharing the bliss of heaven with the sleeping world of earth. Vajda imagines God giving the angels their marching (flying?) orders to go to the shepherds, telling them to 'tear the sky apart with light' and, evocatively, to

Give earth a glimpse of heavenly bliss,
A teasing taste of what they miss:
Sing bliss, sing endless bliss.

Vajda ends his hymn by putting these words on to God's lips:

The love that we have always known,
Our constant joy and endless light,
Now to the loveless world be shown,
Now break upon its deathly night.
Into one song compress the love
That rules our universe above.
Sing love … sing God is love.
Copyright © 1981, Concordia Publishing House.
Used with permission.

'Into one song compress the love that rules our universe above.' Christmas is divine love compressed into a song that humans can hear. A story that humans can tell and retell, as we do Christmas by Christmas. Each year we hear that 'teasing taste of what we miss' when we hear that the Word became flesh and lived among us and we have seen his glory; that to all who received him he gave power to become children of God. Another hymn-writer, Samuel Crossman, sang of 'love to the loveless shown that they might lovely be'. Love, strong and passionate and tender love, is what God speaks to us through his Son, Jesus Christ.

There is no reason for the joy and hope of Christmas to be a one-night wonder. Christmas is the love of God compressed into one song and, with that love, comes an invitation to sing it for the rest of our lives in a tragically loveless world, that it might lovely be. The Word dwells among us. In the post-communion prayer we pray, 'May the light of faith illumine our hearts and shine in our words and deeds.' Only then will people in the places of tragedy across the world know that the Word of God dwells with them.

First Sunday of Christmas

Isaiah 63.7–9; Hebrews 2.10–18; Matthew 2.13–23

DARING TO LIGHT CANDLES IN THE DARKNESS

Almighty God, who wonderfully created us in your own image and yet more wonderfully restored us through your Son Jesus Christ: grant that, as he came to share in our humanity, so we may share the life of his divinity; who is alive and reigns with you, in the unity of the Holy Spirit, one God, now and for ever. Amen.

A wise yet demanding juxtaposition of readings plunges us, just days after Christmas with its songs of heavenly bliss, into the violence of the world into which the Son of God was born. There can be no cocoon that isolates Christmas from the harsh realities of daily life.

After two millennia, the massacre in Bethlehem is all too familiar in its horror. In November 2013 the Oxford Research Group reported that over 1000 children had been deliberately killed in Syria and, shockingly, 112 – including infants – were first tortured. The same week, *The Guardian* (23 November 2013) quoted a father in the Central African Republic: 'They started to attack my [four-year-old] son. They tried to shoot him but the gun was not working. So they slit his throat instead. What threat does this child pose …?'

This is the world in which we hear this Sunday's readings. If Matthew tells the story, Hebrews gives a theological commentary: God has made the pioneer of our salvation perfect through suffering which began almost immediately; the Son, through whom God speaks to us, was in danger as a toddler and Joseph did not wait for farewells before becoming a refugee.

It is likely that Joseph and Mary settled with the Jewish community in Egypt. Coptic Christians in Egypt are proud that their country offered sanctuary to the Son of God; that the place of slavery and deliverance became the place of sanctuary and deliverance. The incarnation took place in the context of fear for survival, fear that Joseph and Mary continued to feel even back in Israel.

Again, Hebrews and Isaiah provide theological insights into this very human story: these were people living with the fear of death, who were being tested and who therefore were the recipients of God's mercy, steadfast love and help, however fragile their existence felt at the time. No messenger or angel would do: in his love and pity God redeemed his people and carried them all the days of old. Through his ultimate death, the Son destroyed the one who had the power of death. His was a cosmic battle.

In the Collect, we pray that as Jesus Christ came to share in our humanity, so we may share the life of his divinity. A world of theology lies behind that prayer, which we pray this Sunday through the lens of the vulnerability of a young child to violence and massacre. No one can accuse God of ignoring the cruelty and suffering of the world so, if we share his life, we cannot ignore what God embraces in his love and pity.

Our problem is that, faced with such horrors, paralysis sets in and we can feel powerless to do anything. Just where do we start? When that happens, we have Joseph's example of doing what he could when God asked him to act, and we can go back to the words we heard at the beginning of Advent, 'Let us walk in the light of the Lord' (Isaiah 2.5). Our response begins with the next step, however small that might be. When we walk, we keep one foot on the ground of our sorrowful world.

At Yad Vashem memorial in Jerusalem six candles, representing the 1.5 million children killed in the Holocaust, are reflected hundreds of times in mirrors. My response to seeing this was a hymn-prayer:

Rachel's voice from Ramah, weeping
as the little children die,
still across the land is sweeping
in the parents' anguished cry.

Jesus, you sought consolation
as you faced the awful cross,
and your cry of desolation
shouts the terror of its loss.

Light a candle in the darkness,
multiply its flickering light,
let it speak in solemn starkness
through the dark of evil's night.

Still today the children's crying,
unwiped tears and broken hearts,
ask of us much more than sighing,
plead for justice grace imparts.

So the cries of lamentation,
Rachel's weeping down the years,
meet, in us, God's inclination
to redeem the mothers' tears.

Light a candle in the darkness,
Multiply its flickering light,
Let it speak in simple starkness
Of new hope born in the night.

Copyright © 1996 Rosalind Brown

On Christmas Day we heard that the light shines in the darkness and the darkness has not overcome it. If we believe that, we can dare to light candles in the darkness of our world.

Second Sunday of Christmas

Jeremiah 31.7–14; Ephesians 1.3–14; John 1.[1–9] 10–18

POWER TO BE GOD'S CHILDREN

> *Almighty God, in the birth of your Son you have poured on us the new light of your incarnate Word, and shown us the fullness of your love: help us to walk in his light and dwell in his love that we may know the fullness of his joy, who is alive and reigns with you, in the unity of the Holy Spirit, one God, now and for ever. Amen.*

This Sunday, we hear the Christmas Day Gospel in an extended form, alongside different readings and a different Collect. From exile, Jeremiah records how God has saved, redeemed, and gathered his sheep, and led them back home.

Yet, in Christ, there is still more. Ephesians falls over itself in a breathless paean of praise about every blessing, being chosen in Christ before the foundation of the world, being redeemed, chosen for adoption as children, experiencing God's good pleasure in Christ, and more, and more … When the author finally pauses for breath, it is to conclude that all this is given so that we might live for the praise of his glory. That leads us to John, who tells us that we have seen his glory, full of grace and truth.

John's opening, 'In the beginning', echoes Genesis. Scientists' discoveries about the scale and beauty of the cosmos are mind-boggling enough for us to cope with, but 'In the beginning was the Word' takes us beyond the beginning of created time, as we know it, to eternity. The ancient hymn, 'Of the Father's heart begotten', gives poetic voice to this mystery.

Part way through John's theological litany of wonder, amazingly, human time and space are suddenly interjected, and become part of the story: 'There was a man sent from God whose name was John.' God's eternal light and life are let loose in the world that we know. We are people upon whom the riches of God's grace are lavished, blessings of which Jeremiah's exiles were promised a foretaste.

John's prologue is like an overture, playing phrases of themes that will be repeated and developed richly throughout his Gospel. 'The light shines in the darkness' looks forward to other references to light and darkness. That the Word is 'the true light' points to another of John's themes: that of truth and what is true.

The statement that the Word 'came to what was his own and his own people did not accept him' is a succinct summary of the first half of John's Gospel. The prologue then turns on verse 12, 'But to all who received him, who believed in his name, he gave power to become children of God.' This is a theme that Jesus explored with Nicodemus and the Samaritan woman.

The Old Testament resounds with the steadfast love of the Lord, now revealed and shared in the Son, through whom we have received grace upon grace. John writes of the Word's dwelling, or pitching his tent, among us. That recalls God's presence in the tabernacle, as his people journeyed through the wilderness (Exodus 25.8), and the prophets' words that God would again pitch his tent among the people (Ezekiel 37.27; Zechariah 2.10). Jeremiah glimpsed this when speaking of God's leading and gathering his scattered people.

Another Old Testament theme repeated in this overture is that of glory (Exodus 24.16, 40.34–35). 'We have seen his glory,' writes John. He does not, like the other Gospel-writers, record the revelation of that glory in the transfiguration, but instead locates the revelation of God's glory in Jesus's signs (John 2.11), and ultimately in the crucifixion (John 12.23, 13.32, 17.1).

This theological overture serves a similar purpose to that of the (quite different) prologue to Job. Both tell the reader more than the people in the subsequent story know; they have to discover it for themselves as it unfolds. John does not name Jesus until the very end of the prologue, and immediately says that no one has ever seen God, not even Moses (Exodus 33.18–23) through whom the law was given. The Son, however, has made him known, and this is the lens that John gives, through which his readers can interpret what they read (John 20.31).

In the light of all this wonder, we pray to walk in God's light, and to dwell in his love. One way to do this afresh, before Christmas ends, is to read through John's Gospel, soaking up the wonderful themes with which he tantalizes us in the prologue.

Writing what we notice by hand (dare I suggest, on good quality paper, with a fountain pen?) slows us down, and allows us to absorb what we record in a way that typing on to a computer screen cannot. Take time to savour God's Christmas gift to you, then perhaps write your own version of Ephesians' outburst of praise.

Epiphany

Isaiah 60.1–6; Ephesians 3.1–12; Matthew 2.1–12

LESSONS FOR THE FINAL MILE

O God, who by the leading of a star manifested your only Son to the peoples of the earth: mercifully grant that we, who know you now by faith, may at last behold your glory face to face; through Jesus Christ our Lord. Amen.

The superbly evocative Christmas poem, 'Leap, world, for joy' by Jaroslav Vajda, includes the invitation: 'Let manger, star and angel choir unhinge us from our sleep and sorrows.' We have heard how the manger and the angels unhinge the shepherds, but what does it mean to be unhinged by a star? Matthew supplies a story. It has something to do with being thrown off balance into risky living.

One year, the day after Epiphany, like the Wise Men, I set off on the longest journey I had ever made: to Australia and New Zealand. For me, unlike them, there was not much risk, because I had everything arranged. They had no travel agent to sort things out; they did not know exactly where they were going, or how long they would be away; they had to fend for themselves rather than arrive for scheduled flights and prearranged hospitality. They probably travelled with a group of merchants for safety, and were unlikely to be regular travellers. So this is a story of an important venture, even a crazy enterprise. Whereas I responded to an invitation, the Wise Men were motivated by curiosity rather than religious commitment – although why foreigners would want to pay homage to a Jewish king is unexplained, except that, for Matthew, it fulfilled Isaiah's prophecy. They were not particularly reputable people but pagan star-gazers or astrologers – the word Matthew uses could be used of charlatans and quacks – and not the sort of people we expect to populate the Bible. A particular star caught their attention and unhinged them enough so that they decided to investigate since, in their interpretative framework, it meant a king.

Their visit to Herod was, with hindsight, a bumbling mistake; so were they really models of wisdom? It is like showing up at passport control in a country ruled by a dictator, and asking to be taken to the leader of the underground resistance that will overthrow him. Their visit lit the blue touch-paper. But they seemed naïvely unaware of the politics of the situation, and, had God not warned them, they would have gone back to Herod.

Despite the carol in which we sing lustily about the star's leading them, Matthew implies that the star disappeared after they first saw it – hence their joy when it reappeared after the potentially disastrous visit to Herod. Until then, they had to travel without its guidance, using their own initiative, living in the light of their hunch that this was worthwhile. Life can be like that: we set out with conviction on a course of action, but soon find ourselves thrown on to our own resources, and beginning to doubt. Once the star started to guide them again, what began as a journey of curiosity, even nosiness, ended up as a pilgrimage, because they rode into God's frame of reference when they encountered the Hebrew scriptures which pointed them to a house in a small town, Bethlehem. Quests can turn into pilgrimages, and pilgrimages can sometimes disabuse us of preconceptions about where God is to be found.

On seeing a baby, most of us, with the honourable exception of grandparents, do not kneel down and pay homage. But that is why these men came all this way. I like to think that they were changed by the experience. Then they had a dream, and returned by another road. Sometimes, especially on pilgrimage, it is the return journey that is more important than the outward one, because it is on the return journey that we do the work of reflection on what we have experienced and begin to integrate it with the life to which we are returning at home.

The Christmas stories can become too familiar. However we read them, they should challenge us, and unhinge us from our sleep and sorrows, because they are startlingly good news. They invite us to risk the first step, to keep going when we feel we are on our own in strange territory, remembering that the meaning might be in the final hard mile.

In his poem 'Twelfth Night' Laurie Lee wrote, evocatively, of 'lessons for the final mile of pilgrim kings'. The revelations of Epiphany are for those who keep going for the mile that is still left, the mile after our first attempt to arrive has failed, the mile to the unexpected encounter.

The Baptism of Christ,
First Sunday of Epiphany
Isaiah 42.1–9; Acts 10.34–43; Matthew 3.13–17

A VOICE FROM HEAVEN

Eternal Father, who at the baptism of Jesus revealed him to be your Son, anointing him with the Holy Spirit: grant to us, who are born again by water and the Spirit, that we may be faithful to our calling as your adopted children; through Jesus Christ our Lord. Amen.

If you are going to announce the arrival of someone important, how do you do it? Spin doctors would be appalled at the thought of choosing a river in a wilderness and a crowd of ordinary people who cannot recognize the person in their midst. But God rarely goes for the predictable grand announcement, seeming to prefer popping up in unexpected places. So the first people to hear of Jesus's birth were shepherds, and now Isaiah tells us that God's servant will not cry out or make himself heard in the street. In the absence of fanfare, we are challenged to the Benedictine virtue of listening carefully.

The readings this week take us to pivotal moments when people grasped the implications of God's unexpected presence in their midst. Peter is in the middle of discovering that Gentiles as well as Jews can receive God's grace. 'I truly perceive that God shows no partiality' sounds like his giving voice for the first time to a realization that had been growing in him since his extraordinary vision on a roof top (Acts 10.9–16). He had to think on his feet in this new theological territory.

John the Baptist was also at a pivotal moment. He was baffled by Jesus presenting himself for baptism, thus confounding John's understanding of his mission and his relationship to the coming One. Far from carrying his sandals, he was to baptize him (but perhaps that *was* carrying his sandals?). In telling John to fulfil all righteousness, Jesus grounded God's new acts in God's past acts. Isaiah assures us that God is doing new things and, like John, we are challenged to live the unfolding new future in the light of the past.

The more usual sound at baptism is a baby's cry rather than a voice from heaven. Either way, the appropriate response is gratitude that, through baptism, we are made members of God's Kingdom. As the Archbishop of Canterbury said in his engaging interview about Prince George's baptism, baptism is not just for future kings, the great thing is that God doesn't care who we are. He invites us all to own the kingship of Jesus Christ.

The Archbishop quoted some words which he wanted to say to all people who are baptized, including a future king:

For you Jesus Christ came into the world. For you he lived and showed God's love. For you he suffered the darkness of Calvary and cried at the last, 'It is accomplished.' For you he triumphed over death and rose to new life. For you he reigns at God's right hand. All this he did for you, though you do not know it yet.

'Though you do not know it yet...' God's grace towards us is not dependent upon our grasping all the implications, just as John and Peter did not grasp all the implications. The Collect refers to our adoption. One of my godchildren was adopted at the time she was baptized. Her godfather and I gave her a baptismal hymn. In writing the words, based on the American baptismal liturgy, I explored what she did know – that her adoptive parents loved and welcomed her to their family – as a context for what she did not know about the implications of baptism.

You're called by name, forever loved,
adopted as a child of God.
Now one with us, the family
of those who know and love the Lord.
 Lord, in your hands we place your own,
 Lord, in her life make your love known.

Marked as Christ's own, signed by the cross
where Jesus for our sins once died.
With Jesus buried in his death,
called to confess Christ crucified.

Raised to new life, a life of grace,
set free from sin in Christ to grow.
His resurrection to proclaim,
his love in all of life to know.

Sealed by the Spirit, Lord of life,
sustained and strengthened by his might.
Joined to the church, to share with us
the inheritance of saints in light.
Copyright © 1989 Rosalind Brown

Why did the voice from heaven come to Jesus at this pivotal moment? Perhaps because in the days and years to come he would need to cling to what he did know of God's love as the gruelling implications of his obedience to God unfolded. In that light, we pray to be faithful to our calling as God's adopted children, whoever we are and at whatever pivotal moment we find ourselves to be.

Second Sunday of Epiphany

Isaiah 49.1–7; 1 Corinthians 1.1–9; John 1.29–42

FROM RAGS TO RICHES IN GOD

Almighty God, in Christ you make all things new: transform the poverty of our nature by the riches of your grace, and in the renewal of our lives make known your heavenly glory; through Jesus Christ our Lord. Amen.

This week we pray that God will make his heavenly glory known in the renewal of our lives. If anyone needed his life renewing, it was God's servant in Isaiah who was so exhausted by his faithfulness to God that he felt he had wasted his time and his life. Was it all over for him? No, because he added, bravely, 'Yet …'. There is always a 'yet' with God.

Hilary Mantel ends *Bring up the Bodies* with this tantalizing paragraph: 'The word, "however" is like an imp coiled beneath your chair. It induces ink to form words you have not yet seen, and lines to march across the page and overshoot the margin. There are no endings. If you think so you are deceived as to their nature. They are beginnings. Here is one.'

Last week Isaiah reminded us that God is declaring new things and this week we encounter some of them. This faithful, exhausted servant is to be given as a light not just to Israel but to the nations; Paul has a troublesome church to write to in what he knew when he started writing would be a hard letter both for him and for them. Yet he could see God's renewal among them and his lines marched across the page, overshooting the margin in praise to God who has enriched and provided for them and will strengthen them and make them blameless. Given what was to follow in the letter, it was a leap of faith on Paul's part, in line with the Collect's affirmation that God will transform the poverty of our nature by the riches of his grace.

Events in the first chapter of the Gospel take place over four days, perhaps a deliberate echo of the days of creation in Genesis 1. After the high Christology of the prologue, we might expect a powerful revelation of God's glory in Jesus. But, no. Suddenly things change and, as with Isaiah and Paul, the revelation of God's glory occurs in a series of ordinary encounters among ordinary people. There is little attempt at persuasion as, first, John leaves people to assess his testimony to what he has seen and heard, letting them decide for themselves what to do about it, and then Jesus asks questions rather than makes statements that push people into responding. Later this will change, but he invites his future disciples to make the first move by asking, 'What are you looking for?'

They respond with another question, 'Where are you staying?', effectively inviting themselves into his company, as disciples of a rabbi would do. Their calling began with Jesus offering them hospitality and, since they remained all day, the conversation obviously flowed, no doubt over food.

John can be quite deliberate in recording times or time spans but we can only wonder at the significance of four o'clock; maybe it was such a significant and life-changing encounter that the time stuck in their memories in the same way that people remember where they were when they heard of President Kennedy's assassination or the attack on the Twin Towers. Whatever the reason, this appears to be the moment when Andrew experienced a 'Yet ...' moment, calling him to set out afresh on a new walk with God. His first response was to find his brother and, with extraordinary certainty (just what had Jesus said after that first almost casual question?), to assert that he had found the Messiah. Then, like us when we pray the Collect, Andrew and his friends offered their lives for renewal without knowing the outcome.

What do we learn about calling, vocation, from these scriptures as we hear them in Epiphany, the season of the revelation of the glory of God? Isaiah reminds us that, when we are exhausted, God opens up new vocation and vision if we dare to pray, 'Yet ...'; Paul can see beyond the problems eroding the witness of the Corinthians to grasp that, perverse and annoying as some of them were, they were called to be saints and were sanctified by God. Divided they might be, but to the eyes of faith they were enriched in every way in Christ. And John places the call to be with Jesus, to come and see, at the heart of everything, holding up John the Baptist who obeyed even without the full picture. God's ink forms words we have not yet seen ...

Third Sunday of Epiphany

Isaiah 9.1–4; 1 Corinthians 1.10–18; Matthew 4.12–23

ENDINGS AND BEGINNINGS

Almighty God, whose Son revealed in signs and miracles the wonder of your saving presence: renew your people with your heavenly grace, and in all our weakness sustain us by your mighty power; through Jesus Christ our Lord. Amen.

Isaiah and the Gospel plunge us into times of endings, beginnings and fulfilment. The tribal lands of Zebulun and Naphtali lay in the fertile hill country north and west of the Sea of Galilee, at the northern end of the Promised Land. On a major trade route, they contained many fortified cities which were needed against invasion from the north – the Syrians ravaged the lands and a century later the people of this region were the first to be deported by the Assyrians.

It is in that Assyrian context that we should hear Isaiah's remarkable prophecy, which must be read with the end of chapter 8 where there is only distress, darkness and anguish. Otherwise chapter 9's life-changing 'But' is robbed of its power. Isaiah dared to anticipate the ending of oppression by a super-power and the beginning of joy for a downtrodden people. As we hear of South Sudan, Syria and the Central African Republic, or whichever other nations are in the news as you read this, we gain an idea of how radical this vision was of God's light shining into places walking in deep darkness. There was an ending because there was God's beginning.

Jesus grew up in this same region. Matthew makes the connection with the centuries-old prophecy, partially fulfilled when the exile ended, for which there was now a less immediately obvious but deeper fulfilment because the light of the world walked this territory: Nazareth was in what was previously Zebulun and Capernaum in Naphtali.

The Gospel is about beginnings and endings. There are two significant endings before there are new beginnings. With John's arrest, his public ministry ended. Traumatic for John, this was a beginning for Jesus who withdrew from his home of 30 years to make a new start by the sea. We can only wonder what went through his mind as he walked there, knowing that everything had changed for him as began to call for repentance because the Kingdom of God came near.

The familiar story of the call of the first disciples differs from John's account heard last week, and both can be seen as part of a process of calling for the men involved. John does not imply a radical abandonment of their nets, so what he describes may have been a first encounter that paved the way for this more decisive response. Sometimes we need to hear the call in different ways and at different times.

There was an ending for the men before there was God's beginning. Yet Matthew indicates that someone else, too, faced a significant ending. Whereas Peter and Andrew left their nets, Matthew records that James and John left their boat and also their father, Zebedee. Peter lived with his mother-in-law, which may hint that his parents were dead. But James and John left their father, precipitating a devastating ending for him. Already sharing his family fishing business with his sons, he would suffer drastically from the withdrawal of their younger, stronger labour.

Recently, sorting through family papers, I found the letter I wrote to my parents when I decided to move to the USA. Memories flooded back of struggling to find words to explain why I was leaving family, friends and a successful career in local government to test my vocation in a Benedictine community in an economically devastated area, trying to express my very mixed emotions at leaving my family behind. Next time I stayed with them, my father took me aside and we both ended up choking on our hard-found words as he gave me the freedom to go with his support. Neither of us could dream where it would lead and he once told my mother he thought I would never return. When I did return to this country he had died and I was ordained. All we knew then was the mutual cost of my following what I believed was my calling.

One of my first journal entries in the USA, while all the farewells were still raw, was, 'Why can't there be beginnings without endings?' At times like that we can pray the petition in the Collect, 'in all our weakness, sustain us by your mighty power', and draw strength from the promise of God's renewal by heavenly grace as well as from the knowledge that Jesus, too, faced endings in order for there to be life-giving beginnings.

Sometimes we have to free those we love to pursue new beginnings, trusting, like Isaiah, there will be God's 'But' in the midst of them.

Fourth Sunday of Epiphany

1 Kings 17.8–16; 1 Corinthians 1.18–31; John 2.1–11

ACTING FOOLISHLY FOR GOD

God our creator, who in the beginning commanded the light to shine out of darkness: we pray that the light of the glorious gospel of Christ may dispel the darkness of ignorance and unbelief, shine into the hearts of all your people, and reveal the knowledge of your glory in the face of Jesus Christ our Lord. Amen.

It all sounds so easy when, centuries later, we read, 'Then the word of the Lord came to Elijah.' God spoke, he heard, he acted. But if we put ourselves in his shoes then suddenly it is *much* harder.

Elijah lived in Tishbe in Gilead, east of the Jordan. After his audacious prophecy of no rain except at his command, the Lord sent him further east to hide by the Wadi Cherith. There he lived a precarious lifestyle, drinking the wadi water and being fed by ravens, birds not known for sharing their food with humans. Then the wadi dried up and there was no special exemption from suffering for Elijah.

So the Lord sent him to Zarephath where he had commanded a widow to feed him. This small coastal town was about 80 miles to the north-west, between Tyre and Sidon. To get there involved a painful walk through land devastated by drought and famine. So much is not said in that simple sentence, 'So he set out and went to Zarephath.' To walk through that devastation must have been heart-wrenching and faith-challenging, but maybe he reasoned that God was sending him that far because God had a widow with secret supplies there?

But no, the scene in Zarephath was one of dire need. When Elijah got there the widow's situation was just as desperate as in the land he had walked through. She was about to scrape some sticks together, cook her last meal, and prepare to die. On the face of it the situation did not add up, and it would be perfectly reasonable to ask why he had trekked 80 miles to die here rather than at Cherith. But even with that question hanging in the air, Elijah never seemed to doubt God. So he told the widow not to fear, but to feed him first and then she would find her supply of basic food would not run out until the day God sent rain. Jesus described this as a three-and-a-half-year famine, so the strength of Elijah's faith was remarkable. So was hers; even allowing for the rules of hospitality in that culture which demanded that a guest be cared for, not everyone literally on their last meal would feed a complete stranger who turned up demanding his share of the scraps. But in an unreported encounter the Lord had commanded her, and we cannot know how or why he chose her or what he said to her. In that sense she shared Mary's later experience of an unlooked-for message from God.

She explained her predicament and Elijah replied, 'Do not be afraid, go and do as you have said.' Mary told the servants, 'Do whatever he tells you.' As the stories turn out, that was effectively saying the same thing. Both were instructing people to do things unfounded on rational explanation, because both believed a previous message from God. The widow had barely enough food for two of them, let alone an unexpected visitor, while filling water jars was not, on the face of it, going to solve the wine problem. The widow and the servants both had to take the risk of looking utterly foolish, as did Elijah and Mary when giving the instructions. And because they did, God's glory was revealed and very practical human needs were met.

Paul knew all about foolishness. He gave his life to preaching the utterly foolish message of the cross. But he also knew it was the power of God to save. Christ crucified was a stumbling block to the Jews Paul met and foolishness to the Gentiles, yet he kept on preaching the cross, knowing that God's foolishness is wiser than human wisdom. He went so far as to describe himself as a fool for Christ's sake (1 Corinthians 4.10), and ultimately died for this godly foolishness.

It is so much easier to imagine God acting elsewhere, or in another century. We risk looking foolish if we anticipate God acting in our situation. The Collect's prayer is realistic: we need God to dispel the darkness of ignorance and unbelief which can arise when we look at our circumstances and lose sight of God. We are called to be fools for God. So we pray that God will reveal in our hearts the knowledge of his glory in the face of Jesus Christ. Like the widow, like Elijah, like the servants, like Mary, that involves acting on what we believe God is telling us to do. Are we open to the life-transforming consequences?

Sunday before Lent,
Proper 1 (3–9 February)

Isaiah 58.1–9a [9b–12]; 1 Corinthians 2.1–12 [13–16];
Matthew 5.13–20

SALT AND LIGHT IN THE WORLD

> *Almighty God, by whose grace alone we are accepted and called to your*
> *service: strengthen us by your Holy Spirit and make us worthy of our*
> *calling; through Jesus Christ our Lord. Amen.*
>
> Collect for the Fifth Sunday before Lent

There are challenging words for us this week. Isaiah, speaking at a time when Israel anticipated deliverance from exile in Babylon, interrupted his messages of hope with stark warnings that, for the promise of God's blessing (v. 6ff.) to be fulfilled, they should live in a way that embodied for others the blessing they themselves wanted, loosing bonds of injustice, freeing the oppressed, so that all creation would experience light rising in the darkness. God's good purposes are for the whole world. The chosen people are agents, not just recipients, of blessing (Genesis 12.3, 18.18, 22.18).

In this context we hear Jesus announce that, far from his abolishing the law, his disciples should keep it more fully than the Pharisees who prided themselves on their superior observance of it. Matthew does not say that Gentiles must become Jews to do this – a hot issue for the Early Church; he simply assumed that all Christians embodied the weighty matters of the law in their lives (23.23).

Since his baptism Jesus had proclaimed that the Kingdom of heaven had come near. Now he linked this with righteousness: it is for those who are persecuted for righteousness' sake (5.10), to enter it their righteousness must exceed that of the Scribes and Pharisees, and they must do the will of his Father (7.21). The Kingdom of heaven, here among them now, is not, as the Pharisees taught, something for the future. So they must go and live accordingly, exploring and embodying what the law looks like when lived not as legal requirement but as a response to being in a world of God's grace and righteousness.

To express the demands of the law as a manifestation of grace they must be able to envisage it that way, and Jesus gave two practical illustrations. This way of thinking makes disciples salt and light in the world. Potentially dangerous on its own, salt is always a means to enhancing something else. It brings out flavour, preserves, seals covenants (Numbers 18.19) and is sprinkled on sacrifices (Leviticus 2.13). Jesus's followers are to enhance God's world, bringing the peace and justice Isaiah envisaged.

Salt came from deposits near the Dead Sea which also contained gypsum.

The two looked similar and gypsum, used inadvertently, was described as salt that had lost its flavour. 'Lost its flavour' could also mean 'become foolish'. Fools do not know God (Psalm 14.1) or recognize God's Kingdom when it comes, thus bringing judgement on themselves. Salt that has lost its flavour is trampled underfoot, an image of God's judgement (Isaiah 14.19, 25), and Matthew ends his Gospel with several parables of judgement on people who fail to embody God's Kingdom (Matthew 7.23, 24.45–25, 46). Being salt carries responsibilities.

The disciples are also light, not just in but – more powerfully – of the world; light which in Genesis 1.3–4 allowed the world to be seen and order to come out of chaos. Again Isaiah anticipated this (42.6), envisaging Israel as a light to the nations.

When I lived in a community in a run-down American town, each Advent and Christmas we put electric candles in our windows, creating a block of light at a bend in the dark road to the town centre. A former resident told us that, for years, painful memories of past prosperity now lost had prevented her going back downtown, but one Advent she had no choice and, seeing the lights, she had wept: 'They said to me, "There is hope, it will be all right".' Years later, amid the deprivation, tenacious light-bearing by Christians working with others for economic and social recovery is bearing seeds of hope.

Like other prophets, Isaiah condemned people who oppressed their employees, quarrelled and ignored the needy. In doing so they made fasting into a personal pious practice and lost the wider vision of being the world's salt and light, bringing wholeness to all God's world. As Isaiah describes, God's fast is very practical and can start small.

Michael Ramsey wrote, 'Openness to heaven is necessary for a Christian … [It] is realized … in every act of selflessness, humility or compassion; for such acts are already anticipations of heaven in the here and now' (Ramsey, 1936). How much time, effort and money have we given to this openness to heaven in the past year? Is there a Lenten discipline waiting to be discovered?

Sunday before Lent,
Proper 2 (10–16 February)

Deuteronomy 30.15–20; 1 Corinthians 3.1–9;
Matthew 5.21–37

UNRULY WILLS AND PASSIONS

> *O God, you know us to be set in the midst of so many and great dangers,*
> *that by reason of the frailty of our nature we cannot always stand upright:*
> *grant to us such strength and protection as may support us through all*
> *dangers and carry us through all temptations; through Jesus Christ our*
> *Lord. Amen.*
>
> Collect for the Fourth Sunday before Lent

As last week, this week we hear about God's commandments. It makes
demanding reading. Moses, in his farewell address, set a stark choice before
the perverse people he had shepherded through the wilderness for years: life or
death. It seems like an unnecessary waste of words on his part, for who would
not choose life and prosperity? But with the choice of life came responsibilities
– obedience, love, steadfastness – and Moses's experience was that these were
not the people's strong suit.

By asking them to make a choice, he asked them to be mature people,
taking responsibility for their future. He had led them from slavery; now they
had to choose to live as free people, realizing the consequences of their choices
and actions.

Paul wrote to equally demanding people who seemed unaware of their
immaturity. The rest of the letter spells out some consequences of their choice of
life in Christ Jesus, requiring them to make radical changes to their communal
life. For now, Paul pointed them to God who gives the growth in their lives as he
and they worked together to bring about their spiritual maturity.

Part of the Corinthians' problem was their division which denied their
unity in Christ. They were jealous and they quarrelled, behaving according to
human inclinations rather than with the mind of Christ (2.16). Relationships had
broken down as they identified themselves divisively with Paul and Apollos,
not grasping their modelling of what it means to be God's servants rather than
human leaders.

Jesus gave more examples of broken or distorted relationships which result
in murder, anger, adultery, divorce and swearing oaths. He was nothing if not
realistic about the field into which he was sowing the seeds of God's Kingdom.
Sadly, the situation is little changed today even if the details differ: the dreadful
situation created in 2013 by Bishop Kunonga in Zimbabwe, where people could

not even offer gifts at the altar, was an extreme example, but, tragically, the Church abounds with less dramatic divisive stories.

Although Jesus used a figure of speech when speaking of cutting off a hand, he drew on his hearers' knowledge that such physical mutilation precluded participation in Old Testament worship (Leviticus 21.5, 17–23). In God's Kingdom come among them, worship no longer required physical perfection, but perfection of life.

In Matthew, Jesus more than once calls for radical action in order to meet God's standards of righteousness. He repeated these exhortations about cutting off anything that causes us to sin (18.8–9), and later (23.16–22) called woes on the Pharisees and hypocrites for failing to do what he taught here. This was clearly an enormously serious matter for Jesus; the coming of God's Kingdom is no soft option. The pure in heart will see God (5.8), and purity of heart, as Kierkegaard said, is to will one thing: in this context, to be perfect as our heavenly Father is perfect (5.48).

This pursuit of purity of heart is not a cause for despair at the enormity of the demands. There is a possible way. Jesus models another attitude of total commitment to God and assumed that his disciples could and would live differently, even at great cost to themselves. They could choose life with all its consequences because, as Moses told the people (Deuteronomy 30.6), God would circumcise their hearts, causing them to love God.

The Collect, as so often, is a helpful prayer in the light of the challenge of the readings. We have unruly wills and passions – ask Paul about that as he wrote to the Corinthians – to which only God can bring order. God does it by giving us grace to love what he commands and to desire what he promises so that we find, increasingly, that we want to fix our hearts on him. As we pursue God, hungering and thirsting for righteousness, we will be filled.

Archbishop William Temple's words, quoted by his successor Michael Ramsey, are apposite to this week's readings as we reflect on how the way we live reflects our relationship with God. Temple reminds us that the inclination of our heart towards God is what directs our living. 'It is sometimes supposed that conduct is primary and worship tests it. That is incorrect: the truth is that worship is primary and conduct tests it' (Ramsey, 1964).

Sunday before Lent,
Proper 3 (17–23 February)

Leviticus 19.1–2, 9–18; 1 Corinthians 3.10–11, 16–23;
Matthew 5.38–48

FOOLISH, HOLY LIVING

> *Almighty God, who alone can bring order to the unruly wills and passions*
> *of sinful humanity: give your people grace so to love what you command*
> *and to desire what you promise, that, among the many changes of this*
> *world, our hearts may surely there be fixed where true joys are to be found;*
> *through Jesus Christ our Lord. Amen.*
> Collect for the Third Sunday before Lent

The Corinthian Christians to whom Paul wrote in about AD 55 lived in a port
city dominated by pagan culture. This fairly small group of recent converts were
an international bunch: of those named, half had Latin names, half had Greek
names, a few were Jews. A few were wealthy and influential, some were slaves
and some fitted in between. And they fell out.

Paul had stayed there for 18 months, establishing the church until opposition
forced him out, leaving a muddled community that lacked secure grounding in
the Christian faith. Influenced by Greek culture's dualism between body and
spirit, they thought that Jesus's resurrection liberated their human spirits, making
what they did with their bodies inconsequential. As the letter unfolds it becomes
clear that they ignored the ethical consequences of the Holy Spirit's work in their
lives.

Paul identified two underlying causes of this anarchic living. First, they
had not grasped that they were God's temple and that God's Spirit dwelt in
them. So he rubbed it in, saying twice, 'you are God's temple' and that God's
temple is holy. The church was not something they joined if they wanted to. No,
they *were* the church; being Christian was their identity, not a hobby. Second,
they deceived themselves with their understanding of wisdom. True wisdom had
nothing to do with what the world around them considered wise; in fact, that was
really foolishness. Instead, true wisdom looked foolish to the world and they had
to become the world's fools in order to be wise in a godly way.

Against that background of being reminded that we are God's holy temple,
in Leviticus and the Gospel we hear some of the extraordinarily practical
implications of being holy because God is holy. Some of them do indeed look
foolish in the world's eyes, but actually reveal God's wisdom for holy and
peaceful living. So, in the days before Social Services when people lived off the
land, they were to leave some food in the fields or on the trees for the landless

poor and aliens to reap. That is how Ruth and Naomi survived when they first returned to Bethlehem as widows. It appears foolish to people whose aim in life is to maximize profits or who, today, assume all people going to foodbanks are scroungers. Underlying several of the injunctions is an attitude that does not take advantage of other people and treats them all as equals, not deferring to the great. Where would the tabloid newspapers be today if we took all that to heart, given our warped ideas of what makes someone great? Then there is no room for the attitude that there is nothing wrong with getting away with whatever we can, expressed vividly here as bullying by making people wait for due payment, getting away with fraud, insulting deaf people who cannot hear the offence or tripping up blind people – the implication being that it is done for the fun of having the upper hand over them. No: foolish wisdom always puts others first.

Jesus picked up the theme of foolish godly living in a culture where retaliation was the basis of life. Not resisting an evildoer sounds more than unwise, it could be positively dangerous. Any slap on the face was humiliating (Isaiah 50.6; Lamentations 3.30) but was particularly debasing if done with the back of the right hand or the left hand (used for dirty work), which was the only way to slap the right cheek. But, if grossly insulted, it was appropriate to offer the other cheek too. If forced by a Roman soldier to carry a load for one mile – which the soldier could demand – holy people were to be foolish enough to offer to do double duty. They were to give and loan without a second thought, including the clothing they needed for warmth. And then, in the ultimate foolishness, they were to do all this not just for friends but for enemies, outdoing even hated tax-collectors in showing love.

Why live in this foolish way? It all comes down to being perfect as our heavenly Father is perfect, being holy because God is holy and we are God's temple. So we pray to love what God commands and desire what God promises, fixing our heart on true joys. If we get that attitude right the practical expression of holiness may remain very foolish, but it comes within reach.

Second Sunday before Lent

Genesis 1.1–2.3; Romans 8.18–25; Matthew 6.25–34

BEASTS AND ALL CATTLE, WORMS AND ALL FEATHERED FOWLS

> *Almighty God, you have created the heavens and the earth and made us in your own image: teach us to discern your hand in all your works and your likeness in all your children; through Jesus Christ your Son our Lord, who with you and the Holy Spirit reigns supreme over all things, now and for ever. Amen.*

Each of this week's readings asks to be read out loud, rather than silently, because hearing helps to articulate its repeated internal theme.

Genesis has 32 action words and phrases. We can domesticate this story, reducing it to an inventory of God's actions, or, if we let the internal rhythm drive the story forward through the repetition of 'God …', it can lead us to marvel as creation takes shape, moving in just nine verses from the cosmic to something we can get our feet on, before narrowing our gaze to birds and creepy-crawlies.

Repeated short sentences, 'And it was so', 'And God saw that it was good', hammer home that God brings only good things into being. Years ago, I was struck by the novelist Stephen Donaldson's portrayal, in *The Wounded Land*, of the terror of a malicious force in creation so people never know whether sunrise will be safe or life-threatening. In contrast to that unpredictable world, we take for granted that we can trust the goodness of God's creation and the way it exhibits the steadfast love of God as we rely on it for security and sustenance. Within that context, events like devastating floods remind us about how fragile is the balance in the relationship we humans have with nature, as they make it temporarily challenging to sense the presence of God in creation.

'Subdue it and have dominion' is best understood in the context in which Genesis 1 was written down. In the sixth-century world of exile in Babylon this was a mandate of hope. God promised the exiles not perpetual landless existence but their own land to subdue and care for. This was no licence to exploit the land, but a promise of a healthy and godly relationship with land they did not then have.

God saw, time and again, that creation was good. Humans made it very good. So something had gone drastically wrong by the time Paul wrote to the Romans, because five times he referred to creation now groaning and yearning for freedom from bondage to decay. The Genesis creation story, with its description of human sin which resulted in the earth being cursed and its relationship with its human stewards distorted (Genesis 3.17–19, 4.10–12), underlies his thinking.

But Paul is not without hope. As so often with lectionary snippets, we must read the previous verses. They speak of suffering with Christ so that we might be glorified with him and, from there, Paul moves seamlessly into the sufferings of the present age. Creation is groaning, yes, but groaning in labour pains because, as for a woman in labour, unstoppable new life is coming to birth. Creation's healing is bound up with human salvation. Thanks to the work of Christ, creation waits with eager longing for the revealing of the children of God in their glory.

In Romans, the thrice repeated words are 'groan' (the third, variously translated, is in verse 26) and 'wait': creation waits with eager longing, we wait with patience. Hope, waiting and longing go together; it is possible to groan with hope and without worrying.

Jesus, however, was dealing with some inveterate worriers. Six times he told them not to worry which suggests that, even living around Jesus, the disciples hovered on the edge of fear and were prone to fret about securing the basic necessities of life. Jesus, whose words must be read in the context of verses 19–24 (which in turn allude to Ecclesiasticus 29.8–11 where laying up treasure in heaven involves almsgiving), sent them back to look at creation – look at the birds, consider the lilies – the very creation which God pronounced good. The foundation for not worrying is the goodness of God. God could rest. So can we.

The Collect's reference to our being made in God's image reminds us of a truth which human sin has not negated: the likeness of God in us may be tarnished, but not the image of God. We are capable of discerning God's hand in all God's works. Since we pray for God to teach us to do that, we should give God the opportunity. If you have never taken ten minutes with a flower or bird, pondering it and letting it tell you of the goodness of God, make time this week. Snowdrops are appearing from barren soil, migrant birds will return from far continents: consider carefully what they reveal of God. Grasping the goodness of God seen in creation will help us to wait with hope, to strive for God's Kingdom, not to worry.

Sunday next before Lent

Exodus 24.12–end; 2 Peter 1.16–end; Matthew 17.1–9

GLORY BEFORE SUFFERING

Almighty Father, whose Son was revealed in majesty before he suffered death upon the cross: give us grace to perceive his glory, that we may be strengthened to suffer with him and be changed into his likeness, from glory to glory; who is alive and reigns with you, in the unity of the Holy Spirit, one God, now and for ever. Amen.

On this final Sunday before Lent, the Collect prays us into a world where suffering and glory belong together, both for Jesus and for us. We pray to be conformed to the image of Christ, to become more Christ-like. Specifically, we ask for grace to perceive Christ's glory and be strengthened to suffer with him. Let there be no doubt, there will be suffering. However, the Collect does not stop there but envisages us being changed into God's likeness from glory to glory.

Last week we heard Paul encouraging the Romans to wait patiently because God's glory is to be revealed to us. He might have had this week's story of Moses in mind; having told Moses to wait, it took seven days before God called to him out of the cloud and God's glory was revealed. God was in no hurry.

The transfiguration was the revelation of God's glory in Jesus Christ. However, perhaps unexpectedly, it also included the appearance of Moses and Elijah and was seen by three disciples. The author of the epistle also describes an eyewitness account of Christ's majesty when he received the honour and glory from the Father. Like Moses, these disciples had an extraordinary encounter with the holiness of God. God's impulse is to draw humans in to share his glory, an instinct that we hear time and again in the biblical story, from God's forlorn 'Where are you?' to Adam (Genesis 3.9) to, ultimately, the ascension when Christ took humanity into the heart of God.

But why Moses and Elijah in particular? Traditionally they represent the law and the prophets which point to and were fulfilled in the coming of Christ. However, I wonder if it is also because both men had known the loneliness and suffering of fidelity to God in the face of the disloyalty of their people. Therefore, they were able to strengthen Jesus at this pivotal moment in his life and ministry.

Next week we will be reminded that Jesus was vulnerable to the temptation to take short cuts to glory, while Matthew has just recorded Jesus's foretelling of his death and resurrection and his call to the disciples to take up their cross and follow him (16.21–28). Jesus knew the terrible cost of his calling and perhaps, like us, needed to be strengthened by people who had proved God's faithfulness.

Matthew refers to the disciples' fear when they heard the voice from the cloud (in Luke the cloud itself caused the fear), and Jesus's response of touching them – so tactile and reassuring amid the ethereal glory and dazzling brightness – and of Jesus's speaking to them, telling them not to be afraid. Again there are echoes of last week's readings when Jesus repeatedly told the same disciples not to worry. Fear and worry are slightly different; fear often being a more instant, involuntary response to threat whereas worry is more of an ongoing condition of unease. However, both share the same root and both need the reassurance of God's present grace.

So, as we tramp around in a world of fear and worry, learning to wait with hope, we end this pre-Lenten season as we began it at Epiphany: assured of the revelation of God's glory in our world. However sharp our fear, in Jesus Christ God's light and glory shine in the darkness. Truly, 'the world is charged with the grandeur of God'.

> The light has come! our world is changed.
> No more can darkness terrify.
> The star shines out, Immanuel's sign
> emblazoned in the sable sky.
>
> The light has come! the Son of God
> transfigured on the mountain stands,
> God's glory seen by human eyes
> disturbs our peace, our hope expands.
>
> The light has come! it seeks us out,
> unmasking secrets long concealed;
> then truths we know but have not faced
> are named and owned, by light revealed.
>
> The light has come! it penetrates
> so deep within where beauty lies;
> from hidden and uncharted depths
> the treasures of our darkness rise.
>
> The light has come! our world is charged
> with glory, dazzling, holy, true.
> God's radiant and resplendent light
> transforms our lives, makes all things new.
>
> *Copyright © 1995 Rosalind Brown*

Ash Wednesday

Joel 2.1–2, 12–17 or Isaiah 58.1–12; 2 Corinthians 5.20b–
6.10; Matthew 6.1–6, 16–21 or John 8.1–11

FACING REALITY

*Almighty and everlasting God, you hate nothing that you have made and
forgive the sins of all those who are penitent: create and make in us new and
contrite hearts that we, worthily lamenting our sins and acknowledging our
wretchedness, may receive from you, the God of all mercy, perfect remission
and forgiveness; through Jesus Christ our Lord. Amen.*

Bill Bryson (Bryson, 2013) tells a story from 1920s Hollywood when quality
control was overlooked in film studios. The head of MGM, told it was wrong to
put a coastal scene in a film about Paris because Paris is nowhere near any sand,
said, 'We can't cater to a handful of people who know Paris.'

'We can't cater to a handful of people who know Paris.' Better to delude
millions for the sake of entertainment than face reality.

Lent is a time for facing reality. So we hear, 'Remember that you are dust
and to dust you shall return.' Using story to convey theological truth, Genesis
tells us that God made us from the dust of the earth, while scientists tell us we
are 99 per cent oxygen, carbon, hydrogen, nitrogen, calcium and phosphorus, or
about 60 per cent water. Both in their different ways cut us down to size.

That makes it more incredible that God lavishes such love on us and makes
us far, far more than a combination of chemicals. God breathed life into us and
we take on a life of our own. No wonder the psalmist exclaimed, 'What are
human beings that you are mindful of them, mortals that you care for them?'

Ash Wednesday is a sobering opportunity to face reality about being human.
Paris is not on the coast. Ashes remind us that we are mortal, finite. God meets us
just where we are, facing joys and sorrows, trials and tribulations. They are the
raw material of Lent.

Paul, writing to the Corinthians, listed a catalogue of hardships, even one
or two of which would scare many off being faithful to God. Christians around
the world suffer similarly today, in and out of the news. Paul was learning not
to be controlled by his circumstances, which did not mean emulating the White
Queen in believing six impossible things before breakfast, but through adversity
learning deeper truths about himself and about God. He was mortal, destined to
die, but until then he would be faithful and do good.

Jesus taught his disciples how to live faithfully. Taking for granted that,
as good Jews, they gave alms, prayed and fasted, he reshaped the way they did
those things. Most of us want to be good Christians so Jesus challenges us, too,
to continue to practise the basics of our religion.

'Remember you are dust and to dust you shall return.' The true test of our living is in our dying. Benedict, instructing his monks to keep their death before their eyes, was not being macabre but realistic. Lent is an appropriate time to prepare for death. Is your estate in good order; your funeral planned; your will up to date? And what will happen your body before it returns to dust? Will you leave either your organs or your whole body for transplant or medical research so that others can live?

To keep a holy Lent we have to give attention to how we live, to stop living in denial about the realities and givens in our life (Paris is not at the seaside); to prepare for dying; to focus on the givens of the Christian life. 'Do not lay up for yourselves treasures on earth, but store up for yourselves treasures in heaven … For where your treasure is, there your heart will be also.'

Posture and body language play a big part in the story in John's Gospel. Were we performing this, we would have all the stage directions but be left to improvise the conversation. Our Lenten journey is as much about discipleship as penitence so, like the woman, we stand before God acknowledging our waywardness, maybe something big and obvious, maybe something hidden and more elusive. Imagine yourself in the scene.

I wonder what posture and body language you adopt in front of Jesus.
I wonder what Jesus's posture and body language are.
I wonder if people around you are saying anything to Jesus about you and if he is ignoring them.
I wonder if you should ignore them too.
Watch the people leave until you are you alone with Jesus.
I wonder how he responds to you.
What are you going to do about it during Lent?

First Sunday of Lent

Genesis 2.15–17, 3.1–7; Romans 5.12–19; Matthew 4.1–11

THE FIRST AND SECOND ADAMS

Almighty God, whose Son Jesus Christ fasted forty days in the wilderness, and was tempted as we are, yet without sin: give us grace to discipline ourselves in obedience to your Spirit; and, as you know our weakness, so may we know your power to save; through Jesus Christ our Lord. Amen.

There are master story-tellers at work in Genesis, along with a brilliant editor, who together do theology through story, presenting universal truths through the story of one particular man. In Hebrew 'Adam', 'human', stands for humanity in general.

In this version of the creation story, dating from the tenth century BC, God had done the back-breaking work of clearing stones to plant a garden and had provided irrigation (2.5–10). These were dream conditions for the farmers then cultivating the stony hills around Jerusalem. By telling it this way, the clear message was, 'God is good.'

The man and woman's responsibility was to sustain and nurture the life God had created so carefully, eating absolutely anything except the fruit of the tree of the knowledge of good and evil. Theologically, this story tells us that to be human is to have freedom with responsibility. It is to be contingent, created for goodness, for enjoyment, for relationship, for creative and caring work, to have permission to act in God's world, and to be subject to restriction.

Then what happened? We hear a story of sly half-truths. Like people ever since, the serpent, a crafty manipulator, used words to devastating effect. Without lying directly, he nevertheless distorted what God had said and cast doubts about God's trustworthiness. The rest is history. Theologically, to be human is to have a basic innocence that makes us vulnerable to manipulation and exploitation, to want what is forbidden, to want pleasure, to rebel, to overstep boundaries that are part of God's design for creation, to doubt God's good intentions.

Adam and Eve wanted wisdom but got knowledge. Their actions brought shame, devastating their relationships. While they did not drop dead, they lost eternal life (2.22–24).

This telling of primeval events becomes even more interesting when we realize that the same themes were around in national life at the time it was written down. The people had wanted a king. Saul's hopeful beginning proved sadly transient and David was anointed. David, too, was a flawed character, but his heart was set on God who called him a man after God's heart. Pertinently, a wise woman described him as able to discern good and evil (2 Samuel 14.17).

Solomon succeeded David and, offered any gift he wanted by God, requested an understanding mind and the ability to discern between good and evil so that he could govern wisely (1 Kings 3.9). God's response was the gift of very great wisdom, discernment and breadth of understanding.

This contemporary history, with kings knowing (or not) good and evil, is exactly what the Genesis story is about theologically. Then, humans did not ask God but grabbed what they thought would give them wisdom. Telling stories like this, which would ring bells with people's experience, is a powerful way to do theology.

We find Paul in the middle of a complex argument, working with the Genesis theme. Death is the end result of sin, the consequence of human disobedience. It was cause and effect rather than crime and punishment. Only after Moses could sin be the breaking of the law, because there was no law to break until then. However, since Adam's disobedience, death affects everyone. Paul expresses theologically what Genesis tells in story, and he goes on to marvel that God's grace has acted through the second Adam, Christ, the perfect man.

In the Gospel, Jesus, with all the human attributes identified in the Genesis story barring sin, also faced temptation. Significantly, he was led by the Spirit into this temptation as, in his humanity, God undid the human mess. Twice he was tempted to presume on his divinity and once to surrender it.

Cardinal Newman's hymn expresses this brilliantly:

O loving wisdom of our God!
When all was sin and shame,
A second Adam to the fight
And to the rescue came.

O wisest love! that flesh and blood
Which did in Adam fail,
Should strive afresh against their foe,
Should strive, and should prevail.

How did Jesus resist temptation? Where is the hope for us as we follow him? Archbishop Michael Ramsey quoted a thought-provoking observation by the Congregational theologian P. T. Forsyth: Christ could be tempted because he loved; he could not sin because he loved so deeply.

As we begin Lent, maybe the question is not what we give up but how we can be open to learn to love more deeply.

Second Sunday of Lent

Genesis 12.1–4a; Romans 4.1–5, 13–17; John 3.1–17

THE ENIGMA OF NICODEMUS

Almighty God, you show to those who are in error the light of your truth, that they may return to the way of righteousness: grant to all those who are admitted into the fellowship of Christ's religion, that they may reject those things that are contrary to their profession, and follow all such things as are agreeable to the same; through our Lord Jesus Christ. Amen.

This year the Lent readings are rich in stories as we hear John's long narratives of some of Jesus's encounters coupled with classic Old Testament stories. This week's are the shortest readings and in some ways the most enigmatic: Nicodemus just drops off the scene, back into the night from whence he came. Abram 'went, as the Lord had told him; and Lot went with him'. I am reminded of books I read as a child, *What Katy Did* and *What Katy Did Next*. It is the 'next' that counts.

John set the theological scene for his telling of the story of Jesus by speaking of light and darkness – the light shines in the darkness and the darkness did not overcome it (1.5). He soon introduces Nicodemus, whose night-time encounter is the first of the events that John indicates took place in the dark.

Unlike other encounters where John is specific about body language, Jesus and Nicodemus could not see each other, look each other in the eye or read each other's expressions. So words counted for everything. Jesus bypassed Nicodemus's opening statement and, by turning the conversation, wrongfooted Nicodemus and forced him to ask a question rather than make assertions. Then Jesus seized the initiative and indicated his high expectations of the teachers of the law.

On the other hand, perhaps the conversation verged on the humorous as Nicodemus used the cover of darkness to risk asking seemingly daft questions without losing face in public, a serious concern for a Pharisee. Jesus responded to the absurdity of his literal interpretation and perhaps made them both laugh before he teased out truth and ended with a touch of amused incredulity in his final question.

Either way, Nicodemus can be forgiven for being confused. We hear no more of him after verse 9 and by verse 16 we do not know if he is still listening to Jesus or if this is John's summative commentary on what happens when light shines in darkness. It concludes that Jesus did not come to condemn the world, and John later puts this assertion on Jesus's own lips (8.12). Here, Jesus says nothing to Nicodemus about condemnation, only new birth.

What did Nicodemus do next? He reappears in two cameo roles. When other Pharisees wanted to arrest Jesus, he asked a question about due processes of the law as applied to Jesus. Whether an innocuous question or an attempt to protect Jesus, it prompted his colleagues' scathing criticism (7.50–52) which he had deliberately avoided in this first encounter. Then, after the crucifixion, with another secret disciple, Joseph of Arimathea, he brought large quantities of spices to embalm Jesus's body and place him in a tomb (19.38–42).

So this nocturnal encounter with Jesus bore fruit eventually, but it is never clear how certain or public was Nicodemus's following of Jesus. Maybe he never committed himself wholeheartedly, or maybe, like many people around the world today, his commitment was secure but he had to be cautious about how public he made it. Whatever the ultimate outcome, Jesus tried to nurture and enlarge that faith rather than condemn him.

So, Nicodemus remains an enigma. In contrast, we know what Abram did next. After his father's death, having previously moved from one urban centre, Ur, to another, Haran in the Fertile Crescent, at God's call and invitation he risked everything by leaving his settled life for a nomadic existence. The evocative phrase is, 'And Lot went with him.' Lot, his nephew, was part of the extended family which Abram now headed. He later caused Abram serious problems. Sometimes the people who come as part of the package of obeying God are not our first choice of companions.

Paul adds a commentary to this. Abraham believed in the presence of the God who gives life to the dead and calls into existence the things that do not exist. God did it by giving him an heir when he was as good as dead (4.19) and making him the father of all who share his faith. Jesus invited Nicodemus to share that faith by believing heavenly things. Nicodemus buried Jesus's body, so he must have also experienced the empty tomb and seen the disciples reborn of the Spirit through the resurrection. What finally came of this nocturnal conversation? What did Nicodemus do next?

Third Sunday of Lent

Exodus 17.1–7; Romans 5.1–11; John 4.5–42

TESTING AND QUARRELLING

Almighty God, whose most dear Son went not up to joy but first he suffered pain, and entered not into glory before he was crucified: mercifully grant that we, walking in the way of the cross, may find it none other than the way of life and peace; through Jesus Christ our Lord. Amen.

Several years ago I was in a coach in the desert beyond Jerusalem. Against all expectations, pouring rain had transformed the desert and our experienced guide was speechless. Dry wadis were flooded and roads blocked. We turned round and went a long way back to safety. Next day we heard of tourist coaches which spent the night in the desert – no food, no toilets, no warm clothing. I was struck by the irony – we wanted to see the desert associated with biblical stories but certainly did not want to spend the night there unprepared.

The people with Moses had no choice. Having come out of slavery they were en route to the Promised Land, moving from oasis to oasis, having trouble trusting God to care for them. All the hope and enthusiasm of the deliverance at the Red Sea had gone, life was tough and they were complaining. I have some sympathy.

So God provided food in the form of manna; but now they had no water. Their predictable response? To quarrel with Moses and demand he give them water or face being stoned. Experienced Bedouins know to hit the rock exactly where water is to be found, dislodging the sediment blocking it. Somehow Moses managed and the people drank.

Note what Moses called the place. Not 'where water came from the rock' or 'where God provided', but 'Massah and Meribah' meaning 'Testing and Quarrelling'. It has gone down in history as where they quarrelled and asked, 'Is the Lord among us or not?' Whenever we say Psalm 95 at Morning Prayer we recall that doleful episode in their history.

The question was not, 'Did they need water?' – they did – but 'Did they trust God?' Did they have any memory of God's care for them in recent weeks, any sense that God would do the same in future? Had they failed to see God's actions in everyday life?

Jesus, too, needed water. He was on a road most Jews avoided. Samaritans and Jews hated each other yet John tells us he 'had' to go through Samaria. Exhausted, by a well but without a bucket (careless, it seems, since people carried their own), instead of complaining to God, he sat to see how God would care for him. God's answer was most unlikely: a Samaritan woman, whose midday arrival indicated she was an outcast among her peers who would avoid the midday heat. Men did not talk to strange women, nor Jews to Samaritans. Would these two play by the rules of how God 'ought' to work or be open to God's providing in unexpected ways?

In an age when women could not initiate divorce, even if innocent, the woman's life included abandonment and desert experience. After an extraordinary conversation when, like Nicodemus, she took Jesus's words over-literally, her response was to run to the city and tell of a man who, knowing her history, did not to want to use her for his purposes but offered her new life, living water. As we heard last week, Jesus did not come to condemn her but to offer re-birth and living water.

We all face situations that seem interminable and threaten to be the death of us. Whether it is the depression that will not lift, the family we dread facing, the addiction we cannot break, the relationship that traps us, or the grief that overwhelms us; at times we end up in the desert.

The question is, how do we respond? Complaining is always tempting. But Paul, who suffered more than most of us will in a lifetime, had a different perspective. Describing a chain of responses and virtues that can flow from sufferings, he concluded with God's love being poured into our hearts. The key is in those last few words: Paul was not involved in mental gymnastics which denied the sufferings or endured stoically without hope. No, he accepted them for what they were, knowing they could set in motion a train of growth in the knowledge and love of God, because God's love was poured into his heart.

Halfway through Lent is a good time to ask whether our natural instinct is to complain when under pressure or to accept God's offer of new life out of situations that feel like death, perhaps focusing on a specific one. It is easier said than done, but we are assured it is possible with God's love, with living water.

Fourth Sunday of Lent

1 Samuel 16.1–13; Ephesians 5.8–14; John 9.1–41

WANDERING AND WONDERING

Merciful Lord, absolve your people from their offences, that through your bountiful goodness we may all be delivered from the chains of those sins which by our frailty we have committed; grant this, heavenly Father, for Jesus Christ's sake, our blessed Lord and Saviour. Amen.

Years ago, visiting the Mount of Beatitudes, our peace was suddenly and rudely interrupted as a screaming, diminutive nun waving a broomstick chased a woman from the church. Her offence? Wearing a sleeveless dress. Someone commented ironically, 'The Lord looks on the outward appearance, not on the heart.'

King Saul, the handsomest and tallest man in Israel, had proved to have better outward appearance than heart, so now Samuel had to anoint his successor. Apparently he was still looking on the outward appearance, for Mr Universe. After Jesse's seven sons stood before Samuel and produced no response from God, the search went out for the youngest.

Preaching on these texts in Durham Cathedral one year, I used the Godly Play approach which works with children's natural curiosity and imagination to build the story, asking repeatedly, 'I wonder what it was like …'. So, imagine yourself as a child standing in front of someone in authority – perhaps the head teacher – who surveys you in silence. I wonder what it was like.

I wonder what it was like for Eliab to stand in front of the famous prophet Samuel waiting for him to say something.

I wonder what it was like for Jesse to see his eldest son standing there.

I wonder what it was like for Jesse and his son to hear, 'No, not this one.'

And then the next, and the next, and the next; down to the seventh. I wonder what each one thought on being called, his older brothers having been rejected.

And still, 'No. The Lord has not chosen any of these.'

To break the impasse Samuel asked the obvious question, 'Are all your sons here?' Jesse had not thought it worth mentioning David. Unlike the nun with the broom, unlike most of us, God looks not on the outward appearance but on the heart, and something about young David made him a man after God's heart (Acts 13.22).

I wonder what it is like to be open fully to, indeed praying for, God's unexpected calling on us or on people we know.

I wonder how we can help them grow into that vocation.

Alongside this story of God's call of young David is the story of the blind man healed by Jesus. It is a rare significant encounter for which John does not give a time. It just happened as Jesus walked along and it was entirely at Jesus's initiative. The man was clearly bemused but did what he was told and had his sight restored. Jesus did not even wait for the outcome. There is food for thought about chance encounters.

Then there is the almost comic situation when his parents were called to account for what had happened. Like the situation with Samuel and Jesse where things did not add up and, in desperation, Samuel asked Jesse, 'Have you got any more children?' in this desperate situation the parents were wheeled in to help. But they were at an impasse.

I wonder what it was like for them to have no explanation for what had happened to their son and to be unable to protect him from the fury of the religious authorities.

I wonder what it is like to be caught up in the ways of God when we do not understand what is going on.

I wonder what it is like to sense that God is doing something in our lives that breaks out beyond what our family or our friends expect of us.

And, on this Mothering Sunday when we hear two stories where parents find their children being led by God into uncharted territory, I wonder what it is like for all of us, parents or not, to nurture other people in the unexpected ways of God and to free them to respond to the call of God?

Perhaps our Lenten discipline can be to let our minds wander into the stories we are hearing week by week and lead us to wonder. Who knows what we will discover?

Finally, notice the man's response to Jesus's questioning: 'Lord, I believe'; and he worshipped Jesus. That is the response John has been working towards in his Gospel. But, as with Nicodemus and the Samaritan woman, we do not know what happened next. I wonder ...

Fifth Sunday of Lent

Ezekiel 37.1–14; Romans 8.6–11; John 11.1–45

DEATH IS NOT AN ILLUSION

Most merciful God, who by the death and resurrection of your Son Jesus Christ delivered and saved the world: grant that by faith in him who suffered on the cross we may triumph in the power of his victory; through Jesus Christ our Lord. Amen.

Just before Christmas one year, my brother and I spent four weeks watching and waiting as our mother died peacefully and gracefully, with wonderful care from the NHS. Death is real.

I cannot forget, years earlier when working as a hospital chaplain, hearing the screams of a young girl who had been taken by her family to see her father who had just died from a horrible cancer. For people who had seen his suffering, death was a relief, but for her a scream of anguish was the only appropriate response. Death is real.

For Jesus, death was real. He went to extraordinary lengths to make this clear and so did not respond on hearing that his friend Lazarus was ill. Only after delaying long enough to ensure Lazarus's death did he suddenly tell his disciples he was heading into the danger zone of Judea, eliciting in the process Thomas's profound loyalty.

Jesus spelled it out, 'Lazarus is dead.' Everyone must be absolutely sure of that. When they arrived he had been buried for four days and Martha was in no doubt his body stank. Whatever Jesus was going to do, it was not the resuscitation of a person with any life in him.

Jesus responded differently to Mary's and Martha's identical declarations that had he been there their brother would not have died. This suggests they used very different tones of voice. In the midst of Martha's grief, Jesus had a theological conversation with her about rising from the dead. This led to her affirmation of faith that Lazarus would rise in the resurrection at the last day. Jesus's response, 'I am the resurrection and the life; those who believe in me, even though they die, will live,' is one of this Gospel's seven statements which embodied the Hebrew name for God, 'I am'. However, it still left her brother dead.

Next Jesus met Mary, who said exactly the same thing yet elicited a totally different response. Jesus wept with her, sharing the pain of death and loss. God has made us for friendship and love ('it is not good for the man to be alone') and, when friendship is severed by death, grief is a natural response. It does not indicate lack of trust in God, but bereavement, and bereavement can be a situation where we meet God most profoundly. Jesus knew the intensity of human loss. Later, when Jesus died on the cross, the Father was bereaved. Nothing we experience is alien to God; even in our loneliest and most forlorn places, we are not beyond God's reach of empathy and compassion.

Jesus knew the reality of death. It is not 'nothing at all'. However, in God's hands, death is the raw material of resurrection. This distinguishes Christianity from all other religions and philosophies.

So Jesus made this dramatic scene at the tomb. Lazarus's emergence must have been unforgettable: bound from head to toe in strips of cloth, hopping out of the tomb, unable to see where he was going. It seems everyone was paralysed into inaction and it took Jesus to break the stunned silence with practical instructions.

The Christian gospel does not diminish death. Doing so denies the power of the resurrection. Only Christianity proclaims that God opens graves, and Ezekiel had a visionary foretaste of this. However, while anticipatory, the story of Lazarus is not definitive of Christian belief because Lazarus was raised from death only to die again. Jesus himself was to die a cruel death and be buried. But, when God raised Jesus from the dead and he ascended to God's right hand in glory, he took his humanity into heaven, opening the way for all humanity. That is definitive.

What can we take with us from this story on Passion Sunday when we brace ourselves to hear again of Jesus's last terrible days? We must not rush the next two weeks, dashing from Palm Sunday's 'All glory, laud and honour' to Easter Sunday's resurrection joy, bypassing Good Friday. Without death there is no resurrection. Death is real but in Christ death is conquered, not sidelined. Our hope as Christians lies in the fact that God raised Jesus from the dead. We can face our mortality but not fear it.

Jesus believed in death. Jesus is the resurrection and the life. We believe in the resurrection of the dead. Thanks be to God.

Palm Sunday

Liturgy of the Passion: Matthew 21.1–11; Isaiah 50.4–9a;
Philippians 2.5–11; Matthew 26.14–27.54

CREATION'S HOLY COMMOTION

> *Almighty and everlasting God, who in your tender love towards the*
> *human race sent your Son our Saviour Jesus Christ to take upon him our*
> *flesh and to suffer death upon the cross: grant that we may follow the*
> *example of his patience and humility, and also be made partakers of his*
> *resurrection; through Jesus Christ our Lord. Amen.*

Once, a visitor at Durham Cathedral asked for directions to the 12.30 service
of 'Holy Commotion'. It seems a rather apt phrase when we hear the Passion
narrative read, since we take bread and wine in the name of one who, according
to Matthew, triggered commotions: his birth caused Jerusalem to be frightened
and his riding into Jerusalem threw the whole city into turmoil. On his death,
the veil in the Temple was ripped and two earthquakes ensued, raising dead
people who later walked around, heralding the arrival of an angel and terrifying
hardened soldiers. It all resonates with Ezekiel's vision that we heard last week
of God's breath upheaving a valley of dry bones.

A programme on Radio 4 asked people how many friends they had.
Some had three or four, perhaps ten. But one said thousands, referring to her
Facebook friends. I imagine the crowd cheering Jesus as his Facebook friends.
That friendship indicates support but costs little. Matthew frequently uses the
description 'the crowds' of disciples *en masse*, people who hung on Jesus's
words, enjoying the miracles, cheering loudly but not necessarily following him.

In contrast to fickle crowds, Isaiah described one who is taught, who does
not turn backwards but sets his face like flint. Being taught and being faithful
are at the heart of being disciples. Jesus formed a community of friends; he did
not have lone disciples. Paul's words to the Philippians, probably a hymn, are
surrounded by exhortations about how to live as a community of disciples. We
can miss the fact that the word translated 'you' in English is frequently plural in
the original.

However, the Passion narrative shows the disciples' friendship crumbling
under pressure. This is not just Judas's fault, although Matthew gives much
attention to Judas who, poignantly, Jesus called 'friend' at the moment of
betrayal. Peter, James and John fell asleep when he asked them to stay awake
with him; Peter denied him; the rest deserted him and fled. This is hardly a
picture of robust friendship in action; Facebook friends cheering from the side-
lines might have seemed preferable at that moment. Only a group of women
stuck it out to the end. Subsequently, Peter and Judas felt intense remorse but

while Matthew tells us that, tragically, Judas could not trust his friendship with Jesus to bear the weight of his betrayal, John records that Peter turned back when Jesus would not let their friendship end. We can only wonder what Jesus would have said to Judas had he lived: 'friend' gives us a clue.

In Matthew's Passion narrative, identity becomes crucial to the rapidly unfolding story. Only Matthew records the city's question when Jesus entered Jerusalem, 'Who is this?' The crowds then described Jesus as the prophet from Nazareth – an oxymoron to Jerusalemites for whom Galilee was virtually off the map of civilization. When Judas asked if he would be the betrayer, Jesus did not identify him directly. Instead his 'You have said so' forced Judas to identify himself while also offering a last opportunity to abandon his course of action and truly be Jesus's friend. Jesus used the same disturbing words, 'You have said so,' with Caiaphas and Pilate when they demanded he identify himself. Breaking his defiant silence, he threw their attempts to define him on their terms back in their faces, forcing them, ostensibly the people with power, to answer their own questions.

It took a pagan centurion to answer Caiaphas's and Pilate's questions. 'Truly this man was God's Son!' takes Matthew's Gospel full circle. He had begun by announcing that Jesus was the Messiah (Matthew 1.1), King of the Jews (Matthew 2.2) and Son of God (Matthew 3.17). Midway through the Gospel, Peter tumbled to that insight at Caesarea Philippi, after which the disciples had to be taught the hard lesson that 'King' and 'suffering' belonged in the same sentence. Therefore Matthew signally omitted 'triumphant and victorious is he' when quoting Zechariah 9.9 to describe the entry into Jerusalem. Unlike a conquering emperor returning triumphant on a war horse, Jesus came not in victory, but on his way to victory *through* suffering and dreadful forsakenness.

To all those world-changing events, the physical creation responded with holy commotion, echoing other biblical imagery of creation responding to God (e.g. Psalm 98.7–9; Isaiah 55.12). I wonder what holy commotion God might stir in us this Holy Week.

Maundy Thursday

Exodus 12.1–4 [5–10] 11–14; 1 Corinthians 11.23–26;
John 13.1–17, 31b–35

LOVE IN ACTION

*God our Father, you have invited us to share in the supper which your Son
gave to his Church to proclaim his death until he comes: may he nourish us
by his presence, and unite us in his love; who is alive and reigns with you in
the unity of the Holy Spirit, one God, now and for ever. Amen.*

'During supper Jesus, knowing that he was going to God, got up from the table
and began to wash the disciples' feet.' Washing feet that were dusty, possibly
muddy, from the street was one of the first things that happened when people
entered a house, before starting a meal. It was a practical act, done by a servant
or by a junior member of the host household, much like taking someone's coat
today, and Jesus and the disciples would already have had their feet washed
by the time the meal started. So when, part way through the meal, Jesus rose
from the table, tied a towel around himself and poured water into the basin,
this was evidently not the routine action. Peter's response could be because he
felt humbled by Jesus's action, or it could be that he was perplexed at what was
going on.

John frames this story with references to love, beginning by recording that
Jesus loved his own who were in the world – his family and friends – to the end.
He ends it with Jesus commanding his friends to love one another just as he has
loved them, because this will be the way that everyone else will know they are
his disciples. Everything about the foot-washing is in the context of Jesus's love.

John also states that Jesus's action was precipitated by the knowledge that
his hour had come. That realization had apparently come to him a few days
earlier when Philip and Andrew brought the group of Greeks who were asking
to see Jesus. Jesus's enigmatic response, 'The hour has come for the Son of Man
to be glorified' (John 12.23), appeared to ignore the waiting visitors entirely.
Instead he was caught up in what their arrival – symbolizing the non-Jewish
world coming to him – meant for him. Then he picked up that theme of glory as
soon as the betrayer had left the room, 'Now the Son of Man has been glorified
and God has been glorified in him.'

How did Jesus express his love to his friends and reveal God's glory? He
washed his disciples' feet. We are rightly stung by the example of his humility
and each Maundy Thursday around the world this is followed as a worked
example of loving and serving one another. Having our feet washed is often
harder than washing other people's feet. It makes us more vulnerable. In part it
is that we become aware of the imperfections of our feet as we expose them (and

perhaps even the smell), but it is also that we are rendered immobile because someone else is gently holding the feet that we rely on to get us around. Foot-washing enforces stillness. For the disciples it enforced attentiveness to Jesus because, almost inevitably, when people have their feet washed in church they look at the person washing them.

Contrast that with the Israelites in Exodus. At the first Passover they were to eat on the run, loins girded, sandals on their feet and staff in hand, and they were to eat it hurriedly. No time for foot-washing there. Again it was an event framed by love, God's love for his enslaved and abused people. Love to which they were to be attentive and which was to shape their life and action for ever after. So the reading begins with the words, 'This month shall mark for you the beginning of months; it shall be the first month of the year for you,' and it ends, 'This day shall be a day of remembrance for you. You shall celebrate it as a festival to the Lord.' From that time onwards, their sense of time was to be ordered, indeed dictated, by memory of God's deliverance.

And so it is for us. Jesus's actions at the Last Supper of taking and sharing bread and wine, as described succinctly by Paul, have shaped the lives of Christians ever since. As Gregory Dix put it, 'The sheer stupendous quantity of the love of God which this repeated action has drawn from the obscure Christian multitude through the centuries is in itself an overwhelming thought' (Dix, 1945). Shoes on or shoes off, that love is expressed in service, in allowing ourselves to be vulnerable, in being ready to move when called, and by ordering our lives within the love of God.

Good Friday

Isaiah 52.13–53.12; Psalm 22; Hebrews 10.16–25;
John 18.1–19.42

PRAYING WITH SHATTERED HOPE AND STUBBORN FAITH

*Almighty Father, look with mercy on this your family for which our Lord
Jesus Christ was content to be betrayed and given up into the hands of
sinners and to suffer death upon the cross; who is alive and glorified with
you and the Holy Spirit, one God, now and for ever. Amen.*

There is a moment in the Good Friday liturgy at Durham Cathedral which always
moves me deeply. It is when, during the singing of the seventh-century hymn,

Sing, my tongue, the glorious battle,
sing the ending of the fray,
o'er the cross, the victor's triumph,
sound the loud triumphant lay:
tell how Christ, the world's Redeemer,
as a victim won the day,

a very large cross, draped with a deep red cloth and carried in procession down
the aisle, finally comes into view in the corner of my eye. If I am presiding at the
service I follow it on its slow progress past row upon row of people, all catching
their first glimpse of it while we sing of the victory won on the cross.

For the first few centuries, art and hymnody proclaimed that Christ reigned
from, rather than suffered on, the cross. Another early hymn sings:

O Tree of beauty, Tree of light,
O Tree with royal beauty dight [dressed or adorned, as for battle],
Elect on whose triumphal breast
These holy limbs should find their rest.

These hymns express the theology of John's Gospel. Having begun with light
shining in the darkness and the darkness not overcoming it, the Passion narrative
brings this confrontation of light and darkness to a head. Pilate – raw Roman
power – was confounded: his world-view treated scars like those of Isaiah's
servant as signs of weakness; now he faced Jesus who, by exercising power
so differently, shone light in Pilate' darkness to the extent that Pilate knew he
should release him.

To quote another Passion hymn, God is 'most sure in all his ways'. At
Morning Prayer on Good Friday we pray with the psalmist (69.15), 'Answer
me, O God, in the abundance of your mercy and with your sure salvation.' Each
Good Friday, Isaiah, Hebrews and John leave us marvelling at God's wisdom

in bringing victory out of horrific cruelty, destroying the power of death. Isaiah's litany of the servant's suffering ends with his making many righteous and dividing the spoil with the strong. He prospers and is exalted, startling the powerful with the scars of his suffering.

Jesus opens the new and living way at which Hebrews marvels. John's Gospel has Jesus ending his life with victorious words of completion, 'It is finished!' However, they went unheard for John has no centurion to recognize who Jesus was, no hint of exaltation of the suffering servant. So we end Good Friday with Jesus in a tomb and the disciples facing a chasm of futility.

What was it like for the disciples? Thomas Troeger writes that 'the church needs a "theology of sighing", a theology of the sound that is made by grief too overwhelming to speak, by grace too extravagant to name, by beauty too intense to articulate and by prayer too profound for our lips to shape into speech' (Troeger, 2010). Those are the sounds of the Passion of Christ, of the suffering of God's world today, and of the victory of the cross.

Each Easter Eve in Durham Cathedral, at Evening Prayer, we sing A. E. Housman's poem of doubt and trust, which explores the troubling territory of meaninglessness and the devastation of shattered hope:

If in that Syrian garden, ages slain,
You sleep, and know not you are dead in vain,
Nor even in dreams behold how dark and bright
Ascends in smoke and fire by day and night
The hate you died to quench and could but fan,
Sleep well and see no morning, son of man.

But if, the grave rent and the stone rolled by,
At the right hand of majesty on high
You sit, and sitting so remember yet
Your tears, your agony and bloody sweat,
Your cross and passion and the life you gave,
Bow hither out of heaven and see and save.

It is when we sing those two words, 'But if', that my heart leaps. They are the hinge of hope. Yet, for now, like the disciples we have to wait to know if death is the whole story. And so, on Good Friday we pray, in stubborn, trusting faith, for God to look in mercy on us, his family:

Christ crucified draw you to himself, to find in him a sure ground for faith, a firm support for hope, and the assurance of sins forgiven. Amen.

Easter Day

Acts 10.34–43 or Jeremiah 31.1–6; Colossians 3.1–4;
John 20.1–18 or Matthew 28.1–10

A SOUND OF GRACE AND BEAUTY

*Lord of all life and power, who through the mighty resurrection of your
Son overcame the old order of sin and death to make all things new in him:
grant that we, being dead to sin and alive to you in Jesus Christ, may reign
with him in glory; to whom with you and the Holy Spirit be praise and
honour, glory and might, now and in all eternity. Amen.*

What happened at dawn on the first day of the week was not instant and
overwhelming joy for those involved. It provoked yet more perplexity. Mary
Magdalene and another Mary (like Judas who was 'not Iscariot' – John 14.22
– she was equally faithful but always named in relation to someone else) went
to see the tomb. Suddenly there was the second earthquake in three days and an
angel, looking like lightning and snow at the same time, descended from heaven
and sat on the stone. It was holy commotion yet again.

Matthew, having previously recorded the setting of the guard, contrasts
those men with these women. All were at the tomb, felt the earthquake, saw
the angel and felt the fear. Unlike the previous earthquake which brought dead
people back to life, this one caused living guards to become like dead people.
The women were bolder – afraid, yes, but they held their ground.

They were invited to see the emptiness that betokened Jesus's absence, to
express the sighing that needed a theology. An empty tomb on its own was not
evidence of resurrection. It was Jesus's going ahead to Galilee that gave them
hope. Galilee, off the political map, where they had first encountered Jesus, was
to be the place where hope was given substance.

Mingled with great joy, fear was not paralysing but gave impetus to action.
These were times full of wonder, and the Authorized Version captures this in a
way that more recent translations do not. Good Friday's, 'And, behold, the veil
of the temple was rent in twain' yields on Easter Day to still more marvels for
human eyes and hearts to behold: 'And, behold, there was a great earthquake
… and behold he goeth before you into Galilee … and behold Jesus met them.'
Behold!

So the women ran but Jesus beat them to it, interrupting their run. Even so,
Jesus does not play a large part in Matthew's account of the chaotic dawn goings-
on. His one word, 'Greetings', was almost a walk-on part, but it was some walk-
on. The women recognized him, touched him and worshipped him, showing
none of the doubt that some disciples experienced subsequently (28.16). Then it
was action stations. Just as once disciples were told to proclaim the good news

(Matthew 10.7), now the women were to tell his brothers to go to meet him, and once there they would be told to go and make disciples of all the nations (Matthew 20.19).

I drafted this reflection one evening. The next day someone came to talk something through, and I write this part with her permission. Maybe because I had been immersed in Matthew's dawn story, as she described what had been going on in her life I heard resonances with the underlying issues for the two Marys, so I simply read the story aloud and we discussed it.

Matthew describes speechless, fearful women who had faced a devastating ending, paralysed into inaction and seemingly not knowing what to do next. The angel had to give them very firm and straightforward directions: 'do not be afraid'; 'come and see the tomb' (take a good look and see it is empty, what you laid there is gone, a thing of the past, so leave it behind); 'go quickly and tell the disciples that he has been raised and is going before you' (move on, there is a way forward); 'you will see him in Galilee' (get on with the journey without understanding everything, God who has acted so radically thus far will provide insight when you arrive).

She made her own connections and her face lit up with new insight and hope. I will not tell you what they were, for they are her story. It renewed my joy and confidence that God, who – as a consequence of the resurrection – turned the women's lives around and gave them confidence to move forward in new mission, is doing the same today in our lives.

In the Collect's phrase, through the mighty resurrection of his Son, the old order of sin and death is overcome. There is a sound of grace and beauty expressed in Jesus's one word, 'Greetings'. All things are made new in Christ. Alleluia!

Second Sunday of Easter

Acts 2.14a, 22–32; Exodus 14.10–31, 15.20–21 or
1 Peter 1.3–9; John 20.19–31

THROUGH THE LOCKED DOOR

Almighty Father, you have given your only Son to die for our sins and to rise again for our justification: grant us so to put away the leaven of malice and wickedness that we may always serve you in pureness of living and truth; through the merits of your Son Jesus Christ our Lord. Amen.

It was hardly a hotbed of faith which Jesus invaded when he bypassed the locked door that expressed the disciples' fear. No wonder his first words were the Jewish greeting of peace. Only when he showed them his hands and side did the disciples rejoice at seeing him. It was all a more muted reaction than the joyful and raucous ringing of bells and blowing of hooters that each year greets the announcement 'Christ is risen!' at the dawn Eucharist in Durham Cathedral: the choristers love it because it is not often that you can bring a football rattle to the cathedral!

We rejoice, and rightly so. But it took time for the message to sink in for the disciples. The tomb was terrifyingly empty, and the Gospels vividly describe people's responses of perplexity, terror, hiding their faces in fear, weeping, shaking, not understanding, alarm, disbelief, amazement and going home alone. Our familiarity with the story blinds us to its unfamiliarity and terror at the time, and to the disciples' sheer exhaustion mentally, physically and spiritually. The resurrection was not an instant panacea for their fears. So, a week later, the doors were still firmly shut.

What must the intervening days have been like? Jesus stretched them, being in no hurry to make it easy. He had imparted the Holy Spirit to the disciples, giving them a commission. Yet they had failed signally to convince the first person they told about the resurrection, their friend Thomas. It is tempting, when we are with someone who has genuine difficulty believing, to rush in with reassurance rather than let doubt run its sometimes necessary course of opening us up in greater depth to God's presence. Just because Thomas had not seen Jesus did not mean that Jesus was not risen. When we are not aware of God's presence, it does not mean that God is absent.

John recorded these signs, among many others, so that we can come to believe that Jesus is the Son of God and have life in him. The Gospel-writer's answer to doubts and unbelief is to immerse ourselves in the Christian story and be open to come to believe.

Studies suggest that coming to believe can take years. As for the disciples, our turning point may be a trauma when life is turned horrifically upside down. In one church I know, the vicar asked during a sermon how the congregation came or returned to faith. Several people said it was through the church's presence with them during bereavement arising from death, job loss or divorce. An impromptu show of hands indicated that one third of the congregation said it was like that for them, that they were in church that day because someone had helped them come to believe in time of loss. Stories like this remind us to be very attentive in caring patiently for our friends and neighbours in times of difficulty or bereavement.

It is very easy to consign these stories of resurrection appearances to history. But salvation history involves a time warp: past and present meet, catching us up in it all. In the Exsultet which is sung at Easter and recalls the deliverance recounted in the Exodus reading, we sing 'this is the night' when you delivered us, not 'that was the night'; in the Eucharist we pray that the bread and wine 'may be to us', not just 'may remind us of', the body and blood of our Lord. The resurrection story is in the present tense. We are in it.

This is also John's Pentecost story, when the disciples received the Holy Spirit and Jesus sent them out. John uses 'sent' about 40 times in the Gospel to describe what God did with Jesus and into which Jesus drew the disciples. Another Gospel theme is that light is shining in darkness, and it is significant that John's resurrection stories mostly take place at night or early morning. God sent his Son, who sends his disciples – us – into the thick of the world where light needs to shine and where sins need to be forgiven, helping people to come to believe in Jesus Christ, risen from the dead. The early chapters of Acts, which we read at Easter, give vignettes of what happened when they did get out and preach the gospel. The locked door was flung open. People came to believe.

Third Sunday of Easter

Acts 2.14a, 36–41; Zephaniah 3.14–end or
1 Peter 1.17–23; Luke 24.13–35

ACTIONS LOUDER THAN WORDS

Almighty Father, who in your great mercy gladdened the disciples with the sight of the risen Lord: give us such knowledge of his presence with us, that we may be strengthened and sustained by his risen life and serve you continually in righteousness and truth; through Jesus Christ our Lord. Amen.

Sometimes we find it easier to risk being vulnerable with other people if we are not looking at them but just keeping company together. While working for a few months as a hospital chaplain in the USA, I visited a patient who was curt with everyone and upset most of the nurses. She was not sure what to make of a chaplain with a British accent, especially when somehow I ended up teaching her to knit. I discovered that as I sat alongside her, sorting things out when her knitting went a bit awry, she started to talk. As her scarf grew, some of her story crept out. When we said a final goodbye she had surprised herself not only by knitting most of a scarf but by expressing things never before articulated, and her anger was gradually being defused. The nurses noticed the change.

So I can understand how these two disciples started to talk as they trudged home from Jerusalem after the extraordinary events about which even strangers in Jerusalem knew. We do not know how much they knew, except that they had heard from people who had gone to the tomb and knew that the apostles did not believe the women's story. How things had changed by the time Peter spoke so boldly to the crowds about God making the crucified Jesus Lord and Messiah, or when the epistle was written with its absolute assurance that God raised Christ from the dead.

But that was later; this was still the third day after the crucifixion with its horrific memories of Jesus's suffering and now wild rumours. Walking side by side rather than facing each other probably freed these disciples to express their doubts and confusion. When Jesus joined them, he specifically referred to their walking, and then Luke records that they stood still. We can imagine it happening: the stopping, turning and raising their heads to look at him. Here was the first eye contact; sad eye contact.

The rhythm of walking broken, they did not answer the question directly but asked one back of him and only resumed their discussion when he pressed again. He coaxed their doubts and fears out of them and gradually all their confusion and grief poured out in a torrent of words. Ultimately, 'We had hoped …' said it all. Somehow we are miles away from the Collect's assurance that the disciples were gladdened with the sight of the risen Lord.

Yet that changed, as a result not of what Jesus said but of what he did – actions spoke louder than words. Incidentally, this is another indication that there were more than just the 12 disciples at the Last Supper: these two recognized Jesus's actions of just four days earlier. Once their eyes were opened, Jesus promptly vanished. Again they were left to make sense of the inexplicable, but this time on the basis of their own extraordinary experience.

In Luke's account this was the first encounter with the risen Jesus because until now, although his body was evidently missing, only angels had been seen. By that evening Peter, too, had had a similar encounter and the rest knew about it. The Collect's petition, for such knowledge of his presence with us as will strengthen and sustain us for continual service, was being answered for them and will be for us.

> In the breaking of the bread we recognize you,
> as you take the bread and bless and break and give;
> in the wine poured out and shared we know forgiveness,
> by your body and your blood, O Lord, we live.
>
> In our pain and in our grief you walk beside us
> staying with us as we voice our deepest fear.
> As the darkness falls around us, Lord, stay with us,
> still the doubts that rise, speak peace we need to hear.
>
> In the opening of Scripture, Lord, we know you;
> as you speak the words of life our hearts are stirred,
> in the truth revealed we understand God's purpose:
> to our slow and doubting hearts, Lord, speak your word.
>
> In the gathering of your people come among us,
> you are risen indeed, we know that to be true.
> Break the bread and bless the wine and feed your people,
> through your Holy Spirit's power our lives renew.
>
> *Copyright © 1988 Rosalind Brown*

Fourth Sunday of Easter

Acts 2.42–47; Genesis 7 or 1 Peter 2.19–25; John 10.1–10

GOD'S POWER TO DESTROY AND DELIVER

> *Almighty God, whose Son Jesus Christ is the resurrection and the life: raise us, who trust in him, from the death of sin to the life of righteousness, that we may seek those things which are above, where he reigns with you in the unity of the Holy Spirit, one God, now and for ever. Amen.*

Over the next three weeks we hear the fabulous flood story, resonant with baptismal imagery that is so appropriate in the Easter season when, in the early centuries, the newly baptized were instructed in the faith they had embraced through baptism. Can we be instructed too?

The earth, which God created very good (Genesis 1.31), had become corrupt and filled with violence, going its own self-destructive way. The flood is described as an act not of God's anger but of sorrow at a spoiled creation. So God offered a new beginning and promised a covenant with Noah who would be saved if he expressed his obedience by building an ark. The exotic exaggeration of Noah's age expresses his righteousness: he had outlived the normal 120-year lifespan which God had decreed (Genesis 6.3).

Archaeological records tell of extensive floods which may lie behind the various flood stories of mythology. The editor of Genesis blended two versions of the story and we need not worry about the discrepancy in animal numbers. What is significant is the way the Bible's flood story differed from those told in other ancient cultures where floods were capricious or malicious acts by the gods; here it was God's judgement on human sin with a view to a new beginning.

In this distinctive theology of the biblical version of the flood story, God remains in control but allows creation to express its natural power; the swirling of waters coming from below and the deluge from above threaten a return to the chaos before God brought order to creation in Genesis 1. God acted to deliver people through the flood and, reading ahead to the next two weeks' portion of the story, once it was over God encouraged Noah and his family to make a new and fruitful beginning, almost repeating the instructions given to Adam. The slate was (literally) wiped clean.

Unlike similar stories from other cultures, this version of the flood story does not allow us to see natural disasters as an angry deity's capricious acts but as a consequence of the way the earth is made and the way we live on it. Nevertheless, the vivid descriptions of the force and extent of the flood and its devastating effect reminded the people of God's power, a theme expressed vividly in Psalm 29. However, the other side of this coin was that God used that power to deliver people.

This theme of deliverance through waters occurs again in the Exodus, as we heard two weeks ago, and in Isaiah's prophetic promise, 'Fear not, I have redeemed you. When you pass through the rivers they shall not overwhelm you' (Isaiah 43.1–2). God's underlying care in seeking the deliverance of his people also shines through in Jesus's words, 'I am the gate. Whoever enters by me will be saved and will come in and go out and find pasture.'

As Christians we also see this symbolism in baptism, and the Church began to baptize from day one. What did people do after they were baptized? They devoted themselves to teaching, fellowship, breaking of bread and prayer. They also ensured that no one was in need: God's generous deliverance of them issued in their generous care of people in need. The phrase 'glad and generous hearts' is wonderfully evocative of the atmosphere in the new Church; no wonder they had the goodwill of other people and many were saved and added to their number. This was indeed a new beginning.

Notice how God personally shut Noah and his coterie in the ark (a vivid image of God slamming the door shut!), and that Jesus is the gate of the sheepfold, thus facing danger to protect those inside. This can help us to make a response to floods and other tragedies that is more reflective of God's care and protection. A few years ago we experienced flooding in Britain as disaster and it brought things close to home, but will we remember the impact when the next disaster strikes somewhere far away? Maybe our Easter thankfulness to God for raising us to the life of righteousness can be expressed through glad and generous caring for people who suffer from the turbulence of our world.

Fifth Sunday of Easter

Acts 7.55–60; Genesis 8.1–19 or 1 Peter 2.2–10;
John 14.1–14

MARTYRDOM AT EASTER

Almighty God, who through your only-begotten Son Jesus Christ have overcome death and opened to us the gate of everlasting life: grant that, as by your grace going before us you put into our minds good desires, so by your continual help we may bring them to good effect; through Jesus Christ our risen Lord. Amen.

I do not want to find out how I would cope with watching someone being stoned to death. What was it like for those disciples who braved the crowd and their distress to watch? Why did God allow it? What sense did the good news of the resurrection make? It makes me wonder about Saul, there in the front row approving of it all. It is a disturbing picture.

Luke casts Stephen's death in the mould of Jesus's death. He wants us to understand that Stephen, the first Christian martyr, followed his Lord to death not only in commitment but also in conduct. So both men faced accusations by the populace at the instigation of leaders, both had the assurance that they were going to be with God, and both prayed for forgiveness for those causing their deaths.

In contrast to this vivid and bloodthirsty story which led to persecution and the scattering of the Church, we have the measured calm of the conversation between Jesus and his disciples. Hearing the reassuring words, 'Do not let your hearts be troubled,' we are immediately in calmer waters, in danger of seeing this as little more than a leisurely theological and philosophical debate about heaven and the vision of God, forgetting that John presents this as Jesus's last proper conversation with his disciples before his death.

If you had an hour, under the pressure of ambient fear at what was about to happen, to say all you wanted to your family and friends, what would you say? Jesus's demanding instruction was a command to be active in stopping their hearts from being afraid. Then he answered Thomas's and Philip's questions about how they could be sure of the way to God's house and how they could see the Father. The question of seeing God is a key one throughout John's Gospel, from the prologue's 'No one has ever seen God, it is God the only Son who … has made him known,' to the end when the disciples see but do not always recognize the risen Jesus. In healing the blind man, Jesus used physical sight as a metaphor for spiritual sight.

In this Easter season of resurrection it jars to hear of an angry crowd, a nasty martyrdom, a young man who positively wants to see another stoned to death, fearful disciples commanded not to let their hearts be afraid. Yet putting Stephen's martyrdom, or any similar terrible contemporary event, in dialogue with Jesus's promises is a challenge to which we must rise.

Easter gives a different frame of reference to stories which, on their own, justify fear and despair. Reframed by the Easter story, while the horror of what is wrong is not diminished – stoning can never be made right or sanitized – the power of Jesus's resurrection brings hope of new life in the midst of death. Stephen's vision of God's glory is the outworking of Jesus's promise to his disciples: 'If I go and prepare a place for you, I will come again and will take you to myself so that where I am, there you may be also.' He could add that 'you know the way to the place where I am going' because he himself is the way: all Stephen had to do at the moment of death was pray, 'Lord Jesus, receive my spirit.' By describing Stephen's assurance, Luke puts flesh on the bones of Jesus's promise to the disciples and reassures us of the reliability of our hope.

But we cannot abandon Saul, the young man seeking the blood of Christians. The Bible does not prettify Saul's past just because he becomes a hero in the future. Yet God turned him round. This Easter, the challenge is to let the story of Stephen's horrific death belong with the comfort Jesus promised his disciples before he died. The only way I know to reconcile the two, letting each add profound depth to the other, is to see both through the lens of the death and resurrection of Jesus. How else can we hold together life and death in our own stories or the stories we hear in the news?

Sixth Sunday of Easter

Acts 17.22–31; Genesis 8.20–9.17 or 1 Peter 3.13–22;
John 14.15–21

ON THE HARROWING OF HELL

God our redeemer, you have delivered us from the power of darkness and brought us into the kingdom of your Son: grant, that as by his death he has recalled us to life, so by his continual presence in us he may raise us to eternal joy; through Jesus Christ our Lord. Amen.

The readings fill out the Collect's bold claim that God has delivered us from the powers of darkness. Paul entered the philosophical framework of his pagan hearers to proclaim their unknown God as known. His message of God who made the world giving life to mortals, enabling them to search for and find God, was a quite extraordinary thought for Greeks used to gods too caught up in their own affairs to be interested in humans.

Noah's watery deliverance is described in the epistle as prefiguring baptism. The epistle's reference to God's patient waiting while Noah built the ark suggests God's passion to save from the consequences of sin. Genesis describes the bow in the clouds as a reminder to God, rather than Noah, of the covenant at times when human sin would again tempt God towards destruction (e.g. Exodus 32.7–10).

Then the epistle alludes to the concept, better understood by the Orthodox Church than the western Church despite its inclusion in our Creeds and hymns, that on his death Jesus Christ entered the underworld (considered the place of the dead rather than punishment) to proclaim to the spirits in prison, before rising with all powers subjected to him. St John of Damascus wrote, 'When he had freed those who were bound from the beginning of time, Christ returned from among the dead, having opened for us the way of Resurrection.' Icons of the harrowing of hell show Jesus bursting its gates, hauling Adam and Eve out, followed by others, while we sing,

He whose path no records tell,
Who descended into hell;
Who the strong man armed hath bound,
Now in highest heaven is crowned.
German fifteenth century, translated Catherine Winkworth

A. C. Cawley, introducing the Chester Mystery Play in which – using verses from Psalm 24 – Christ bursts the gates of hell and frees those held captive, commented: 'The cooks and innkeepers of Chester who acted this pageant no doubt enjoyed themselves, rushing in and out of the monstrous jaws of hell-mouth and clashing their pots and kettles. But it should be remembered that medieval men and women took the devil and his works more seriously than we do today, and that the merriment of the spectators probably had an uncomfortable edge to it' (Cawley, 1993).

We are not so different from our forebears, although we might express things slightly differently. Our society is full of fear and a sense of being powerless, whether we are facing international terrorism or the difficulty of getting good care for our elderly relatives. In *Praying with Icons*, Jim Forrest comments:

> The icon of Christ's descent into hell can be linked with an ongoing prayer not to live a fear-centred life. We live in what is often a terrifying world. Being fearful seems to be a reasonable state to be in – fear of violent crime, fear of job loss, fear of failure, fear of illness, fear for the well-being of people we love, fear of war, and finally fear of death … We can easily get ourselves into a paralysing state of fear that is truly hellish. The icon reminds us that Christ can enter not just some other hell but the hell we happen to be in, grab us by the hands, and lift us out of our tombs.' (Forrest, 1997)

What about us today? It is fine to talk about all this in theological terms, but where is the good news in this for us? On Easter Sunday we proclaimed triumphantly, 'Christ is risen!' That victory does not simply set us an example but has a creative effect upon us and upon all creation. Our hearts and wills are transformed, we are released from bondage, made whole, brought into the kingdom of God's Son.

'The Word became flesh and dwelt among us,' proclaimed John at the beginning of his Gospel, and last Sunday we heard that the Father dwells in Jesus. On the cusp of Ascension-tide with Jesus's promise of another Advocate to dwell with us for ever ringing in our ears, like Paul's pagan audience, Jesus's beloved disciples and 1 Peter's persecuted readers, Christ's continual presence dwelling with us raises us to eternal joy. I am left pondering what difference this glorious truth makes in my life day by day.

Ascension Day

Acts 1.1–11; Daniel 7.9–14 or Ephesians 1.15–23;
Luke 24.44–53

A NEW BEGINNING

> *Grant, we pray, almighty God, that as we believe your only-begotten Son our Lord Jesus Christ to have ascended into the heavens, so we in heart and mind may also ascend and with him continually dwell; who is alive and reigns with you, in the unity of the Holy Spirit, one God, now and for ever. Amen.*

Final farewells are sad occasions, whether they take place at an airport or by a graveside. When I moved to the States in 1991, I recall kneeling in the hall of my house, holding my five-year-old godson as he sobbed his little heart out. I wrote in my journal, 'Why can't there be beginnings without endings?' The hymn 'Blest be the tie that binds' was written by a Baptist minister in Bradford for his farewell service before he moved to London in 1762, but, having packed his belongings on a wagon, he found the farewell service so emotional that he changed his mind and stayed!

So it is surprising that Jesus's final goodbye to his disciples appears positively joyful. Gone were the fears and the doubts mingled with joy at his resurrection appearances; now the disciples returned to Jerusalem with great joy and were continually in the Temple blessing God.

St Luke has two accounts of the event we know as the ascension. One brings the story of Jesus's earthly life to an end, and the other opens up the story of what happened next when the Holy Spirit took the lead. In the cosmology of the time, people thought in terms of up and down to express different realms. Luke is expressing physically the theological truth spelled out in Ephesians about God's immeasurable power raising Christ from death and seating him in the heavenly places. The ascension affirms that no part of the universe, the extent of which is beyond our imagining, is barred to God; no authority or power is not subject to him.

Resurrection and ascension belong together. Without the ascension, while knowing that God raised Jesus, we do not know what happened ultimately to the risen Jesus and have no firm hope for ourselves. The ascension completes the incarnation – the Second Person of the Trinity who took human flesh and was born among us has taken humanity into heaven, opening the door for us to enter heaven too.

In Luke's Gospel, the ascension brings Jesus's life on earth to its fulfilment. He took his companions (not necessarily just the disciples) to Bethany where he had experienced so much hospitality from Martha, Mary and Lazarus. There he blessed them and withdrew into heaven. Luke's Gospel, which began with heaven opening and divinity coming to earth, ends with heaven opening to receive humanity into heaven.

Acts describes the same event as the first chapter of a new story about the Church, which was promised the Holy Spirit and commissioned to be Jesus's witnesses. A cloud – biblically, a sign of the presence of God – removed him from the disciples' sight. The ascension is the work of the triune God, Father, Son and Holy Spirit, whose love reaches out, sending witnesses to all creation.

Whether the ascension is a story of an ending or a beginning, Jerusalem, the city at the centre of religious worship and government, became the place of dispersal. The disciples were to begin their witness in Jerusalem and to go from there to all nations and the ends of the earth. For a group of manual workers from the backwater of Galilee, that was some calling. So, while the ascension is about Jesus returning to heaven, it is also about a new beginning for all who follow him.

Why can't there be beginnings without endings? Sometimes things have to die in order for there to be new life. Luke's two accounts underline this. Ascension as the ending of Jesus's physical presence on earth must have been a bittersweet moment. Ascension, as the beginning of the mission of the Church, anticipates the wonder of Pentecost.

We are caught up in this beginning. Each of us is challenged by Jesus's ascension to be witnesses of the wonderful works of God who has raised Christ from the dead and seated him in the heavenly places. At the beginning of Jesus's ministry, Luke described Jesus's vocation as bringing good news to the poor, release to the captives, recovery of sight to the blind and letting the oppressed go free. Jesus changed people's physical as well as their spiritual situations, since both are interlinked. That work goes on today. The consequence of Christ's ascension, translated for us, is to be witnesses wherever we are placed.

The ascension led to joyful worship and service for the disciples. Nothing has changed.

Seventh Sunday of Easter

Acts 1.6–14; Ezekiel 36.24–28 or 1 Peter 4.12–14, 5.6–11; John 17.1–11

TRIED, BUT NOT COMFORTLESS

> *O God the King of glory, you have exalted your only Son Jesus Christ with great triumph to your kingdom in heaven: we beseech you, leave us not comfortless, but send your Holy Spirit to strengthen us and exalt us to the place where our Saviour Christ is gone before, who is alive and reigns with you, in the unity of the Holy Spirit, one God, now and for ever. Amen.*

Sometimes it is easier to gaze into the heavens than get on with life on earth. Eastertide's readings from 1 Peter remind us that, although Christ is exalted with great triumph to the Kingdom in heaven, here on earth all is not so overtly glorious. In the words of the Lord's Prayer, God's Kingdom is still coming. The epistle pulls no punches; Christians should not think it strange to face fiery ordeals or a prowling adversary, lurking in the shadows waiting to pounce. In fact, these trials offer an opportunity to rejoice in sharing Christ's sufferings.

This is an unlikely message of resurrection joy. Yet, both Peter and the Collect use the word 'exalt'. Because God has exalted his Son we, who are in Christ, can pray with confidence to be exalted because the Holy Spirit both strengthens and exalts us.

Ezekiel's promise, radical in the historic political manoeuvres involved and the people's change of heart, was that God would gather his people from exile among other nations to be their God, bringing them to their own land as God's people. Jesus, speaking of the Spirit who would cause living water to flow from believers' hearts (John 7.38–39), drew on Ezekiel's promise of a new heart and spirit responsive to God. Our familiarity with the idea should not breed contempt of its radicality.

In John's chronology, Jesus's prayer, for the Father to glorify the Son and for those who follow him, was prayed in the shadow of his betrayal, arrest and death. God's promise through Ezekiel of a new beginning when people would want to be faithful was fulfilled less through miraculous signs and wonders than in the day-to-day faithfulness of the vulnerable people left behind after Jesus's violent death.

Acts lists some of the early beneficiaries of this prayer by naming the eleven, some women, and Jesus's mother and brothers. The fact that men and women prayed together was one new manifestation of God's life among them, while the presence of Jesus's siblings – previously unbelieving (John 7.5) – was another. The promised new heart and new spirit were given to ordinary people facing confusion and threatened opposition as they came to terms with the resurrection and ascension. In God's hands, glory and exaltation are not estranged from suffering and trials. They can and do coexist.

So while this week's Collect describes Jesus's departure as a great, triumphal entry into God's Kingdom in heaven, it promptly prays that we who are left be not comfortless. Exaltation is not inimical to suffering or bereavement. We can forgive the disciples for being confused since, after the potent combination of grief, fear, doubt and joy involved in coming to terms with the crucifixion and resurrection, they faced the uncertainty of when and where they would see Jesus. His comings and goings were not under their control until, finally, he entered a cloud and disappeared for good. They were stretched to what could feel like breaking point and we should not simply read back into this account their later understanding of Jesus's prayer for them.

Significantly, their response was to devote themselves to prayer. The epistle instructs Christians to humble ourselves, not with Uriah Heap's ingratiating obsequiousness but in honest recognition that, warts and all, we are under God's mighty hand. So, Jesus's parable of the wedding banquet with its invitation to 'move up higher' ends with, 'all who exalt themselves will be humbled, but those who humble themselves will be exalted' (Luke 14.7–11). Only when we own our dependence on God's power, can God exalt us.

As Easter ends with celebration of the ascension of our Lord into the glory that he shared with his Father, the daily news reminds us that, like the disciples and Peter's readers, we live in a troubled world. If we believe that the world is God's and he will strengthen us, then we can dare to be quite specific in our prayers to be given a new spirit, to be God's people in the world. As I write this, headlines include kidnapped schoolgirls in Nigeria, controversial Ukrainian elections, and fantastic insights into the evolution of the world after the big bang. Prayer for God's world remains challenging. We pray with confidence.

Pentecost

Acts 2.1–21; Numbers 11.24–30 or
1 Corinthians 12.3b–13; John 20.19–23

TALE OF THE UNEXPECTED

*God, who as at this time taught the hearts of your faithful people by sending
to them the light of your Holy Spirit: grant us by the same Spirit to have a
right judgement in all things and evermore to rejoice in his holy comfort;
through the merits of Christ Jesus our Saviour. Amen.*

Bishop Michael Ramsey once wrote:

The power of the Holy Spirit is mighty, but intimate and personal too. The
effects of God's actions are seen in human behaviour: the actions themselves,
in minds, hearts and consciences are describable in symbols alone … What
does *fire* tell us about the Holy Spirit? …The Holy Spirit keeps the light of
Jesus glowing within us: that is how we may see as Christians should see.
Fire also gives warmth; so the warmth and love of God can warm your heart
to love Him in response …

Light, warmth, and burning too: the Holy Spirit will burn us. If we
are to have vision and warmth of love, we must be exposed to the pain
of burning … only by such burning can our hearts be exposed fully to his
warmth, and our minds be exposed fully to his light. There is no seeing and
no warming without burning. (Ramsey: 1974)

In the concealment of a locked room in an unnamed house, Jesus appeared to
his frightened disciples, repeated words of peace and gently breathed on them,
imparting the Holy Spirit. Little did they guess how that would work in practice,
how they would be burned. At Pentecost, one minute they were praying together,
the next a violent wind and divided tongues as of fire disrupted things. They
spoke in other languages. A bewildered crowd gathered, all talking at once.
'Amazed and perplexed' is an understatement. I was once present when a friend
spoke in tongues and someone from another continent, recognizing a rare tribal
dialect spoken fluently, confirmed the translation given. Everyone was astounded
this happened to people we knew. So, one message of Pentecost is that God does
extraordinary things with and through ordinary people. The cast list in his story
is very unexpected.

Put ourselves in the shoes of the people in the biblical stories and we would
be very surprised at ourselves. Moses was in the desert with a disgruntled crowd
of people and God sending fire to destroy parts of their camp (Numbers 11.1)
when Eldad and Medad, whoever they were, experienced the spirit resting on
them. They kept on prophesying even though they were not in the group Moses

had registered as elders who, having been taken to the tent of meeting, prophesied but once. Paul's motley Corinthian readers received varieties of spiritual gifts and experience of the Spirit within the one body.

It is not just humans who respond to the vivifying power of the Spirit: creation joins in too. The psalm appointed for Pentecost (104.26–37) describes physical creation trembling and smoking at God's presence, an allusion Peter picked up in his impromptu sermon. We cannot be so presumptuous as to assume that only humans respond to God's presence.

The Durham Cathedral Confirmation group relished their exploration of the biblical story and their growing understanding of its revelation of the First and Second Persons of the Trinity. Comprehending the Holy Spirit was harder until we talked about how we see the signs of the Spirit bringing life in people, in the church, in creation and the world. Then, at dawn on Easter Day, we prayed that the Holy Spirit would rest on each of them with wisdom, counsel, knowledge and true godliness, and it is happening already, differently for each.

As a child, I remember the dawning realization that not all recordings of Rachmaninov's second piano concerto were the same. It seems obvious now! I discovered that musicians interpreted what the composer wrote. Similarly, this extraordinary cross-section of people we encounter at Pentecost played the music of their lives to God's glory as, in Ramsey's words, the fire of God burned them. In his poem, 'As kingfishers catch fire', Gerard Manley Hopkins brilliantly described what happens when humans catch fire for God and make their music to God's glory, revealing Christ in their lives.

> I say more: the just man justices;
> Keeps grace: that keeps all his goings graces;
> Acts in God's eye what in God's eye he is –
> Christ – for Christ plays in ten thousand places,
> Lovely in limbs, and lovely in eyes not his
> To the Father through the features of men's faces.

Trinity Sunday

Isaiah 40.12–17, 27–31; 2 Corinthians 13.11–13;
Matthew 28.16–20

GREEN AVENUE TO ADVENT

*Almighty and everlasting God, you have given us your servants grace,
by the confession of a true faith, to acknowledge the glory of the eternal
Trinity and in the power of the divine majesty to worship the Unity: keep
us steadfast in this faith, that we may evermore be defended from all
adversities; through Jesus Christ our Lord. Amen.*

In 1987, preaching at Durham Cathedral, Canon Professor Dan Hardy said:

Let me be completely straightforward. Trinity Sunday is the most exciting
day of the year, because it celebrates the simple heart of Christian faith, and
wraps all the excitement of the other great festivals of the Church's year
into one sunburst of a celebration. But there is also a sense in which this
excitingly simple heart of the Christian faith is an open heart; and for that
reason it cannot be wrapped up.

Over one hundred years earlier, also in Durham Cathedral, the then Precentor
encouraged the rare practice of singing hymns. Not finding suitable music, he
composed his own and tried it out on Sunday afternoons with his family and
friends who gathered in the Galilee Chapel (the nave was a step too far!). And
so it was there that the tune Nicaea, named for the creedal faith, was matched to
Bishop Heber's text, 'Holy, holy, holy'. With its rising thirds raising our hearts to
heaven, John Bacchus Dykes etched his place in the story of hymnody and gave
the Church a hymn with which to celebrate Trinity Sunday.

As Dykes used his creativity to express his love for God, he reflected
back God's creativity which expresses his love for the world. I think of that
convergence of creativity each February when Dykes's grave in St Oswald's
churchyard is smothered in snowdrops: the first flowers of the new year and, in
their own way, fragile and beautiful signs of God's creativity.

Trinity is how God is: holy, glorious, creative, beautiful, life-giving;
everything that is not isolated and static. Theologians talk of *perichoresis*, derived
from 'around', 'make room for', and 'dance', to describe God's Trinitarian life.
Trinity Sunday is God's invitation to dance and is, indeed, exciting. So we hear
today of the uncontrollability and unmeasurability of God's life: 'Who has
measured the waters in the hollow of God's hand?' asks Isaiah. 'Who taught him
knowledge?' Who indeed?

Paradoxically, Jesus's claim to have been given all authority in heaven and
earth was made to a rather bedraggled and confused group of 11 disciples who

were not sure whether to doubt or worship. His closest friends were unprepared to have an impossible commission entrusted to them. They were thrown on to what Paul, at the end of his sometimes painful correspondence with the Corinthians, described quite simply as the grace, love and communion of God.

That grace had down-to-earth implications, and he told them to put things in order in their disordered church, to agree and live peacefully with each other. We who are made in the image of God are to live peacefully and steadfastly day by day as people who trust the God we confess. There are consequences for our living.

Having excoriated the attitude that the Church can go through 'all those interminable Sundays after Trinity', as he once heard them described, as if nothing happened, Hardy concluded his sermon,

> We make a big mistake not connecting Trinity Season with Advent, as far off as it is. The season of Trinity looks forward to Advent and the coming of the Last and Great Day, and so it should. There is hardly enough time during the many Sundays between now and Advent to complete the movement of God which has begun in us.

This Trinity Sunday, in a sunburst of celebration, we worship a holy God who invites us, with mutual excitement, to launch out into the dance of God's life throughout the coming days until Advent, guided this year by Matthew. Playfully, perhaps Lewis Carroll can have the last word about risking that leaping out:

> 'You can really have no notion how delightful it will be
> When they take us up and throw us, with the lobsters, out to sea!'
> But the snail replied 'Too far, too far!' and gave a look askance –
> Said he thanked the whiting kindly, but he would not join the dance.
> Would not, could not, would not, could not, would not join the dance.
> Would not, could not, would not, could not, could not join the dance.
> 'What matters it how far we go?' his scaly friend replied.
> 'There is another shore, you know, upon the other side.
> The further off from England the nearer is to France –
> Then turn not pale, beloved snail, but come and join the dance.
> Will you, won't you, will you, won't you, will you join the dance?
> Will you, won't you, will you, won't you, won't you join the dance?'

Sunday after Trinity,

Proper 4 (29 May–4 June)

Deuteronomy 11.18–21, 26–28;
Romans 1.16–17, 3.22b–28 [29–31]; Matthew 7.21–29

ON WISDOM AND WISE LIVING

O God, the strength of all those who put their trust in you, mercifully accept our prayers and, because through the weakness of our mortal nature we can do no good thing without you, grant us the help of your grace, that in the keeping of your commandments we may please you both in will and deed; through Jesus Christ our Lord. Amen.

Collect for the First Sunday after Trinity

In Matthew's Gospel, wisdom has everything to do with the way disciples express in their lives the perspective that they live not just in the present but with attention to the coming Kingdom of God. So, wise people build their house, their life, on a secure foundation; they live astutely and shrewdly amid people who wish them harm (Matthew 10.16); and, whatever the seeming delay which causes others to give up, they are like servants who are prepared at all times for their master's return, and like bridesmaids who are ready at all times for the arrival of the bridegroom (Matthew 24.45–25.13).

The reference to building on a rock carries multiple meanings for Matthew's readers who were familiar with the rest of the Gospel and the Hebrew scripture. God is the one who brings water from rocks in wilderness areas to refresh his people (Numbers 20.11; Deuteronomy 8.15; Psalm 78.16), so to build on the rock is to build on this life-giving provision by God. The psalmists sing of God as our rock (Psalms 18.2, 61.2, 62.2) and draw from that the assurance that God is our security, our defender, our refuge. So the wise person predicates his or her life on the trustworthiness and protection of God. The imagery of building on a rock anticipates Simon's confession that Jesus is the Messiah, the Son of the living God (Matthew 16.18), which leads Jesus to rename him Peter (*petros*), 'rock', and say that this is the rock (*petra*) on which he will build his Church. The Church has debated ever since whether he was referring to Peter himself or his confession that Jesus is the Messiah, the rock.

The description of the storm resonates with storms in the region where the soil cannot absorb sudden heavy rain and there is extensive run-off. I saw it once in the Judean desert where even our local guide was amazed at the flash flood from an unseasonal storm. In the Bible, rain, flood and wind are associated both with God's powerful presence (Psalm 29; Exodus 19.16–19) and also with chaos and judgement (Isaiah 28.17; Ezekiel 13.11–15). Matthew appropriates this imagery elsewhere in the Gospel to describe Jesus's power over this chaos (Matthew 8.23–27, 14.22–33) which led the disciples to wonder and worship.

In contrast, in Matthew's Gospel to be foolish was to ignore the signs of the times which point to God's presence in Jesus. To be foolish is to be blind to God's ways (Matthew 23.17).

All three readings are concerned with how we live. So what can we do to grow in wisdom and avoid foolishness? Deuteronomy points us to the centrality of God's words for wisdom expressed in wise living. Faithful Jews were literally to place God's law centrally on their foreheads and on the doorposts and gates of their house as a constant reminder, and they were to teach God's law to their children in all situations. We hear how God gives a choice to obey and choose life or to turn from the wise way and thus choose to be cursed. Paul, a faithful Jew, moved wise living forward from keeping the written law to living by the law of faith in Jesus Christ. In doing so he claimed not to overthrow the law but to uphold it: the one who is righteous will live by faith. The glory of the gospel is that this is now open to Gentiles as well as Jews.

The Collect for the first Sunday after Trinity acknowledges the weakness of our mortal nature which does not always steer us towards wise living and building our house on the rock. So we pray for the help of God's grace to keep his commandments and please him in will and deed. Building on the rock is not an act of law but of faith, but it still requires a right disposition of our will and positive action. Whether Jew or Gentile, God will justify us on the grounds of faith: faith in the God who is our rock, the God who saw Moses and the people through the barren wilderness, who saw the disciples safely to land from a stormy sea, and who holds out to us the opportunity to choose the blessing, to obey the Lord, our life-giving God.

Sunday after Trinity,
Proper 5 (5–11 June)
Hosea 5.15–6.6; Romans 4.13–25; Matthew 9.9–13, 18–26

'SUDDENLY'

> *O God, the strength of all those who put their trust in you, mercifully accept our prayers and, because through the weakness of our mortal nature we can do no good thing without you, grant us the help of your grace, that in the keeping of your commandments we may please you both in will and deed; through Jesus Christ our Lord. Amen.*
>
> Collect for the First Sunday after Trinity

Twice things happen 'suddenly' to Jesus: suddenly a leader of the synagogue came in; suddenly a woman came up behind him. Matthew rarely uses 'suddenly'; it is more Mark's style and, where Matthew does use it, it is in the context of heaven and earth colliding in some way – angels appear suddenly or demons react suddenly. In this Gospel Jesus is doing one thing when someone else appears. That is hardly unusual, so why does Matthew use the word 'suddenly' to describe the encounters?

Several stories are compressed. Jesus, walking along, saw Matthew and called 'follow me', the same phrase he used when calling other disciples: 'suddenly' would be appropriate here, at least from Matthew's perspective since his life was instantly re-shaped. His fellow tax-collectors and the people with Jesus would be astounded because tax-collectors were not respectable company and people avoided them rather than requested their company. Things became weirder still as many tax-collectors and sinners joined Jesus at dinner. The Pharisees were understandably bothered but Jesus simply said his place was with the dregs of society. Words the Church might remember.

The lectionary skips Jesus answering a question from John the Baptist's disciples, during which a leader of the synagogue suddenly barged in and knelt in front of him asking him to come and heal his daughter. Then suddenly a woman came up behind him and touched him. Try walking in a crowd without being touched, yet Jesus knew this was a special touch. For 12 years religious law had barred this woman from touching anyone, even her husband or child, leaving her isolated from society and now very deliberately breaking the law. When Jesus stopped to talk to her we can imagine the desperate father fuming at the delay. But Jesus was paying attention to the sudden interruption to the sudden interruption.

Matthew does not link the two women as the other Gospels do: the girl was 12 years old and the woman had been suffering for 12 years. In biblical thinking, 12 is a number of completeness and perfection. So in a society in which women did not count for much, the healing of these two women was linked to the religious symbolism of the coming of God's Kingdom when creation is healed and perfected at the end of time.

In both cases Jesus was asked to make himself ritually unclean: to touch a dead body, to be touched by a menstruating woman. Both the ruler of the synagogue and the anonymous woman asked something quite unthinkable if Jesus was to be faithful to religious tradition. Matthew knew exactly what he was doing when using 'suddenly': orderly life was being disrupted. Jesus had called Matthew, a tax-collector, to follow him. Jesus had been touched by and commended a woman who was religiously outcast. And then he took a dead girl by the hand and restored her to life. Heaven and earth were meeting. Not just that miracle but all his engagement with uncleanness was far, far more radical in his culture than we realize.

In answer to criticism from the religious conservatives, Jesus sent them to go and learn to show mercy, quoting the prophet Hosea. Hosea had married a prostitute and learned through that relationship just how God's love and compassion for unfaithful Israel were stretched to breaking point. Through Hosea's love for his unfaithful wife we hear God's lament for Israel. God's exhaustion with unfaithful Israel and exasperation at the fleetingness of her love led him to leave her to her fate until she came to her senses. To which Israel's hollow response was all words and no action.

When Jesus quoted Hosea's 'I desire mercy not sacrifice' to the Pharisees he put them in the place of their faithless forebears and criticized their hollow religious observances. Could they see how, in Jesus's calling of Matthew and eating with outcasts, God's love was breaking out in acts of mercy?

As he was saying this, suddenly the leader of the synagogue appeared, suddenly a woman appeared. Matthew is showing us Jesus being tested by these sudden events to embody mercy rather than sacrifice. Often it is sudden events that shape our lives, that act as God's way of challenging us. So we pray for the help of God's grace to please him in will and deed, even when sudden events mean there is no time to think.

Sunday after Trinity,
Proper 6 (12–18 June)

Exodus 19.2–8a; Romans 5.1–8; Matthew 9.35–10.8 [9–23]

UNPROMISING DISCIPLES

> *O God, the strength of all those who put their trust in you, mercifully accept*
> *our prayers and, because through the weakness of our mortal nature we*
> *can do no good thing without you, grant us the help of your grace, that in*
> *the keeping of your commandments we may please you both in will and*
> *deed; through Jesus Christ our Lord. Amen.*
>
> Collect for the First Sunday after Trinity

When Jesus went about proclaiming the good news of God's Kingdom, he told the disciples to pray for people to send out to share the harvest. He promptly made some of them the answer to their own prayers by choosing 12 of them and sending them out. We heard their names: they are a motley crew.

Jesus built in conflict and the potential for disaster with his inner circle from the beginning. He chose impetuous Peter, who acted first and thought later, and cautious Thomas who always needed to work through every possible outcome before committing himself to action: imagine decision-making in a group with those two. He chose Simon the Zealot and Judas Iscariot, both of whose names suggest strong connections to Jewish freedom-fighters who – like terrorists around the world today fighting what they perceive to be oppression – were not averse to bumping off the odd Roman soldier, and Matthew who had sold out to the occupying Romans by becoming a hated tax-collector. How safe did he feel around them? If that were not enough for group dynamics, add in two sons of thunder, James and John.

Jesus worked with that unpromising, conflicted group for three years to form the basis of the church. They were at times unbelieving, at times scared; they fled when danger came, betrayed him or denied knowing him. Probably none of them had spoken in public before, let alone spoken about God. He chose people used to working with their hands rather than their minds, and he did not look for like-minded people. There were times when the disciples fell out with each other and when Jesus despaired of them, becoming totally exasperated. 'You faithless generation. How much longer must I be among you?' (Mark 9.19) was probably the edited-for-publication version of what he thought about them. But he never gave up on them, never waited for them to get their act together.

Jesus followed Moses in having to deal with an assorted, at times recalcitrant, group. The difference was that he chose them whereas Moses was presented with his companions. Having been in the wilderness of Sinai, I have sympathy for Moses in that environment with a reluctant bunch of nomadic wanderers. Already they had more than made their mark as grumblers, while their rebellious streak had shown itself in their readiness to stone him when they were thirsty and there was no obvious water supply (Exodus 17.1–4). So God preceded the giving of the Ten Commandments by telling Moses to remind them what they had been – slaves in Egypt – and how God had delivered them and kept them safe. Sometimes, when life feels precarious, we need to remind ourselves of God's faithfulness through the years. Miraculously but over-optimistically, they promised to obey God. Then, as soon as they suffered again, they complained.

Paul, on the other hand, regarded suffering as something of which to boast because he could see the chain of character-building consequences that it set in motion – through suffering, endurance, character and hope to an experience of God's love poured into his heart through the Holy Spirit. He knew he was weak and sinful, but he also knew that Christ had, through his death, saved him and, through the gift of the Holy Spirit, made him more than he could have dreamed of becoming in his pursuit of God.

So I wonder what these 12 apostles thought as they were sent out with authority to cast out unclean spirits and cure every disease and sickness. Like Paul, they knew their weakness – they were like sheep among wolves (an image more vivid to them than to us) – but, like Paul, they discovered that when they were put to the ultimate test, being handed over to hostile authorities, they could indeed boast in their sufferings, not because suffering is good but because in it they were not disappointed in their Christian hope.

Since God gave Moses such an awkward group of people and Jesus chose people like the 12 apostles and Paul for his disciples, it's no wonder that we, just as odd and idiosyncratic an assortment of people, can be and are called to be his disciples today.

Sunday after Trinity,
Proper 7 (19–25 June)

Jeremiah 20.7–13; Romans 6.1b–11; Matthew 10.24–39

MOURNING AND WEEPING IN THIS VALE OF TEARS

O God, the strength of all those who put their trust in you, mercifully accept our prayers and, because through the weakness of our mortal nature we can do no good thing without you, grant us the help of your grace, that in the keeping of your commandments we may please you both in will and deed; through Jesus Christ our Lord. Amen.

Collect for the First Sunday after Trinity

The opening phrase of Jeremiah takes me back to 1996 when, during a summer of hospital chaplaincy, I was visiting a woman I will call Maria who had married into a family that dominated and effectively silenced her. In the few remaining days of her life she began to tell me how that felt, to weep about her disappointments and to dare to reach out to God whom she believed in but who had always seemed distant.

On my way home from overnight duty on the first Sunday after Trinity, I went to church. The preacher quoted an alternative translation of Jeremiah's words: 'O Lord, you have seduced me and I was seduced.' I wrote in my journal:

> The reading came to me with Maria's voice, 'O Lord, you have enticed (seduced, raped) me and I was enticed, you have overpowered me and you have prevailed. I have become a laughing stock all day long, everyone mocks me.' Suddenly I had a frame of reference for Maria: she appears to me as a woman who has been overpowered all her life and feels powerless to fight back, even to speak her name as an individual with self-esteem and dignity. Her identity is defined in relation to others.

There are many Jeremiahs and Marias in the world, people for whom, in their loneliness and desperation, God appears at best untrustworthy, seeming to play with our lives and hold them of no account, at worst letting people abuse us. In a time of violent upheaval, the young Jeremiah was called to a dangerous, thankless task of speaking to people being overpowered by the Babylonians. He had persevered doggedly but had been reviled. We hear from him soon after he had been struck in the face and left ignominiously in the stocks overnight by a priest, Pashur, son of the chief Temple officer.

On his release, Jeremiah lambasted Pashur and launched into this lament to God about the impossibility of his task and his helplessness in resisting God's power of persuasion. It may sound familiar. Benedict understood the feeling and told any monks asked to do an impossible task to explain to the abbot why it seemed unmanageable but, nevertheless, to do what the abbot, having heard their perspective, asked. He would have empathized with Jeremiah's lament.

So was Jeremiah hopeless? No; he lamented, and lament usually ends up in hard-won praise. Jeremiah lamented his way to hope by recalling that the Lord was with him as a dread warrior. The lament that 'they that hate me without a cause are more in number than the hairs of my head' (Psalm 69.4) provides the context for Jesus's reassurance that 'even the hairs of your head are all counted. So do not be afraid.' It is a challenging, hope-filled assertion that God knows what we are up against, has counted our enemies and calls us to traverse the path from sharing Jeremiah's feeling of being inveigled by God to the security of which Jesus speaks. Knowing that we are known delivers and deepens praise from trite blandness into honest dependence, honouring the lament without rushing to easy resolutions that deny the pain of Jeremiah's accusation, of Maria's silencing, of our own desolations.

Jeremiah kept going. Paul reminded the Romans that there is no going back. Having been baptized into Jesus's death, they cannot go on living in sin; having died with Christ they will live with him. They must move forward, deliberately, walking in newness of life as an ontological imperative in hope, the hope which allowed Jeremiah to lament, which turns us to pray the Collect.

Jesus said, 'A disciple is not above the teacher ... it is enough for the disciple to be like the teacher.' Later he cried in abandonment, 'My God, my God, why have you forsaken me?' He, too, has felt discarded by God. After reflecting on the sermon, I took Maria a postcard of the Dominus Flevit Chapel in Jerusalem and wrote on the back the description of Jesus weeping over Jerusalem. She literally held on to that postcard and even her domineering husband thanked me for it. The life of faith is not always serene but it is filled with hope.

Sunday after Trinity,
Proper 8 (26 June–2 July)

Jeremiah 28.5–9; Romans 6.12–23; Matthew 10.40–42

THE UNWELCOME PROPHET IN OUR MIDST

Lord, you have taught us that all our doings without love are nothing worth: send your Holy Spirit and pour into our hearts that most excellent gift of love, the true bond of peace and of all virtues, without which whoever lives is counted dead before you. Grant this for your only Son Jesus Christ's sake. Amen.

Collect for the Second Sunday after Trinity

Alas, readings taken out of context! There are advantages to the lectionary's thematic pairing of the Gospel and Old Testament readings, but sometimes verses are shorn of their setting and lose the strength of their meaning. This Sunday's reading from Jeremiah is one of them. It sounds like a debate between two people over how the words of prophets are received which complements Jesus's comments about prophets. In context it is more uncomfortable.

Before we come to that, notice that Jesus is concerned with how we receive people or things, not how we give them. Repeatedly he says that it matters how we welcome others, how we offer even a cup of cold water, and how in welcoming one person we might just be welcoming God. Vulnerability to God is expressed in vulnerability to whoever knocks on our door.

Benedict devotes a whole chapter (66) to how to answer the monastery door. Joan Chittister comments:

> Of all the questions to be asked about the nearly 1500 year old Rule of St Benedict … one of the most pointed must surely be why one of the great spiritual documents of the Western world would have in it a chapter on how to answer the door … The way we answer the door is the way we deal with the world … The chapter on the porter of the monastery is the chapter on how to receive the Christ in the other always. It is Benedict's theology of surprise. (Chittister, 1992)

God surprised the people of Israel at the perilous time of the threat of Babylonian invasion, the context in which Jeremiah spoke the words we hear rather blandly this week. For centuries God delivered his people from enemies, moving them traumatically, but ultimately safely, from exile in Egypt to the Promised Land, and then kept faith with them through their centuries of apostasies. Now, between 598 and 587 BC, they faced the surrounding Babylonian armies, and two prophets emerged to speak the word of God. Behind the words that we hear lay a vitriolic encounter: Jeremiah claimed that the Babylonians knocking at their door, the enemy, were in fact the messengers of God to the people who had gone too far in their rebellion against God.

Read through chapters 26–28 and the fuller story emerges. This was but part of a battle of words and wits between Jeremiah and other prophets who thought they were hearing God's promise to deliver the people yet again from their enemies. When Jeremiah countered this with words of judgement from God, the priests and prophets responded with death threats (26.8–9, 11). The ordinary people argued back that Jeremiah was speaking God's word to them – not that they did much about it. Finally, Jeremiah acted out his message, putting an oxen's yoke around his neck as a message to the King of Judah and the kings of the surrounding nations who were also threatened by the Babylonians, telling them to submit to the Babylonian yoke because in a perverse way the Babylonians were God's messengers of judgement. Read on, and we hear how, following violence and bloodshed, the people were deported into exile.

That was a very serious surprise. Could they welcome this command to submit to their hated enemy and to receive in that the judgement of God? Suddenly the passage from Jeremiah becomes much tougher. Hananiah emerged as Jeremiah's main opponent, disputing his interpretation of the message from God and going so far as to accuse him of misunderstanding and misleading people. He shamed Jeremiah, undermining everything he said and substituting soothing words the people wanted to hear.

We cannot divorce God's coming to us from the political and social contexts in which we live. There is not always a clear answer and it takes courage to discern faithfully how we should act. In the context of Jeremiah's struggles to be a faithful prophet, Jesus's words become much edgier: 'Whoever welcomes a prophet in the name of the prophet will receive a prophet's reward.' Because the rest of this passage is about receiving good things – welcoming Jesus unexpectedly, receiving a righteous person's reward – we assume that a prophet's reward is to be welcomed too. But Jeremiah points us to the cost of fidelity and the determination needed to welcome the uncomfortable prophet in our midst. God, being a God of surprises, sometimes comes to us by the hard route.

Sunday after Trinity,
Proper 9 (3–9 July)

Zechariah 9.9–12; Romans 7.15–25a;
Matthew 11.16–19, 25–30

A WORLD IMBUED WITH HOPE

> *Almighty God, you have broken the tyranny of sin and have sent the Spirit*
> *of your Son into our hearts whereby we call you Father: give us grace*
> *to dedicate our freedom to your service, that we and all creation may be*
> *brought to the glorious liberty of the children of God; through Jesus Christ*
> *our Lord. Amen.*
>
> Collect for the Third Sunday after Trinity

Once, at a school governors' meeting, I said to a teacher, 'I'm sorry I can't come
to the concert tonight.' Everyone laughed, and I looked blank until someone
explained that they had just been talking about why some people say, 'I can't
come to something,' and others, 'I can't go to something.' I had just proved
and disproved their point. Thinking about it, I said 'come' because my point of
reference was the person who issued the invitation and where she was, inviting
me to join her there.

Both Zechariah and Matthew use the word 'come': 'Behold, your king
comes to you'… 'Come to me.' How different it would be had they said, 'Behold
your king goes to you', 'Go to me.' 'Come' implies presence and proximity – the
prophet speaks to the people where they are and the king comes to the people
where they are. Jesus invites his hearers to be close to him where he is, not to go
and find him somewhere else altogether. So, before his death he promised the
disciples, 'I go to prepare a place for you and I will come again and take you to
myself, that where I am, there you may be also.' Even when he did say, 'Go into
all the world and preach the gospel,' he immediately followed it with, 'I am with
you always, even to the end of the age,' providing the assurance that, wherever
we go, we go with him.

'Come' is a word we use when giving invitations. 'Come to me,' says Jesus,
'all who are weary and carrying heavy burdens.' The criterion for coming is
simple: being weary and burdened. No wonder people who come to Jesus find
themselves with other people who are worn out, under pressure and at the limits
of their patience, and therefore not always easy companions.

Why come? So that Jesus can give rest. But Jesus says more: 'Take my
yoke upon you and learn from me.' Rest is part of what Jesus offers people who
come to him, but so too is the opportunity to keep in step and learn from him.

Jesus's words of invitation were spoken to people who were totally unpleasable, as we all can be in our worst moments. They would neither dance when there was music nor cry when there was mourning. John the Baptist's strict ascetical life was too conservative; Jesus's joyful life too liberal. Whatever God offered was wrong. If the so-called wise missed the point entirely, who had got the message? The infants, the ones who did not know to do anything other than trust the goodness of their heavenly Father. It is in that context that Jesus invited the weary to come to him for rest.

Zechariah's message to the dispirited people of Israel was, essentially, similar: 'Your king comes to halt the warring, to restore hope.' He spoke of people being prisoners of hope, a powerful image of being simply unable to escape hope, bound to and with hope. It makes me wonder what a world imbued with unpreventable hope might look like.

This king is a rest-giver, a hope-giver, who comes to us. What is the incarnation, if not God coming among us? What is Jesus's ministry, if not coming to the people in villages and towns largely overlooked, even despised, by Jerusalem? Sometimes, as a southerner now resident in the north-east, I have an idea what it feels like for this region to be overlooked by the capital. The kidnapping of school girls in north-east Nigeria highlighted how that area is not central to Nigerian life, while the news is relentlessly full of stories of people whose daily lives go unheeded by the rest of their nation, let alone the world, until something shocking happens.

What would it be like to live as though no one is overlooked, as if our King has come to everyone to offer rest and hope? What would it be like to dedicate our freedom to God's service so that all people, even exhausted people in forgotten backwaters, may come to the glorious liberty of the children of God who calls them to come? Maybe this week we can let our imaginations wander and wonder.

Sunday after Trinity,
Proper 10 (10–16 July)

Isaiah 55.10–13; Romans 8.1–11; Matthew 13.1–9, 18–23

TRUTH IN THE TRIVIAL ROUND

> *O God, the protector of all who trust in you, without whom nothing is strong, nothing is holy: increase and multiply upon us your mercy; that with you as our ruler and guide we may so pass through things temporal that we lose not our hold on things eternal; grant this, heavenly Father, for our Lord Jesus Christ's sake. Amen.*
>
> Collect for the Fourth Sunday after Trinity

The biblical story returns time and again to gardening and farming in order to express something important. God is a gardener creating and planting a garden in Eden; the Promised Land was crammed full of mouth-watering crops; Elijah fulminated against Ahab's murder of Naboth and annexation of his family's vineyard to grow luxury vegetables; Isaiah sang about a vineyard and God's deep disappointment that, despite his careful gardening, the people were like wild grapes in the cultivated vineyard. Farming was central to the people's survival and thus central to their understanding of God, because God is always to be known in the midst of ordinary life.

In Isaiah, God's rich invitation to, and promises of, food and drink were given to people settled into relatively comfortable Babylonian exile. Ignoring God was an easy possibility: why change when they were all right? That attitude is dangerous when we consider responsibility for, and the implications of, issues like climate change. If the people listened, Isaiah's message was that God's good world is for all people to enjoy and care for responsibly because God is generous and wants life to flourish. But to benefit, we must respond.

Jesus described a farmer scattering seed with rather wild abandon, letting it fall all over the place, knowing that the harvest will vary but sowing it nonetheless. Not for this sower the assurance of a bumper crop, but rather a generous lashing of opportunity as seed and soil are given the chance to produce a harvest. This is risk taken in order to offer the chance for life without the absolute guarantee of success. In the world today with its joys and sorrows, can we risk creating the opportunity for life, even if this opens us to failure?

The sheer ordinariness of the story is remarkable. We hear it followed by Jesus's explanation to his disciples, but miss some intervening verses which indicate there was no explanation for the crowd. They simply heard a story about a farmer doing something familiar, something they saw happening around them. For them there was no punchline to the story as Jesus told it. It was just an account of everyday farming life which ended with a variable harvest and some patches of land that yielded nothing. It was hardly worthy of an episode of the first-century equivalent of *The Archers*.

The disciples, however, received an explanation which related this account of mundane life to the Kingdom of God. It was not an obvious connection, but one that Jesus taught them to make as they listened to him. This connection of our daily life with the Kingdom of God is one we must learn to make because, if we cannot make such connections day by day, how can we do it when events turn our lives upside down? How can we begin to answer questions that people challenge Christians with, like 'Where is God in the wars in Syria or South Sudan?', if we have not asked that same question day by day in our own lives?

George Herbert prayed,

Teach me, my God and King,
in all things thee to see,
and what I do in anything
to do it as for thee.

Every simple task – sweeping a room is one of Herbert's examples – provides an opportunity to serve and be aware of God. Theological insight is often born in the midst of daily routine done faithfully. If the parable of the Sower is about nothing else – and it is about other things too, as Jesus explained – it is about the need for disciples to probe what God is saying in the midst of ordinariness. We can all be theologians in the midst of the magnificent commonplaceness of everyday life, even when it is a hard grind, if, attentively and prayerfully, we ask questions of ourselves and God. Then, when triumph or tragedy strike, we need not be like seed that is choked by weeds, eaten by birds or shrivelling for lack of roots, but can produce a crop that befits the Kingdom of God. As the Collect puts it, 'We may so pass through things temporal that we lose not our hold on things eternal.'

Sunday after Trinity,
Proper 11 (17–23 July)

Isaiah 44.6–8; Romans 8.12–25; Matthew 13.24–30, 36–43

CREATION YEARNS IN HOPE

Almighty and everlasting God, by whose Spirit the whole body of the Church is governed and sanctified: hear our prayer which we offer for all your faithful people, that in their vocation and ministry they may serve you in holiness and truth to the glory of your name; through our Lord and Saviour Jesus Christ. Amen.

Collect for the Fifth Sunday after Trinity

Imagine yourself in the turbulence of mid-50s Rome. Claudius had expelled 40,000–50,000 Jews from Rome at the end of the previous decade. When he died (AD 54), returning Jewish Christians found the church had changed and was now predominantly Gentile. Inevitably, there was tension. Who finds it easy to accept it when something we love changes in our absence?

Paul gave a theological framework to this heart-searching over the relationship of Jews and Gentiles in a church he had not visited. We land in the middle of his dense argument that expands the meaning of the righteous life, beginning with the law's inability to change a person but God's power to do so through the Spirit's transforming work (8.3).

Paul ranges over themes of wider interest that transcend his context: how we should live, not knowing how to pray, God's purposes for us, suffering – our own and that of creation – and hope. The suffering was not abstract but seriously practical: the Romans suffered from the devastating impact of Claudius's rule, while Paul suffered with Christ.

Five times in five verses Paul refers to 'creation'. Nowhere else does he address the relation of humans to the non-human world, and he packs it in tightly. Contrasts are drawn: 'eager longing' and 'futility'; 'its own will' and 'the will of the one who subjected it'; 'bondage to decay' and 'freedom of the glory of the children of God'; 'groaning in labour pains' (birth) and 'adoption'. The creation story underlies these verses which also link back to earlier in the letter; in one sense this is the final answer to the problem of 1.18–32.

Paul believes in a cosmic outworking of salvation, that creation's suffering is not without hope. It waits with 'eager longing' (in J. B. Phillips's memorable phrase, 'on tiptoe') for the revealing of the children of God. Human redemption is coming and has implications for creation. Paul's 'we know that' (8.22) presupposes knowledge of the apocalyptic tradition that, if creation suffers by human action and disobedience (Genesis 3.17–

19; 2 Esdras 7.11), then it will be set free when humans come into their freedom and glory and the Messiah delivers his creation (2 Esdras 13.26).

How can we put today's flesh on these theological bones? The thought of creation subjected to futility and bondage to decay is vivid when we are all too aware of ecological issues. Jesus spoke, memorably, of the stones crying out (groaning in labour pains and hope?) if people were silent when the Messiah came bringing redemption. Can we hear the cries of the ravaged earth and the people who suffer on it? Do we respond with action?

These verses lead to Paul's next thought: creation waits in hope, we were saved in hope, and we too hope and wait for what, by definition, is not yet seen. Creation waits with eager longing, we wait with patience – not resigned 'patience on a monument' but patience invigorated by hope that glory is about to be revealed to us. Hope and revelation are inextricably linked.

From Paul's complex theology we move to Jesus's story which is drawn, like others, from familiar farming life. Farmers know all about hope. This farmer had bold hope of an excellent harvest despite the very practical reservations of his slaves who, doing the weeding, saw the problem at first hand. With Jesus's explanation, we realize the connection with Paul's theology and with Isaiah's redeemer and king. There will indeed be a harvest, we are right to wait in hope, but until then evil is allowed to continue, ironically to avoid destroying the good. Maybe that helps us to understand why Claudius (and his successors today) could devastate the lives of thousands, why Paul suffered with Christ, why creation still yearns in hope, why we wait for adoption.

I am challenged by how I cope with what I think are annoying weeds messing up my life, situations I wish would change. But this is not the whole story, and Paul's matchless scene-setter (Romans 8.18) is that there is a double time-perspective, this present age and the glory about to be revealed. Creation will obtain the freedom of the glory of God's children and the righteous will shine like the sun in their Father's kingdom. We live in confident hope.

Sunday after Trinity,
Proper 12 (24–30 July)

1 Kings 3.5–12; Romans 8.26–39;
Matthew 13.31–33, 44–52

INTERCESSION WITH GROANINGS

> *Merciful God, you have prepared for those who love you such good things*
> *as pass our understanding: pour into our hearts such love toward you that*
> *we, loving you in all things and above all things, may obtain your promises,*
> *which exceed all that we can desire; through Jesus Christ our Lord. Amen.*
>
> Collect for the Sixth Sunday after Trinity

Continuing his line of thought from last week's reading, Paul has entered the
court-room. Assuming knowledge of the Jewish tradition, including the satan,
the accuser (Job 1.6–12), he asks if charges can be raised against God's people
and who is laying them.

Echoing Isaiah 50.7–9, Paul concludes that only Christ Jesus has the
authority to condemn, yet he is interceding for us. Without prosecuting counsel
there is no trial, but the debate begun in last week's reading continues. The
motion is, 'This house believes that the sufferings of the present age are not
worth comparing to the glory that is to be revealed.'

First: evidence for the motion. God has given his Son for us and, with him,
everything else. When we do not know how to pray in the turmoil we face, God
has already acted on our behalf and the Spirit intercedes for us. Similarly, Jesus
assures us that, even when we cannot see it, God's Kingdom is steadily growing
as from a tiny mustard seed. Christians live by faith and not by sight. Equally,
yeast works unseen to make bread happen. Jesus compares the Kingdom of God
to the yeast rather than the bread, thus making God's Kingdom the invisible
catalyst for growth rather than the finished product. That is dynamic.

Second: evidence against the motion. Paul's reference to being killed for
God's sake (Psalm 44.22) and Jesus's parables assume that the Kingdom of God
exists alongside suffering and wrong. Unfortunately, the lectionary separates
Paul's three references to 'groaning' (8.22, 23, 26) while the NRSV's 'sighs
too deep for words' obscures the repetition. Paul asserts that creation groans
while waiting for the revealing of the children of God who groan as we wait for
adoption. Creation groans in labour pains (loudly!), we do it inwardly because
we have the first-fruits of the Spirit, and the Spirit does it wordlessly and deeply.
Biblically, birth pangs have eschatological associations of anguish and turmoil:
Paul cannot keep his eyes off the glory about to be revealed to us.

Third: surprise evidence. Pious Jews described themselves as 'those who love God and keep his commandments', whereas Paul astounds the Roman church, struggling to hold together Jews and Gentiles, by changing the end to 'who are called according to his purpose'. That changes the role of the law radically.

Jesus similarly startled his hearers. Instead of choosing an exotic or beautiful plant to describe the Kingdom of heaven he preferred the mustard seed, an analogy he used of faith (Matthew 17.20). The Kingdom of God is like this common invasive weed growing rampantly, seemingly from nowhere, into a tree 8–10 feet high. Then it does something life-giving: it offers shelter and shade. When I wrote this, we were dealing with a cathedral visitor's need which we could not solve but the vergers, chaplain and I did what we could. When the visitor thanked me, I realized that the temporary shelter we offered was experienced as a hitherto unknown foretaste of God's Kingdom.

Fourth: summing up. Paul approached the question from another angle: who will separate us from the love of Christ? The processes of the law could not, so a catalogue of potential separators was rolled out, to no avail.

Finally, 'I am convinced' (8.39) develops 'I consider' (8.18) in the light of evidence. If 'consider' means 'think over' rather than 'believe', then all the evidence has been debated – creation's suffering, our sharing in it, the place of hope, the Spirit's help, what we know of God's ways, that we are to be glorified. Finally the motion under consideration is carried: 'I am convinced'.

What does all this tell us about God at work in the world today, where there is suffering, we are weak, and many people are burdened with guilt? Yeast and a buried mustard seed cannot be seen but do their work nonetheless. The Spirit intercedes for us with sighs we cannot even hear. How would the world be transformed if we followed Solomon's example in the Old Testament reading and, recognizing our failure to know how to act, yearned for wisdom; if we made sure that seeds were scattered and yeast kneaded into the dough? Then they can do their work through us, miraculously providing shelter and food for whoever needs it.

Sunday after Trinity,
Proper 13 (31 July–6 August)
Isaiah 55.1–5; Romans 9.1–5; Matthew 14.13–21

A STORY WITH SIX ENDINGS

> *Lord of all power and might, the author and giver of all good things: graft in our hearts the love of your name, increase in us true religion, nourish us with all goodness, and of your great mercy keep us in the same; through Jesus Christ our Lord. Amen.*
>
> Collect for the Seventh Sunday after Trinity

Do we think of Jesus rowing a boat?

He needed space to grieve the execution of his cousin but the crowds would not leave him alone and compassion got the better of him. That resulted in a food shortage. The disciples suggested, 'Get rid of the problem, send people away to fend for themselves,' but Jesus expected them to come up with food and sat the crowd down. Everyone was watching and there was no escape for the disciples.

And we know the rest. Jesus took the bread and fish, looked up to heaven, blessed and broke the loaves and gave them to the disciples for distribution. He did the same at the Last Supper. We do it week by week. This alfresco meal was a foretaste of heaven's banquet, could people but see it. Because it was a heavenly meal there was more than enough – 12 full baskets left over. God is a God of abundance.

Jesus could have fed the people himself. Instead, he threw the situation to the disciples who could see the problem all too well. The Church's vocation is to be so closely involved with our broken and hurting world that we know what is going on and articulate the needs to God. Even then, we cannot just dump the solution on to Jesus; the disciples had to do something about it with their measly resources.

How often Jesus seems to break what we offer him, and then give it away to others. Afterwards, he wanted the leftovers to be collected. With God, the author and giver of all good things, nothing is wasted or too scrappy to be collected up and celebrated as a sign of God's abundance.

This story has six potential endings, each of which tells it differently. It could conclude with the disciples giving food to the crowds, but it goes on, 'and all ate and were filled'. Then, 'and they took up what was left over of the broken pieces'. Then, '12 baskets full'. Then 'and those who ate were about five thousand men'; and, finally, 'besides women and children'. Matthew's extra details move this from being a story about meeting an immediate need to one where there is not just enough, but more than enough. There was overflow for others not present, and we never know who ate the leftovers.

This has implications for our celebration of the Eucharist. Jesus's actions of taking, blessing, breaking and giving the bread are in the context not of a meal with friends but of the overwhelming needs of a very large crowd. He expected the disciples to find the resources to meet that need, which they did – to their own surprise – by bringing the five loaves and two fish that they could muster.

Eucharist is about God's generous love for this world. There can be no celebration of Holy Eucharist without prayers for God's world, for the crucial theological reason that our sharing in the heavenly banquet can never be divorced from our sharing in the life of the world, with its needs and confusions. Eucharist is the foretaste, the anticipation, of God's Kingdom come on earth as it is in heaven. So, in the eucharistic prayers we pray, for example, 'Lord of all life, help us to work together for that day when your kingdom comes and justice and mercy will be seen in all the earth.' Eucharist is about justice and mercy, because our communion is with Christ who makes his communion with people in need.

We pray to be nourished with all goodness, a vivid image, and then, at the end of every Eucharist, we commit ourselves to serve Christ in this world. 'Send us out in the power of your Spirit to live and work to your praise and glory'; 'May we who share Christ's body live his risen life, we who drink his cup bring life to others, we whom the Spirit lights give light to the world.'

If we do that, then Isaiah's prophetic vision of the thirsty, poor and hungry delighting in rich food can begin to become reality in our corner of the world. Only those adjusted to a healthy diet can cope with rich food: it is not occasional emergency handouts but regular, healthy food for everyone that is God's vision for the world, of which the Eucharist is foretaste and commission.

Sunday after Trinity,
Proper 14 (7–13 August)

1 Kings 19.9–18; Romans 10.5–15; Matthew 14.22–33

THE SILENCE AND THE STORM

Almighty Lord and everlasting God, we beseech you to direct, sanctify and govern both our hearts and bodies in the ways of your laws and the works of your commandments; that through your most mighty protection, both here and ever, we may be preserved in body and soul; through our Lord and Saviour Jesus Christ. Amen.

Collect for the Eighth Sunday after Trinity

'What are you doing here, Elijah?' is one of the most profound and penetrating questions in the Old Testament, perhaps matched only by the angel's question (Genesis 16.8) to the distraught and fleeing Hagar, 'Where have you come from and where are you going to?' Ponder that and there is no need for the rest of this column.

Elijah appears to be trying to go back in Moses's footsteps, to recreate Moses's experience at Mount Sinai (Horeb) of thunder, lightning, thick cloud, earthquake and noise like a trumpet, all associated at one time or another with God's mysterious presence. Elijah wanted the reassurance of a similar display of God's tremendous power.

So God asked what he was up to and Elijah's answer was a mixture of utter fidelity to God tinged with despair and self-pity. Not answering the complaints, God sent him to face all the destructive power that Moses faced and Elijah apparently wanted. It was terrifying – he started by standing on the mountain but ended deep in a cave. And then there was a sound of sheer silence, noiselessness: a silence so intense you could hear it, the exact antithesis of the commotion.

And then the repeated, persistent question, 'What are you doing here, Elijah?' The silence that is God's presence confronts us with uncomfortable questions about ourselves. Only once we face our own situation can God meet us where we are.

Jesus also faced pressure. From the way the Gospel-writers tell the story, we know that John's execution was a turning point in Jesus's ministry as he began to face his own death. Like Elijah, he tried to get away from people into lonely places with God.

The disciples, meanwhile, were on familiar territory, the Sea of Galilee, when suddenly life lurched out of control. A storm blew up and they, hardened sailors, feared for their lives. Jesus did not come to the disciples as soon as the storm blew up, but kept praying. Then, in the dim light of early morning, Jesus walked towards them on the water and identified himself as God by saying, 'It is

I', 'I Am': the name of God. The water responded to his presence by bearing his weight; the storm subsided. Like his feeding the crowd from a few loaves and fishes the day before, this was another foretaste of the healing of the relationship between humans and creation that Jesus's incarnation, death and resurrection brought about.

Peter, in a burst of impetuous, perhaps incredulous, bravery, responded, 'If it is you, tell me to come to you.' And Jesus did, and Peter did, and it was all brilliant until he looked at the waves around him and started to sink. Then Jesus rescued him, got into the boat, and the storm ceased. We have to admire Peter's boldness rather than criticize his lack of faith. Which of us would have dared to put a foot over the side of the boat?

God, in Jesus Christ, came to him. God comes to us in the midst of our distress, of whatever we fear is out of control and threatening to us, perhaps to our very survival. Yet God does not always make everything right immediately. Elijah's story reminds us that we cannot dictate terms to God or expect God to do an automatic repeat performance of what he has done for someone else. Instead, after experiencing the absence of God, despite the power of the natural events which for others signalled the presence of God, he had to face sheer silence. Maybe that is what he needed most of all.

Similarly, God did not spare Jesus the anguish of John's execution. So Jesus, having fed the people, and still distressed by the news of John's brutal execution, deliberately took time to be with God – and Matthew is mute on the subject of his prayer.

These stories, and the Collect, tell us that God does not abandon us in our distress but meets us in totally unexpected ways. For me, it can be summed up in the words of Professor Leander Keck, who taught me New Testament when I was training for ordination: God is reliable but never predictable.

Sunday after Trinity,
Proper 15 (14–20 August)

Isaiah 56.1, 6–8; Romans 11.1–2a, 29–32;
Matthew 15.[10–20] 21–38

THE DOGS EAT OF THE CRUMBS

> *Almighty God, who sent your Holy Spirit to be the life and light of your Church: open our hearts to the riches of your grace, that we may bring forth the fruit of the Spirit in love and joy and peace; through Jesus Christ our Lord. Amen.*
>
> Collect for the Ninth Sunday after Trinity

Isaiah had words of hope and promise for foreigners who, barred from the inner Temple, nevertheless, in the lovely way he described it, 'joined themselves to the Lord'. Specifically, and radically, he mentioned outcasts. Centuries later Paul, writing to a church struggling with Jewish–Gentile relationship, stressed God's mercy to all peoples.

With this background, it is shocking that Jesus turns away a Gentile, Canaanite woman: a classic outcast. The affront is all the more pointed because Matthew has placed Canaanite women in Jesus's genealogy (Matthew 1.3–5). So all may not be as clear-cut as it seems.

Although Matthew repeatedly shows Jesus as the fulfilment of the law and the prophets, with a mission priority to the Jews and sending his disciples only to Jews, that did not prevent his scathing critique of empty religious tradition. His gospel was more radical than most of his fellow Jews could tolerate: God purposed, through blessing them, to bless the world. This had been envisaged in God's promise to Abram (Genesis 12.3) and was a theme developed in the latter chapters of Isaiah. That worldwide mission and blessing took full shape after Jesus's resurrection.

Probably to escape pressure after his confrontational teaching, Jesus went to Gentile territory which most Jews avoided. There he was confronted by a Canaanite woman who was unclean in Jewish religious terms. But what came out of her mouth was faith-filled, and thus she forced him to embody in his ministry what he had just taught about cleanness and uncleanness.

Rabbis did not talk to women in public. Jesus was silent while the disciples reiterated their mantra, 'send the problem away' (Matthew 14.15). But the woman knelt before him, called him by a Jewish title and, a loving mother at her wits' end, pleaded, 'Lord, have mercy on me.' Matthew places mercy at the heart of Jesus's message (9.13, 12.7), so surely she was pushing at an open door?

Jesus's answer was offensive. Jews called Gentiles 'dogs'. Perhaps inured to abuse, she accepted the insult but also retaliated. By saying, 'Even foreigners can grab the crumbs that Jews reject,' she put Jesus, who had recently had 12 baskets of crumbs on his hands, on the spot by demanding some of them.

By positioning the story as he did, Matthew made more connections than crumbs. He contrasted the woman with the Jewish leaders who had just rejected Jesus (15.1–9) and used this story to put flesh on the bones of Jesus's recent teaching.

Kenneth Bailey (Bailey, 2008) suggests that Jesus was deliberately teaching the disciples and began by voicing and appearing to share their beliefs as faithful Jews. Playing along with deeply embedded prejudices about Gentiles, ultimately he turned the tables and commended the woman at their expense. 'Woman, great is your faith' was in stark contrast to 'You of little faith, why did you doubt?', so recently addressed to Peter (Matthew 14.31).

This is the only recorded time that someone took Jesus to task and emerged victorious. That person was neither a disciple nor a Jew, but a Gentile woman. In that social climate she was a classic example of Isaiah's outcasts. The Church, facing the divisions to which Paul referred in his letter written about 30 years before the Gospel, had to grasp that the mission to the Gentiles began in the mission of Jesus. This gospel is for all nations, as Isaiah, radically, foresaw. Our inclusion in the Church is a product of this encounter.

The woman challenged Jesus. She challenges us, too, about how we view interruptions in life. If, like the disciples, we want to send them away, we may miss out on what God is doing to bring health and hope in the world. She also challenges us about persisting with God in the face of all-consuming, unmet need. Maybe Jesus had her in mind when telling his parable of the Persistent Widow and the Unjust Judge.

The woman got more than she wanted: not just her daughter's healing but mercy for herself and public praise for her great faith. Some of the greatest answers to prayer have a life-changing effect, way beyond the actual thing for which we asked.

There is, indeed, 'a wideness in God's mercy'. So we pray, 'Open our hearts to the riches of your grace.'

Sunday after Trinity,
Proper 16 (21–27 August)

Isaiah 51.1–6; Romans 12.1–8; Matthew 16.13–20

A NEVER-FORGOTTEN MOMENT

Let your merciful ears, O Lord, be open to the prayers of your humble
servants; and that they may obtain their petitions make them to ask such
things as shall please you; through Jesus Christ our Lord. Amen.

Collect for the Tenth Sunday after Trinity

I find it hard, whenever I hear the epistle reading, not to be back in my shoes
as a student hearing a very powerful talk, from someone whose name is long-
forgotten, on presenting our bodies as a living sacrifice to God which is our
spiritual, or reasonable, worship. The details are lost but the impact remains.
This was one of those moments that crystallized some of the implications of
saying 'yes' to God years earlier.

I also recall one of the people who taught me in the preaching courses I took
when training for ordination saying that we should always pay attention when
we are hooked back to previous memories by the text we are to preach on. To
remember is good, but it may distract us when preparing to preach by focusing
us too narrowly on personal memory at the expense of engagement today with
this scripture for this situation.

Having said that, I doubt that Peter ever forgot the moment we hear in the
Gospel reading. He blurted out his answer to Jesus, perhaps never dreaming the
implications but knowing that he loved his friend and had come to realize that
there was more than met the eye in this Galilean carpenter turned rabbi. Paul,
too, would find it impossible to forget the moment when his life was turned
upside down by Jesus in the episode on the road to Damascus.

The aphorism that, when we see 'therefore', we should ask, 'What is it there
for?' draws our attention to Paul's line of thought to this point: he predicates what
follows on the fact that we are called to be saints and to belong to Christ Jesus
(1.6–7), who has broken down barriers between Jew and Gentile. The bottom
line is that we are to present our bodies as a living sacrifice.

The international Celtic tradition, of which the Anglo-Saxon church was
part, recognized three forms of martyrdom. Red martyrdom was literally to spill
your blood for Christ. Few Anglo-Saxon saints faced that fate because their
approach to mission, exemplified by Aidan and Cuthbert who are so beloved at
Durham Cathedral and elsewhere in the north, was irenic, getting alongside their
pagan neighbours.

White martyrdom was separation for God's sake from everything a person held dear, choosing the way of exile for the sake of Christ. To leave one's tribe in that culture was to become a nobody, to lose your identity and your protection from the tribe. People called to a monastic or missionary vocation today fit this category.

Green martyrdom was the unseen, inner, way of daily repentance, refusing to be controlled by one's desires, self-sacrifice without leaving home. It remains the unspectacular way of commitment and discipline, self-control and simplicity in daily life, chosen because love for Christ is reordering our priorities.

In Romans Paul wrote about presenting our bodies to God as a living and holy sacrifice – in essence martyrdom without dying. That appeal is what I recall being moved by in my student days. Paul immediately spells out what that means in a very specific way. We cannot get away with a purely 'spiritual' conversion; it involves all my life – my body and thus what I do with it. Sin is not to have dominion in our mortal bodies (Romans 6.12), so there may be a conflict between our desires and our actions (Romans 7.14–25). St Benedict understood this and his Rule has much to say about our bodies as well as our prayer life because discipleship is all-embracing.

What does this mean for us today? When we pray for the Christian virtues like love, joy, peace, patience and self-control, we only gain them when we are in situations where we need them. I cannot learn patience if I am never in a situation where my instinct is to be impatient, just as I cannot learn to love if I am surrounded only by people it is easy to like. It is in the nitty-gritty of life when we annoy each other or don't live up to each other's expectations, when things go wrong and people are upset or tempted to blame others for what has happened, that Paul's challenge, 'Let love be genuine', makes us feel the pinch of confessing, with Peter, Jesus Christ as Son of the living God. That is all part of pursuing righteousness, as Isaiah so presciently envisaged.

Sunday after Trinity,

Proper 17 (28 August–3 September)

Jeremiah 15.15–21; Romans 12.9–21; Matthew 16.21–28

OVERCOME EVIL WITH GOOD

O God, you declare your almighty power most chiefly in showing mercy and pity: mercifully grant to us such a measure of your grace, that we, running the way of your commandments, may receive your gracious promises, and be made partakers of your heavenly treasure; through Jesus Christ our Lord. Amen.

Collect for the Eleventh Sunday after Trinity

'Do not be overcome by evil, but overcome evil with good.'

In July 2014, anticipating the beginning of the four-year commemoration of the First World War, we held a study morning at Durham Cathedral on Hensley Henson, Dean of Durham during that war. His copious journals, letters and sermons shed light on how he tried to respond faithfully to the shock of his world being plunged into conflict. Always aware of his pastoral responsibilities, to the troops who hastily assembled and to the people of Durham who were being asked to send their men to war, inevitably he worked with the themes in this week's readings. So, preaching in the first days of the war, Henson drew parallels between Jerusalem being invaded by Antiochus Epiphanes and the Belgian people who did not deserve the cruel treatment they received from the Kaiser and his army.

A few weeks ago Jeremiah was berating God for enticing him; now God has deceived him. He had been utterly faithful, had truly delighted in God's word and was glad to be called by God's name. So it was reasonable to ask why his pain was unceasing and his wound incurable, like a running sore that will not heal. He was extraordinarily bold, given God's impatience with grumblers. Yet, because Jeremiah's heart was set on God, his was a lament not a whinge and God took him utterly seriously, responding with profound promises.

Jeremiah's situation leaps across the centuries. People still struggle to be staunch in their commitment to God through dreadful situations, and many Christians are supporting people through unfair and unrelieved suffering. Paul exhorted a church which, in its short life, had already faced cruel persecution, martyrdom and, for its Jewish members, exile.

'Be patient in suffering, do not lag in zeal, be ardent in spirit' were very real, gritty and tall orders for his readers, given what the Romans endured. Paul went on relentlessly, with demanding words that describe Jesus Christ's example to us 'Do not repay anyone evil for evil … if it is possible, so far as it depends on you, live peaceably with one another … Do not be overcome by evil, but overcome evil with good.' It is worth noting that Paul said, 'if it is possible, so far as it depends on you': sometimes it is not possible and does not completely depend on us. Then, like Henson, we face hard decisions about how to respond to evil.

From the start of his wartime preaching, Henson was resolute that there be no animosity against the German people whom he saw as hoodwinked by their leaders. So, preaching in Sunderland on 'salt and light' in July 1915, he described as anti-Christian the inevitable demand for reprisals and vengeance which would arise as the war continued and fresh provocations provoked exasperation. The test of the English church, revealing whether salt had lost its savour or light had been darkened, would come when, ultimately, the German nation learned how its leaders had wronged it. For his congregation in Sunderland, after a year of 'unprecedented slaughter and devastation', those were prophetically uncomfortable words which echo Jeremiah's entrusting of his yearning for retribution to God.

In commemorating the Great War and also hearing the ongoing, dreadful, news reports of the continuing slaughter of innocent people, of revenge killings on more innocent people, of there being more refugees than at any time since the Second World War, these readings confront us. Few of us face such absolutely desperate situations, but we do encounter situations when it is hard to rejoice in hope, be patient in suffering and persevere in prayer. Jeremiah's brutally honest response was to plead to be remembered by God and to entrust to God his instinctive desire for vengeance, rather than taking it himself. Paul made extraordinary demands of his readers, given their circumstances: contributing to the needs of the saints was one thing, but feeding their merciless enemies was another. Radically counter-cultural, it could only spring from an attitude that 'take[s] thought for what is noble in the sight of all'.

Bringing this together, while Peter wanted Jesus to bypass suffering, Jesus held his life in a different perspective and faced it head on. Paul's final words sum it up: 'Do not be overcome by evil, but overcome evil with good.'

Sunday after Trinity,
Proper 18 (4–10 September)

Ezekiel 33.7–11; Romans 13.8–14; Matthew 18.15–20

AN ABUNDANCE OF MERCY

Almighty and everlasting God, you are always more ready to hear than we to pray and to give more than either we desire or deserve: pour down upon us the abundance of your mercy, forgiving us those things of which our conscience is afraid and giving us those good things which we are not worthy to ask but through the merits and mediation of Jesus Christ our Lord. Amen.

Collect for the Twelfth Sunday after Trinity

Grace, forgiveness and opportunity pervade this week's readings but, unless we read the whole chapter of Matthew, we miss the context and inadvertently turn grace into law.

Jesus has described a crazy shepherd, probably caring for other people's sheep as well as his own, who risks everyone's livelihood – 99 sheep – for the sake of one sheep who messes things up for everyone by getting lost. His hearers would have laughed at the sheer irresponsibility of the shepherd. But for Jesus this is a good model for the Father's loving action to avoid losing even one little one. Who are the little ones? Go back to the beginning of the chapter and it is children who are models for the greatest in the Kingdom of heaven. In the thought of the time children counted for little; Jesus was getting more and more absurd.

Against this background, Jesus outlines what his disciples should do when one sins against another. Matthew switches to the language of the Church and reads his contemporary situation back into the teaching he inherited through the tradition. But things are none the worse for that and we apply scripture to our situations today.

The readings are all concerned with how God's people live, together, in less than ideal worlds. Ezekiel, in exile, is reminded that those whom God calls have a responsibility for the welfare of others, offering every opportunity to reform and turn back to save their lives. God desires people to have life. In Romans Paul writes to persecuted Christians and at the same time anticipates the day of judgement. His message? Salvation is coming and they owe each other nothing except love.

Matthew's process for dealing with someone who sinned against another is carefully designed to reclaim the offender with as little fuss or publicity as possible. Not for him tweeting another person's failings. Deuteronomy (17.6, 19.15) specifically excluded reliance on just one witness, going straight for more, but Jesus slips in an earlier stage in which the wronged person offers the chance to heal the relationship quietly. Should that fail, others are called in, not to back up the offended person or to reinforce the condemnation but as independent witnesses of what is said. Only if that fails is the whole Church involved. Even then there is a surprise in store because a person who still refuses to listen is to be treated as a Gentile and tax-collector. How did Jesus do that? He was their friend (Matthew 11.19).

Matthew continues (18.21–22) by using Peter to clarify the limitlessness of the mercy expected of them. Put that alongside Paul's instructions to owe nothing except love and to love our neighbours as ourselves (two phrases that trip off our tongue but should trip us up) which lead him to urge action: to put on the armour of light, leave behind dark, sleep and night with their revelling and drunkenness, awaken to the light and to the day, to honourable action as we are clothed in Christ and together await the day of the Lord. Transparency of life is called for.

This week there is a particularly happy coincidence of the readings and the Collect, which is a paean of God's excesses: more ready to hear than we to pray, giving more than we desire or deserve, pouring down abundance of mercy, giving good things we are not worthy to ask. In the middle is that phrase which echoes the people Jesus may have had in mind: people whose consciences are afraid and who dare not ask for forgiveness or mercy, perhaps because they fear they will not get it, or feel unworthy of it, or will not know how to receive it.

So, if we find the benchmark is set very high in today's readings, if we do not know how we can bring ourselves to forgive someone who has sinned against us or how we can love someone who is plain impossible, then the Collect is the place to start. Jesus said, 'Blessed are the merciful, for they shall receive mercy.' It is a symbiotic process, all rooted in the excess of God's grace. There is always another chance to show and receive mercy.

Sunday after Trinity,
Proper 19 (11–17 September)

Genesis 50.15–21; Romans 14.1–12; Matthew 18.21–35

OF DEBTS AND DEBTORS

Almighty God, who called your Church to bear witness that you were in Christ reconciling the world to yourself: help us to proclaim the good news of your love, that all who hear it may be drawn to you; through him who was lifted up on the cross, and reigns with you in the unity of the Holy Spirit, one God, now and for ever. Amen.

Collect for the Thirteenth Sunday after Trinity

The Roman Christians were embroiled in a conflict that was dividing the church. The presenting issue was religious observance and dietary laws, the deeper issue was the church's relationship with Jesus Christ which was affected by this dispute. In judging one another and quarrelling over opinions they were denying the truth that they were all welcomed by God and all lived and died to the Lord. Paul made it clear that judging and despising one another were not only ruled out, these were inconceivable actions if they really knew who they were and grasped that one day all would stand before the judgement seat of God. Paul quoted from an early hymn, possibly a version of the hymn that he quoted to the Philippian church (Philippians 2.10–11), which had begun by holding up Christ's self-emptying as the example for their common life.

So what might this way of life look like in practice? Peter no doubt thought he was being extravagant in going so far as to forgive someone seven times, since rabbinical tradition limited it to three times for the same offence. Seven symbolized fullness, but Jesus expanded Peter's ideas beyond fullness, effectively to infinity. The number recalls Lamech's boast of 77-fold vengeance (Genesis 4.24): infinite vengeance in the family of the first Adam is overcome by infinite forgiveness in the family of the new Adam.

The parable Jesus told to illustrate this is another of his over-the-top stories where exaggeration is used to press a point home. The servant's debt ran into the trillions, so to plead for time to repay was laughable. Josephus records that in the year 4 BC the total taxes collected in Judea, Idumea and Samaria came to 600 talents, and it has been calculated that, taken literally, this debt would take 150,000 years to pay off. The king had two options, to sell the man and his family into slavery, but still never to see his money, or to forgive. He chose the latter.

The forgiven slave then chased and refused to forgive a debt worth about one third of a year's wages. That provoked the king to spell out his expectation of how forgiven debtors live in the light of his clemency. Matthew's version of

YEAR A

the Lord's Prayer refers to 'debts' where Luke refers to 'sins', so Jesus made the explicit connection to his heavenly Father's expectation of Peter and the others listening: if you do not forgive from the heart, you will not be forgiven. Seen in this light, the Roman Christians were on dangerous ground when they judged one another. They had lost sight of what the Collect describes as the vocation of the Church, to bear witness that God in Christ was reconciling the world to himself, and in that light to proclaim the good news so that others will be drawn to God through Christ.

The Old Testament story is poignant. We all know the brilliantly told Joseph saga about a family that had deception down to a fine art and could not, it seems, tell the truth if it tried. This part of the story comes at the very end, after all the reconciliations and forgiveness for past wrongs. Yet, perhaps understandably given the family's history, there was still not the level of trust necessary for the family to live peaceably without their father's presence as family patriarch to restrain them. The wrongs done by the brothers were so grievous that they were still wary of Joseph and the sincerity of his words and actions. It can be very hard to know ourselves to be forgiven when we are conscious of the depth of the wrong we did in the first place which has put us in the position of needing to be forgiven.

Joseph's response to their rather ham-fisted way of dealing with this – concocting another story – was to weep and to spell out again his belief, expressed when he first identified himself, that God had used him to preserve life. Their actions had been cruel, but God had redeemed the situation. His ability to forgive them and speak kindly to them was remarkable. It flowed from deep awareness of God's merciful purposes. If we can grasp that perspective we can take the hard step of forgiving and also knowing ourselves to be forgiven.

Sunday after Trinity,
Proper 20 (18–24 September)
Jonah 3.10–4.11; Philippians 1.21–30; Matthew 20.1–16

A DAFT STORY OF OUTRAGEOUS BEHAVIOUR

> *Almighty God, whose only Son has opened for us a new and living way into your presence: give us pure hearts and steadfast wills to worship you in spirit and in truth; through Jesus Christ our Lord. Amen.*
>
> Collect for the Fourteenth Sunday after Trinity

When hard lessons have to be learned, the Bible has an uncanny way of using ludicrous stories of outrageous behaviour to make us face reality. We take them too seriously, missing their sheer daftness, nodding piously rather than laughing loudly, only to find the tables turned.

Take Jonah. His story has all the hallmarks of comedy, even pantomime. The word of the Lord comes out of the blue to Jonah, somewhere near Joppa. His story starts in mid-sentence, pitching us into the middle of an argument with no explanation of why Jonah is furious with God about something to do with the city of Nineveh, the capital of the enemy Assyrians. Like the people in the parable who cannot cope with the landowner's generosity, Jonah cannot cope with God's mercy to the city. So when God says, 'Go east overland for 600 miles to Nineveh', Jonah heads west by sea for 1500 miles to Spain. That is not a promising start for a prophet. A storm blows up, the ship threatens to sink and the sailors throw cargo overboard. Meanwhile Jonah, who has told the sailors he is fleeing from God, sleeps on peacefully. When they wake him he suggests throwing him overboard. They do, the storm stops and a fish swallows Jonah. After three days he is thrown up on to the land.

We join the story in the middle of a battle of wills between God and Jonah. When God again sends him to Nineveh he goes, reluctantly. He announces the city will be destroyed in 40 days. Astonishingly, there is an instant reaction – from king to animals they repent, fast and put on sackcloth, crying to God for mercy. It is a preacher's dream reaction and, like the whole story, totally over the top. Jonah should be thrilled at his success as preacher of the year. But instead he is furious, lashing out and complaining he fled to Spain because God is forgiving and ready to relent from punishing. So, 'Please God, take away my life because I cannot cope with all this mercy for sinners.'

Then, in a Jack and the Beanstalk episode, God grows an instant bush, providing shade and making Jonah happy. Next day God sends a worm which attacks the bush which withers as fast as it grew. Then God turns up the sun's heat and, for good measure, adds a nasty sultry wind. Inevitably, Jonah complains again and God asks if he is right to be angry. Jonah says he certainly is. God has the last word, saying that just as Jonah is upset about losing a bush which God gave him in the first place, so God can be upset about a city full of people and animals (it seems the story-teller is an animal lover) who do not know the way. And there the story suddenly ends.

The reading is less about Nineveh than about Jonah in his lonely rage, reluctant discipleship and two God-given opportunities to change. Jonah did it with bad grace, in the process having an unsettling experience with a big fish and making a fool of himself over a bush. We never hear what ultimately happened to Jonah, but leave him sulking in the desert. Did God get to the bottom of Jonah's anger and resistance to the people of Nineveh's repentance? Why did God choose Jonah when it would have been easier to find someone less stubborn?

God has a way of undermining our religious trappings to get at what is really underneath. Even if we appear to be faithful disciples, what about our underlying motives and driving forces, our own besetting sin that we manage to cover up most of the time?

We can nod sagely at the responsive example of the people of Nineveh. But what about Jonah, resisting God who would not let him get away with his anger, stubborn resistance and sheer self-centred concern for what was best for him? What about the underlying loneliness and rebellion that drove him to act in this way? We pray for pure hearts and steadfast wills, which may mean God asks us a few questions about our discipleship, our motivation. What is our equivalent of Jonah's simmering and raging anger? How does God put a finger on it, as he put a finger on Jonah's basic problems? We are stunned by Jonah's behaviour, but perhaps we should be equally outraged by some of our own behaviour.

Sunday after Trinity,

Proper 21 (25 September–1 October)

Ezekiel 18.1–4, 25–end; Philippians 2.1–13;
Matthew 21.23–32

TEACHING WITH AUTHORITY?

> *God, who in generous mercy sent the Holy Spirit upon your Church in the*
> *burning fire of your love: grant that your people may be fervent in the*
> *fellowship of the gospel that, always abiding in you, they may be found*
> *steadfast in faith and active in service; through Jesus Christ our Lord.*
> *Amen.*
>
> Collect for the Fifteenth Sunday after Trinity

Authority is the issue in the Gospel. It was reasonable for religious leaders to ask the source of Jesus's authority, given that he was in the Temple where he had caused disruption the previous day. If someone came into Durham Cathedral and started proclaiming things contrary to what we believe, we would have a duty to ask similar questions. The Church is very careful, when commissioning people for ministry, to indicate where their authority lies: it is God-given but expressed through the actions of the Church.

The crowds had seen that Jesus taught with authority; indeed, they glorified God for giving such authority to a human (Matthew 7.29, 9.8). Jesus claimed authority when healing (Matthew 9.6) and gave authority to his apostles in a limited way when sending them in mission (Matthew 10.1). After his resurrection, claiming that God had given him all authority, he sent his apostles out with authority to make disciples of all the nations. There is no doubt in Matthew's Gospel where Jesus's authority lay and that he used it for good.

The reading from Philippians sheds another perspective on this: Jesus's authority over everything in heaven, earth and under the earth (a comprehensive cosmology in the thought of the day) derives from God in response to Jesus's disregarding his equality with God and being put to death as a human. Total self-emptying led to total exaltation and authority – the name above every name.

However, Jesus refused to discuss the source of his authority with the chief priests whose questioning was clearly hostile. Instead he put them on the spot. Like a good rabbi who answered a question by asking a question – thus teaching his disciples to think – he asked a question. But this one trapped them. Their problem was not just the crowds they feared but the fact that some Pharisees had previously gone to John the Baptist for baptism (Matthew 3.7), thus accepting John's authority as God-given, even though John rebuffed their own claim to authority, 'We have Abraham as our ancestor.'

Having gained the upper hand, Jesus rubbed it in with a parable about a vineyard which everyone understood to represent Israel. The parable was linked to their question and his opponents knew it: they were the people charged with working in God's vineyard. The second son could easily be the Pharisees who went to John for baptism but did not act on their repentance (Matthew 3.7–8). We can almost hear the reluctance in their answer when Jesus asked which son did the will of his father. There are echoes of Jesus's solemn words: 'Not everyone who says to me "Lord, Lord" will enter the kingdom of heaven, but the one who does the will of my father in heaven' (Matthew 7.21).

Then Jesus made it worse; he made prostitutes and tax-collectors appear more righteous than the Pharisees, claiming they did the will of the Father. This was all said in the Temple – the religious leaders' territory – and it was acutely embarrassing. As we will hear next week, Jesus was still not finished: yet another awkward parable followed hot on the heels of this one.

This parable acts as a vivid commentary on the reading from Ezekiel because both are about turning, however slowly, from wickedness to righteousness, from disobedience to obedience. It can be embarrassing to have to change our minds, but it can also be a sign of maturity. So as we ponder the readings this week and pray the Collect about being steadfast in faith and active in service, it might be worth pondering what causes us to change our minds when we need to, and what stops us changing our minds when we ought to.

The Benedictine vows of stability, obedience and conversion of life can reframe, helpfully, what lies behind this. Obedience raises the question of the source of authority in our lives, while Michael Casey's graphic image of stability as what it takes to stay upright on a surf board (Casey, 2005) clarifies that stability is never stagnation but being able to handle in a godly way whatever happens in life. Our aim is conversion of life to become more Christ-like. Is there a pinch-point in all that for us?

Sunday after Trinity,
Proper 22 (2–8 October)

Isaiah 5.1–7; Philippians 3.4b–14; Matthew 21.33–46

IN THE VINEYARD OF THE LORD

O Lord, we beseech you mercifully to hear the prayers of your people who call upon you; and grant that they may both perceive and know what things they ought to do, and also may have grace and power faithfully to fulfil them; through Jesus Christ our Lord. Amen.

Collect for the Sixteenth Sunday after Trinity

Isaiah, the faithful and at times beleaguered prophet speaking to the nation shortly before Israel was to be wiped off the map by the conquering Assyrians, sang a song of a vineyard. Gardeners will recognize the scenario: the landowner has lavished his best care on the vineyard, clearing it of stones, digging it, building a watchtower so he could watch to keep predators off (a scarecrow of its day), constructing a vat to hold the produce. Yet after all this it yielded wild grapes – essentially, weeds. What wasted effort and care. The landowner laments, as on *Gardeners' Question Time*, 'What did I do wrong?'

Isaiah's lament would have evoked sympathy among his hearers – and the sting in the tail was that they, God's people, were the vineyard which had not produced the good fruit expected after all this care. God was furious and disappointed with them.

Having come with a love song and loving action that did everything possible to help them flourish, God's patience ran out and his intense disappointment at their rejection of his love led him to enraged, destructive action. In a frenzied attack by a rejected lover on the object of his love, God tore down what he had built up so carefully over the years, turning it into a wasteland.

Centuries later, Jesus's parable about a vineyard ratcheted up the tension that was building in last week's readings. Now he accused the Pharisees not just of not doing the will of God but of instigating murder and direct rebellion. His parable pushed the boundaries of reality in order to make the point. The farmer was extraordinarily, some would say stupidly, patient. The tenants' reaction was so over the top as to be ridiculous: even if the son did die, they would never inherit because contractually they remained tenants, accountable to the owner.

The verbs used to describe the careful hard work of the owner are interesting. In Matthew he planted, fenced, dug, built, leased, and left before sending to collect the harvest. In Isaiah, similarly, he dug, cleared, planted, built, hewed, and expected. But then things changed. In Isaiah the owner then removed, broke, allowed it to be trampled, made it a waste, no longer pruned or hoed, but abandoned it to become overgrown and parched. In Matthew, however, Jesus let his hearers decide what happened and did not disagree that the tenants who wrought the havoc should face their fate, while the vineyard was spared and leased to other tenants. Lest there be any doubt he spelled it out to the chief priests and elders, 'The kingdom of God will be taken from you and given to a people that produces the fruit of the kingdom.' Given what he had previously said about prostitutes and tax-collectors, the meaning was clear and offensive.

George Herbert's poem 'Redemption' addresses these themes of tenancy, God as landowner and Jesus as the son in a slightly different way, coming at it with an attitude of humility which the tenants in the parable so notably lacked:

> Having been tenant long to a rich lord,
> Not thriving, I resolved to be bold,
> And make a suit unto him, to afford
> A new small-rented lease, and cancel the old.
> In heaven at his manor I him sought;
> They told me there that he was lately gone
> About some land, which he had dearly bought
> Long since on earth, to take possession.
> I straight returned, and knowing his great birth,
> Sought him accordingly in great resorts;
> In cities, theatres, gardens, parks, and courts;
> At length I heard a ragged noise and mirth
> Of thieves and murderers; there I him espied,
> Who straight, 'Your suit is granted,' said, and died.

As Herbert knew, with God there is always redemption for those who turn to him through Jesus Christ. Paul's reflection on his life as a zealous Pharisee who before he was converted persecuted Christians to death provides a steadying reminder that, despite the waywardness of God's people, thanks to the mercy of God we may surprise ourselves, when we end up doing 'things we ought to do' even when this is exact antithesis of what we once did. Only by God's mercy is that possible.

Sunday after Trinity,
Proper 23 (9–15 October)
Isaiah 25.1–9; Philippians 4.1–9; Matthew 22.1–14

THE VESTURE OF MINISTERS

*Almighty God, you have made us for yourself, and our hearts are restless
till they find their rest in you: pour your love into our hearts and draw us
to yourself, and so bring us at last to your heavenly city where we shall see
you face to face; through Jesus Christ our Lord. Amen.*

Collect for the Seventeenth Sunday after Trinity

We hear Jesus's parable in the context of Isaiah and this week's psalm, Psalm 23, where banquets and celebration point us to joy of the Messiah's heavenly wedding feast. Isaiah spells it out vividly: a feast of rich food and matured wines strained clear (a luxury in those days). More than that, the shroud of death hanging over people is destroyed and, like a tender parent with a distressed child, God himself wipes away remaining tears.

Turn back one chapter in Isaiah and we grasp his context of impending or actual exile in Babylon when Jerusalem was razed to the ground in ghastly, bloody actions that are echoed too frequently around the world today. I have pictures of people weeping over the ruins of their homes to help me to hold them before God. It can take courage to hope in redemption, but Isaiah insists, 'let us rejoice and be glad in his salvation'.

In contrast to the previous parable with its contractual relationship of the people to God, here God is not landowner but host and joyful father of the groom, while the people are not tenants but invited guests. Both parables contained judgement and were told in the Temple where Jesus faced calculated opposition. In contrast, Luke's version of this parable (Luke 14.15–24) was told in the home of a Pharisee who had invited him for a Sabbath meal – a meal traditionally shared with family, which indicates that Jesus had close friends among the Pharisees who were not all hostile.

Matthew had set the scene for this parable much earlier in his Gospel (Matthew 8.11–12). Speaking then of a Roman centurion, Jesus envisaged many from east and west coming to eat with the patriarchs in the Kingdom of heaven while the heirs were thrown out. This parable develops that theme as the invited guests threw etiquette to the wind and, having accepted the invitation, came up with lame excuses for not fulfilling their commitment to attend. Like the second son in the earlier parable, they said 'I go' then failed to do so.

As with the tenants we heard about last week, some guests went way over the top by seizing and killing the messengers sent to call them to the son's wedding feast. The point could hardly be lost on Jesus's hearers who were party to plots to arrest and kill him. Still reeling from the previous parable, they would be appalled by Jesus's audacity and the threat he posed to them.

The NRSV puts a paragraph break in the middle of the parable, but it is really all one story. Too many attempts to make sense of the final verses, which sound to us at best nonsensical if not malicious, fail because we do not understand and enter the culture of the time. Unlike today, when a wedding is often an excuse for a trip to the shops, then it was the host of the wedding banquet who provided wedding garments for all the guests who had accepted his invitation. So to show up without the wedding garment was to have gate-crashed your way in by the back door and come on your own terms.

As last week, George Herbert, this time in his poem 'Aaron', has words for this. Drawing on Old Testament imagery and writing about being dressed in Christ to be a priest, the words nevertheless apply to everyone who is in Christ:

> Holiness on the head,
> Light and perfections on the breast,
> Harmonious bells below, raising the dead
> To lead them unto life and rest:
> Thus are true Aarons drest.

> Profaneness in my head,
> Defects and darkness in my breast,
> A noise of passions ringing me for dead
> Unto a place where is no rest:
> Poor priest, thus am I drest.

> Only another head
> I have, another heart and breast,
> Another music, making live, not dead,
> Without whom I could have no rest:
> In him I am well drest.

> Christ is my only head,
> My alone-only heart and breast,
> My only music, striking me ev'n dead,
> That to the old man I may rest,
> And be in him new-drest.

> So, holy in my head,
> Perfect and light in my dear breast,
> My doctrine tun'd by Christ (who is not dead,
> But lives in me while I do rest),
> Come people; Aaron's drest.

Sunday after Trinity,
Proper 24 (16–22 October)
Isaiah 45.1–7; 1 Thessalonians 1.1–10; Matthew 22.15–22

THE THINGS THAT ARE CAESAR'S

Almighty and everlasting God, increase in us your gift of faith that, forsaking what lies behind and reaching out to that which is before, we may run the way of your commandments and win the crown of everlasting joy; through Jesus Christ our Lord. Amen.

Collect for the Eighteenth Sunday after Trinity

How do we balance our loyalty to God and to secular governments? There is no monochrome view in the Bible. God's people lived under different circumstances at different times, and we hear one perspective when, in 587 BC, they were taken into exile. Their Babylonian conquerors exiled conquered nations to Babylon where they allowed them to settle in their own communities. But soon the Babylonians were conquered by King Cyrus of Persia, who adopted a different policy, permitting conquered nations to return to their homelands. So, in the 540s, Cyrus issued an edict allowing the Jews to return to Jerusalem and rebuild their city.

The Bible interprets secular events through theological eyes. This unexpected turn of events was surely a manifestation of God's power and ultimate authority. Isaiah reiterates that, although Cyrus did not know God, nonetheless God worked through him. Even more startlingly, Isaiah claimed Cyrus as God's anointed – in other words, God's Messiah or Christ. This raises all sorts of hard questions about how we discern God at work in the world.

If nothing else, it alerts us to the dangers of identifying a particular regime with divine intention or opposition. As a student in the 1970s, I recall a rash of dubious American books claiming with undue confidence that Russia was the anti-Christ in Revelation. Subsequent events have shown this to be far too simplistic. So, in due course the Persians were conquered by the Greeks, and we should read Isaiah less as a description of Cyrus (or Brezhnev, or anyone else) in particular, than of God's authority in the world.

Jesus lived in a fraught political situation. His encounter with the religious leaders was the first of a string of such head-to-heads in these last days of his life. Tellingly, Matthew uses 'malice' to describe their motives. They tried to trap Jesus into either sedition (denying the authority of the emperor) or denial of God's authority. The tax referred to was a tax on agricultural harvests and personal property, liability for which was established through census registration. This prompted violent opposition (Acts 5.37), and what made matters worse was the collaboration of Jewish authorities in its collection. Ultimately it contributed to the catastrophic rebellion against Rome in AD 70.

At Jesus's request, the religious leaders produced a coin that should never have been in the Temple precincts because it bore the blasphemous image of the emperor whom the Romans considered divine. Notably, Jesus and his disciples did not carry this coin on this sacred ground. Jesus then edged his way out of the trap. Matthew carefully places this story close to Jesus's parable of the Wicked Tenants who denied the landowner what was his by right (Matthew 21.33–46). In that light, Jesus's words about giving Caesar his due were qualified by the earlier parable. He left no doubt who was entitled to the income from the vineyard which, in the thought of the time, represented Israel.

Like Isaiah centuries earlier, Jesus claimed God's authority over earthly rulers, whether or not they recognized it. The rider to this was that duty owed to rulers is, ultimately, duty owed to and determined by God. That raises all sorts of very difficult and very live questions with which theologians through the centuries have tussled.

It is simpler to be wholly given to one extreme or another – to deny God, succumb to secular authority and avoid persecution, or to be religious fanatics who decry worldly authorities. Neither will do. The harder way of discipleship is to live faithfully in a world that, while not always acknowledging God's authority, nonetheless is God's world in which we have to go on making difficult choices about how, in practice, to be faithful to God day by day.

Paul wrote to Thessalonian Christians who were in this situation of living under a pagan emperor, being persecuted (1.6) even to death (4.13). Having turned from idols, how were they to live? As Christians today in Iraq, Syria, Nigeria, Sudan and too many other countries know, it was searingly demanding. There is more than meets the eye when Paul gives thanks for 'your work of faith and labour of love and steadfastness of hope in our Lord Jesus Christ', and we should be praying for Christians who run the way of God's commandments in such situations.

Sunday after Trinity,
Proper 25 (23–29 October)

Leviticus 19.1–2, 15–18; 1 Thessalonians 2.1–8;
Matthew 22.34–46

HOLINESS IN OUR HUMANITY

O God, forasmuch as without you we are not able to please you; mercifully
grant that your Holy Spirit may in all things direct and rule our hearts;
through Jesus Christ our Lord. Amen.

Collect for the Nineteenth Sunday after Trinity

There can be fewer Collects shorter and more to the point than this one. It allows
no get-out clause as it sums up our problem and points to the source of our help.
The readings provide a commentary on this succinct prayer.

Paul's appeal to the Thessalonian Christians to have regard to how he
and his companions presented themselves to this new church is a powerful
summary of how Christians can support one another. Having escaped 'shameful
mistreatment' in Philippi, including, as a Roman citizen, wrongful arrest, Paul
walked 100 miles to Thessalonica, a city about the size of York or Milton Keynes
today. It might have been a forced arrival but it 'was not in vain', as nothing is
with God.

Paul's actions exemplify Leviticus's focus on holiness and purity. How did
he come? With pure motive, with the gospel, desiring to please God, without
flattery or pretext for greed, with gentleness and deep care for hitherto unknown
people. What happened? There was uproar, a mob formed, and Jason and other
believers were hauled before the city's leaders before being bailed. Meanwhile
the Christians packed Paul and Silas off in an undignified exit (Acts 17). Our
best attempts to do good can meet with extraordinary opposition.

Sometimes we can have too pious a picture of what it means to obey the
command in Leviticus, 'You shall be holy, for I the Lord your God am holy …
you shall love your neighbour as yourself: I am the Lord.' For Paul it meant chaos
and fleeing for his life to unknown places while remaining driven and shaped by
his love for God. I suspect that, both en route from Philippi to Thessalonica and
from Thessalonica to Beroea, he had some vigorous fellowship with God about
what had happened. The Old Testament frequently reminds us that being holy
may involve asking faithful but demanding questions of God.

Matthew quotes this passage from Leviticus three times, indicating how
deeply it was embedded in Jesus's understanding. But it was not unique to Jesus:
a lawyer quoted it to him (Luke 10.27). Here Jesus quotes it in response to a
malicious question freighted with animosity and designed to 'test' him (Matthew

22.18, 35). Nothing could be further from Paul's lack of deceit, impure motives and trickery. There are, perhaps, deliberate echoes of Psalm 2.2, 'The rulers take counsel together against the Lord and his anointed.'

Jesus's answer was as adroit as the question. He combined the instruction in Leviticus with the Shema, the nearest thing his questioners had to a creed (Deuteronomy 6.4–9), which – as faithful Jews – they recited every morning and evening. Jesus had greater and wiser insight into the law than they, yet we should not fall into the trap of assuming that his divinity made this automatic. It was gained in his humanity through study and commitment. We can all study: Jesus was a Jewish peasant with few of the opportunities available to us. His whole orientation of life was towards God; he loved what God loves – his neighbour. In the fourth century, Evagrius Pontus wrote that love of the neighbour is equated with love of God because it is love of the image of God in humans. Jesus was about to come to that more explicitly (as we will on Christ the King Sunday) ,and had already addressed it when castigating the hypocrisy that allowed people to claim their love for God justified neglecting to care for their needy parents (Matthew 15.1–9).

Jesus seized the initiative with his question. The reference is to Psalm 110 and the only way to resolve the conundrum he presented is to believe that he, Jesus, is the Messiah. As Christians, we read that back in, but the people present could not and were silenced. How is it resolved? Since the ascension, there is a human at the right hand of God who is both David's son and David's Lord: Jesus Christ, incarnate God, now seated at the Father's right hand in glory. Their answer should have been not silence but worship with pure and holy hearts.

We are to be holy. Kierkegaard said, famously, that purity of heart is to will one thing. He went on to pray, as we can in words that expand the Collect, 'In prosperity, grant perseverance to will one thing; amid distractions, collectedness to will one thing; in suffering, patience to will one thing.'

All Saints' Day
Revelation 7.9–17; 1 John 3.1–3; Matthew 5.1–12

LIVING ON EARTH AS IF IN HEAVEN

Almighty God, you have knit together your elect in one communion and fellowship in the mystical body of your Son Christ our Lord: grant us grace so to follow your blessed saints in all virtuous and godly living that we may come to those inexpressible joys that you have prepared for those who truly love you; through Jesus Christ our Lord. Amen.

The Collect begins by reminding us of the mystery into which we are inevitably drawn on All Saints' Day: that God has knit together his elect in one communion and fellowship in the mystical body of his Son, Jesus Christ our Lord. Knitters know that once you knit something together it is impossible to undo it, short of unravelling the whole piece of work. You cannot just lift a stitch out and expect the garment to be usable. The image of knitting together is a powerful one when applied to Jesus Christ and his elect – the Church, both on earth and in heaven. We are so caught up in Jesus Christ that we cannot be isolated from the rest of the Church or from Jesus Christ. We are living in the realm of mystery, just by virtue of who we are in Christ. When it is so easy to get stuck in the ruts of everyday living, All Saints' Day shakes us out of that and reminds us that we are living a mystery, God's mystery.

The vision of John in the book of Revelation takes us into this world of holy mystery. John, who lived at a time of persecution of the Early Church, had a vision of the unending worship in heaven that we join every time we gather for worship. Our worship never begins at 10.00 on Sundays and lasts for an hour; instead, at 10.00 on Sundays we join in for an hour with the ongoing worship of heaven, and occasionally we are lifted out of ourselves and have the numinous sense that we are caught up in something bigger than ourselves, greater than our corporate effort.

In apparent contrast, we hear difficult words from Jesus speaking to his disciples – including John who, decades later, was to have this extraordinary vision which set his years of faithful discipleship in a heavenly perspective. The beatitudes are not directives but statements of fact, inviting us to a new way of seeing which incorporates the outlook and way of life of people who live fully on earth, wading into life with both feet and with their sleeves rolled up. They are merciful and meek, they mourn, they are peacemakers, they hunger and thirst for righteousness, they are reviled and persecuted. Their perspective is that of heaven – they know that this life is not all there is, but that grief will be comforted, righteousness will come in fullness, the pure in heart will see God, the peacemakers will be called children of God, and they have a reward in heaven. This perspective frees them from the necessity to seek reward in this life, and thus enables them to be more fully involved because they have no ulterior motive except to live as those who know they are blessed by God.

The beatitudes describe a way of life that is not unworldly, but immensely worldly and in the thick of things. We cannot live the beatitudes without getting messy, because they involve living amid the grief and mourning for a world that is not as it should be, in the midst of unjust and unrighteous situations, in the places where mercy is missing, where there is no peace, where purity of heart is undermined at every turn, where power-hungry people scorn and manipulate meekness for their own ends. People who live this way, the saints we remember today, live risky lives as fully and as passionately as they can. In a sense they gamble with their lives for the sake of Jesus Christ.

Saints who live in the way of the beatitudes also have a sense of balance between heaven and earth. They know that the present moment counts in God's purposes. Some religious people are so heavenly minded they are no earthly good, and some non-Christian people are very earthly minded, driven by an admirable desire to right the injustice they see, but with no knowledge of the ultimate redemption of all creation in Christ. A saint is someone who can move between the heavenly and earthly worlds, totally immersed in each, letting each inform the other as the light of heaven shines through their lives. So we pray to emulate the saints who have gone before us, thereby adding to their number.

Fourth Sunday before Advent

Micah 3.5–12; 1 Thessalonians 2.9–13; Matthew 24.1–14

AN INCORRUPTIBLE PROPHET

Almighty and eternal God, you have kindled the flame of love in the hearts of the saints: grant to us the same faith and power of love, that, as we rejoice in their triumphs, we may be sustained by their example and fellowship; through Jesus Christ our Lord. Amen.

A map helps us to understand Micah's message. He was from Moresheth, one of a string of named places (Micah 1.1, 11–15) in the foothills about 30 miles south-west of Jerusalem, between the coastal plain (near today's Gaza, then Philistia) and the mountains around Jerusalem. That gave him a very different perspective on life from that of people living in or near Jerusalem. This is a cry from the margins.

In 721 BC the northern kingdom fell to the Assyrians, whose demands for tribute from the southern kingdom created economic instability and a social crisis. While, for Isaiah, Jerusalem was impregnable because it was the city of God (Isaiah 31.4–5), for Micah, living more vulnerably in an area attacked by the Philistines and now occupied by the Assyrians (2 Chronicles 28.16–21, 32.9), the destruction of Zion was a real threat (Micah 3.12). Even the fortified hill city of Lachish, about five miles from his home, had fallen. Yet Micah explicitly inveighed not against the Assyrians but against the cruelty and injustice of his own rulers (Micah 3.1–4). He blamed all this on the sinful way of life of Judah and Samaria, north of Jerusalem (Micah 1.1–7).

Kings frequently sought the will of God or the gods, and Micah accused prophets in the royal courts of prophesying what the king wanted to hear, since they depended on him for their food. Years earlier, Micah had been struck and put on reduced rations for refusing to prophesy to order (1 Kings 22). Like Jeremiah (6.14, 8.11) and Ezekiel (13.10–16), Micah stood bravely against lying, self-interested prophesying of peace. A century later his stance was remembered (Jeremiah 26.17–19). Describing himself as filled with power and the spirit of the Lord, fearless for justice and might, ready to name sin as sin and unable to be bribed, he denounced his nation's perversion of justice and equity. Today's reading sounds like condemnation of the prophets but, heard in context, was essentially judgement on a whole nation.

There is a felicitous juxtaposition with the lectionary's course reading of 1 Thessalonians where Paul, who had suffered at the hands of a mob in Thessalonica (Acts 17.1–10), described himself in not dissimilar terms to Micah. Coming to them without deceit, flattery, greed or a desire for praise, and expecting nothing from his hearers (1 Thessalonians 2.3–7), he described his way of life in positive terms – pure, upright, blameless, fatherly, encouraging.

Then we find Jesus leaving the Temple, which had been rebuilt twice since Micah prophesied, the city having been destroyed as Micah anticipated. Herod's rebuilding, begun before Jesus's birth, took 46 years (John 2.20), so as a boy visiting Jerusalem for the Passover Jesus would have seen it as a building site. His disciples were examining its enormous stones but, when they admired its impregnability, Jesus echoed Micah's warning of its destruction, fulfilled by the Romans in AD 70.

The world is in convulsion yet again. I wrote this during the centenary of the war that decimated the fabric of Europe, when wars were doing the same in the Middle East. The same human hatreds and capacity for cruelty manifest themselves as in biblical times. Now as then, local geography renders people living away from the centre of power vulnerable in ways that people in secure locations cannot comprehend.

Despair is always a possibility. But Micah, Paul and Jesus deny us that option. 'God's word is at work in believers,' says Paul; 'I am filled with power, with the Spirit of the Lord, with justice and might,' says Micah. We can choose to live righteously, as Micah did. That much is within our power, albeit sometimes searingly hard.

Today the Church refocuses its gaze towards Advent and the coming of God's Messiah. At All Saints' and All Souls' tide we remember all the faithful people of God, famous or unremarked. Both our world situation and our liturgical context should shape our response to the readings. We remind ourselves that God has kindled the flame of love in the hearts of the saints, and pray for the same faith and power of love, asking to be sustained by their example and fellowship. Micah and Paul join the ranks as our companions on the way and, taking courage from their examples, our response must be to pray for those who face similar sufferings today.

Third Sunday before Advent, Remembrance Sunday

Amos 5.18–24 or Wisdom 6.12–16;
1 Thessalonians 4.13–18; Matthew 25.1–13

USHERING IN THE KINGDOM

Almighty Father, whose will is to restore all things in your beloved Son, the King of all: govern the hearts and minds of those in authority, and bring the families of the nations, divided and torn apart by the ravages of sin, to be subject to his just and gentle rule; who is alive and reigns with you, in the unity of the Holy Spirit, one God, now and for ever. Amen.

As last week, geography is important. This is another message from the margins where things look different from the perspective at the centre of power. Amos was from Tekoa, a fortified wilderness hill city ten miles south of Jerusalem from which King Jehoshaphat once defeated neighbouring enemies who had ended up killing each other (2 Chronicles 20.20–30). A century later, that triumph of Jerusalem's king was remembered vividly.

Now, in the mid eighth century BC, there was over-confidence in Jerusalem where another king, Uzziah, had won battles in this wilderness region; he built towers and, loving the soil, farmed the lowlands west of Tekoa (2 Chronicles 26). Meanwhile, north of Jerusalem, King Jeroboam of Israel was also consolidating his nation's security. Both kings were long-lived, and archaeological finds confirm the biblical accounts of widespread prosperity, at least for the upper classes.

Yet the Chronicler records tersely, '[Uzziah] became strong and grew proud, to his destruction' (2 Chronicles 26.16). So enter Amos, like King Uzziah a herdsman and arboriculturist (Amos 7.14). The occasion seems to be a harvest festival (Amos 8.1). Amos's message was as devastating as it was unexpected, given the pervading sense of well-being in both nations. But Amos, like Micah soon after him, saw below the surface to the rotten heart of both nations, to the oppression of the poor by the rich which he spelled out in gruesome specificity (Amos 4.1, 5.10–13, 6.1, 4–7, 8.4–6).

About 30 years before the Assyrians conquered the northern kingdom, Amos voiced God's lament over its future fall (Amos 5.1–3) before pleading for the people to seek God and live. God had not changed, yet justice was perverted amid the people's prosperity. He warned them not to seek refuge through offering sacrifices in Bethel, Gilgal and Beersheba: places of previous theophanies and displays of God's power (Amos 5.4–5, 4.4). Then came the dire, vivid warnings we heard, effectively, of being thrown out of the frying pan into the fire. Announcing God's absolute hatred and rejection of sham religious observances underpinned by injustice and unrighteousness, Amos pleaded for justice and righteousness to roll down like rushing waters.

This Remembrance weekend we describe ourselves in the Collect as nations divided and torn apart by the ravages of sin. We are all too aware of the complexities of world situations that lead nations into wars that rarely have clear political answers. Yet Amos insists that there are clear ethical answers: the prosperity of nations cannot be allowed to conceal the suffering of the poor – worse their oppression – behind a façade of well-being. No one can seek the day of the Lord in the future as the alternative to pursuing justice now.

So Amos calls us to dare to live faithfully in, and responsively to, the world and national situations in which we find ourselves. He shouts that our God is coming with justice. As the centenary of the First World War reminds us, all too cogently, this makes enormous demands on us, whether we live in the UK or Iraq, Syria or African nations where there is injustice.

Jesus, teaching his disciples privately (Matthew 24.3), touched on this in a different way. The scene was a typical village wedding but the focus was not so much the centre of the festivities – the coming of the bridegroom – as how people managed the consequences of his delay. That was also the issue for the Thessalonians: did they live expectantly and appropriately? Because people worked during the day, weddings took place at night and, as now in Middle Eastern cultures, for a woman to be out at night without a light was unthinkable, yet five of the bridesmaids risked their reputations and their participation by being unprepared. With echoes of Matthew 7.21–22, they were locked out.

We can debate the details of the parable and whether we should read it allegorically, but the point is clear: how we act now must express our vocation to be utterly faithful to God who is coming among us with justice. There are consequences for the future and our pilgrimage begins with the first step. I am reminded of the evocative phrase used as the title of Eugene Petersen's autobiographical book, 'a long obedience in the same direction'.

Second Sunday before Advent

Zephaniah 1.7, 12–end; 1 Thessalonians 5.1–11;
Matthew 25.14–30

JUDGEMENT DRAWS NIGH

Heavenly Father, whose blessed Son was revealed to destroy the works of the devil and to make us the children of God and heirs of eternal life: grant that we, having this hope, may purify ourselves even as he is pure; that when he shall appear in power and great glory we may be made like him in his eternal and glorious kingdom; where he is alive and reigns with you, in the unity of the Holy Spirit, one God, now and for ever. Amen.

Zephaniah, like Micah and Amos in the last two weeks, destabilizes things, hacking away at over-confidence and misplaced religiosity. Living under different kings, all three reframed the picture, sometimes radically, sometimes using poetic imagery. Zephaniah's visions of impending disaster are not unlike Jeremiah's picture of a desperate woman in labour abandoned to an enemy (Jeremiah 4.31). Nothing can save the people of Judah and, shockingly, it will be God's wrath that does the damage (Zephaniah 1.18) because a holy God will turn against his sinful people (Joshua 24.19–20).

Zephaniah, a contemporary of the young Jeremiah, denounced the cultic and ethical sins deriving from Manasseh's reign (687–642) when, as a loyal vassal of the Assyrians, he allowed pagan cults, divination and magic to flourish even within the Temple (Zephaniah 1.4–9) and human sacrifice to be practised. Zephaniah may have been a foreigner – his father's name suggests Ethiopian (Cushite) origins – yet his earlier genealogy suggests connections to the royal household of Judah, thus associating him with this abomination. Like him, we are both the heirs of our past yet freed and called to carve out our own path in life.

Around 610 BC the previously dominant power, Assyria, its temporary alliance with the Egyptians having failed, fell to the Babylonians. Judah became by default a free country, and its new young king Josiah annexed lands north of Jerusalem and instituted sweeping reforms. He restored the Temple and its worship, purging foreign cults. A law book (probably Deuteronomy with its appeal for a return to the covenant and Mosaic tradition) was found and read (2 Kings 22.8–13).

But then the Babylonians began to threaten Judah. Zephaniah and other prophets announced the impending day of the Lord and called Judah to repentance so that God could save a faithful remnant from judgement.

Zephaniah began with divine judgement against both infidel Judah and other nations. All creation, including the natural world (1.3), was implicated. In that light, Judah was called to be silent, or, as we might put it, 'Shut up and listen for once.' Centuries later Benedict began his Rule with the injunction, 'Listen!' and later added, 'speaking and teaching are the master's task: the disciples' is to be silent and listen' (*Rule*, 7). As we approach Advent, that can be a command to us. God is coming to us. Listen!

The problem in Zephaniah's day was apostasy, coupled with violence and fraud. The nation had long been warned against this because their God was holy: 'If you forsake the Lord, then he will turn and do you harm, and consume you, after having done you good' (Joshua 24.19–20). Now God was on the warpath, searching out the people who were complacent, complicit in evil and relying carelessly on a sense of God's benign purposes (Zephaniah 1.12ff.).

Last week we heard Amos on the subject of the day of the Lord, now it is Zephaniah's turn. Far from being a joyful event, the prophets emphasized its element of judgement. It is in that light we hear the other readings. Paul exhorts us to vigilance. Active preparation for the coming of our Lord is required. Jesus told another story, this time of a rich man who, unlike last week's delayed bridegroom, surprised his servants with the earliness of his return.

In the parable, extraordinary sums of money were entrusted to the servants, each according to his previously proven ability. One talent would sustain a person for 15 years at subsistence level. To preserve what was entrusted to him the servant had to take risks since maintaining the status quo was not adequate. Just as God has taken a risk with his creation, ultimately by sending his Son to live in it as a human, so risky, faithful holiness is required – a combination from which many shy away.

There is urgency in all the readings about how we live as the people of God. We are two Sundays away from Advent Sunday: our God is coming with the joy of salvation but also the judgement of his holiness. Are we ready to risk everything to prepare his way? The Collect makes for demanding praying.

Christy the King,
Sunday next before Advent
Ezekiel 34.11–16, 20–24; Ephesians 1.15–23;
Matthew 25.31–46

THE COMPASSIONATE SHEPHERD-KING

> *Eternal Father, whose Son Jesus Christ ascended to the throne of heaven that he might rule over all things as Lord and King: keep the Church in the unity of the Spirit and in the bond of peace, and bring the whole created order to worship at his feet; who is alive and reigns with you, in the unity of the Holy Spirit, one God, now and for ever. Amen.*

'Who do you say that I am?' Jesus's question, in the middle of Matthew's Gospel, hovers in the background on Christ the King Sunday. Matthew's whole Gospel is the answer, opening with the bald and bold assertion that Jesus is the Messiah, the Son of David and Abraham, and concluding with Jesus's claim to have been given all authority in heaven and earth, sending his disciples to make disciples of all nations, promising his presence to the end of the age. Ephesians echoes it: Jesus Christ, seated far above all rule and authority, calls people to recognize and know him.

So, on the one hand, Matthew makes no secret of the answer to the question. On the other hand, he does. Today's Gospel pitches us into the heart of the complexity. If Jesus is the Messiah, with all authority, incarnate among us, coming in glory, why do people not recognize him when they meet him?

Isaiah proclaimed (61.1–2):

> 'The Spirit of the Lord God is upon me, because the Lord has anointed me; he has sent me to bring good news to the oppressed, to bind up the broken-hearted, to proclaim liberty to the captives, and release to the prisoners; to proclaim the year of the Lord's favour, and the day of vengeance of our God; to comfort all who mourn ...'

The Spirit's empowering precipitates compassionate action for the oppressed. Because Matthew told us that Jesus was conceived and anointed by the Spirit (Matthew 1.20, 3.16), fulfilling Isaiah's prophecy that God's Spirit was upon him and he would not break a bruised reed or quench a smouldering wick (Matthew 12.18–20), it is no surprise to find Jesus identifying himself with the poor and needy. That is where we will find and know him if we look hard enough.

The head verger at Durham Cathedral and I meet regularly with three central Durham churches to coordinate ministry for people who turn up in need. During one meeting, a young woman barged into the room unannounced and, in very colourful language, expressed her anger at having nothing in life. Abruptly, what we were discussing was, yet again, in front of us in flesh and blood demanding help. There was not a lot we could do. The irony was not lost on us.

Our readings help us with the dilemma we faced on not being able to fix her life instantly. We worship a God whose idea of kingship is being involved in compassionate action. Ezekiel described God as the true shepherd who personally seeks out his lost sheep, rescuing the scattered and returning them to the safety of good, secure pasture. This was a vision of woolly heaven. But the picture is even better because God's kingship is about compassionate action to secure not just relief but justice.

As Ezekiel describes, shepherds had to be hands-on. In the previous chapter he, exiled in Babylon, received the message he dreaded. Jerusalem was razed to the ground and the nation's freedom over. He was so distressed that he was literally unable to speak. Then the Lord came with a message of judgement on the leaders of the people who had brought this disaster on the nation, accusing them of being false shepherds refusing help to people who were like sheep at the mercy of predators. In this context of severe judgement of false shepherds who did not care for the vulnerable people, God made the extraordinary promise to humble himself to become a shepherd – a very lowly job in the pecking order of the day – for his defenceless people.

The prophets we have heard from in the last three weeks were more like godly irritants than pastors, although ultimately that may be pastoral ministry if people need to be jolted to attention. On Christ the King Sunday, who do we say that Jesus is? If he is who he claims to be, then he is both prophetic irritant and pastor. So we will meet him in the poor and needy as well as in the breath-taking foretastes of his heavenly glory which the Ephesians experienced in worship. Are we to be found in all the places where he can be found?

YEAR B

Advent Sunday

Isaiah 64.1–9; 1 Corinthians 1.3–9; Mark 13.24–37

WHEN GOD CANNOT WAIT

> *Almighty God, give us grace to cast away the works of darkness and to put on the armour of light, now in the time of this mortal life, in which your Son Jesus Christ came to us in great humility; that on the last day, when he shall come again in his glorious majesty to judge the living and the dead, we may rise to the life immortal; through him who is alive and reigns with you, in the unity of the Holy Spirit, one God, now and for ever. Amen.*

Advent, and thus the church year, begins with a cry, 'O', as we hear an impatient Isaiah wanting God to go on something of a rampage, 'O that you would rend the heavens and come down.' Advent invites us to express our yearning for something to happen that is beyond our power to do anything about, except to desire it. This is not the 'Oh' of surprise, but the passionate, vocative 'O' of address, of imploring God to come among us and change things. It is a prayer of penitence and of hope, and our 'O' is predicated on active remembering because, like Isaiah, we can remember that God forgives sin and meets those who gladly do right.

We make this cry for God to come among us, not because we are longing for deliverance from this world, but for God's glory to be revealed in this world, in the time of this mortal life. There is a 'now and not yet' dimension to the prayer that God's Kingdom will come on earth as it is in heaven. The basic ache for God to act transcends the years, and is as potent today in our world of injustice, oppression, and suffering as it was when the exiles prayed centuries ago. It would be a good Advent discipline to pray with the daily news for God's Kingdom to come in the suffering places of earth.

All three readings presuppose that we have to wait faithfully for the answer to this cry that God will rend the heavens and come among us in power and glory; and Paul assured his readers that God will strengthen them to the end. Jesus dispels any idea that we can twiddle our thumbs while we wait, and so the prayer in the Collect elaborates the readings: 'Give us grace to cast away the works of darkness and to put on the armour of light.' God rends, God strengthens; we cast away, and we put on. These are not delicate actions, but decisive and determined. Advent is a time for active and energetic waiting.

But if 'O' is the cry of Advent, 'Yet' is the basis of that cry: 'Yet you are our father,' pleads Isaiah. If we dare to address our plea to God then we begin to know who we are: yes, we are clay in the hands of a potter, but this potter is our father. There is unbridled power, and there is passionate love. There are echoes of this mystery in Mr and Mrs Beaver's description of Aslan in *The Lion, the Witch and the Wardrobe*:

'If there's anyone who can appear before Aslan without their knees knocking, they're either braver than most or else just silly.'
'Then he isn't safe?' said Lucy.
'Safe?' said Mr Beaver … 'Who said anything about safe? 'Course he isn't safe. But he's good. He's the King, I tell you.' (Lewis, 1950)

The cry of Advent, for God to come among us, is, paradoxically, both wildly risky and gloriously secure because the God to whom we pray is a good and faithful God, who has called us into the fellowship of his Son, Jesus Christ our Lord. Our Advent longing will be fulfilled in the stories we will hear and inhabit during the coming year: in the incarnation when God tears open the heavens and comes among us; when Jesus is baptized; and again at the transfiguration. Then, at the moment of Jesus's death in the earthquake, comes the tearing of the veil of the Temple which separated humans from God's holy presence, from top to bottom. God cannot wait to come among us, and, in Jesus Christ, bursts in on the scene.

Gate-crashing God who took our flesh
and heaven's hope to earth unfurled:
Your kingdom come! Oh, raise our sights
until your ways transform our world.

Astounding God, once tortured, killed!
you broke the power of lies and fear:
Your kingdom come! Let justice roll
on earth as heaven. O God, draw near!
Copyright © 1993 Rosalind Brown

Second Sunday of Advent

Isaiah 40.1–11; 2 Peter 3.8–15a; Mark 1.1–8

THE HOPE OF A ROAD IN THE WILDERNESS

O Lord, raise up, we pray, your power and come among us, and with great might succour us; that whereas, through our sins and wickedness we are grievously hindered in running the race that is set before us, your bountiful grace and mercy may speedily help and deliver us; through Jesus Christ your Son our Lord, to whom with you and the Holy Spirit, be honour and glory, now and for ever. Amen.

This is a noisy reading from Isaiah. Last week, he was crying to God to rend the heavens and come down; now heaven answers with several cries. It seems heaven has to cry in order to be heard above the clamour of earth.

The time is round about 550 BC. The location is Babylon, where the people of Israel have been exiled, hundreds of miles across the desert from their home, and where they cry and rail against their fate. In Psalm 137 they are lamenting: 'By the rivers of Babylon, there we sat down and there we wept when we remembered Zion.' Above this noise, a voice cries out that a highway is to be prepared for the Lord in the wilderness. Babylon was a magnificent city (as we know from the exhibition at the British Museum in 2009) with wide, straight streets, along which gods and kings processed, asserting their brazen power and rubbing in how useless are the exiles' gods and how hopeless any thought of rebellion.

So it is staggering for exiles to hear that there is to be a similar highway for their God. With echoes of the Exodus way through the wilderness, this can mean only one thing: it is going away from Babylon, and towards Jerusalem. But that is too much for dispirited people to take in. They have lost hope of ever returning, because they believe that their exile is God's perpetual punishment for their sins. When a voice from heaven says: 'Cry out,' the cynical response is: 'What shall I cry? There's nothing to say – we are like grass or flowers which are here today and gone tomorrow. It's too late; there is no hope.' So the message from heaven has to be a series of imperatives: 'Comfort, O comfort, my people; speak tenderly; cry to her; prepare a way; do not fear.' These people who have lost all hope need to be stirred up to become people of hope; they cannot do it themselves. As Charles Wesley put it in his hymn: 'Kindle a flame of sacred love On the mean altar of my heart.'

It is the same today. From the same part of the world as ancient Babylon, Zainab Salbi, an Iranian woman, writes movingly about the contemporary version of the sounds Isaiah knew:

I grew up with the sounds of war. The staccato sounds of gunfire, the wrenching booms of explosions, the ominous drones of jets flying overhead, and the wailing warning sounds of sirens. Those are sounds you would expect. But there's also the dissonant concert of a flock of birds screeching in the night, the high-pitched, honest cries of children, and the thunderous, unbearable silence. The silence is the worst. It is the silence of children so terrorized they do not scream. War, said a friend of mine, is not about sound at all, but about silence: the silence of humanity. (Salbi, 2011)

So, at the same time as an audacious cry about a road in a wilderness, there is a tender message of comfort for a bruised Jerusalem in the midst of her silences of fear. Before the exile, the people had lamented that there was no one to comfort them, and the roads to Zion mourned (Lamentations 1.2, 17); now, in a complete reversal, God comforts them that there is to be a highway to Zion.

If the hinge for hope in last week's words from Isaiah was 'yet', this week it is 'but': 'But the word of our God will stand for ever.' That is the basis for these cries of hope from heaven. God has remembered, and, in the words of the Collect, is with great might succouring them.

Noise and silence are both sounds that can drown out hope. In a world of despair, our message of hope that God is making a new way in the wildernesses of life and that there will be a place where (as the epistle puts it so evocatively) righteousness is at home may have to be shouted to some people and spoken tenderly to others. How shall we proclaim it this Advent?

Third Sunday of Advent
Isaiah 61.1–4, 8–11; 1 Thessalonians 5.16–24;
John 1.6–8, 19–28

ALL THE EARTH IS TO BE BLESSED

O Lord Jesus Christ, who at your first coming sent your messenger to prepare the way before you: grant that the ministers and stewards of your mysteries may likewise so prepare and make ready your way by turning the hearts of the disobedient to the wisdom of the just, that at your second coming to judge the world we may be found an acceptable people in your sight; for you are alive and reign with the Father in the unity of the Holy Spirit, one God, now and for ever. Amen.

The focus is narrowing as Advent progresses. We began with Isaiah's passionate cry to God, 'O that you would tear open the heavens and come down,' which was met by God's returning cry, 'Comfort, O comfort, my people.' Now it is not nations that are addressed, but individuals, as we hear from and of the servant of the Lord about God's anointing and commissioning to bring good news to the oppressed and to proclaim the year of the Lord's favour. Heaven's big picture is coming down to earth, and it will burst the confines of earth's expectations. This astounding belief is captured in some of our wonderful, stately Advent hymns, which should shake us to the core of our being as we gasp in awe at what God has in mind. They wade into the deep things of life, our own and our world's hopes and fears, and they both undo and remake us as people of extraordinary hope and deep compassion for those who suffer.

This part of Isaiah dates from around 538 BC, when the Persian King, Cyrus, defeated the Babylonians who had originally taken Israel captive into exile. Cyrus's policy was to return enslaved people to their homelands, and Isaiah interprets this political approach in theological terms, presenting it as God's turning again to restore his people. This third part of the book of Isaiah proclaims the daring idea that, through God's blessing of Israel as a nation, all the earth is to be blessed. Israel can no longer boast of being the sole recipient of God's favour; now she is to be the means of God's blessing of all creation. It has to be said that Israel has never entirely grasped this message, which radically and disturbingly expanded the people's understanding of themselves. Trapped in exile, how could they hope to be described as the planting of the Lord, the rebuilders of generations of devastation? God works through individuals, and so the servant of the Lord speaks of God's anointing by the Spirit for the tender ministry that a bruised and broken people needed. Here is hope beyond anything that they could imagine in exile: their tears of grief will turn to shouts and tears of joy; once more, there will be singing and dancing, righteousness and praise in front of all nations.

The servant of the Lord is identified by life-giving action, and not as a particular person. The same can be said of John, who is faced with religious leaders desperate to find out who he is. We sense their mounting anger, as they fire questions at him like frustrated interrogators. John confounds them by refusing to define himself except by who he is not, and by his vocation to prepare the way of the Lord – that straight path in the wilderness which we heard of in last week's readings.

Isaiah anticipated God's blessing of the whole world through the liberation of his people, Israel. John the Baptist anticipated the revealing of the unknown coming one – standing among them, but as yet unrecognized. Paul encourages the Thessalonians to 'rejoice always, pray without ceasing and give thanks in all circumstances' – 11 words that model an attitude in life that is not triumphalist or unrealistic, but a faithful way to hold fast to what is good when facing adversity or prosperity. Like them, we are invited to live as people of confident hope in God.

In the Collect, we pray for all who are entrusted with preparing God's way today, and, as with all prayers that we pray, we may find ourselves becoming part of the answer. The opportunity before us this Advent is to be caught up in God's audacious ways of responding to earth's cry, not just with the brazen power that we heard Isaiah yearning for on the First Sunday in Advent, but through the hands-on, compassionate actions of binding up the broken-hearted, comforting the mourners, providing for those unable to help themselves, and bringing God's joy into situations of despair.

It does not take much imagination to see how God might call us to this, in our economically inept, politically confused, and exhausted, war-torn world. If we gave half the money or time that we spend on Christmas with our families and friends to embodying the joy of Christmas for the needy in God's world, that would be a radical start.

Fourth Sunday of Advent

2 Samuel 7.1–11, 16; Romans 16.25–27; Luke 1.26–38

NOT YOURS, BUT YOU, DAVID

God our redeemer, who prepared the Blessed Virgin Mary to be the mother of your Son: grant that, as she looked for his coming as our saviour, so we may be ready to greet him when he comes again as our judge; who is alive and reigns with you, in the unity of the Holy Spirit, one God, now and for ever. Amen.

David's well-intentioned desire to build a house for God is, at first, endorsed by Nathan – it seems a good and pious aim. But both of them are in danger of attempting to domesticate God, who has never been contained in time and space. Can we hear echoes of Peter's experience at the transfiguration, when, in response to his suggestion that the disciples should build booths for Jesus, Moses, and Elijah, the voice from heaven directs them not to try to control things, but to listen to the Beloved Son?

Sometimes it is easier to find a project to do than it is to remain open to God in relative stillness. The emphasis was not to be on what David could do for God, but on David's openness to receive what God would do for him – God wanted to turn the tables and make him a house, a dynasty. That would not be easy for a man used to fighting for his survival, and who had seen his own son try to usurp the throne. His every instinct would be to consolidate his power, and to be seen to do so by building a magnificent temple where national worship could be focused. But, instead, he was reminded of the faithfulness of God, and effectively told to go on trusting God in this time of relative security, in the same way as he had in past times of fear and insecurity. Essentially, what God was saying to him can be summed up in the motto of St Chad's College in the University of Durham: *'Non vestra sed vos'*: 'Not yours, but you'; in other words, not what you have, but you yourself.

David could not have known it when he was told to put his plans on hold, but his desire to build God a house would, ultimately, be answered through Mary, a young member of the house that God had given him. Through her openness to the overshadowing of the Holy Spirit, God indeed came to dwell among us. On the face of it, the Collect is rather disingenuous in its description of Mary's being prepared to be the mother of God's son: Luke tells of an angel dropping in unannounced with the news, and her understandable response of perplexity and fear. Some preparation, we might say.

Perhaps we are underestimating Mary, who shows all the hallmarks of being a very faithful young Jewish woman, as well as a very brave one. As such, her preparation would have gone back to her childhood, when she was steeped in the stories of her heritage, and, before her birth, to the heritage itself, with its sometimes turbulent relationship with God and the passionate yearnings for God to come as Saviour. God's response to that yearning – one that, time and again, we are told that God shares – had been to remind the people that coming to save meant also coming to judge them, and not just their enemies (something they were not backward in praying for at times), holding them to their calling to be the people of God through whom all nations would be blessed. This is the inheritance that prepared Mary for the sudden visit of the angel, and for her readiness to greet him once the initial shock was over. In these last days of Advent, we can ask ourselves how secure we are in our Christian heritage: if an angel dropped in on us, would we have the spiritual wherewithal to make sense of what God is asking of us?

So our prayer today is answered not so much by gearing ourselves up spiritually to be ready when Christ comes again to judge the world, but by our day-in, day-out preparation to meet our God through our routine faithful living. If we are not making the effort to prepare for God's coming among us in our ordinary life, and cannot trace his presence with us now, we have missed the point.

This Advent prayer is answered by our commitment to seeking God in the ordinary rather than the spectacular. Our response when God acts dramatically will be determined by our fidelity now.

Christmas Day

Isaiah 9.2–7; Titus 2.11–14; Luke 2.1–20

TRUSTING A BABY TO STRANGERS

Almighty God, you have given us your only-begotten Son to take our nature upon him and as at this time to be born of a pure virgin: grant that we, who have been born again and made your children by adoption and grace, may daily be renewed by your Holy Spirit; through Jesus Christ your Son our Lord. Amen.

Every year, Durham Cathedral hosts many carol services. Our organists and vergers have harked the herald angels singing more times than they might wish, while serving visiting organizations that, because of pressures on the cathedral calendar, have been singing carols here from early December. But now it is really time to celebrate the incarnation, and to do so with joy.

In the midst of the round of carol services at Durham, there is one that never ceases to move staff and volunteers alike. Although it has exactly the same script year by year, it is always fresh and powerful. The local Mencap branches present a nativity play in which members of Mencap, along with their siblings, parents, and friends, form a tableau, while a narrator and cantor tell the story and the congregation joins in the carols. The costumes are fabulous; the acting is simple. The tableau is created by a series of processions down the cathedral aisle, first of Mary and Joseph, then of a host of angels of all shapes and sizes, followed by equally assorted shepherds, and finally Wise Men, with their little page boys to help them. One year, the cathedral waited expectantly as a Wise Man laboriously hauled himself out of his wheelchair, stood on tiptoe, and tottered forward for a couple of steps, held safely by his wheelchair-pusher, determined to place his gift at the feet of the baby. The devotion was palpable.

And it is that baby who, year by year, speaks powerfully to me of the meaning of the incarnation, and the risk that God took in being born among us. In the tableau, when Mary and Joseph are seated at the manger, a young mother carries her newborn baby the length of the aisle, and places him or her in the manger at the feet of two people who are too vulnerable to care for themselves independently, let alone a baby, but who depend on the care of others. Then the mother walks away, leaving her tiny baby there, helpless at the mercy and in the care of strangers, but strangers who are totally focused on what they know they have to do. Her action is more eloquent theology than a thousand words. It is what God did in the incarnation. Mary and Joseph were not, perhaps, as vulnerable as the actors in the nativity play, but they lived in an occupied country in violent times, and would soon become refugees in order to save their baby from massacre. God risked all to share our life so that we might share his.

Once again, we hear Isaiah announce with breathtaking vision and certainty: 'The people who walked in darkness have seen a great light; those who lived in a land of deep darkness, on them light has shined.' But are we ready? Will we recognize this light when it comes shining in our darkness, perhaps not in ways we expect? We prayed at the beginning of Advent: 'O that you would tear apart the heavens and come down,' and now God answers, not with quaking mountains, but in awe-inspiring vulnerability.

A few years ago, in Salisbury Cathedral, I sat with hundreds of people in the silent darkness as we waited for the Advent procession to begin. Suddenly, from another part of the cathedral, a baby's cry pierced the air. A woman behind me said huffily to her neighbour: 'They shouldn't bring babies to a service like this.' But what is Christmas about, if it is not about a baby crying in the night? Emmanuel, God is with us. God has torn apart the heavens and come down.

Mary laid her baby in a manger because there was no place for them in the inn. God laid his beloved Son at our feet when the grace of God appeared, bringing salvation to all. Christina Rossetti's words say it all:

Love came down at Christmas,
Love all lovely, love divine;
Love was born at Christmas,
Star and angels gave the sign.

First Sunday of Christmas
Isaiah 61.10–62.3; Galatians 4.4–7; Luke 2.15–21

THE MIRACULOUS AND THE MUNDANE

> *Almighty God, who wonderfully created us in your own image and yet more wonderfully restored us through your Son Jesus Christ: grant that, as he came to share in our humanity, so we may share the life of his divinity; who is alive and reigns with you, in the unity of the Holy Spirit, one God, now and for ever. Amen.*

This is the time of the church year when we are left holding the baby. The world is at the January sales, while we hear of shepherds getting to the stable and Jesus being circumcised.

Mary and Joseph might remember an angel with a message from God, but then there was silence. For nine months they got on with life before making the unexpected 90-mile journey to Bethlehem because the Roman emperor called a census. It would be tempting to think something had gone wrong. God had asked Mary to bear this baby but had not fixed the arrangements for the birth. When the time came, Jesus's birth was without any divine glamour as, in the mess and pain of birth in a stable, away from home, God kept quiet.

God did send an angel, eventually. But not to Mary and Joseph. Instead God disturbed the night watch of some shepherds on a hillside outside Bethlehem who apparently had no intention of seeking God. They were outcasts because their work prevented their attendance at the Temple. Yet to these unlikely people, minding both their sheep and their own business, God's angel appeared. So a band of breathless shepherds became God's messengers to Mary and Joseph. They would not expect anyone to believe their far-fetched story yet Mary and Joseph probably took comfort from it. This was the only miraculous part of the actual birth of Jesus, otherwise Mary and Joseph were on their own discovering, after the event, that God's silence is not God's absence.

Jesus was circumcised and named as Gabriel instructed. 'Jesus' was a common name and, on the face of it, there was nothing special in the event beyond the joy of taking their firstborn for circumcision, recognizing his membership of the Jewish race. For Mary and Joseph, this was the start of raising him in the Jewish tradition that would shape his life and ministry as he lived into the full meaning of his name, Jesus, Saviour. He was a Jewish boy, with a good Jewish mother (if we see Mary as saccharinely pious we lose sight of an essential part of who she was), and he imbibed the Jewish worship and culture from his birth. As the Collect puts it, he was circumcised in obedience to the law for our sake. Galatians puts it more strongly, 'born of a woman, born under the law in order to redeem those who were under the law, so that we might receive adoption as children'.

Circumcision first appears before the law was given, in the context of covenant. Mary and Joseph placed Jesus within the response of God's people to God's unflinching holiness, goodness, and faithfulness. Jesus was obedient to the law for our sake and it began eight days after his birth when he was circumcised and brought under the authority of the law. Had there been no circumcision, there would be no fulfilment of the law.

This is the transition between the miraculous elements of the birth narratives and 30 years of humdrum life in a backwater village when Mary and Joseph raised their son as a faithful Jew. No doubt they thought Jesus the best baby ever, regaling the grandparents with accounts of his first smile, his first words, his first steps. Mary sang nursery rhymes to him, whispered nonsense in his ear as she stroked his hair, cleaned up the grazes and tears of childhood. They taught him to pray, to study, and to observe the Jewish festivals. This child was fully human, born of woman, born under the law, circumcised on the eighth day: a good Jewish boy.

Mary and Joseph had to hold together the miraculous and the mundane, the divine and the daily. Occasional angels were not enough; stability in their daily life as faithful Jews was what they needed if Jesus was to fulfil his vocation, expressed in his name, to save his people from their sins. The answer to our prayer in the Collect will come in the midst of daily fidelity to God. Whatever our hopes and dreams, the circumcision and naming of Jesus reminds us that we live an earthed life where our love for God is expressed in ordinary ways in ordinary situations. What that opens up is divine.

Second Sunday of Christmas
See Year A

Epiphany
See Year A

The Baptism of Christ,
First Sunday of Epiphany
Genesis 1.1–5; Acts 19.1–7; Mark 1.4–11

THE NEED FOR FORGIVENESS

Eternal Father, who at the baptism of Jesus revealed him to be your Son, anointing him with the Holy Spirit: grant to us, who are born again by water and the Spirit, that we may be faithful to our calling as your adopted children; through Jesus Christ our Lord. Amen.

In the Epiphany season, we are plunged into the revelation of the glory of God in Jesus. Beginning with the Wise Men, now in his baptism, over the next few weeks in his life, and ultimately in the transfiguration, Jesus is revealed to be the Christ, the anointed one. At his baptism, the voice from heaven, which once spoke creation into being and pronounced it good, declares that this outwardly unremarkable human being is God's beloved and well-pleasing son. Then our Advent prayer for God to tear open the heavens and come down is answered, as Jesus sees the heavens ripped apart by God, and the Spirit descends on him.

One year, when we began a lectionary year of reading Mark's Gospel, I challenged the congregation at Durham Cathedral to read this Gospel from start to finish in order to grasp the whole picture. Several people did; it takes about an hour. In his opening sentence Mark tells us, the readers, that Jesus is the Son of God, but then shows Jesus's contemporaries – friend and foe alike – struggling, sometimes almost comically, to grasp their way to this truth, as they pick up the clues in Jesus's life. They do not hear the voice from heaven at his baptism, but there are moments of revelation and realization: halfway through the Gospel, three terrified disciples hear the voice from heaven repeat the words: 'This is my Son, the beloved,' adding, 'listen to him'; and at the end, a Roman soldier, inured to the horrors of crucifixion, realizes that the man he has just killed is 'truly God's Son'. If you read Mark's Gospel through their eyes, it becomes almost a detective story: when will they discover what we know from the outset?

Much scholarly thought and ink has been spilled on why Jesus, who was without sin, deliberately walked 40–50 miles to be baptized with John's baptism of repentance for the forgiveness of sins. It may help to remember that Jesus was not 50 per cent human and 50 per cent divine, but fully divine and fully human; and, as a human, he shared the human experience of alienation from God because of sin – he was born in a violent, occupied country, and was wise to the deceptions of the human heart. What is so astounding is that, at his baptism, this fully human person was revealed as fully divine. 'This is my Son, the Beloved' brings together Old Testament understandings of divine sonship (Psalm 2.7) and servanthood (Isaiah 42.1), and defines his ministry. The incarnate Second Person of the Trinity, the son and the servant, identifies with humans in our need for repentance and forgiveness, even though he has no need to do so for himself.

Jesus's submission to John's baptism of repentance for the forgiveness of sins makes sense because repentance is not an ending, but a glorious beginning. The heavens are torn open, the Spirit descends: baptism is no longer merely a human act, a response to conviction of sin. Now, through the baptism of Jesus, the divine response to this sign of repentance is not merely forgiveness of sin – amazing as that is – but the coming of the Holy Spirit. In baptism, we are caught up into new life in the family of God, and John ends his Gospel with Jesus's breathing on the disciples so that they might receive the same Holy Spirit who descended on him, a blessing which the apostles then enabled those baptized for repentance to receive.

Because of this, we pray to be faithful to our calling as God's adopted children. Jesus was not adopted by God – an early heresy – he is God, but adoption is one of the vivid images and insights that we are given into our relationship with God. Adoption brings with it new identity within a new family, where the adopted person learns the ways in which a family lives its life.

It is the same with adoption by God, whose family we join through baptism: we learn to live as God's beloved, adopted children, and find ourselves growing in faithfulness in daily life. So we can repent with joy, knowing that baptism is not only for the forgiveness of sin; it is God's reaching out to us, and transforming us through the Holy Spirit.

Second Sunday of Epiphany

1 Samuel 3.1–10 [11–20]; Revelation 5.1–10;
John 1.43–51

GOD CALLS TO SAMUEL

*Almighty God, in Christ you make all things new: transform the poverty of
our nature by the riches of your grace, and in the renewal of our lives make
known your heavenly glory; through Jesus Christ our Lord. Amen.*

Put yourself in Eli's shoes. His track record as a priest was abysmal. He had
failed to deal with the appalling actions of his two sons, who had turned the
shrine of the Lord into a brothel, and was complicit in their greedy extortion of
people who came to worship. Then, when a woman in deep distress was praying,
he was so pastorally insensitive that he accused her of being drunk. Surprisingly,
that woman, the childless Hannah, had the guts to stand up to Eli and gain a
blessing.

A few years later, the child born as a result of that blessing was, amazingly,
entrusted by Hannah to the care of this elderly man, despite his incompetence
in raising his own sons. The spiritual life of the nation had reached such a low
ebb that 'the word of the Lord was rare in those days and visions were not
widespread'. That was hardly surprising, given the behaviour of the priests, but
Hannah was true to her vow, and set an example of radical trust in God's power
to redeem the situation.

Then, some years later, one night God acted, and called to Samuel. Although
this was a shrine, set apart for the worship of God, its spiritual life was so lax and
Eli so unused to God's doing anything like this that it took three attempts by God
before it dawned on Eli that maybe this was the Lord calling. The breakthrough
came only because of Samuel's naïve persistence, but, having tumbled to this
radical turn of events, Eli guided Samuel in how to respond, and the next day
demanded to know the message. We rarely know the tone of voice used in the
dialogues in the Bible; so we cannot tell whether Eli's question, 'What was it
that he told you?', was said with a heavy heart, fearing the worst, or with hopeful
expectation. The news was indeed disastrous: God would not overlook his failure
to control his sons, and no amount of sacrificial offering would change God's
mind because of the horror of the outrage perpetrated over the years. To give Eli
his due, he had the courage to accept this judgement.

At this rock-bottom point in the nation's and Eli's life, Eli could sink into
despair and give up. But God did not abandon him: Samuel continued to live
at the shrine and, as he grew up, the Lord was with him and he becomes a
trustworthy prophet of the Lord. This could not happen without Eli's oversight;

so perhaps this call of Samuel was as much a call of Eli to pick up the shreds of his ministry and keep going with renewed commitment and faithfulness – in the words of the Collect, to have the poverty of his nature transformed by the riches of God's grace, and in the renewal of his life to let God's glory be known.

Put yourself, now, in Nathanael's shoes. Philip, your friend, comes to you with the outrageous proposition that the One about whom Moses and the prophets have written is the son of a man from Nazareth, a small village in the backwaters of Galilee – truly the back end of nowhere. Nathanael's incredulous, cynical retort, 'Can anything good come out of Nazareth?', is apposite. Nazareth is off the religious map, and this is not what is supposed to happen when the Messiah comes. But Jesus catches him by surprise, ignores the derogatory remark, praises his integrity, and suddenly Nathanael finds himself the recipient of a promise that he will see God's glory revealed in a way that will demand his lifetime commitment. God has made even Nazareth new.

Epiphany is the season when the Church focuses on the revelation of the glory of God in Jesus Christ. Last week, it was overt, in the words from heaven at his baptism. This week, it is more covert because God's glory is revealed in the unlikely circumstances of an ineffectual old man with a lifetime of failure to regret, and a young man who is over-confident about the parameters within which God should work.

God can make all things new, and in Epiphany we are invited – even if we feel as burned-out as Eli or sceptical as Nathanael – to offer our lives to be transformed and renewed, so that God's glory may be revealed through us.

Third Sunday of Epiphany

Genesis 14.17–20; Revelation 19.6–10; John 2.1–11

SAVING THE BEST UNTIL LAST

Almighty God, whose Son revealed in signs and miracles the wonder of your saving presence: renew your people with your heavenly grace, and in all our weakness sustain us by your mighty power; through Jesus Christ our Lord. Amen.

I am ashamed to admit that my memories of being a bridesmaid for the first time have nothing to do with the service, but are all about the reception. I was given a glass of orange drink and was disgusted because it was fizzy and I disliked anything sparkling. Consternation: there were no still drinks to be found. So I sulked, as over-excited seven-year-olds do so well, went thirsty for a while, and then drank tap water. Years later, the lack of orange squash at a wedding is lodged in my memory.

Food and drink can make or break a party, which perhaps explains why Jesus performed a non-essential miracle. Wedding parties lasted several nights (people went to work in the day); so these guests had already had a great deal to drink. The family was wealthy, with servants and the more hygienic stone water-jars that only the rich could afford. To run out of wine at a wedding was not a matter of life and death, but it was a social faux pas. Apparently, it might even be cause for a lawsuit if a disgruntled guest did not receive hospitality appropriate to the value of his wedding gift. John tells us that this was the first of Jesus's signs, and through it he revealed his glory. John does not have any parables in his Gospel, and calls his seven miracles 'signs', which alerts us to probe more deeply than face value.

We are not immersed in the Jewish mind-set, which, on hearing 'marriage-feast', immediately thought also of the expected banquet heralding the Messiah. The reading in Revelation gives us the foretaste of the joy at the marriage-feast of the Lamb of God. Weddings have wine, and God has the best cellar of all: Isaiah tells us about God's supply of well-aged wines, strained clear (Isaiah 25.6). That detail – strained clear – was significant in an age when wine was pretty rough and needed to be diluted with water to make it palatable; hence the bemused head steward's comment to the bridegroom that, very unusually and perhaps stupidly, he has saved the best until the end. God, however, offers only the best, all the time.

So this sign, performed in the village of Cana, points us to the lavish extravagance of God's messianic banquet. Just as Jesus produced the best wine at the end, so God has saved his very best gift to Israel and the world to the last; for something better than the law is given in Jesus Christ. No wonder John begins his Gospel with a wedding banquet. This sign demonstrates the dawn of the messianic age that comes in Jesus Christ. As Christians, we celebrate a foretaste of the wedding banquet of heaven, which the reading from Revelation describes for us, when we take bread and wine, and give thanks for the saving death and resurrection of Jesus Christ.

For one of Jesus's disciples, Nathanael, this sign was particularly astounding. Three days earlier, Nathanael had met Jesus for the first time, when Jesus startled him by saying: 'You will see heaven opened.' It all happened astonishingly quickly because, John tells us (21.2), Nathanael came from Cana; so this revelation of Jesus's glory happened in his home town. Whatever he was expecting when he went with Jesus to the wedding, it cannot have been this. Sometimes it is easier to expect miracles to happen elsewhere – in fact, anywhere but on our doorstep. But this sign challenges us to believe that God will reveal his glory in our daily lives. In this season of the Epiphany, of the revelation of God's glory, Nathanael's experience dares us to be open to the revelation of God's glory and generosity among us, whether or not we expect it.

This revelation should challenge us when we run into situations where the world's shortages and needs – whether of food, medical supplies, justice, or peace – tempt us to despair. John's Gospel does not have a Last Supper story but, instead, in two of Jesus's signs there is lavish abundance: here, the best wine; after five thousand have eaten, 12 baskets left over. Since the God we love is so generous, and has plans for the ultimate wedding banquet in heaven, the least we can do is be generous ourselves in our giving and our celebration.

Fourth Sunday of Epiphany

Deuteronomy 18.15–20; Revelation 12.1–5a;
Mark 1.21–28

SPIRITUAL BATTLE COMMENCES

God our creator, who in the beginning commanded the light to shine out of darkness: we pray that the light of the glorious gospel of Christ may dispel the darkness of ignorance and unbelief, shine into the hearts of all your people, and reveal the knowledge of your glory in the face of Jesus Christ our Lord. Amen.

St Mark launches into his Gospel with 'a week in the life of Jesus', which begins when Jesus comes to Galilee and calls some disciples. Then they go to the synagogue on the Sabbath, where he is known to the leader of the synagogue who invites him to teach from the scriptures. Mark emphasizes Jesus's teaching ministry, and often links it to miracles that show his power and what happens when he teaches. So, in this first description of Jesus's teaching, Mark does not bother to tell us what Jesus taught; instead he is far more interested in the impact Jesus has, which is first astonishment and then a commotion. The astonishment is at his authority. Unlike scribes who deferred to the authority of the law, Jesus has authority in himself. This has already been shown in his imperative to the fishermen: 'Follow me.'

Whatever we think about demons, we mishandle Mark's Gospel if we do not enter his first-century world-view where evil spirits were part of Satan's forces but would be afraid and flee in the presence of a righteous person, and where to know a person's name was to have advantage over him or her. When people recognize Jesus's authority, he is challenged by an unclean spirit who is threatened by his presence and who tries to control him by invoking his name. Radical evil has encountered radical good and is afraid. The unclean spirit knows that Jesus comes from Nazareth, which emphasizes his humanity, and names him as the Holy One of God, which acknowledges his divinity and his power to destroy the evil spirit. Jesus exercises his authority over the spirit, to everyone's astonishment. They link this turn of events to Jesus's teaching, and word spreads rapidly. This is the end of any privacy that Jesus had – he is now on the public stage. We never hear what happened to the man because the focus is on people's reaction to Jesus.

John the Baptist had said that Jesus was the 'more powerful one' (Mark 1.7), and Jesus has already had a 40-day encounter with Satan (Mark 1.12–13), the details and outcome of which Mark (unlike Matthew and Luke) does not tell us. Instead, it is in this encounter that Mark describes Jesus's victory over Satan

– it is displayed in the way that he brings health and wholeness to a suffering man. Jesus is taking his battle against evil into his daily ministry. The prophecy we heard in Advent is being fulfilled: liberty is being proclaimed to the captives and release to prisoners (Isaiah 61.1).

Mark shows us that Jesus's teaching has a devastating impact on forces that oppress people. While the story embodies beliefs about demons, which many people dismiss today, there is no doubt that evil exists in our world and that lack of belief in demons will not make evil go away. Enforced slavery in any of its forms – from people-trafficking into this country to child soldiers in Africa – is evil, and is not hard to name as such. We are less ready to name other indulgences as evil. Whether or not they are crimes in the eyes of the law, there is evil behind the headlines about invasion of privacy through phone-hacking, or enormous bonuses that manifest an underlying culture of greed. The attitude that men have a right to use women for sex, whether with a prostitute, a hotel maid, or through grooming, economic decisions by multinationals, as well as our own love of consumer goods that encourage sweat shops and destroy environments – all these are just as oppressive of their victims as the unclean spirit that Jesus cast out.

In the Collect, we pray to the God who commanded light to shine out of darkness, as Jesus commanded the light to shine in the darkness of this man's life. If we believe that God answers prayer, and if we pray (as we do) 'deliver us from evil', then we should be asking ourselves how we respond to evil in the world that oppresses people today. Jesus's hearers were stunned at the impact of his teaching, and so should we be: it should be changing our lives and, through us, the lives of others.

Sunday before Lent,
Proper 1 (3–9 February)
Isaiah 40.21–end; 1 Corinthians 9.16–23; Mark 1.29–39

A MIRACLE IN THE HOUSE

Almighty God, by whose grace alone we are accepted and called to your service: strengthen us by your Holy Spirit and make us worthy of our calling; through Jesus Christ our Lord. Amen.

Collect for the Fifth Sunday before Lent

It is dark! Most of the events in the Gospel reading took place at night. After sunset on the Sabbath, Peter's house was bombarded with people wanting Jesus to heal their sick, probably in chaotic scenes of noisy crowds. Then, in the morning, Jesus got up in the dark and escaped to a deserted place to pray. Despite, or perhaps because of, the demands the previous day had made on him, Jesus made prayer a priority, in this case over sleep. Mark is setting out early in his Gospel what undergirded Jesus's ministry: encounter and prayer.

Sometimes the Bible is specific about which watch of the night an event happened in – something we tend to ignore. Mark specifies that Jesus got up in the morning while it was still dark. This was during the fourth watch, known as the dawn, or morning, watch. The Jews had added a fourth, Roman, watch to their previous three watches, thus dividing the night for watchmen into four three-hour watches, which Jesus referred to by name in Mark 13.35. A parish priest once commented to me that this fourth watch of the night is when many people find sleep most difficult: they lie awake, going over things, often worrying. Problems seem enormous when we cannot sleep, but, equally, new perspectives sometimes emerge. Monastics, however, who follow the Rule of St Benedict, and get up early to pray the monastic offices, the *Opus Dei*, are also awake in the fourth watch of the night: that prayer is a gift that they offer to others. As John Ellerton put it in his hymn: 'The voice of prayer is never silent, Nor dies the strain of praise away.'

When trying to imagine the scene in Capernaum on that dark early-Sunday morning, we know that Jesus was awake and praying somewhere outside on his own. Perhaps he had been sleepless while the previous day's events, when he had suddenly become a celebrity, replayed in his mind. We do not know the content of his prayer, but can make a guess that he focused with God on the message that he had begun to proclaim (Mark 1.15) and came to realize that he had to move on (Mark 1.36).

It is speculation, but perhaps Peter's mother-in-law was also awake, pondering what had happened to her when this young man, a friend of her son-in-law, had simply walked over to her, taken her by the hand, and lifted her off her sleeping mat, and her fever had suddenly disappeared. As she lay on that same sleeping mat just a few hours later, the mystery of what had happened was perhaps running through her mind, while she tried to comprehend what had taken place and who this Jesus was.

Our homes are places where meaning and memories are made; walls enclose stories, and places evoke remembrance. Bill Bryson writes: 'Houses aren't refuges from history. They are where history ends up' (Bryson, 2010). History certainly happened in this house: a miracle occurred. Now Peter's mother-in-law and the rest of the family had to make meaning out of this memory, which probably became a family legend. Perhaps it made it easier not to complain when Peter was away travelling with Jesus. This home had become a place of healing and restored life.

Our homes are the places where we sleep, and thus may wake in the night. How we use that waking time is the challenge, especially when time drags, and sleep eludes us. The hymn-writer Frederick Hosner wrote that 'the slow watches of the night not less to God belong'. In those slow watches, we can take our cue from Jesus – if not physically getting up, then, as the Collect prays, fixing our minds where true joys are to be found. This time, in the dark before dawn, is an opportunity to pray for others who are sleepless, and for those who are working through the night, including the emergency services, and it may be helpful to have simple prayers committed to memory for such occasions.

And, yes, this reflection came together in my mind in the fourth watch.

Sunday before Lent,
Proper 2 (10–16 February)
2 Kings 5.1–14; 1 Corinthians 9.24–27; Mark 1.40–45

UPSTAGING THE POWERFUL

O God, you know us to be set in the midst of so many and great dangers,
that by reason of the frailty of our nature we cannot always stand upright:
grant to us such strength and protection as may support us through all
dangers and carry us through all temptations; through Jesus Christ our
Lord. Amen.

Collect for the Fourth Sunday before Lent

There is an element of pantomime when the poor and powerless constantly get the better of the rich and powerful. It is there in Naaman's story.

It is the ninth century BC in Israel. A strong king has restored political stability, although enemies still threaten. Worship of God is confused with pagan worship, the rich have got richer and the poor have got poorer. The prophets, many rather colourful characters, are vitriolic in their condemnation of the king.

The story begins with a crisis in the enemy camp. Naaman the army captain has a skin disease. Fear of leprosy meant instant isolation, ending his military career and family life. No wonder his wife would try anything. Although a serious story for those involved, the way it is told is not. The author has a joke at just about everyone's expense; people are at cross purposes and the powerful are upstaged by the poor and powerless. Enter a little slave-girl, young and powerless: 'I know someone who can help. You will have to go to my land and find a prophet.' Captain and king decide to go for it. But they have not listened. The little girl said 'find the prophet', the person on the edge of society, the scourge of powerful people. Instead, using their power and influence, they go to the enemy king, softening him with gifts. The worst happens and a serious diplomatic incident ensues.

News reaches Elisha, no friend of the king, who sends a message, 'Send him to me.' Exit stage left chariots, horses, soldiers and hangers-on. At Elisha's house, which is not the palace Naaman might have expected for so worthy a person as he, there is no reception committee. Elisha does not bother to show up, just sends a messenger with the humiliating instruction to wash in the Jordan seven times. Naaman loses his temper. Again the powerless come to the rescue: his servants, who obviously knew how to handle their master, talked him out of his rage. So he washed and was healed. Reading on, we hear that he was so bowled over by this that he converted immediately and went home with a good lump of Israelite soil on which to worship. Political incident over.

Although the rich and powerful assume they are where power lies, the poor and powerless subvert this left, right and centre, cutting the powerful down to size. There is also a landmark in theological understanding of the power and influence of the God of Israel. We are told that Naaman was successful in battle because the Lord gave him victory. God was not supposed to do that! Quite apart from supporting the enemy, there was a question whether God's power extended beyond the borders of Israel or whether God was another territorial god whose power stopped at the border. Then, as events unfold, power is seen to lie not with the kings but with the prophet. And finally came the idea that Israel's God could be worshipped in Aramea of all terrible places. Profound theology was worked out in events and told in story form.

So who discovered what? A young slave-girl discovered that her small, seemingly stupid, idea to send her master to a prophet in Israel set something epic in motion; an army general learned humility and was given back his life in society and a new faith; a king was challenged – although we cannot be sure he learned from it – to listen to the word of God as well as his political ambitions; and the people as a whole, whether involved directly or reading about it later, learned that God is God of all the earth not just their own geographic bit of territory.

What do we learn from events in our lives? Do we pay attention to what is happening? Do we expect to encounter God in everyday events? If not, why not? Paul wrote about an athlete and discipline, running to win the prize. We can only do that if we train. As Christians, we can train ourselves to notice what God is doing in our midst, and train to be open to discovering more about God in all events of life, however insignificant or dramatic.

Our lives are too valuable to let God's activity go unnoticed, and if we do not let God meet us in daily life where can God meet us?

Sunday before Lent,
Proper 3 (17–23 February)
Isaiah 43.18–25; 2 Corinthians 1.18–22; Mark 2.1–12

OFF WITH THE ROOF

Almighty God, who alone can bring order to the unruly wills and passions of sinful humanity: give your people grace so to love what you command and to desire what you promise, that, among the many changes of this world, our hearts may surely there be fixed where true joys are to be found; through Jesus Christ our Lord.

Collect for the Third Sunday before Lent

'After I was paralysed all I wanted was to do something for myself instead of being dependent on others. I never adjusted to being unable to stop people doing things I did not want. There was one day when I would have given anything to be able to stop my friends taking advantage of my paralysis.

It started normally. My brother and the man next door carried my pallet into the shade so I could beg. They went off to work but discovered that Jesus from Nazareth, who was creating a stir ever since he healed Simon's mother-in-law, was back. They stopped to listen. Then they hatched the idea of taking me along so Jesus could heal me.

Having had experiences of sham healers, I was not keen. But they would not take no for an answer. They grabbed my pallet and set off, throwing me all over the place as I protested loudly. At Simon's house the crowds blocked the way. I suggested going home, but they ignored me. Then someone suggested the roof.

"Suppose it is not Simon's house?"

"Of course it is his."

"But you cannot do a demolition job on Simon's house. You would be livid if he did it to you."

"We can mend it afterwards. And, besides, he will be delighted that you are healed."

"But suppose I do not want to go through the roof, and suppose Jesus does not heal me."

I lost the argument.

I wanted to disappear and die. What if they dropped me through the hole? I would be in full view of everyone, embarrassed and paralysed on the outside, seething with rage and terror inside.

The sounds inside the house indicated we had been noticed. Someone said, "The dirt is coming down. Mind out." People rushed up the outside stairs to see what was happening. My companions ignored them and just kept pulling away at the roof.

Jesus went silent. I wondered how to apologize to him, what to say to Simon about the damage to his roof.

Then I was pulled over to the hole, and ropes were tied to the ends of my mat. I'll never forget the descent. All eyes were on me as I swung precariously through the air. I barely realized I had landed safely at the feet of a man who must be Jesus. He looked at me with penetrating eyes. I could not think what to say. Then I looked up at the sky and saw my brother and the others staring through the hole. After all their bravado on the roof, they were silent too but they were smiling and I realized Jesus was looking at them.

Then Jesus spoke. No question to me or to the men on the roof. No condemnation for interrupting his sermon. Just, "Son, your sins are forgiven."

That shot through me like a streak of lightning. Who had mentioned sins? But it certainly cleared my head, I even felt gratitude because somehow I felt safe with Jesus.

It seems I was not the only one taken aback by Jesus's words. Whispers came from near the door, and then Jesus raised his voice to ask why they raised questions. Then he went on, "So that you may know that the Son of Man has authority on earth to forgive sins, I say to you, stand up, take up your mat, and go to your home." Suddenly I realized he was talking to me. "Stand up!" he said. And, do you know, I did! I stood up! "Go home" he said. He did not even ask who I was, or hear any of my protests, apologies or thanks. So I went.

Can you imagine the scene when we got home? My wife was frantic, wondering where I had got to, and then I just walked in. I never heard what happened at Simon's place after we left. I went to see Jesus next day when he was out by the sea – the sea I never expected to see again. I paddled in it, felt the water and the sand between my toes.'

'In Jesus Christ every one of God's promises is a "yes."' (2 Corinthians 1.20)

Second Sunday before Lent

Proverbs 8.1, 22–31; Colossians 1.15–20; John 1.1–14

THE MYSTERY OF GOODNESS

> *Almighty God, you have created the heavens and the earth and made us in your own image: teach us to discern your hand in all your works and your likeness in all your children; through Jesus Christ your Son our Lord, who with you and the Holy Spirit reigns supreme over all things, now and for ever. Amen.*

We get too many opportunities to reflect on evil in our world. This week, we are invited to reflect on the mystery of goodness, as the readings place us squarely in the midst of God's sheer unadulterated love.

Unlike the other Gospels, John begins not with human time, but with eternity. The incarnation can be summed up in the eternal love of God, and God's desire to scoop us into that love which is great beyond our comprehension. The early Christians spoke of God's sharing our humanity in order that we might share his divinity. In the incarnation, God disrupts old ways of living: in Christ, he is inextricably part of our world, and makes us part of his, when, at the ascension, he took his, and thus our, wounded humanity into heaven.

And what is revealed of God by the Son? Today's readings run out of words. Christ is the image of the invisible God, the firstborn of all creation, before all things, and in him all things hold together. The wonder is that this unknowable, unseeable God is now known and seen as Jesus Christ. As John puts it: 'The Word became flesh and dwelt among us, and we have seen his glory … as of a father's only son, full of grace and truth.' When my brother's first child was born, I saw a whole new side to my brother. He was still the same brother whom I had always known – in that sense, he did not change – but he was revealed by his son in a new way because he was made known as father. This helps me to understand how the Son has made God the Father known. God is revealed in a new way as the father of our Lord Jesus Christ: like father, like son.

It is no accident that we have these readings on this Sunday. Having celebrated the incarnation at Christmas and the revelation of God's glory during Epiphany, we are ten days away from Lent, when our sights will suddenly turn towards the Passion and death of Jesus. Today we hear about Jesus Christ's divinity, his existence in the Godhead from before time came to be, so that next week we are ready to hear about that glory's being revealed, and then to go straight into Lent, when we have to hold that truth in creative tension with his suffering. Taking time to ponder the mystery of God's glory and love, which are revealed by the Son and lavished upon us, is no excuse for complacency in our war- and disaster-ravaged world. Instead, it is the most compelling catalyst for sacrificial living that there can be: something to keep in mind as we prepare for Lent.

All humans are made in God's image, even if they are not all Christ-like in their behaviour. If we all really understood that, there would not be the appalling incidents of abuse, rape, people-trafficking, violent crime, domestic violence, sexual or emotional abuse of children, and the other degradations that sully the news and tarnish our dignity as humans. Theologically, at the root of all of these abuses of our common humanity is a lack of respect for a person who is made in the image of God. So we pray this week for discernment to see that image and likeness of God, and, it goes without saying, to act accordingly.

The Gospels are amplifications of the basic wonder that God's boundless and eternal love is compressed into human flesh and blood, which we can see and know in daily life. Our inspiration in discipleship, which can be costly, is the wonder that this holy and incomprehensible God is made known in Jesus Christ, and invites us to share his life – in him to become children of God. That is what sets Christianity apart from all other religions, which are serious attempts to find and be faithful to God and with which there is scope for fruitful dialogue. But ultimately Christians come back to the truth that, in Jesus Christ, God has made himself known to us; that the impulse for communion comes not from us, but from God.

Sunday next before Lent

2 Kings 2.1–12; 2 Corinthians 4.3–6; Mark 9.2–9

STRENGTHENED TO SUFFER

Almighty Father, whose Son was revealed in majesty before he suffered death upon the cross: give us grace to perceive his glory, that we may be strengthened to suffer with him and be changed into his likeness, from glory to glory; who is alive and reigns with you, in the unity of the Holy Spirit, one God, now and for ever. Amen.

There are a few pivotal days in the church year, when our focus is redirected in an instant. The classic one is Palm Sunday, but today is another, epitomized in the Collect. The readings tell of Christ's heavenly glory revealed on earth, but in the Collect, our task is to get ready for Ash Wednesday, when we are turned round to take a long hard look at our human shortcomings, and, despite them, at God's amazing and insistent call to us to be disciples.

In the readings we are back with Epiphany's theme of the revelation of Christ's glory, to which the appropriate response is awe and wonder. The best that Mark can do is to describe Christ's transfigured clothes as brighter than any fuller or bleach can wash them; in other words, God is better than the best washerwoman. But everything will change. Ash Wednesday faces us with our sinfulness, and makes no compromises to human sensitivities; this politically incorrect day brooks no excuse, no plea of mitigating circumstances. Then we have the rest of Lent to come to terms with our sin, and with God's mercy and forgiveness. In preparation for this, the Collect has three linked petitions.

The first, 'give us grace to perceive his glory', takes its cue from today's readings: the disciples perceive Christ's glory, and Paul reiterates what we heard last week about knowing the glory of God in the face of Jesus Christ. In 2010, at Durham Cathedral we installed a Transfiguration window in memory of Michael Ramsey, former Bishop of Durham, Archbishop of York and of Canterbury, for whom transfiguration and glory were theological wellsprings. The window stops people in their tracks with its shaft of white light which in low winter sunlight is dazzling. Its immensely detailed images and scenes etched into the glass are perceived only if people stop and look. Its theological artistry challenges me to be attentive, to stop and look as God's glory sheds light on the events of daily life.

Then there is the awkward petition that this perception will strengthen us 'to suffer with him'. Normally we want out of suffering, not strength to endure it. There is a steadiness about what we pray for here – a stability that, enabled by our perception of glory, is not thrown off balance by suffering. After the revelation of his glory, Jesus went straight to a scene of suffering, a cameo of the millions of such incidents of suffering in our world: some beyond human control, others all too horrifically the result of human action. Sharing Jesus's suffering – his own and that of the world to which he brings light – is inevitable if we pray to perceive his glory.

The third part of the prayer anticipates the Easter message of hope, resurrection, ascension, and our transformation into his likeness from glory to glory. Vladimir Lossky wrote: 'The fire of grace, kindled in the hearts of Christians by the Holy Spirit, makes them shine like tapers before the Son of God' (Lossky, 1957). Kallistos Ware reminds us that, in this life, the glory of the saints is normally an inward splendour of the soul, but at the day of resurrection, the glory of the Holy Spirit comes out from within, decking the bodies of the saints (Ware, 1963). As Charles Wesley sang, we will be 'changed from glory into glory'.

On the threshold of Lent, we are called to become more and more Christ-like, and thus to share his glory. Lent is a time to take stock, as we focus on discipleship in a world of suffering. But we do so against the backdrop of the revealed glory of God, and with the assured hope of Easter, and our transformation more and more into Christ's likeness. Most of us are not prone to visions, but can be alert to perceive God's glory in daily life, as we look for what a friend calls 'hairline cracks of God'; these reminders that God is gloriously and rampantly present, if we will but notice. Perhaps a Lenten discipline could be to look for and respond to the glory of God revealed in other people.

Ash Wednesday
See Year A

First Sunday of Lent

Genesis 9.8–17; 1 Peter 3.18–22; Mark 1.9–15

THE MUD AND THE RAINBOW

Almighty God, whose Son Jesus Christ fasted forty days in the wilderness, and was tempted as we are, yet without sin: give us grace to discipline ourselves in obedience to your Spirit; and, as you know our weakness, so may we know your power to save; through Jesus Christ our Lord. Amen.

Lent is not tidy, because it faces us with the effects of sin. This year, Lent begins with timeless stories of floods – and therefore mud everywhere – temptation, wild animals, and a wilderness. Water and wilderness go together, and the epistle links these robust stories of Noah's deliverance through the flood with baptism and deliverance from the power of sin.

In Genesis, Noah picks up the pieces after the flood. Pictures of the devastation that floods wreak today come to mind: destruction everywhere and relentless clearing of debris. Noah's burnt offering pleases God (Genesis 8.20–22), but past experience indicates that rebellion will ensue; so God takes the initiative, launching into a speech: 'As for me, I will establish my covenant with you.' Although a covenant requires agreement between two parties, God does not negotiate or consult Noah when setting the ground rules in an outlandishly generous manner – not just with Noah, but with all his descendants and every living creature.

This part of the flood story is by the priestly author of Genesis 1, where God also took the initiative, spoke, and creation happened. After the flood's devastation of the first creation, the same Creator begins again with this universal, unilateral covenant: salvation and blessing are entirely at God's initiative. As before, the charge is to 'be fruitful and multiply' (Genesis 9.7), but some things have changed: now human sin is in the equation; the rest of creation will fear humans, who now can eat not only plants but animals, and murder has to be specifically prohibited. God promises never to destroy the earth again through a flood, and gives the sign of the covenant, the bow in the clouds. We immediately think of the rainbow, but, in the Old Testament, where battles involved bows and arrows, the word usually meant 'the bow of war'. When the rainbow appeared, significantly it was not Noah, but God – who had the power to override the covenant and destroy the earth – who would remember the everlasting covenant. So the rainbow would 'remind' God, and reassure Noah that God had abandoned his bow of war. It would rain again; there would be thunder and lightning again. When that happened, Noah might well be afraid that water would again destroy the earth. The sun would, however, shine again, sometimes while it was raining. Noah saw rainbows only when it rained, when 'what I dread has befallen me' (Job 3.25). Sometimes, it is in the midst of what we dread rather than beforehand that we discover God's faithfulness, much as we would like to avoid being in that situation in the first place.

In Mark, Jesus, after he, too, has been immersed in water through baptism, is driven – Mark uses a strong word, unlike Luke's more gentle 'led' – into the wilderness, where wild beasts and Satan await him. For him, just as for the people whom Moses led through the Red Sea into the wilderness, there is no respite. Deliverance by God is followed by the testing of human trust in God in less favourable times.

After the temptation in the wilderness, the sun came out, metaphorically, for Jesus: angels ministered to him. But then John was arrested: in Noah's language, it rained again, or, in Jesus's recent experience, wild animals came again. What did he do? Undeterred, he began preaching the good news of God's Kingdom's coming near, acting as though he saw in the midst of this cruel event the rainbow of God's covenant.

Lent is a time for dealing with the disorder in our lives, the mud that messes up God's world, addressing not just the effects but the causes. A report in *Church Times* (30 December 2011) quoted Linda Tiongco from Christian Aid alerting us to the logging in river watersheds in the Philippines and other environmentally destructive practices that were causing or exacerbating flooding. In addition to tending our own concerns, our Lenten discipline might involve engagement with such hard, big issues that devastate people's lives. As Christians observing Lent, we should get our hands dirty, and clear the mud – whether literal, metaphorical or spiritual – that ruins lives. At the same time, we follow Jesus's example, and, undaunted by the recurrence of testing, proclaim God's good news. With God, there are rainbows.

Second Sunday of Lent

Genesis 17.1–7, 15–16; Romans 4.13–end; Mark 8.31–38

KEEP GOING FOR THE LONG HAUL

Almighty God, you show to those who are in error the light of your truth, that they may return to the way of righteousness: grant to all those who are admitted into the fellowship of Christ's religion, that they may reject those things that are contrary to their profession, and follow all such things as are agreeable to the same; through our Lord Jesus Christ. Amen.

Lent is a time for honing our discipleship. This week we have two stories of the struggle that this may involve. Genesis tells a story of a man whose faith wobbled as he tried to hold his situation in creative tension with the promise of God. Mark recounts how Jesus upset the disciples' beliefs as soon as they recognized him as the Messiah.

Abraham, hitherto childless, had a son through his wife's slave – a not uncommon way of doing things in those days. He appeared to think that that was it: God had blessed him, as promised, with a son. But, disconcertingly, God appeared again, and renewed the promise, spelling it out that his elderly wife would become the mother of the child of promise. Abraham had to trust all over again. Like him, we never outgrow this challenge. Abraham had to believe and act on this promise. Writing to the Romans, Paul summarized it by saying that no distrust made Abraham waver concerning the promises of God. Paul was drawing a theological conclusion in the light of the whole Old Testament, but Genesis was concerned with narrative and was far more honest about the struggle involved, as chapters 12–22 show.

Mark, at the mid-point of his Gospel, has shown us people trying to understand who Jesus is, and then, at last, how Peter recognized Jesus as the Messiah. Immediately, Jesus reinterpreted this in a shocking way. The second half of the Gospel changes focus to the suffering and death of the Messiah, an unimaginable scandal that culminated not in a confession of faith, but in frightened people running from an empty tomb. Jesus made this reinterpretation quite openly. In today's terms, the leader went off-message, in public, and his press office had to act to stop him before he ruined his reputation. So Peter took Jesus to one side to talk some sense into him, apparently with the collusion of the rest of the disciples, since Jesus looked at all of them before silencing their spokesman. I wonder what was in his eyes at that moment. We may sympathize with the disciples who, in their love for Jesus, wanted to stop him making a seemingly disastrous mistake. It is easier for us, with the benefit of hindsight, but they had to enter uncharted territory, let go of all that they had understood of God's ways, and turn again in commitment in faith.

Lent is a time for the renewal of our commitment to God when it is tested, stretched, or in danger of faltering. Peter and the disciples were challenged to think the unthinkable – that God's Messiah would suffer – and to remain faithful. Abraham's faith was put under pressure because he could not conceive the greatness of God's promises, and was content to settle for a compromise. Paul's assertion that no distrust made him waver, even though he had some dodgy moments, is an encouragement when we want to be committed to God but vacillate in the face of particular circumstances. Lent is a good opportunity to refocus our gaze on faith's long horizon, not its short-term view. In doing this, we follow Jesus, the pioneer and perfecter of our faith, who, for the joy set before him, endured the cross, despising its shame (Hebrews 12.2).

In the light of these readings, the Collect's prayer to reject those things that are contrary to our profession refers not just to wrong actions or attitudes that turn us from the way of righteousness, but also to the narrowness of vision that is paralysed by what is in front of us, and cannot see beyond that to God's bigger, life-giving picture: for Abraham, the possibility of a child through Sarah; for Peter and the disciples, the possibility that taking up the cross would lead through death to resurrection.

The psalmist (119.33) prays: 'Teach me, O Lord, the way of your statutes and I will observe it to the end.' Lent is a time for turning back if we have wavered, taking the risk of trusting God, and keeping going for the long haul.

Third Sunday of Lent

Exodus 20.1–17; 1 Corinthians 1.18–25; John 2.13–22

THE DELIGHT OF OBEDIENCE

Almighty God, whose most dear Son went not up to joy but first he suffered pain, and entered not into glory before he was crucified: mercifully grant that we, walking in the way of the cross, may find it none other than the way of life and peace; through Jesus Christ our Lord. Amen.

The Ten Commandments were given to a people as they emerged into a nation that had to shape its way of being the people of God. The Commandments have to do with their, and now our, individual behaviour, certainly, but essentially they are about relationships with God and one another, and only have meaning in the context of community. We can see that if we read into the next chapter in Exodus, where they are expanded and applied to everyday life in the culture of the time.

We can start to get blind spots when we look at the application of the commandments in our culture and time. In the 1860s, Anthony Trollope wrote of the commandment 'Thou shalt not steal,' and the man 'who stands high among us and who implores his God every Sunday to write that law on his heart, spends every hour of his daily toil in a system of fraud, and is regarded as a pattern of the national commerce' (Anthony Trollope, *Phineas Finn*). In 2012, Christian Aid highlighted the way tax havens and tax evasion cost poor nations millions of pounds. At root, it is stealing, and we should ask ourselves how honest we will be about untaxed income when the next round of tax forms arrive.

There is no way to escape the public effects of our private actions. King David discovered, after his adultery with Bathsheba, that forgiveness included facing in front of others the consequences of his affair. Equally, it is in our private actions that our public trustworthiness is revealed: Jesus spoke of the servant who had proved trustworthy in a few things as being put in charge of many things (Matthew 25.14–30). So, when a 2012 US presidential candidate claimed his adultery, concealed while pursuing a former President on the same subject, was forgiven because he believes in a forgiving God, he ignored the impact on his public trustworthiness. Religion cannot be privatized.

The Early Church knew this. So, in addition to keeping Lent as a time of baptism preparation, notorious sinners who had brought the Church into disrepute were excommunicated for a period of public repentance. Their sin had affected the community. Only if they showed clear signs of contrition and repentance were they readmitted to the fellowship at Easter. It was not long before the whole Church decided to keep a penitential Lent in solidarity with them and with baptism candidates. This approach to Lenten observance has to do not only with our relationship with God, but also with the impact of our lives on Church and society: we are members one of another.

We are not saved by our actions, but are 'created in Christ Jesus for good works which God prepared beforehand to be our way of life' (Ephesians 2.10). That takes us way beyond the Ten Commandments, which can be taken as given, and are about the wrong we should not do rather than the good we are created to do. So how can we keep a holy Lent?

St Benedict describes, in the prologue to his Rule, a life-giving way that echoes the prayer of the Collect:

> As we progress in his way of life and faith, we shall run on the paths of God's commandments, our heart overflowing with the inexpressible delight of love. Never swerving from his instructions, then, but faithfully observing his teaching in the monastery until death, we shall through patience share in the sufferings of Christ that we may also deserve to share in his kingdom.

The commandments are a pathway of joy! At the Benedictine days and weeks held in Durham Cathedral, many people discover how relevant the Rule is for us today, living non-monastic lives. I remember one young mother having an 'aha moment', as she realized that her approach to helping her children to do what is right was the same as St Benedict's with monastics. At Durham Cathedral, our baptism and confirmation candidates attend a Benedictine day as part of their Lenten preparation for Easter, so that they, too, can not just keep, but run, in the path of God's commandments with overflowing, delighted hearts.

This Lent, we are invited to walk the way of the cross; the promise is that it will be the way of life and peace. Thanks be to God.

Fourth Sunday of Lent
Numbers 21.4–9; Ephesians 2.1–10; John 3.14–21

TEMPTED TO GRUMBLE?

> *Merciful Lord, absolve your people from their offences, that through your bountiful goodness we may all be delivered from the chains of those sins which by our frailty we have committed; grant this, heavenly Father, for Jesus Christ's sake, our blessed Lord and Saviour. Amen.*

Several years ago, during a visit to Israel, our guide, a local man, could not believe the amount of water in the desert; there were waterfalls where he had never seen them before and rivers flowing across normally dry roads. This was before mobile phones, but our coach driver heard from other drivers that roads ahead were impassable, and turned back. At one stage, it seemed we might be stranded between rivers, as indeed some coaches were overnight. Suddenly, the desert was not something to look at, but something that might overwhelm us, and we had no food, no water, no lavatory. It did not take long for voices to be raised in potential complaint: we had entered the desert on our terms: we did not want an unplanned night there.

Remembering that experience makes me sympathetic to the Israelites who became impatient when faced with the relentlessness of the desert. Then, to make it worse, poisonous snakes appeared. I am sure I would have grumbled, too. If we try to rationalize the odd story of a serpent on a pole providing deliverance, we miss the basic fact that life in the wilderness was harsh, and when life is hard we tend to complain. Difficulties like this reveal what is in our hearts, things normally so well covered up that even we are not aware what is there.

Benedict has much to say in his Rule about murmuring, that unremitting undercurrent of muttered discontent that can destroy the life of a community. It grows into grumbling, but it starts smaller than that, which is why Benedict is so concerned to nip it in the bud before it grows and takes on a life of its own. The catalyst can be anything that disconcerts us.

In the Collect, we pray to be delivered from the chains of those sins which by our frailty we have committed – not just the sins, but their chains. Last week, we were reminded that actions have consequences, and grumbling can have consequences that bind us like chains long after we have forgotten what the original complaint was. By inculcating an attitude of complaint, grumbling undermines trust in other people because we doubt their goodwill, and undermines trust in God because we doubt God's goodness. The antidote to this, in the Collect and the epistle, is God's bountiful goodness: God is rich in mercy. As a colleague once said in an Ash Wednesday sermon in Durham Cathedral, too often we assume that God's more means our less – the bane of zero-sum economics – whereas the invitation of Lent is to experience that God's more means our more. If we spend Lent focusing on ourselves, we miss the beauty and generosity of God's loving goodness, which leads us to repentance more effectively than anything else.

The wilderness is a place of paring back, indeed of deprivation for those of us who do not know how to live there, but God sometimes takes his people into the wilderness so that they can experience blessing. Hosea (2.14) spoke of God's luring Israel into the wilderness and speaking tenderly to her there, bringing her new life. We can treat that as a lovely idea in theory, keeping it at arm's length in practice, or we can engage with it in our daily lives, as Belden Lane does in his powerful book, *The Solace of Fierce Landscapes*, where he reflects on his love of wilderness and mountains, alongside the hard experience of accompanying his mother through her long final illness, confined in a small room. The mutual giving and receiving of loving care, sometimes in wilderness-like circumstances, is at the heart of what we celebrate on Mothering Sunday, whether in relation to our natural mothers, or to those who have nurtured us in their absence.

Lane writes:

> Allurement – that careful and passionate fixing of our attention, drawing us often to love – can be triggered by an experience of being unstrung, made very observant, mindful of things we might not otherwise notice because now our safety depends upon it. The desert teaches us to watch for mercy in the least likely places … [It] becomes a good place for distinguishing between what is a threat and what is actually another way of being loved. (Lane, 2007)

Perhaps Lent can be a time to learn not to grumble, but to find a new way to be loved by God when we find ourselves in a desert.

Fifth Sunday of Lent

Jeremiah 31.31–34; Hebrews 5.5–10; John 12.20–33

CHRIST, THE PATTERN OF OBEDIENCE

Most merciful God, who by the death and resurrection of your Son Jesus Christ delivered and saved the world: grant that by faith in him who suffered on the cross we may triumph in the power of his victory; through Jesus Christ our Lord. Amen.

There is an old story about the child who is reprimanded and told to sit down, and who eventually does so unwillingly, with the retort: 'I may be sitting down on the outside, but inside I'm standing up.' We all know about doing what is asked of us with bad grace, only because we know it is futile to resist. That is not true obedience; it is compliance. It involves only our actions, not our hearts. How different is Benedict's approach to obedience in his Rule: 'Listen carefully, my child, to your master's precepts, and incline the ear of your heart (Proverbs 4.20). Receive willingly and carry out effectively your loving Father's advice, that by the labour of obedience, you may return to Him from whom you had departed by the sloth of disobedience' (Prologue). Benedict knows from experience that obedience takes work and involves the inclination of our heart towards God (Joshua 24.23).

Abbot Christopher Jamison writes:

> The monastic way invites people to listen, and then to choose what voices to follow. This is a double exercise of freedom: the freedom of discernment and the freedom of choosing to follow what has been discerned. Obedience that is blind does not exercise discernment and simply follows the most assertive voice or the voice of the one to whom life has been surrendered. (Jamison, 2006).

Jeremiah spoke God's word to a wayward people whom God had been excoriating for their relentless disobedience. Despite God's persistent loving care for them, they had not learned to incline their hearts towards God. So, in a stunning move, God promised a new covenant with them, in which he would put his law within them, and write it on their hearts. Centuries later, Paul wrote that not only Jews, but also Gentiles who keep God's law, have it written on their hearts (Romans 2.15). In Hebrew thought, the heart is the seat of the will rather than of the emotions; so what was required of the Hebrews, and now of us, is to listen with our hearts, and not just to feel that we love God, but to act accordingly by choosing the way of obedience. We are not enslaved and forced into compliance: there are still free choices to be made in any situation, and God does everything to help us to obey in love.

The writer to the Hebrews tells us that Jesus learned obedience to God through what he suffered, with loud cries and tears in prayer. It was not blind or enforced obedience, but resolutely offered obedience, and it was something that he had to go on offering as his life unfolded. In the Gospel reading, Jesus realized that his ministry was reaching its climax when Gentiles responded to his coming. This precipitated yet another willed act of facing a cruel death. Despite being deeply troubled, Jesus articulated his options, and, shaped by his overarching commitment to God, again chose the path of obedience.

Reflecting on the Rule of Benedict, Joan Chittister writes:

> No one really has full control of their own lives. We're all limited by something. The difference is that some people decide what they will allow to control them, and some people simply find themselves controlled by the whims and fancies of life. All of us meet and wrestle with authority. The only question is to what authority I have surrendered, and how do I myself use authority when I have it? (Chittister, 1991)

For Jesus and for Christians, obedience offered to God is a response to and of love. It is not always easy, but, as the hymn puts it, we are drawn by 'love to the loveless shown that they might lovely be'. On this Passion Sunday, we hear again in the Gospel the invitation to follow Jesus like faithful servants. We are invited to have obedient hearts, hearts inclined to God that are sitting down on the inside as well as the outside. That is what God has promised, indeed longs, to give.

George Herbert's prayer 'The Call' is an appropriate response:

Come, my Joy, my Love, my Heart:
    Such a Joy, as none can move;
    Such a Love, as none can part;
    Such a Heart, as joys in love.

Palm Sunday

Liturgy of the Passion: Isaiah 50.4–9a; Philippians 2.5–11;
Mark 14.1–end of 15

LOVE SO AMAZING, SO DIVINE

*Almighty and everlasting God, who in your tender love towards the human
race sent your Son our Saviour Jesus Christ to take upon him our flesh and
to suffer death upon the cross: grant that we may follow the example of
his patience and humility, and also be made partakers of his resurrection;
through Jesus Christ our Lord. Amen.*

There are many people with bit parts in the Passion narrative. Jesus, who until
now initiated the action, is suddenly passive. Things happen to him, and he
rarely speaks. He has entered a different world, which is peopled by a new cast
of characters, many of them nameless. However, if Jesus is passive, others have
their say about him in word or action.

The Passion narrative is framed by stories about women: one who anoints
his body for burial, and two who watch that burial. Jesus describes the anointing
as a 'beautiful thing' that the anonymous woman does for him. This is a rare
description in the Bible of an action as beautiful. The woman's act of extravagant
love was one of the few kind things done to Jesus that week. Her touch was in
marked contrast to the touch he experienced when he was manhandled, spat
on, flogged, pierced by thorns, and ultimately crucified. Actions that should be
tender – a kiss, being dressed, receiving homage – were distorted into acts of
cruelty.

In the powerful stage and film adaptations of Michael Morpurgo's book *War
Horse*, the central character, Joey the horse, cannot speak, but elicits responses
from the people around him, drawing out love in the cruel theatre of war. Touch
is important: the nuzzling of two horses; the whipping as they struggle to drag
a gun carriage up a steep muddy hill; and the exquisitely gentle touch of two
soldiers – enemies brought together by compassion – who free the exhausted
horse from the barbed wire that traps him. There is always room for beauty in
the midst of suffering, if only we will bring it.

The gentle touch of compassionate action, the beautiful gift that the woman
gave Jesus in her anointing, is the touch that Jesus probably yearned for in his
Passion. He had used touch to heal and restore people, including those deemed
untouchable by others, and yet he was not touched that way again until after his
death.

Other people move in and out of the narrative, making their small mark.
An unnamed person leads the disciples to a large room that Jesus borrowed
from another unnamed person for the Passover meal. Its largeness indicates

the presence of many people at the Last Supper. We know his mother and brothers were in Jerusalem, and there were always children at a Passover meal, because a child has particular questions to ask as part of the proceedings.

Outside Jesus's circle, there are numerous walk-on parts: the priests buy Judas's betrayal; Judas brings an armed crowd; the curiosity of a slave-girl and bystanders leads Peter to deny knowing Jesus; another bystander, Simon of Cyrene (a place that is now part of Libya), is forced to carry Jesus's cross, leading to speculation that his family was converted (cf. Acts 13.1; Romans 16.13); a mysterious young man flees naked from the garden – scholars say he is not Mark, but perhaps there are evocative resonances of Adam and Eve, naked and later cast out of another garden, or of the young man in the empty tomb? It is these bit players who move the story on to its relentless conclusion: Jesus's cry of agony and abandonment on the cross – one of the few times when God is mentioned in these chapters. Jesus's suffering draws vastly different responses out of others, and also completes Mark's storyline about people's gradual recognition of Jesus.

It began at his baptism, when the voice from heaven proclaimed: 'You are my Son, the Beloved.' It moved forward when Peter said: 'You are the Messiah,' which led Jesus to begin speaking of his suffering. Now, finally, a Roman centurion, inured to the harshness of crucifixion, said of the suffering man: 'Truly this man was God's son.'

As we hear this Passion story read in its entirety, we can imagine ourselves in the scene, playing a bit part. It is tempting to want to be an uninvolved bystander, but Paul's challenge is to be participants who have the same mind that was in Christ. That mind-set includes responding in grateful, beautiful love when we see Christ's suffering in his people today – and in his animals, such as the war horse.

> Love so amazing, so divine,
> Demands my soul, my life, my all.

Maundy Thursday
See Year A

Good Friday

Isaiah 52.13–end of 53; Psalm 22; Hebrews 10.16–25;
John 18.1–19

THE FOOT OF THE CROSS

*Almighty Father, look with mercy on this your family for which our Lord
Jesus Christ was content to be betrayed and given up into the hands of
sinners and to suffer death upon the cross; who is alive and glorified with
you and the Holy Spirit, one God, now and for ever. Amen.*

*Behold the wood of the Cross, whereon was hung the Saviour of the world.
Come, let us worship.* (The Liturgy for Good Friday)

On Good Friday, the focus narrows. We are no longer thinking about the cross
and reflecting on its implications; instead, the Gospel reading leaves us at the
foot of the cross, looking on the one who was pierced. We sing that we 'survey'
it, giving our focused attention. But it is not just us looking at the cross. The
Collect for Good Friday asks nothing for us, except that God graciously behold
us, God's family for whom our Lord Jesus Christ was content to be betrayed and
to die. We have run out of words: in the face of the cross, all we can ask is that
God look on us with grace.

God beholds us; we behold the cross.

In the liturgy, this silence of God's gaze on us is broken, as we hear the
reproaches, God's questions to us: 'O my people, what have I done to you? How
have I offended you? Answer me! What more could I have done for you?' And
our answer? We have nothing to say, only to acknowledge: 'Holy is God! Holy
immortal one, have mercy on us.'

*Behold the wood of the Cross, whereon was hung the Saviour of the world.
Come, let us worship.*

My memories from my first visit to the Church of the Holy Sepulchre, built over
the supposed site of Calvary, were that from the outside it is an architectural
accident that does nothing to inspire devotion, while inside it resembles a dark
rabbit-warren. So when, years later, I returned to the Holy Land, I had mixed
feelings about going there again. But, of course, I did. I stood in the slowly
moving queue, shuffling forward towards the spot identified as the place of
crucifixion, past devotional images that leave everything and nothing to the
imagination. The place of crucifixion is marked by a hole in the floor under an
altar; pilgrims kneel down, lean under the altar, and place their hand in the hole,

feeling for bedrock that they cannot see. It requires an enormous stretch of the imagination to visualize it as it was 2000 years ago.

As the queue moved inexorably forward, I found myself saying to God: 'I don't know what I am doing here; I am ten feet from one of the most holy sites of Christendom, and I am so bemused that I don't know what to think or feel or pray.' Then I was at the front of the queue, and, ready or not, it was my turn to kneel and reach out for the rock. As I did so, from nowhere, the thought hit me: at this moment, you are the only person in the world literally at the foot of the cross. Stunned, my instinctive reaction was a sense of responsibility to pray for our world, asking simply that God have mercy on us.

Behold the wood of the Cross, whereon was hung the Saviour of the world. Come, let us worship.

However we explain it theologically, the cross is where the Son of God died, and, through his death and resurrection, opened the way for our reconciliation to God. Speechlessness may be the most appropriate way to come on Good Friday because, in the face of the cross, there is nothing to say. All we can do when faced by God's grace and love is be there, and be grateful.

In John's Gospel, Jesus always seems to be in control of events, even in his death, and his final words, 'It is finished,' were no cry of hopelessness or despair, but of triumph at the work of salvation completed. In the words of the ancient hymn:

Sing, my tongue, the glorious battle,
Sing the last, the dread affray;
O'er the Cross, the victor's trophy,
Sound the high triumphal lay,
How, the pains of death enduring,
Earth's Redeemer won the day.

The cross is inseparable from the resurrection of Jesus Christ. But, for now, on Good Friday, we are at the foot of the cross.

Behold the wood of the Cross, whereon was hung the Saviour of the world. Come, let us worship.

Easter Day
Acts 10.34–43; 1 Corinthians 15.1–11; Mark 16.1–8

THE PERPLEXITY OF THE TOMB

Lord of all life and power, who through the mighty resurrection of your Son overcame the old order of sin and death to make all things new in him: grant that we, being dead to sin and alive to you in Jesus Christ, may reign with him in glory; to whom with you and the Holy Spirit be praise and honour, glory and might, now and in all eternity. Amen.

The empty tomb, on its own, is not good news. Like other empty spaces that once were occupied, it merely signifies that something is missing, possibly stolen or lost. Our instinctive reaction is a distressed lurch of emotions when we realize something is badly wrong.

Mark makes no concessions: rather than provide a glorious climax to the story, he brings his fast-paced Gospel juddering to a halt with terrified women fleeing from the tomb, not daring to tell anyone what has happened. There is no joy in this episode for them, and Mark spares them no blushes: they are alarmed, seized with terror and amazement, and afraid. They have waited through the enforced rest of the Sabbath, no doubt with exhausting emotion, to anoint the body, to touch it and lavish care on it as a necessary part of their grieving. And now it is not there. Anyone who has mourned without a body to bury, or who is troubled by important things left unsaid to a dead person, will understand the awfulness of their situation.

The confusion engendered by the empty tomb and the untidiness of Mark's abrupt ending are overlooked if we glide seamlessly from Palm Sunday and Jesus's entry into Jerusalem, via a hot cross bun on Good Friday, to resurrection appearances on Easter Day. Those who have seen the Triduum through – Maundy Thursday, Good Friday, Holy Saturday – know that there was a tomb holding a mutilated body. If we enter Mark's world, we cannot rush to the assurance of resurrection with a politician's knock-down argument, but are forced to come to terms with a void in which faith is stretched to its limit.

In his inimitable way, Mark tests any glibness in our confidence in the resurrection by confronting us with the perplexity of an empty tomb. There is no easy way to encounter resurrection, and Mark does not rescue the women from their confusion. But, since he has been showing us perplexed disciples throughout the Gospel, we should not be surprised. He has told us (Mark 14.8) that another woman anointed Jesus's body for burial before his death. These women are too late to do that. Instead, although they do not know it, they are at a pivotal moment in history and theology, a *kairos* rather than chronological moment, when 'the time is fulfilled' (cf. Mark 1.15).

As the Collect puts it, the old order of sin and death has been overcome by the mighty resurrection of God's Son. In this new order, they are in the wrong place, for the wrong purpose, with the wrong things in their hands. They are standing in the confined space of the tomb, the ultimate symbol of the old order, and somehow they have to be pushed out of it. Once Jesus came to Galilee with the good news of God (Mark 1.14), and called his disciples; now he is going there again, and the women are to ensure the disciples get there, too. They are being recalled.

Much in human life is unfinished, from symphonies to relationships, and this is the Gospel for people living with unfinished business. Mark's Gospel ends with a theological comma rather than a full stop. Once the emptiness of the tomb was established, there were indeed resurrection appearances, as we hear from Peter and Paul. But Mark's story ends without tangible evidence for the disciples of Jesus's resurrection. Perhaps Mark knew that seeing is not always believing; faith is part of the resurrection equation. Everything that has happened since was left in the hands of terrified women and the male disciples who had not even been brave or devoted enough to make it to the tomb. God's good news did not depend on the disciples' readiness, and, mercifully, it does not depend on ours. Instead, God's grace catches us up in the story wherever we are.

God's mighty resurrection breaks into a world of loose ends and frightened people. Mark is the Gospel for people who recognize themselves in that situation. We, too, are called to leave the confines of the tomb and whatever holds us back from faith, and follow where the risen Jesus leads. Alleluia!

Second Sunday of Easter

Acts 4.32–35; 1 John 1.1–2.2; John 20.19–31

A TOUCH TO OVERCOME DOUBT

Almighty Father, you have given your only Son to die for our sins and to rise again for our justification: grant us so to put away the leaven of malice and wickedness that we may always serve you in pureness of living and truth; through the merits of your Son Jesus Christ our Lord. Amen.

The Pietà by Fenwick Lawson is a larger-than-life-size sculpture in Durham Cathedral. Jesus lies on the ground at Mary's feet, and the sculptor has worked with the grain of the wood to bring out the sorrow of the figures. There are nail holes in his hands and feet, while pock marks from when the sculpture was spattered by lead from the roof of York Minster, where it was displayed at the time of the fire, add to the sense of the suffering borne by Jesus's body. Jesus's right arm is raised very slightly in an anticipation of resurrection. One of the guides told me of a group of children she took to see the sculpture. While they were talking about the story it portrays, one little boy was busy putting his fingers into the nail holes. The guide asked him his name, and says she should have guessed the answer: 'Thomas.'

The biblical Thomas was a twin. I wonder whether he was an identical twin who, as a child, sometimes swapped places with his brother to confuse adults. If so, it would be natural to insist on touching the wounds of Jesus to be sure that this was not a lookalike impostor. Jesus knew that Thomas would need to touch in order to make sense of things, as he put the fact of the empty tomb together with the unbelievable stories that the other disciples told of seeing Jesus, risen from the dead. It seems, however, that Jesus was in no hurry to relieve Thomas's doubts, but waited a whole week before appearing to him. Thomas, the one who had been so faithful during Jesus's life, being ready to go to Jerusalem to die with him (John 11.16), was the only one missing on that first day when Jesus appeared. Many of us, like people who live with remorse for not being present when someone whom they love has died, would let it prey on our minds if we were in Thomas's shoes. Such regrets are deep-seated and powerful. Like the women in last week's Gospel, his was a difficult – and much longer – experience of the empty tomb. When Jesus did appear, he went straight to the heart of Thomas's need: to touch and to believe.

Thomas is the disciple and John the epistle for people who are 'sensers' on the Myers-Briggs personality-type indicator – people who trust their experience and work from facts to the bigger picture. Only when Thomas saw and touched Jesus could he grasp what he could not take in from the disciples' words. It then became his testimony: 'What we have looked at and touched with our own hands we declare to you.'

Thomas and the other disciples, who had seen and touched Jesus for three or more years, were so sure that they had also seen and touched him after he was raised from the dead that they all went to death or exile rather than deny that conviction. Some travelled across the known world, an extraordinary feat for Galilean peasants who had once met in fear behind locked doors. According to early Christian tradition, Thomas went to Edessa in Syria, and then, in AD 52, to India, where the Mar Thoma Syrian Church claims him as its founder. There he was martyred by being stabbed: he who wanted to touch Jesus's wounds received his own wound. Long before then, he had been part of the group in Acts for whom retaining personal possessions mattered less than eliminating poverty. This, too, was part of their powerful testimony to the resurrection: not only their beliefs but their lifestyles were transformed by the resurrection of Jesus Christ. This Easter, we might ask ourselves what impact the resurrection has on our lifestyle and life-plans.

John wrote his Gospel so that readers could come to believe that Jesus is the Messiah. Jesus invited Thomas to touch him in order to overcome his doubts. Years later, his young namesake in the cathedral touched nail holes, and someone explained to him what it was all about.

'We declare to you what we have seen and heard so that you may have fellowship with us.' The proclamation of the risen Lord goes on because: 'As the Father has sent me, so I send you.'

Third Sunday of Easter
Zephaniah 3.14–end; Acts 3.12–19; Luke 24.36b–48

THE ANGELS GAZE IN WONDER

Almighty Father, who in your great mercy gladdened the disciples with the sight of the risen Lord: give us such knowledge of his presence with us, that we may be strengthened and sustained by his risen life and serve you continually in righteousness and truth; through Jesus Christ our Lord. Amen.

The disciples had a hard time believing. On Easter Day, we heard of women who were too afraid to believe; and last week, we heard about Thomas, who wanted more evidence to believe. Today, there is too much joy for some to believe. Luke's powerful description of the disciples 'disbelieving for joy' reminds us of the pastoral truth that there is room for doubt within faith: the presence of Jesus in the room was too much to comprehend, especially with the horrors of the cross etched in the mind. Resurrection is not easy to encounter. Only as Jesus calmed the disciples' disbelief by eating broiled fish – the detail that it was broiled providing something graspable in an event beyond belief – could he begin to interpret, as he had done earlier on the Emmaus road, everything written about him in scripture. As they began to believe, they could begin to understand. Recall Augustine's dictum: 'I do not seek to understand that I may believe, but I believe in order to understand.'

In a lecture in 1907, P. T. Forsyth said that the cross interprets the Father, not the Father the cross. The God of Israel is the God of the cross and resurrection. The disciples were forced by the events that they witnessed to rethink their understanding of God, without letting go of their inherited tradition. They could not isolate their unbelievable experience from God's action through the centuries, and soon, as Acts tells us, they proclaimed boldly Christ's resurrection as an act of the God of Abraham, Isaac, and Jacob.

By this time, resurrection was not unfamiliar in the Jewish tradition; Daniel concludes with the promise of resurrection, and the Pharisees believed in the resurrection. So how could what was fine in theological theory about the end of days become so shocking when Christians claimed that resurrection occurred with Jesus? Resurrection is about God, not merely an example of the principle of dying and rebirth in nature. Leander Keck, the New Testament scholar, has said that if the resurrection were just resuscitation or reanimation, then nothing would change except the corpse. Instead, resurrection is what God is up to in a world already changed by the incarnation. God has made the future tense into the present tense.

What of us? Belief in the resurrection of Jesus requires that we, like the disciples, understand the scriptures, and ponder how the cross interprets God. That takes time and effort.

> Ponder long the glorious mystery,
> breathe, in awe, that God draws near;
> hear again the angels' message,
> see the Lamb of God appear.
> God's own Word assumes our nature:
> Son of God in swaddling bands;
> Light of light, and God eternal
> held in Mary's gentle hands.
>
> Ponder long the glorious mystery
> of the Lamb who once was slain,
> now at God's right hand in glory:
> he who in the grave had lain.
> Once he bid the doubting Thomas,
> 'See my hands and touch my side.'
> Now the angels gaze in wonder,
> Jesus' wounds are glorified.
>
> Ponder long the glorious mystery,
> 'This my body, this my blood.'
> Bread and wine reveal God's presence,
> love engulfs us like a flood.
> Human longing meets God's yearning,
> words fall silent, all is grace;
> mystery with hope is brimming,
> earth is held in heaven's embrace.
>
> *Copyright © 1997 Rosalind Brown*

The disciples were caught up in the mystery of God, which, through the incarnation, is earthed mystery – mystery involving someone they had touched and known. Having opened the disciples' minds to understand the scriptures, Jesus opened their minds to understand where they fitted into this new twist to the story, and then sent them to proclaim the good news to all nations. When we pray this week for such knowledge of Jesus's presence with us that we may be strengthened and sustained to serve God continually in righteousness and truth, we are asking to follow in the disciples' footsteps. The 50 days of Easter are a time to give close attention to deepening our understanding of God, who is revealed and interpreted by the cross and resurrection. Perhaps some study or focused reading is appropriate.

In Zephaniah's language, God is rejoicing and exulting over us with loud singing. The resurrection is God's victory dance. We are invited to be embraced by unbelievable joy.

Fourth Sunday of Easter

Genesis 7.1–15, 11–18, 8.6–18, 9.8–13; Acts 4.5–12;
John 10.11–18

WATER TO DESTROY AND SAVE

Almighty God, whose Son Jesus Christ is the resurrection and the life: raise us, who trust in him, from the death of sin to the life of righteousness, that we may seek those things which are above, where he reigns with you in the unity of the Holy Spirit, one God, now and for ever. Amen.

The Easter liturgy involves water. At the Easter Vigil we hear of waters parting so slaves can flee captivity; water is poured over baptismal candidates and sprinkled on the rest of us to remind us of our baptism. The interruption of the Boat Race when it was rowed on Holy Saturday one year reminded us that water is deep, powerful and holds things that stop even trained athletes in their tracks. A few years ago we were shocked by terrifying footage showed tsunami waves rolling inland in Japan and a year later Fiji suffered from floods. Ultimately we are at the mercy of water, not in control.

The early chapters of Genesis tell theological, rather than historical, truth in narrative form. God created a good world, humans spoiled it and, in a mythological story in Genesis 6, God limited mortal lifespan to 120 years. Enter Noah, aged 600, so well beyond this limited lifespan. In the mind-set of the time, this indicated his righteousness.

Meanwhile God had set in motion an anti-creation story in which he would undo and destroy the creation so lovingly wrought in chapters 1 and 2. Water will be the means of judgement on the corruption and violence of humans. Two original sources are blended here and the editor is not bothered that the details do not quite match. However, we get the idea, vividly. A cunning plan involves a boat that will, amazingly, hold multiple pairs of all living creatures (imagine the smell and the noise!) thus allowing God to destroy the humans he now regrets creating while saving righteous Noah. Noah and the animals got into the ark just in time before, touchingly, God shut the door on them so they were safe. It then rained for 40 days, a biblical time frame that indicates a period when significant things happen.

Flood stories from contemporary cultures told of gods whose sleep was disturbed by the overpopulation and noise of their troublesome human slaves. The gods reacted by sending destructive floods to limit human numbers. In the Bible, the primal myth is slightly different. The erring humans were not God's slaves but were created to be God's friends and companions and to enjoy caring for and cultivating the fruitful world God made. The problem was not over-population but human disobedience which broke that life-giving relationship.

In the biblical world, water is destructive but also has a sacramental role in salvation. In this story, one of the great theological scene-setters of the Bible, Noah and his boatload were saved through water, foreshadowing the Exodus deliverance through the sea and, ultimately, the water of baptism. Theologically unlike flood stories in other cultures, this one ended with a promise; when they were back on terra firma, God's generous love was again extended to humans through a covenant. Never again would all flesh be destroyed by a flood. Out of the destruction came a new beginning and a new promise to last for all time; its sign, a bow in the clouds, would only appear when it rained and there was the potential for another destructive flood. God's judgement was tempered with mercy; God's purpose was to enable, not to destroy, his relationship with humans.

It is that steadfast love which Jesus embodied when he described himself as the good shepherd who placed the well-being of his sheep above all else and, ultimately, laid down his life for them. The same care that locked Noah into the ark so he would be safe was manifest by the good shepherd who did not run away in the face of threat but stayed put and saved his sheep from destruction. As Peter proclaimed: health and salvation are given in Jesus's name.

Jesus was raised from death by the God who saved Noah from and through the chaos of water and we, who with water, are baptized into Jesus's death have been raised from the death of sin to the life of righteousness. Water which can bring death can also bring life. Salvation is sheer gift of God who cares for us beyond our imagining. It is fitting, in these 50 days of Easter, that we pray to seek the things that are above so we can live God's new beginning, this life of righteousness.

Fifth Sunday of Easter

Genesis 22.1–18; Acts 8.26–end; 1 John 4.7–21;
John 15.1–8

OBEDIENCE BEARS GOOD FRUIT

Almighty God, who through your only-begotten Son Jesus Christ have overcome death and opened to us the gate of everlasting life: grant that, as by your grace going before us you put into our minds good desires, so by your continual help we may bring them to good effect; through Jesus Christ our risen Lord. Amen.

The story in Acts tells of events for which more detail would be wonderful. How did Philip, then based about 40 miles north of Jerusalem, know that he had to take a trip down the wilderness road south-west of Jerusalem, for no apparent purpose? It was hardly an everyday thing to do. What would he say to people he met on the way who asked: 'Where are you off to, Philip?'

'Oh, just a quick trip to the wilderness. I suddenly felt like seeing if there was anyone in the desert, or how it had changed since I was last there.'

How could he be sure that this sense that he should go was not some wild figment of his imagination? Did he know why he was going? Was it wise to enter the wilderness alone? We do not know the answers, and probably Philip pinched himself to see whether this was real. Was he really setting off and leaving his family, which included four daughters, without any explanation, except that God had called him? Who was Philip, anyway – someone given to wild ideas and crazy action? No: anything but that. He was chosen by the early Christians for the work of serving widows at the daily distribution of food, and had gone to Samaria to preach the gospel, becoming known as an evangelist (Acts 6.3, 8.5, 21.9). Acts tells us that he was of good standing in the community, full of the Spirit and of wisdom; so he was reliable, good with people, not given to flights of independent fancy, and the last person to do anything impetuous, or to let people down by taking off at short notice. But, when God called this steady, reliable pillar of the church, he went off to the wilderness, not knowing why, just convinced that God had called him to do so. Although the resulting action may appear odd to us, it was in character for someone who could trust God not to lead him down the garden path. There must be a reason for this strange command, and God would make it clear.

We know the reason. An Ethiopian government official was setting out on this road in his chariot, his time in Jerusalem over. He had been worshipping God – there was a Jewish community in Ethiopia at the time – and had acquired a scroll of the scriptures to study on the way home. It was not just any part of the scriptures, but the part of Isaiah that Philip and the other early Christians now understood to refer to Jesus: the Lamb sent to the slaughter. He needed to have it explained, and Philip, the evangelist, was the one to do it. It seems that God even gave Philip a few days' head start; otherwise he could not have caught up with a chariot. Later tradition identifies the man as the founder of the Christian Church in Ethiopia, so Philip's obedience had immense consequences. With hindsight, knowing the end of the story, we can see that this makes perfect sense – except that we do not live our lives with the benefit of hindsight. For us, as for Philip, the bigger challenge is what we do in the middle of daily life, when there is no hindsight to affirm our action, and it seems that we are being called to do something unusual or demanding.

In the Gospel, Jesus exhorted his disciples to abide in him, and let his words abide in them. We pray this week for God's grace to put good desires into our minds, and to bring them to good effect. Abiding in Christ is the way to ensure that we are sensitive to the Holy Spirit's nudge, but not at the mercy of our whims.

There is still another twist to the tale. Philip was dropped off by the Spirit in Azotus. Azotus? That must have been a surprise, because, although it was on the way back, it was not where he started from, being near the coast, 40 miles south-west of Jerusalem. So he simply made his way back north, preaching as he went.

Our gifts and vocation come into play wherever we find ourselves.

Sixth Sunday of Easter

Isaiah 55.1–11; Acts 10.44–end; John 15.9–17

QUICK-EY'D LOVE

> *God our redeemer, you have delivered us from the power of darkness and brought us into the kingdom of your Son: grant that, as by his death he has recalled us to life, so by his continual presence in us he may raise us to eternal joy; through Jesus Christ our Lord. Amen.*

The reading from Isaiah brims with imperatives: Come; buy, eat, come, buy, listen carefully, eat, delight yourselves, incline your ear, come to me, listen; see, see, seek the Lord, call upon him, forsake, return. I cannot read them without thinking of George Herbert's poem, 'Love (III)':

> Love bade me welcome: yet my soul drew back,
> Guilty of dust and sin.
> But quick-ey'd Love, observing me grow slack
> From my first entrance in,
> Drew nearer to me, sweetly questioning,
> If I lack'd anything.
>
> A guest, I answer'd, worthy to be here:
> Love said, You shall be he.
> I the unkind, ungrateful? Ah, my dear,
> I cannot look on thee.
> Love took my hand, and smiling did reply,
> Who made the eyes but I?
>
> Truth, Lord, but I have marr'd them: let my shame
> Go where it doth deserve.
> And know you not, says Love, who bore the blame?
> My dear, then I will serve.
> You must sit down, says Love, and taste my meat:
> So I did sit and eat.

Herbert's poem embodies God's invitation given through Isaiah. Its resolution, with its succession of one-syllable words and the final imperative 'You must sit down,' would not have been easy for Herbert. We know from his other poetry that he faced many inner conflicted feelings, and his consciousness of his sin and unworthiness shows in this dialogue with Love. The exhortation to listen to and seek the Lord appears to have come more easily to him than to come, sit and eat, which required him to forsake his sense of unfitness.

Before ordination, Herbert had been Public Orator at Cambridge, and served briefly in Parliament. In Bemerton, his little church needed repair, and his rectory was badly dilapidated. That existence must have felt a world away from his former life at the intellectual and political heart of the nation's life. Although he lived by a peaceful, tree-lined river a couple of miles from Salisbury Cathedral, where he attended evensong and enjoyed making music with friends, life was not all tranquil. He lived in the tumultuous time when the king had dissolved Parliament, church politics were entangled with national politics, and Archbishop Laud's determined reforms were meeting opposition. Herbert died young, in 1633, before the conflicts escalated into civil war. In this poem, we glimpse the source of his sustenance through those times of worry, tension, and illness, which did not diminish his capacity for joy.

In the Gospel reading, Jesus speaks about love. Again, the times were troubled. John places this discourse shortly before Jesus's crucifixion, when the atmosphere was threatening, time was short, and every word counted. Jesus had to choose carefully what to say and what to leave unsaid. He chose to speak at length about the Father's love, which held and motivated him, and would hold the disciples through the tumultuous life of the Early Church, as they were appointed and bore fruit that has lasted through the centuries. Their responsive love was not to be wishy-washy, but love expressed in obedience and action – in forsaking evil, bearing fruit, and being friends of God. The vignette in Acts when the Holy Spirit fell upon all who believed, Jew and Gentile (the shock of which is lost on us today), is the powerful precursor of the mission to the Gentiles, which led the disciples into far corners of the world, ultimately to lay down their lives for their friend.

Isaiah spoke God's message when the people were in exile, enslaved, and struggling to keep faith in their God. Jesus spoke to disciples who felt the fear of the opposition in Jerusalem. George Herbert wrote in a time of looming conflict in the nation and Church. God's invitation is unchanged: 'Everyone who thirsts, come to the waters.'

Once, I took my copy of Herbert's poetry when visiting someone facing a difficult operation with an uncertain outcome. Without hesitation, she asked me to read 'Love (III)', and said that I could write in this column that through it she experienced God's deep peace. The assurance of Love's welcome, the invitation simply to sit down and receive Love's tender care, remains one of the greatest gifts of God in times of trouble.

Ascension Day
See Year A

Seventh Sunday of Easter

Ezekiel 36.24–28; Acts 1.15–17, 21–26; John 17.6–19

CHRIST'S ASCENSION WHICH IS OURS TOO

O God the King of glory, you have exalted your only Son Jesus Christ with great triumph to your kingdom in heaven: we beseech you, leave us not comfortless, but send your Holy Spirit to strengthen us and exalt us to the place where our Saviour Christ is gone before, who is alive and reigns with you, in the unity of the Holy Spirit, one God, now and for ever. Amen.

After seeing Jesus ascend into heaven, the disciples were left waiting in Jerusalem. Acts tells us of the changes the resurrection was already bringing: men and women prayed together, which they would not do in a synagogue; and Jesus's previously unbelieving brothers were there, too. Peter's suggestion that they should replace Judas in order to maintain the symbolically significant number of 12 apostles led to the choice of Matthias. But we never hear of Matthias again. With hindsight, perhaps the ascension made this a case of new wine in old wineskins. The disciples were living through rapid change, and yet again they had to learn that, in the title of the old book, 'Your God is too small.'

If (and the jury is permanently out) Peter wrote the letter 2 Peter, then he developed a much bigger vision than that of the 12 disciples representing the 12 tribes of Israel. He came to realize that, in Christ, Christians become participants of the divine nature (2 Peter 1.4). The ascension had much to do with this insight.

Ascension Day is one of the most woefully neglected days in the church year. The person who ascended is human, one with us; he is God, one with the Father. Theologically, the ascension completes the incarnation: God in Christ assumed our humanity, entered our world, and through his death and resurrection conquered death; but only with his ascension is heaven opened, as Jesus Christ takes his and thus our humanity into heaven. We are baptized into Christ, and in him (only in him: this is not pantheism), we share the Father's divine glory through being made, in Christ, participants of the divine nature. 'The glory which you have given me I have given them, so that they may be one, as we are one. I in them and you in me, that they may become completely one, so that the world may know that you have sent me and have loved them even as you have loved me' (John 17.22–23).

Christopher Wordsworth's hymn captures the wonder of this:

Thou hast raised our human nature
On the clouds to God's right hand;
There we sit in heavenly places,
There with thee in glory stand;

Jesus reigns, adored by Angels;
Man with God is on the throne;
Mighty Lord, in thine Ascension
We by faith behold our own.

The Collect is already turning our eyes towards Pentecost, linking the promise of our exaltation in heaven to the sending of the Holy Spirit to strengthen us. We are not yet exalted, but called to live faithfully. In praying this Collect, we ask for the promises through Ezekiel of a new heart of flesh, not of stone, and of God's Spirit within us to guide us in God's way.

Today's Gospel takes us back before Jesus's death. Knowing that he was returning to his Father, Jesus prayed that his disciples would be one, as he and the Father are one, and that the Father would protect them from evil in the world rather than take them out of it. Although he had spoken of the coming of the Spirit, or Advocate, to the disciples, Jesus's prayer to the Father in John 17 does not mention the Spirit by name. Instead, he prayed: 'As you have sent me into the world, so I have sent them into the world.' How had Jesus been sent? John began his Gospel by describing the Spirit descending and remaining on Jesus (John 1.33) and, without naming the Spirit, this prayer is for the disciples to be empowered and sent with that same awareness of abiding in God's presence.

In the ascension and exaltation of Jesus Christ, heaven opened to a human. Ten days later, at Pentecost, heaven overflowed with sounds and fire. The Holy Spirit rested on the people whom Jesus had asked the Father to protect, and the Spirit to empower and send into the world. Not understanding what was coming, in the days between Ascension and Pentecost, they devoted themselves to prayer. In this in-between week, we could follow their example, and the Collect is a prayer with which to begin.

Pentecost

Ezekiel 37.1–14; Acts 2.1–21; John 15.26–27, 16.4b–15

HEAVEN BREAKS IN NOISILY

God, who as at this time taught the hearts of your faithful people by sending to them the light of your Holy Spirit: grant us by the same Spirit to have a right judgement in all things and evermore to rejoice in his holy comfort; through the merits of Christ Jesus our Saviour. Amen.

Perhaps because the River Wear had been overflowing its banks in Durham when I first wrote this column, the image of flood came to mind more readily than wind and fire. At Pentecost, heaven bursts its banks, floods earth, and carries us along in its powerful flow.

We jump to conclusions that the Christians experienced strong wind at Pentecost. In fact, all we know is that they experienced the sound like the rush of a violent wind. The description of the divided tongues of flame resting on them suggests that they were not being blown about by a gale, even if it sounded like one. That in itself must have been unnerving, because sound and experience did not match up.

Centuries earlier, Ezekiel experienced noise when the Spirit of God was at work. In his case, it was the eerie sound of rattling, as he surveyed a valley of skeletons before flesh was added to the bones, in the reverse of the natural process of decomposition. When Ezekiel was first called, he had described hearing sounds from heaven like the sound of mighty waters, the thunder of the Almighty, the sound of tumult like the sound of an army (Ezekiel 1.24), and a loud rumbling (3.12). These were echoes of heaven: look in Revelation, and the sounds in heaven are described as being like that of many waters and mighty thunder peals (Revelation 19.6). Heaven is noisy. That is why silence in heaven for half an hour (Revelation 8.1) was remarkable.

When the Spirit acts, the sounds of heaven are heard on earth. This happened at the incarnation, when heaven spilled over on to earth, as God took human flesh in Jesus, and shepherds heard a multitude of the heavenly host singing heaven's songs of glory to God, very similar songs to those that John heard in his visions (Revelation 4.11). At Pentecost, God's noisy life again burst on the scene, when the Spirit of God was poured out on the people who had followed Jesus and for whom he had prayed. People whom Jesus had described as once filled with sorrow were filled with the Holy Spirit. This was total immersion.

To set the experience of Pentecost in context, we should go back to Jesus's life. At his baptism, the heavens opened, and the Spirit of God descended on him in bodily form like a dove, filling him (Luke 3.21–22, 4.1, 14). Then, at his ascension, the heavens opened again, and received him (Acts 1.9 10). Now, at Pentecost, the heavens opened once more, and the Holy Spirit fell among and upon the disciples, filling the house and transforming them. Once, God had said of Jesus: 'This is my Son, the beloved.' Now, the disciples spoke of God's wonderful works, as the Spirit gave them ability. Jesus had promised that if he went away, he would send the Advocate, the Spirit of truth, who would testify on Jesus's behalf. As the disciples discovered, perhaps to their surprise, this was done through them. Not only did they experience the sounds of heaven: they were caught up in the action of heaven.

Ezekiel was charged to prophesy to the dry bones (a seemingly thankless task, and he sensibly hedged his bets when God asked whether the bones could live) and to call for breath to come into them, to fill them. Amazingly, they lived and stood up.

Peter and the disciples found themselves speaking to the crowd, and found themselves remembering – as Jesus said they would – what he had told them of the Father and the Spirit. Read on in Peter's speech, and we discover a fearless proclamation of the crucifixion and resurrection of Jesus, and an assurance that God had fulfilled a centuries-old promise to pour out the Spirit on all people. Jesus had promised that the Spirit would glorify him and guide them into all truth; the immediate outcome was that the disciples glorified Jesus, and guided others into the truth about him.

Pentecost is about heaven's catching earth up into its life. The impetus comes from God; to be a Christian is to be caught up in and find ourselves being guided by the Spirit of God. We do not do things for God: we are filled by God's Spirit, and go where he is going.

Trinity Sunday
Isaiah 6.1–8; Romans 8.12–17; John 3.1–17

THE GRANDEUR OF GOD

Almighty and everlasting God, you have given us your servants grace, by the confession of a true faith, to acknowledge the glory of the eternal Trinity and in the power of the divine majesty to worship the Unity: keep us steadfast in this faith, that we may evermore be defended from all adversities; through Jesus Christ our Lord. Amen.

I have a postcard from Durham Cathedral Library propped up in front of me as I write, showing a late-fourteenth-century miniature of, and prayers to, the Trinity. God the Father, book in hand, points both to God the Son and God the Holy Spirit. Father and Son sit on an altar. The Son shows his wounded hands, still bleeding, and points to the chalice and host, indicating his presence in the Eucharist, and the Holy Spirit descends from above them as a dove, with gold and red flames emanating from his head. Like the better-known icon by Andrei Rublev, the figures invite us into the scene as participants, not just observers. In this miniature, our point of entry is the Eucharist, embodying Christ's work for our salvation.

On Trinity Sunday, it is too easy to be distracted by attempts to 'explain' the Trinity and to miss the invitation to share, in Christ, in the life of the Trinity. For the past six months, we have been observing the events surrounding God's initiative to save a wayward world, moving from Nazareth and Bethlehem to Pentecost in Jerusalem. Salvation is an act of the Trinity. Now we move from these seismic events of salvation history into six months of reading through a Gospel, focusing on the life of Jesus and our discipleship. The hinge is Trinity Sunday. This year's readings on Trinity Sunday point us to our communion with God. Isaiah's terrifying vision of the worship of heaven, replete with the noise we encountered last week at Pentecost, ends not with his banishment for being unclean, but with heavenly action and invitation to share in God's life and mission. Paul reminds the Romans that we are not slaves, excluded from the intimate life of the household, but heirs – part of the family. If we are led by the Spirit, we are children of God; we share God's life; we belong in the picture in the manuscript.

In his encounter with Jesus by night, Nicodemus tried to go over the ground of 'How can this be?' but Jesus was focused on the work of the Spirit, who, as we recall from last week, is not known for staying within boundaries when bringing life to God's world. Jesus held Nicodemus to the foundational truth that God is love, and that God's love cannot be contained, only shared and lived in. He, Nicodemus, was invited to share that love and be saved by it.

It is too easy to be anthropocentric in our understanding of God's love. It is cosmic in scope. Jesus told Nicodemus that the world is loved and saved by God. Similarly, it was not just the disciples, but the house where they were praying that was filled with the Spirit at Pentecost. Isaiah saw the hem of God's robe filling the Temple (an amazing description), and the house filled with smoke.

Gerard Manley Hopkins expressed it so evocatively in his poem 'God's Grandeur':

> The world is charged with the grandeur of God.
> It will flame out, like shining from shook foil;
> It gathers to a greatness, like the ooze of oil
> Crushed.

Just as the natural world was affected by the Fall, so it is healed in Christ. I remember vividly how, at a retreat centre a few years ago, one candle went on smoking for about five minutes after the candles were extinguished at the end of a service. We sat silently, while the plume of smoke played in the air. It was sheer gift to watch this beautiful, creative ballet, as the smoke ebbed and flowed, widened and narrowed, twirled in excited circles or broke into droplets that hung in the air. It simply and exquisitely filled the space, as the candle added its 'Amen' to the worship. The world is filled with God's glory.

As the medieval miniature shows, we are invited to share the life of the Trinity. On Trinity Sunday, Father, Son, and Spirit point to Christ's saving work as our way in to share this divine love that fills and saves the world. In these coming months of attention to following Jesus, the Saviour of the world, this cosmic context reminds us that sharing God's life means loving God's world, with all the consequent practical implications for discipleship.

Sunday after Trinity,
Proper 4 (29 May–4 June)
Deuteronomy 5.12–15; 2 Corinthians 4.5–12;
Mark 2.23–3.6

BEING HOLY

O God, the strength of all those who put their trust in you, mercifully accept our prayers and, because through the weakness of our mortal nature we can do no good thing without you, grant us the help of your grace, that in the keeping of your commandments we may please you both in will and deed; through Jesus Christ our Lord. Amen.

Collect for the First Sunday after Trinity

At the heart of the readings this week is the question of what it means to be holy. The reading from Deuteronomy is part of a long speech by Moses to the people of Israel, who have experienced God's deliverance and been made heirs of the covenant, reminding them of what it means that 'I am the Lord your God, who brought you out of the land of Egypt, out of the house of slavery' (Deuteronomy 5.6). Most of the reading is an explanation of the implications of the commandment, 'Observe the Sabbath day and keep it holy.'

In Exodus 20.8–11 the people were to 'remember' the Sabbath day and keep it holy because its origins are in relationship to creation: in six days God created the world and rested on the seventh. However, in Deuteronomy, the Sabbath was to be 'observed' not because of its source but because of its purpose which is to rest and enable others, even animals, to rest. What the people were to remember was not the origin of the Sabbath but their slavery in Egypt and God's deliverance from the burden of enforced labour.

It is against that background that we hear Jesus's observation of the Sabbath being called into question. His actions were already raising questions as he had healed in a synagogue on the Sabbath (Mark 1.21–28). This, while not prompting overt criticism, had led to publicity, while his subsequent eating with tax-collectors had provoked hostile questioning. By the end of this second healing in the synagogue his life was in danger.

So what had Jesus done to upset established notions of how to remember or observe the Sabbath? His disciples had plucked grain as they went through the field. Deuteronomy 23.25 makes a distinction between plucking and harvesting, the latter being an intentional act that was ruled out on the Sabbath since it was clearly work. Deuteronomy allowed plucking by hand as a person walked through a field. Jesus's response to this reproach was based not on the original ruling in Deuteronomy, even though it sanctioned his disciples' action so would have been the easiest retort, but on a biblical precedent in 1 Samuel 21.2–7 (where the name of the high priest is misquoted) which illustrates a broader principle that meeting human need is more important than keeping the letter of the law. In other words, they were to remember that they were once slaves in Egypt and God had delivered them and then to act accordingly.

Then Jesus healed a man with a withered hand on the Sabbath. Two millennia later we can feel the tension in the air with his opponents watching his every move. Jesus sidestepped the trap by reframing the whole situation. The question was not 'to work or not to work?' but 'to do good or to do harm, to save life or to kill?' The man was not literally going to die if Jesus did not act but, in Jesus's frame of reference, to fail to do good was, strikingly, the equivalent of condemning someone to death. The man could not enjoy rest while he suffered in this way and the Sabbath was and is about sharing God's rest after the creation of a good world. Then, in a final adroit move, by first asking the man to come forward and then telling him to stretch out his hand, Jesus did not do anything that might be called work but the man was healed anyway. Jesus had bested his opponents and off they went to conspire against him because they missed the law's purpose and thus missed experiencing God's life-giving way.

Paul writes about this to the Corinthians. Recalling the creation where God said 'let light shine out of darkness' he says that God has shone in our hearts to give the light of the knowledge of God in the face of Jesus Christ. Jesus's opponents resisted God's light shining in their hearts and thus missed seeing the glory of God revealed in the face of this man from Galilee who was doing extraordinarily good things in their midst. It is a salutary reminder to us not to miss the glory because we are so concerned with the minutiae of what we think passes for holiness.

Sunday after Trinity,
Proper 5 (5–11 June)
Genesis 3.8–15; 2 Corinthians 4.13–5.1; Mark 3.20–35

PROTECTING AND INCLUDING

O God, the strength of all those who put their trust in you, mercifully accept our prayers and, because through the weakness of our mortal nature we can do no good thing without you, grant us the help of your grace, that in the keeping of your commandments we may please you both in will and deed; through Jesus Christ our Lord. Amen.

Collect for the First Sunday after Trinity

This is the first time that Mark has mentioned Jesus's family. When reading this Gospel, we have to forget what we know from the birth narratives of Matthew and Luke because, for Mark, Jesus is a charismatic young man who appeared on the scene in a whirlwind of activity, with no background information except that he came from Nazareth and lived in Capernaum. Mark's readers had some additional information: that Jesus was empowered by the Holy Spirit, and was then driven into the wilderness to be tempted by Satan. People in Mark's story who met Jesus, however, did not know of this earlier conflict, or the source of his power, which was displayed so frequently in the early part of the Gospel. So, confronted with a miracle-worker, they were confused, and asked questions – as, later, did people who knew his family background (Mark 6.1–3).

The pace of Mark's story is breathtaking. Jesus drew crowds wherever he went: this is the ninth time in three chapters that Mark has reported enormous crowds around Jesus, or that he had no privacy, or was too busy to eat. He performed miracles, including exorcisms, and people flocked to be healed. Local life was turned upside down as news spread. The religious leaders should have recognized when God was at work, but they accused Jesus of blasphemy (Mark 2.7). In response, Jesus, grieved by their hardness of heart, challenged them to weigh the evidence of his power to do good. Now, faced with more miracles, they went too far, and ascribed the Holy Spirit's empowerment of Jesus to Satan. It was that intentional denial of the holiness of God's Spirit, confusing good and evil, which Jesus described as unforgivable, and put him on the offensive. This is the last of the dramatic, confrontational events that open Mark's Gospel. Already, Mark has shown us people divided in their responses to Jesus: while the crowds were thrilled by miracles, the Scribes misread him terribly, and thereby condemned themselves; and Mary did not understand. Indeed, Mark frames the Scribes' confrontation with Jesus with the story of Mary, drawing attention to their contrasting responses.

This frenetic pace of life was unsustainable, and took its toll on Jesus; so people questioned his mental state. Whereas the Scribes placed themselves outside God's family, Mary tried to close the natural family around Jesus for his protection. We can picture this strong Jewish mother, bringing her other children with her for support, arriving on the scene to tell her eldest son off. Any mother of a young man who appears to be going off the family rails will understand. This miracle-worker had a family history, was human, and his mother was concerned. But she could not get into the house, and so resorted to sending a message. Jesus was not to be distracted, and his brusque response was the passion of a young man caught up in the intensity of his mission. His answer was not to reject his family as his nearest kin, but to expand his family circle, drastically, to include anyone who did the will of God and wanted to follow him. This was not easy for Mary.

In pairing this story of Mary seeking out Jesus with the poignant episode in the creation myth from Genesis, the lectionary draws our attention to the pain of rejected love. Mary searched out her son with his well-being at heart; God searched for the man to whom he had given life with his well-being at heart. We read that God missed the close fellowship for which Adam was created, and which brought joy to God as well as to Adam.

Mary sought Jesus because she wanted to protect him from his popularity; but his impulse, like that of God with Adam, was and is to seek human company, and to include more people than might be on our invitation list for family events. If we find that disconcerting, so did the religious leaders of Jesus's day. From the other perspective, some people find it hard to believe that they are welcomed, and, like Adam, may hide for shame. God's presence among us today may be equally disturbing to our way of life before it can be liberating.

Sunday after Trinity,
Proper 6 (12–18 June)
Ezekiel 17.22–end; 2 Corinthians 5.6–17; Mark 4.26–34

OPENNESS TO UNEXPECTED HARVESTS

Lord, you have taught us that all our doings without love are nothing worth: send your Holy Spirit and pour into our hearts that most excellent gift of love, the true bond of peace and of all virtues, without which whoever lives is counted dead before you. Grant this for your only Son Jesus Christ's sake. Amen.

Collect for the Second Sunday after Trinity

When John Major was Prime Minister, I was living in the United States. A friend told me that he had discovered Prime Minister's Question Time on cable TV, and was hooked. 'There's one thing I can't work out,' he said. 'Where is Mr Major's autocue?' I explained that politicians have to debate knowledgeably on their feet, and that, although there might have been advance warning of the questions, the to-ing and fro-ing across the despatch box was indeed that. Today's Gospel reading reminds us that, even if he had the option, Jesus would be at home with that thinking on his feet. He thrived on personal contact to proclaim the Kingdom of God, preferring conversation to speeches.

Mark is essentially an oral Gospel. Sadly, we will never know the tone of voice, the facial expression, or the body language that people used. As a result, sometimes we read the Bible with far too straight a face. On this occasion, Jesus, in a boat on the edge of the Sea of Galilee, appears to have cast his eyes around for a way to describe the Kingdom of God, as he wondered aloud: 'With what can we compare the Kingdom of God, or what parable will we use for it?' He hit on the mustard growing on the hills around the seashore. Jesus probably had a broad grin when coming up with this parable to describe the Kingdom of God, because it was verging on the ludicrous. Far from its being a glorious example of first-century Mediterranean arboriculture, mustard was a tall annual herb, grown for mustard-seed oil. Anyone listening would laugh at the thought of birds' trying to nest in it: they couldn't even perch on its spindly stems. Taken literally, it was plain daft. Jesus appears to have chosen this example to catch people's attention.

Mark began his Gospel with the news that the Kingdom of God had come near. In the first three chapters, Jesus brought God's healing and wholeness through his miracles. Now it was time to explain what was going on. These are Mark's first parables, and he grouped together several about things that grow. So, like Jesus's hearers, we should think in terms of agriculture, because the Kingdom of God is something that grows in ways beyond human control.

Although we can nurture it, like any crop, we cannot grow it ourselves, but should expect to be surprised and delighted at what happens when the seed is sown. I had a taste of this parable one year as what I had thought was a sweet-pea seed in a seed-tray grew into something totally unlike a sweet pea. I simply let it grow to see what emerged.

If people laughed at the idea of birds' nesting in mustard, some would know from the scriptures that Jesus was alluding to Ezekiel's prophecy to exiles in Babylon about birds of the air who would nest in the branches of trees. But Jesus was subverting it. Ezekiel was talking about enormous, solid cedar trees that could house dozens of nesting birds. His prophecy looked forward to the Messianic age, when God would make the restored nation a blessing to all nations on earth. Jesus, meanwhile, talked about the most lopsided shrub imaginable with skinny stems and big branches.

Jesus was not arguing detailed points of the law with scribes, but lodging unforgettable images in the minds of a large crowd. So he threw out, unscripted, the startling idea of the Kingdom of God's being like a common-or-garden herb that grows everywhere, and then unexpectedly sprouts large branches for birds to nest in. Its bite lay in the fact that it was not a totally wild idea; theologically, it indicated that Jesus's arrival was fulfilling the situation of blessing foreseen by Ezekiel. The obvious challenge is whether we are open to unexpected harvests when God gives the growth. God may just be growing a new form of shelter – of blessing – for his needy world, and trying to expand our imagination to cope with this manifestation of the Kingdom of God. He might even want us to laugh with him at this outlandish outcome to his propagation.

Sunday after Trinity,
Proper 7 (19–25 June)
1 Samuel 17.57–18.5, 10–16; 2 Corinthians 6.1–13;
Mark 4.35–41

A KIND OF *CANTUS FIRMUS*

> *Almighty God, you have broken the tyranny of sin and have sent the Spirit of your Son into our hearts whereby we call you Father: give us grace to dedicate our freedom to your service, that we and all creation may be brought to the glorious liberty of the children of God; through Jesus Christ our Lord. Amen.*

Collect for the Third Sunday after Trinity

If we want a complaint against Jesus to stick, not caring would be one of the last we might think of. Yet, twice in the Gospels, Jesus is asked 'Don't you care?' and on both occasions (the other is in Luke 10.40), the question is put by a close friend, who, of all people, should have known better.

The panic-stricken disciples, seasoned fishermen, were terrified that they would die in a storm through which Jesus had the temerity, or the tiredness, to sleep. Mark describes him as absolutely exhausted; so no wonder his reply was rather short. Once woken, Jesus did what was necessary, and then asked, in effect: 'What is the matter with you?' Jesus expected better of them. His sharp question was partly annoyance at being woken up, but also part of Mark's theme of people's recognizing Jesus. Under pressure, the disciples had failed to grasp Jesus's power, or his care, even though they had seen all his miracles. It's a very human fear – that we are being ignored.

Paul was writing to the Corinthians, a new church with which he had a rather fraught relationship. People there were undermining his authority; so his catalogue of hardships was not so much blowing his own trumpet as an attempt to persuade them of his apostolic credentials. We rattle off the list, but, if we pause to think about what he had been through, the fact that he kept faith in God becomes remarkable. Think what a few sleepless nights or delayed meals do to our temper, add in beatings, imprisonment, riots, hardship, and calamities, and his list becomes quite a package of fidelity to God.

Probably, at times, Paul asked God: 'Don't you care?' It is a healthy question to ask in prayer at times of distress; it keeps God in the dialogue, when the easier option is to dismiss God from the equation. The Psalms, Job, and Jeremiah show how much a part of Jewish religion it is to question God from a position of faith. What enabled Paul, with a few more years' experience of following Jesus, to be more secure in his response to crises than the disciples? Again, we can rush over his words. It is one thing to be kind and truthful when all is going well, and quite another when we are under intense pressure or falsely imprisoned.

Purity and holiness of spirit sound pious, but are desirable, and we think of people such as Mother Teresa. After her death, her journals revealed her daily struggle with doubts: her holiness was not an easy attribute, but a hard-won purity, forged in hundreds of daily decisions made in the slums of Calcutta, and the commitment to prayer, whether or not she felt like it.

Dietrich Bonhoeffer, the German pastor murdered by the Nazis in 1945, wrote from prison of

> ... A kind of *cantus firmus* to which the other melodies of life provide the counterpoint ... where the ground bass is firm and clear, there is nothing to stop the counterpoint from being developed to the utmost of its limits ... Only a polyphony of this kind can give life a wholeness, and assure us that nothing can go wrong so long as the *cantus firmus* is kept going. Put your faith in the *cantus firmus*. (Bonhoeffer, 1953)

Put simply, the *cantus firmus* is our deep-seated song at the core of who we are, which enables us to live with vivacity and faith.

Michael Mayne, the late Dean of Westminster, wrote in his final book, *The Enduring Melody*, of his discovery, when he was diagnosed with cancer of the mouth, of his own *cantus firmus*. He described this as the truths that lay at his deep centre, tempered and pruned over a lifetime.

Paul did not know that phrase, but knew the experience, as in time did the disciples, of having the inner resources to face whatever life threw at him. It takes slow, deliberate, and at times unexciting work, as we build our Christian character and our trust in God. It is the work of a lifetime. It enables us to trust in God when waves rock our boat.

Sunday after Trinity,

Proper 8 (26 June–2 July)

Wisdom of Solomon 1.13–15, 2.23–24 or 2 Samuel 1.1, 17–20;
2 Corinthians 8.7–24; Mark 5.21–43

A RITUALLY UNCLEAN WOMAN

*O God, the protector of all who trust in you, without whom nothing is
strong, nothing is holy: increase and multiply upon us your mercy; that
with you as our ruler and guide we may so pass through things temporal
that we lose not our hold on things eternal; grant this, heavenly Father, for
our Lord Jesus Christ's sake. Amen.*

Collect for the Fourth Sunday after Trinity

Writing about a financial collection for people facing famine, Paul commended
the Corinthians for their faith, speech, and knowledge, and then urged them to
take action and do something practical. His example was Jesus, who for our
sakes became poor, so that we might become rich through his poverty. In today's
Gospel, Jesus's poverty is expressed in his sharing the uncleanness of outcasts.

Jairus, a leader of the synagogue, did the first-century equivalent of a
churchwarden falling down at the feet of a revivalist preacher who has wandered
into town. Jairus faced the dilemma whether to risk his reputation by going to
Jesus for help, or to give in to embarrassment and miss out on healing for his
daughter. He believed that Jesus could heal his daughter, but also knew that
Jesus could be ritually unclean, since he broke religious laws to help people.
On this occasion, Jesus had just come from Gentile territory, where he had been
dealing with demons and pigs.

Jairus acted, and Jesus responded, but the crowd slowed down progress.
Anyone who has been stuck in traffic when trying to get someone to hospital will
understand the desperation. Then Jesus stopped to ask the ridiculous question:
'Who touched me?' Crowds can't help touching each other. But Jesus persisted,
and met the woman with the 12-year haemorrhage.

When we understand her situation, we can understand why she was so
desperate for help. Anyone with severe anaemia is physically weak, and even
simple tasks are exhausting. She had no iron tablets. Worse, since women were
unclean during and for a week after their period, she had been excluded from
society for the whole lifetime of Jairus's daughter. If she had children, she had
been unable to touch them or her husband without making them unclean for the
rest of the day and needing to purify themselves. That was no life.

The woman made Jesus unclean by touching him, and the crowd would expect him to be angry. Mark, however, by using certain words to describe her suffering that he uses elsewhere only of Jesus's suffering, indicates that Jesus shared this woman's rejection and shame. He also links them by the experience of feeling a change in their bodies. Of all people, Jesus was identified with a woman excluded from society. By forcing her into the open, Jesus could assure her that she was healed (literally, 'saved'), and restored to society; that, as much as the physical healing, turned her life around. Furthermore, Jesus called her 'my daughter'. Having said earlier that whoever does the will of God is his family, Jesus assured this outcast that she was his daughter; that, in seeking healing, she had done the will of God. Then, unperturbed by the delay, Jesus raised another daughter, a little girl, who, unlike the woman, had someone to speak for her.

Each Petertide, at the end of June, many deacons and priests are ordained. Deacons are ordained so that the people of God may be better equipped to make Christ known, and priests are charged with leading God's people in the proclamation of the gospel, and, with God's people, in telling the story of God's love. This is a shared responsibility; the clergy do not do this for others, but with others. All baptized Christians are sent in mission to God's world of crowds and desperately lonely people; so churches that receive a new curate can expect their mission to be sharpened.

Paul urged people to be practical in service, following Jesus's example. Jesus noticed individuals in the middle of crowds. Our baptismal vocation is to be attentive, and ready to stop and help; to get our hands dirty; to encourage discouraged and fearful people not to give up in seeking God's help. Next time that you are in a crowd, pay attention to what is going on around you. Pray for people as you walk by them or stand next to them. Get involved in outreach to people in need. Visit housebound people. Stand up for people who, like this woman, have no voice in society. Give generously to charities that can help people whom you cannot reach yourself.

In the stories we heard, healing and new life came because Jesus was willing to take notice of people in need. It is his example that we follow.

Sunday after Trinity,
Proper 9 (3–9 July)
Ezekiel 2.1–5; Corinthians 12.2–10; Mark 6.1–13

JESUS RETURNS TO NAZARETH

Almighty and everlasting God, by whose Spirit the whole body of the Church is governed and sanctified: hear our prayer which we offer for all your faithful people, that in their vocation and ministry they may serve you in holiness and truth to the glory of your name; through our Lord and Saviour Jesus Christ. Amen.

Collect for the Fifth Sunday after Trinity

This week we hear of visions, but neither Ezekiel's nor Paul's visions alleviated their troubles. One minute Ezekiel was with fellow exiles by the river in Babylon (Ezekiel 1.1); the next, he was having extraordinary visions, and hearing that he was being sent to impudent and stubborn rebels. Psalm 137 expresses the exiles' despair and yearning for revenge on their captors and betrayers; speaking to them about the ways of God would be very hard work. A few centuries later, another man committed to serving God, whatever the cost, had to make sense of indescribable visions. To boast or not to boast? Paul settled for boasting of his weakness, which was brought into sharp focus by the power of God seen in the visions. A thorn in the flesh, from which the God who could give these immense visions did not act to free him – despite three appeals – was an unwelcome aid to keeping his perspective. Through it, Paul had learned that God's power was sufficient, and was made perfect in the weakness that he experienced through his trials and persecutions.

Jesus, too, had a vision from God at the beginning of his public ministry (Mark 1.10–11), followed by trials in the wilderness, from which he emerged to proclaim the reign of God in word and in action. Now, after some extraordinary and exhausting events, he had made the long walk to see his family, and was worshipping with his neighbours. There were no overt visions; instead, the power of his teaching and actions – which should have been vision enough – raised questions, and provoked doubts as well as faith. When the miraculous hits the familiar, belief can be difficult. The neighbours knew too much of Jesus's family to reconcile this with the authority they saw in him. We can be sympathetic to their perplexity: few of us would do better in their shoes. On the other hand, we can be sympathetic to Jesus: being rejected, or at the very least doubted, by your friends and family is hard (John 7.5). Life was lonely back at home.

There is a poignant irony to the comment: 'He could do no deeds of power there except that he laid his hands on a few sick people and healed them. And he was amazed at their unbelief.' 'Except that ...': healing even a few sick people is some exception, yet the contrast of Jesus's limited ministry with the many miracles performed by the Twelve when he sent them out (Mark 6.13) is notable. Jesus risked sending the disciples out, despite this uncertain response. They had seen miracles, and they had seen people refuse to believe. Like Ezekiel, they were going to stubborn people as well as receptive people. Like Paul, they were going in weakness, with no basic necessities for travel, placed in total dependence on the people they met. If they were rejected, all they could do was to move on to another uncertain reception, and remain faithful.

This week's Collect prays for all faithful people in their vocation and ministry to serve God in holiness and truth. Mercifully, with God, holiness is manifest in the middle of the muddle of life, as well as in its glorious moments; holiness is not circumstantial, but the fruit of intentional faithfulness to God, whatever our situation. Ezekiel, Paul, Jesus, and the disciples all experienced God's holiness in the midst of their tribulations, their tangles and struggles. To have visions or see miracles is not enough: if they are granted, they may encourage us (and perhaps unsettle us), but what matters is how we live as a result, especially in the midst of people who do not have faith in God. Ezekiel, Paul, and the disciples all struggled – the Bible is honest about that – but kept going. Our example is Jesus, who, despite disappointing, astounding unbelief, still performed a few miracles, and transformed a few lives.

> Come, holy God, refine your Church,
> hallow to us our poverty:
> we would be rich in holiness,
> servants of him who sets us free.
> Our listlessness transform with power,
> our meagre love with love divine,
> come, Holy Spirit, breath of God,
> as wind disturb, as fire refine.
>
> *Copyright © 2001 Rosalind Brown*

Sunday after Trinity,
Proper 10 (10–16 July)
Amos 7.7–15; Ephesians 1.3–14; Mark 6.14–29

KEEPING THE FIRST LOVE

Merciful God, you have prepared for those who love you such good things
as pass our understanding: pour into our hearts such love toward you that
we, loving you in all things and above all things, may obtain your promises,
which exceed all that we can desire; through Jesus Christ our Lord. Amen.

Collect for the Sixth Sunday after Trinity

The contrast between the epistle and the Gospel is stark and inescapable. The glorious and expansive vision of all the blessings described in Ephesians was not the experience of John, or indeed of Herod and his family, who were locked into a cycle of fear and revenge. The juxtaposition of these readings gives us pause for thought. John's experience, as he lived for the praise of Christ's glory, despite his being imprisoned, prevents the epistle from becoming completely otherworldly. Equally, the epistle does not allow John's distressing experiences to be meaningless.

John's reward for his faithfulness as forerunner of the Messiah, and his proclamation of the message of repentance, was, seemingly, to be overlooked by God when he was in dire need. Jesus was healing the sick and releasing captives, but had not brought freedom to John. Luke records that John appeared to doubt that Jesus was the Messiah, to which Jesus's response was to point to his works, and challenge John not to be offended that he remained in prison (Luke 7.18–23); in other words, not to lose his first love for God. John's was a hard calling, and Herod's fickle curiosity, which allowed him to enjoy listening to John when he fancied intellectual titillation but not to lift a finger to help him, must have grated.

Life in Herod's palace was deeply miserable. Herod, despite officially being the powerful one, was at the mercy of his wife's jealousy, and finally was trapped, probably when drunk and showing off in front of his guests, into an action that he hated. It was too late: he was cornered, and John was the victim. Herod was not physically imprisoned like John, but he was imprisoned in other ways, and, in that sense, John was the freer man, however uncomfortable his situation.

In contrast, there is the Ephesian church that was built up by Paul, after the work of others (Acts 19, 20.17–38). It was a cause of joy that the church was full of faith in the Lord and love for the saints. The writer poured out this breathless paean of praise to God, unable to contain his wonder at all that God had done and would do from the foundation of the world to the fullness of time. We can imagine the excitement when the Christians gathered and heard this description of who they were in Christ read publicly for the first time. If they had been struggling with the difficulties of being Christians in a city dedicated to and dominated by the pagan goddess Diana, then this was encouragement and new vision indeed.

We read in Revelation (2.1–7) that, by the end of the first century, the Ephesian church, despite enduring faithfully and bearing up for the sake of the Lord's name in the face of false apostles, had lost its first love. Somehow, despite the theological insights in this epistle, which no doubt remained a treasured part of this church's memory, things had slipped. The epistle goes on to spell out in practical detail how to live as the people of these amazing promises, and how to be strong in the Lord, wearing all the armour God provides, and praying at all times in the Spirit. The letter in Revelation assures them that they had done this, but sees beneath the surface that, in the process, they had lost their first love.

John, in prison, kept his first love, and was faithful to the end, despite his doubts and the harsh treatment meted out to him. The Ephesians, facing the difficult ups and downs of life as Christians in a pagan society, and strengthened by the encouragement of the epistle, had faltered. While remaining faithful, they were no longer in love with God as once they had been. That danger is always before us; hence the wisdom of the petition in the Collect that God will pour into our hearts such love towards him that we, loving God in all things and above all things, may obtain his promises, which exceed all that we can desire. Ephesians spells out some of those promises; the juxtaposition of that reading with John's story alerts us to the possibility of retaining our first love, however hard our situation.

Sunday after Trinity,

Proper 11 (17–23 July)

Jeremiah 23.1–6; Ephesians 2.11–22; Mark 6.30–34, 53–56

FORMING GOD'S COMMUNITY

Lord of all power and might, the author and giver of all good things: graft in our hearts the love of your name, increase in us true religion, nourish us with all goodness, and of your great mercy keep us in the same; through Jesus Christ our Lord. Amen.

Collect for the Seventh Sunday after Trinity

As I write, homes and livelihoods are being devastated by floods and I find myself praying for them and for people around the world without emergency services, like ours, to help. Topically, the readings describe people unable to help themselves. God looked at a flock of people abandoned by those who should care for them. Jesus was surrounded by a crowd of people who were like sheep without a shepherd and wanted attention. The author of Ephesians wrote to a community that had been alienated through the divisions between Jew and Gentile – divisions replicated through the ages as the Church has found issue after issue on which to define its members over and against one another.

Jesus, too, was in need – for the second time Mark describes him as too busy to eat. His exhausted disciples, just back from their first mission trips, had him on their own for once and were telling him their adventures. Then others barged in. What was his response to the intrusive crowd which interrupted his time for rest with his friends? Not irritation, even if he felt it, but compassion. This was not because they were hungry – in the missing verses he fed them – but because they were like sheep without a shepherd. He saw deeper into the source of the problem. So, hungry and exhausted as he was, he taught them not briefly but about many things. He gave lavishly of himself for, as the Collect prays, God is the author and giver of all good things.

In all three readings, the consequences of seeking healing and wholeness included being turned from a crowd into a community. God promised to make a single flock out of his scattered people under a righteous King; Jesus drew the people together and became their shepherd as he taught them; the Ephesians, people who had been alienated and strangers, without hope, were brought together in Christ and the dividing wall of hostility between them came down. That is a powerful image. At an event in Durham Cathedral, Sir Thomas Allen who was in Berlin when the Iron Curtain fell, described his enduring memory of the sounds of hammering as the wall was chipped away and of breaking glass as champagne bottles were trampled underfoot when separated people rushed towards each other in unforgettable scenes.

YEAR B

Those sounds of joy and exhilaration are rightly ours because, in Christ, dividing walls have fallen, peace is made between alienated people and all have access in one Spirit to the Father. Yet sometimes in the church we barely walk towards each other. The Collect and the readings remind us that we are God's community and are learning God's ways. While it is one thing to like the principle of having a good shepherd and being one flock in Christ, it is another to build community. Other people crowd in, mess up our ideal arrangements and stretch our love. We discover that we have to work at welcoming and loving the people God sends our way. Love is costly.

For St Benedict it is not enough that people simply get together or even live together – that can happen in any institution without it having a common life. His goal is people who, conscious of their shared life in Christ, work to build God's community and do not just reap its benefits. So he says in chapter 72 of the Rule, 'This is the good zeal which monks must foster with fervent love, they should each try to be the first to show respect to the other.' The power to do this lies in the Collect's petition that God will graft in our hearts the love of his name.

Michael Casey comments, astutely, why we need God's loving gift of each other, 'We are all unavoidably both unique and incomplete. Someone with a grand vision will simultaneously be grateful to and irritated by another with the knack of delving into detail' (Casey, 2005). In God's community the gifts we need may come from unlikely people when we are built together spiritually into a dwelling place for God (Ephesians 2.22). No wonder we pray in the Collect for the deeper experience, the staying power, to live into this wonderful, demanding, reconciling vocation.

Sunday after Trinity,
Proper 12 (24–30 July)
2 Kings 4.42–44; Ephesians 3.14–21; John 6.1–21

CREATION IN CHRIST'S HANDS

> *Almighty Lord and everlasting God, we beseech you to direct, sanctify and govern both our hearts and bodies in the ways of your laws and the works of your commandments; that through your most mighty protection, both here and ever, we may be preserved in body and soul; through our Lord and Saviour Jesus Christ. Amen.*
>
> Collect for the Eighth Sunday after Trinity

This little-known story of Elisha involves an unexpected gift from an unknown man who made a miracle possible – we will never know how far he travelled to fulfil his obligation to bring the first-fruits, or if he realized how urgently his gift was needed. This prefigures the story of Jesus's feeding the crowd which depends on an unknown boy's offering, on the face of it, a pointless gift: six months' wages were inadequate; so why bother with a packed lunch? It took courage by Andrew to make such a stupid suggestion, but, sometimes, reckless courage is needed to unlock a miracle.

If the provision for 5000 was a miracle, then so were the leftovers, which comprised far more than the boy offered. I wonder what the disciples did with this tangible reminder that God not only met needs, but provided in abundance. This early example of not letting anything go to waste raises questions. Do we throw out food too readily? Do we recycle all we can? There is also a spiritual application: do we miss part of God's blessing through failing to gather up the fragments around us in daily life?

The satisfaction of the crowd is juxtaposed with the later terror of the disciples. Both wanted to do something to Jesus. The crowd wanted to make him king; so, to avoid being thrust into the political arena, Jesus withdrew to be alone. The disciples wanted to take him into the boat, once he had calmed them down. Enigmatically, John does not tell us whether Jesus let them do this (unlike Mark, who says that he complied), but simply reports that, immediately, the boat reached the land towards which they were going. For John, Jesus is never someone to be controlled by others.

For a few weeks, we switch from Mark's action-packed Gospel to John's more reflective Gospel. John does not let the miracle of the feeding go unremarked, but uses it as the basis for Jesus's teaching about the bread from heaven. Intertwined with this are questions about Jesus's identity, which, in John's Gospel, is proclaimed openly, and people must respond rather than guess at the secret that Mark makes it.

These two miracles involve creation, and are foretastes of the ultimate healing of creation in Christ. Paul looks forward to this when writing of the glory to be revealed: 'The creation was subjected to futility … the creation itself will be set free from its bondage to decay and will obtain the freedom of the glory of the children of God' (Romans 8.18–21).

Storms were stilled, water bore the weight of Jesus walking on it, bread and fish fed more than they should, the sky darkened at the crucifixion, and the earth shook at Christ's death and resurrection. Here was a person whose relationship with the physical creation was not scarred by the effects of sin. Creation responded to his presence.

Stories of the relationship between the saints and the physical creation are part of our heritage; whatever we think about otters warming St Cuthbert's feet, birds nesting in St Kevin's hand, wild beasts becoming docile, timid animals frolicking joyfully with saints, these stories illustrate this theological understanding, that God's redemption in Christ restores all of creation to its intended freedom to flourish.

This is a very holistic understanding of salvation as including, but not restricted to, humans: Jürgen Moltmann has said, 'All that is created longs to participate in the divine glory' (Moltmann, 1992).The Eastern Orthodox Church sings to Christ on Holy Saturday: 'The whole creation was altered by your Passion, all things suffered with you, knowing that your Word holds all things together in unity'; and, in the Easter Vigil, sings the words of John of Damascus: 'In Christ's resurrection the whole creation is established and made sure.'

As we pray to be open to the riches of God's grace, on the one hand, we pray with the author of Ephesians for power to comprehend the scale of God's love which surpasses knowledge, so that we can be filled with the fullness of God; on the other, we are reminded to be attentive to God's blessing of creation, to offer what we have, however little, and to notice and gather the fragments that are the surplus abundance of God's goodness.

Sunday after Trinity,

Proper 13 (31 July–6 August)

Exodus 16.2–4, 9–15; Ephesians 4.1–16; John 6.24–35

MANNA IN THE WILDERNESS

Almighty God, who sent your Holy Spirit to be the life and light of your Church: open our hearts to the riches of your grace, that we may bring forth the fruit of the Spirit in love and joy and peace; through Jesus Christ our Lord. Amen.

Collect for the Ninth Sunday after Trinity

One year the post-Confirmation group at Durham Cathedral explored Benedictine wisdom for daily Christian living. The members were happy for me to describe their discussion about the demands of caring for dying relatives, when, despite their love, exhaustion sapped their strength to keep going. They had read of the monks martyred in Algeria in 1996, having refused to flee from danger because of their commitment to their neighbours, a story told in the film *Of Gods and Men*. They made a connection with their different experience: in both cases, people were sustained by drawing on foundations laid over the years – for the monks, steady commitment to their vows and daily showing up for prayer together; for the carers, routine loving commitment in family life. As the group looked back on their lives, they recognized signs of God's compassionate care; some noticed only now that they were more open to God. When we are under stress, events can overwhelm our awareness of the riches of God's grace.

Having seen the place associated with the complaints of the Israelites in the wilderness, I have some sympathy for them. In this harsh territory, Egypt suddenly seemed very appealing as selective memory kicked in: they remembered the food, but forgot the oppression. They were beginning a completely new life, and had to learn to live with freedom. That involved taking responsibility for themselves. It is a part of all growing up, and they were to grow up as people of God. They floundered when, exactly a month since they kept the first Passover, in the first test of their trust in God's rich grace, they forgot their miraculous deliverance. Graciously, in this early stage of their journey from slavery, God understood their predicament, and did not deal with them harshly.

God's rich grace was expressed through bread with bemusing properties. The only answer to their question: 'What is it?' was that this odd provision was from God. It was intended both to feed them and to help them understand that they lived not by bread alone but by every word from God (Deuteronomy 8.3). The food denoted something much more wonderful: God was sustaining them; they would be cared for on their journey; and this involved living with hearts open to God, despite their questions. In Durham, we talked about how God's provision, today's manna, comes in many forms – from random acts of kindness by colleagues to the hospice's respite care.

Jesus was dealing with people who needed to see beyond wanting food to the one who provided it. Like the Israelites faced with manna, they were full of questions. Unable to live with those questions, they ordered a miracle, so that they could measure Jesus's performance against God's in the wilderness, and perhaps deign to believe in him. Refusing to play their game, Jesus challenged them to look more deeply, and to open their hearts to God's presence with them now.

The Ephesian Christians were set a high benchmark. Exhorted to mature to the measure of the full stature of Christ, they were to grow up as people of God, to live with their freedom in Christ. This reading marks the transition in the epistle from ecstatic, otherworldly, wonder at what God in Christ has done – our deliverance – to the down-to-earth implications of living a life worthy of our calling, which the Durham group discussed: living with the questions raised by God's presence among us, and keeping our hearts open to the riches of God's grace.

Only by being aware of the cosmic scope of God's grace and translating that into humble, gentle, patient human living can we grow up into Christ, and promote the growth of the body of Christ which, in turn, we need to help us remain faithful under pressure. Preaching at an ordination service in Durham Cathedral, Canon Professor Mark McIntosh reminded everyone that God has known and loved us from all eternity, so completely that we can open our hearts to him. That takes us back to the Collect; it all begins with hearts that are open to God's overwhelming love, enabling us to bring forth the fruit of the Spirit in love and joy and peace.

We are pushing at a door that is already open, entrusting ourselves to the God who knows us inside out with unfailing love, to become bearers of joy and peace in God's world.

Sunday after Trinity,
Proper 14 (7–13 August)
1 Kings 19.4–8; Ephesians 4.25–5.2; John 6.35, 41–51

GOD'S BELOVED CHILDREN

Let your merciful ears, O Lord, be open to the prayers of your humble servants; and that they may obtain their petitions make them to ask such things as shall please you; through Jesus Christ our Lord. Amen.

Collect for the Tenth Sunday after Trinity

'Who do you think you are?' asks the television programme that delves into family trees. Elijah's despairing answer was: 'I am no better than my ancestors.' Jesus said he came from heaven and was the bread of life. The people around Jesus insisted that he was simply Joseph's son. The Ephesians were described as God's beloved children.

There are two extremes: being paralysed because we think we cannot outdo our ancestors, and being rejected because we dare to challenge expectations that we are nothing but our parents' children. Who had said that Elijah had to be better than his ancestors? Certainly not God, and, since he was isolated and imagined himself to be the last faithful person, it was not other people. So it must have been an internal voice, accusing him of failure to live up to, or exceed, family expectations. The drive to prove ourselves better than others is a cruel pressure to face, and is dangerous in ministry. On the other hand, the people around Jesus had spiritual tunnel-vision, were unable to encounter him as more than the son of Joseph, whose family they knew, and so criticized him for breaking moulds of their making.

There is a godly alternative. If we let God answer 'Who do you think you are?' like the Ephesian Christians, we know ourselves to be God's beloved children, marked with the Holy Spirit of God. Once we know that, consequences follow, because our vocation is to be imitators of God, kind to one another, living in love, as Christ loved us and gave himself for us. As we experience for ourselves the goodness and kindness of God, we become imitators of God and bearers of God's goodness and kindness in the world: in the words of the hymn: 'Love to the loveless shown, That they might lovely be.'

We see this in God's care of the exhausted and depressed Elijah, who was duly fed, watered, allowed to rest, and – if we read on – given a new commission to fulfil. Probe in any church, and there should be contemporary stories of the kindness of God to us that lead to further kindness by us. When did your church last gather the crumbs, as the disciples did after 5000 people ate, and tell some of the stories?

YEAR B

The lovely but challenging commission given to the Ephesians was to speak so that their words gave grace to those who heard. In our world, where words are used to such devastating effect, and then broadcast around the world (footballers' language was in the news when I first wrote this), or used shrewdly to evade responsibility (for example, the Leveson inquiry elicited some highly equivocal testimony), how different it would be if Christians, by their speech and action, gave grace to those who hear. This does not mean being naïve. The speech that gave grace to Elijah was not merely comforting, but dared him to keep going; and Jesus's speech confronted the people, undermining their limited vision. Ultimately, the Jewish authorities found this speech too hard to hear, but it was grace-filled none the less. If, like Elijah and the people around Jesus, we need God to expand our horizons, graceful speech may unsettle us as a prelude to building us up.

The epistle points us to tough practicalities if we are true to ourselves as God's beloved children and give grace to those who hear us. It means that there is no evil talk, only talk that builds up; it means putting away bitterness, wrath, anger, wrangling, slander, and malice – in other words, the things in which many headlines revel.

Preaching at the Durham Miners' Gala service in 2012, the Revd Lord Griffiths affirmed that hope can survive if and when words are turned into action. If we turn words that give grace into actions that give grace – into the kindness, tender-heartedness, forgiveness, and love to which the Ephesian Christians were exhorted – the result may be less newsworthy, but will imitate God and bring life to the world. To do that, we need to know who we are. I remember hearing, on the *Sunday* programme on Radio 4, someone prefix an answer to a question by defining herself with a long string of classifications of her faith and churchmanship. I longed to say to her: 'Cut through the labels: who do you think you are?' You and I are God's beloved children – no more, and no less.

Sunday after Trinity,
Proper 15 (14–20 August)
Proverbs 9.1–6; Ephesians 5.15–20; John 6.51–58

THE MELODY OF THE HEART

O God, you declare your almighty power most chiefly in showing mercy and pity: mercifully grant to us such a measure of your grace, that we, running the way of your commandments, may receive your gracious promises, and be made partakers of your heavenly treasure; through Jesus Christ our Lord. Amen.

Collect for the Eleventh Sunday after Trinity

On this Sunday in 2000 I was the visiting preacher at a rural church in Wiltshire. I decided to preach on the exhortation to the Ephesians to be filled with the Spirit as they sang psalms and hymns and spiritual songs among themselves, singing and making melody in their hearts. The churchwarden greeted me at the door and told me that, since most people were on holiday, they had decided not to sing hymns that week. We laughed when I told the congregation the theme of the sermon, and at the end they said: 'Perhaps we should sing anyway, even if there are only five or six of us.'

Numbers do not matter, although it is wonderful to be part of a big congregation singing with joy and conviction. We do not know the size of the Ephesian church, but, whether five or 50, they were to sing among themselves when they met, and also to make melody in their hearts – which sounds more like what they did on their own, humming away quietly, keeping their hearts fixed on God, whatever they were doing. When we sing, apart from offering worship to God, we are transformed (something I explore in *How Hymns Shape our Lives*). Many things can happen: we are formed more closely as the body of Christ; our faith is lifted; we are challenged by prophetic words to serve God with boldness, and be comforted in distress. I am always haunted by Etty Hillesum's courageous words about arriving at a Nazi death camp: 'We entered the camp singing' (Hillesum, 1983). She did indeed sing in her heart, helping others until her death, and moving towards renewed faith in God.

It is not possible to worship truly while the daily life is far from God; and it is not possible to bring the daily life much nearer God except by the best worship of which we are capable ... Worship includes all life and the moments spent in concentrated worship, whether 'in church' or elsewhere, are the focusing points of the sustaining and directing energy of the worshipper's life. It would strike many people as absurd to say that the cure for unemployment is to be found through worship; but it would be quite true.

This startling thought by William Temple (Temple, 1940) written during the depression of the 1930s, when unemployment was a significant problem, does not claim that worship is the solution to unemployment, but that the cure is found through worship, because worship informs the way in which we engage with the hard issues of national and international life. As we are transformed, so we help to transform the world.

The Ephesians were to live wisely. In Proverbs, the personified Wisdom invites us to enjoy her feast. Paul describes Christ as the wisdom of God (1 Corinthians 1.24). We are invited to become wise in a way that transforms our living, and, through worship, helps to transform the world. In Proverbs, all things were created through Wisdom (Proverbs 8.22–31); so the house that Wisdom has built is the created world, with pillars (in ancient cosmology) holding up the sky. To come to Wisdom's banquet is to feast on and enjoy creation, while to fear the Lord (Proverbs 9.9–10) is the beginning of wisdom.

Like Wisdom calling to all who would hear (Proverbs 8.1–5), Jesus invited everyone into communion with him and his teaching about bread; his body and blood was given not to his friends, but to the confused crowd and antagonistic religious leaders. Many refused. With hindsight, the Church reads eucharistic allusions into the dialogue that John – who has no Last Supper bread-and-wine story – set at Passover (John 6.4).

Wisdom invites us to the banquet; no qualifications are needed except simple hunger for God. The outcome will be a life of communion and commitment, of worship and wise living. William Temple continued: 'The Eucharist divorced from life loses reality; life devoid of worship loses direction and power. It is the worshipping life that can transform the world.' So, at the end of the Eucharist, we go in peace to love and serve the Lord.

To the church in Shalbourne: greetings. I hope that you are still singing and making melody in your hearts.

Sunday after Trinity,
Proper 16 (21–27 August)
Joshua 24.1–2a, 14–18; Ephesians 6.10–20; John 6.56–69

THE COST OF FOLLOWING HIM

> *Almighty and everlasting God, you are always more ready to hear than*
> *we to pray and to give more than either we desire or deserve: pour down*
> *upon us the abundance of your mercy, forgiving us those things of which*
> *our conscience is afraid and giving us those good things which we are not*
> *worthy to ask but through the merits and mediation of Jesus Christ our*
> *Lord. Amen.*
> Collect for the Twelfth Sunday after Trinity

Jesus followed his feeding of the 5000 with uncompromising teaching to the crowd and in the synagogue. Since people had experienced such amazing displays of his power, they could be expected to be receptive to his message. Instead, even some of his disciples complained that it was too difficult to accept, and turned back, as in the Synoptic Gospels had the man who found it too hard to give up his wealth.

We sell people short if we dumb down discipleship. Jesus presented both the cost and the rewards. He faced the painful consequences of losing some of his followers, even asking his closest disciples whether they would stay or go. This was a turning point in their commitment. Peter remained when others left. In the words of Ephesians, he was strong in the Lord and standing firm (albeit wobbling when Jesus was arrested), and aware of his liminal status. An exile from his former way of life, he was committed too far to go back, and had nowhere else to go to. Peter clung to his belief that Jesus had the words of eternal life and was the Holy One of God. His words: 'We have come to believe and know that you are the Holy One of God' look forward to John's explanation that he wrote his Gospel so that people might come to believe that Jesus is the Messiah (John 20.30–31).

Dietrich Bonhoeffer, the young leader of the Confessing Church that resisted the Nazis, had the opportunity to leave Germany and go overseas, but chose to stand firm in the Lord, remaining to be a pastor to the people. His famous phrase, 'When Christ calls a man, he bids him come and die,' was literally true for him; after a failed plot to kill Hitler, he was imprisoned and then hanged a few days before the Allies liberated his prison. In 1937 he wrote:

> The disciple is dragged out of his relative security into a life of absolute
> insecurity (that is in truth the absolute security and safety of the fellowship
> of Jesus) … it is nothing else than bondage to Jesus Christ alone … The life
> of discipleship is not the hero-worship we would pay to a good master, but
> obedience to the Son of God. (Bonhoeffer, 1937, 2001)

The Ephesians faced the spiritual forces of evil; Bonhoeffer's discipleship meant contesting the evil of Nazism, and it cost his life. For others, it means struggling to remain faithful, despite terrible personal circumstances. For some, this means the mundane daily grind of keeping a family together and fed; dealing with children in trouble, domestic violence, or sexual abuse; or confronting corruption in public life. For others, life is good, and discipleship relatively easy. There is no one form that discipleship takes, but there is one call to follow Christ. When the going is tough, we each have to choose whom we will serve and give our own answer to Jesus's question: 'Do you also want to go away?' For Peter, Bonhoeffer, and countless others, commitment to Christ means accepting suffering and death as a sharing in Christ's way. To sustain them and us in proclaiming the gospel of peace wherever we find ourselves, we, like the Ephesians, can wear God's armour, stand firm, and pray in the Spirit.

Jesus faced his disciples with a paradox: he had called them and wanted them with him, but he was willing to let them go, because he loved them and respected their freedom. His question is actually a liberating one which we have to answer time and again through life, as we receive opportunities to reassess our faith and to mature in our commitment. Each week, as we say the Creed, we give our answer: 'We have come to believe and know that you are the Holy One of God.' But we follow the Creed with our prayers, acknowledging that there is still much that does not make sense to us about God's world, and that we need God's help in our desire to be faithful disciples. Wonderfully, this week's Collect assures us that God will hear.

Sunday after Trinity,

Proper 17 (28 August–3 September)

Deuteronomy 4.1–2, 6–9; James 1.17–27;
Mark 7.1–8, 14–15, 21–23

REFLECTING AND ADJUSTING

> *Almighty God, who called your Church to bear witness that you were in*
> *Christ reconciling the world to yourself: help us to proclaim the good news*
> *of your love, that all who hear it may be drawn to you; through him who*
> *was lifted up on the cross, and reigns with you in the unity of the Holy*
> *Spirit, one God, now and for ever. Amen.*
>
> Collect for the Thirteenth Sunday after Trinity

Put yourself in the shoes of a Pharisee, and the Gospel reading is turned on its
head. It becomes a story of pesky peasant from a rural backwater, who draws
large crowds with dangerous teaching that undermines the faith that you, as a
religious leader, strive so hard to uphold. Worse, he could prompt civil unrest. So
no wonder you act to enforce the traditions that you have inherited.

Mark cleverly structured his Gospel so that Pharisees keep reappearing,
like annoying pedants, to challenge Jesus. In the other Gospels, Jesus has more
sympathy with the Pharisees, but in Mark he is on a collision course with their
interpretation of inherited religious traditions. We might be less worried about
the religious washing of pots and pans which bothered the Pharisees, but we
have our own disagreements over how tradition applies today.

Jesus reframed the challenge by saying that outward shows of religion are
useless if our hearts are not right. So would Jesus disagree with James's stress
that what we do is paramount? Martin Luther called James's work an epistle of
straw, having fought, at great personal cost, the theological battle to reclaim the
insight that we are saved by grace through faith, not by our actions. With the
wisdom of hindsight and in less pressured times, James is not as simplistic as
Luther may have made out.

James emphasizes our actions in the theological context that every generous
act of giving comes from God. We behave in a godly way because we have been
given such good gifts by God, and we are to be the exemplars of his love. Our
actions are a response to God's grace and an expression of it, not an attempt to
win it. James, in telling us to welcome with meekness the implanted word that
has the power to save our souls, seems to be alluding to Old Testament insights
about God's words' being written on the tablets of human hearts, so that our
response is the internal one that Jesus spoke of: that of loving obedience.

St Benedict tells us that the Lord waits for us every day, to see whether we will respond by our deeds to his holy guidance, and that we must prepare our hearts and bodies to serve him under the guidance of holy obedience. Have you ever thought, when you wake up, that the Lord is waiting for you?

The Pharisees could not be faulted for their intent to live absolutely by what they believed that God wanted of them. But they had lost their perspective, and keeping the law had become an end in itself, the only guarantee of their security with God – a security that Jesus challenged. For James, as for Jesus, godly action comes from within, and is the expression of a heart that is given to God. When James told his readers to be doers of the word and not hearers only, he said that if they only heard and did not act, they were like people who look at themselves in the mirror and forget what they see. They do not know fully who they are, and cannot respond to what they see.

When I look at myself in a mirror, I respond to what I see, perhaps combing my hair or adjusting my clothing, or perhaps just smiling at myself. We should be doing the same spiritually, looking at ourselves every so often, and making necessary adjustments in the light of what we see. If we don't check in with ourselves regularly, we will forget who we are and what we should do. We are called to be reflective people who look at ourselves in God's mirror, to see what is going on; people who welcome the word of God implanted in our heart, and act on it, knowing that it is what comes out of us that can defile us, or can express our love for God. The suffering world needs us to live as people who know that God is a generous giver of perfect gifts, and as people who are doers of that good word. How we do that is different for each of us. That we do it is an imperative for all of us.

Sunday after Trinity,
Proper 18 (4–10 September)
Isaiah 35.4–7a; James 2.1–17; Mark 7.24–37

BREAKING WITH TRADITION

> *Almighty God, whose only Son has opened for us a new and living way into your presence: give us pure hearts and steadfast wills to worship you in spirit and in truth; through Jesus Christ our Lord. Amen.*
>
> Collect for the Fourteenth Sunday after Trinity

The epistle and Gospel seem to clash head-on when heard together. Jesus rudely refuses to help a woman because of her race, whereas James insists Christians must not make any distinction on the basis of wealth, appearance, race, or education.

The context is important. Jesus, wanting privacy, had hidden in a house in Tyre, north of Galilee, where he had challenged the Pharisees' obsession with purity laws. There was no escape, however, and the tables were turned when he was challenged by a woman who had broken purity laws on several counts. She was a Gentile; her daughter had an unclean spirit, and so she was unclean from touching the girl; and she lived in Tyre, which was the Old Testament epitome of unfaithfulness and pride. The woman bowed down to Jesus. In that culture, a man bowing down showed respect, but a woman brought disgrace on the person to whom she bowed. This woman should never have been pleading in public. A father would protect and provide for his daughter, but there was no sign of her husband; so she was in an impossible situation with no option but, ignoring tradition and culture, to plead. Self-respecting rabbis did not talk to women, and it appears that Jesus was silent; so she resorted to begging him. Finally, Jesus broke with tradition, spoke to her, and even gave her public credit by commending her faith.

The woman challenged Jesus in more ways than one. Apart from challenging any sense he had that his mission was focused on Jews, she faced him with the tension between the command to care for the widow and orphan, and the tradition that rabbis did not deal with Gentile women. For us, one of the hardest things is that Jesus appeared to be offensively rude to a woman. Most Jews at this period despised Gentiles; so, shockingly to us, being called a dog was only what she expected to hear. She, however, threw Jesus's own words back at him, confronting him as he had earlier confronted the Pharisees. The woman defied Jesus to be free to do good, and not to be bound by his culture. Using the derogatory language of dogs, Jesus said, in effect: 'Let the Jews receive the word of God first; it is not fair for their scripture to be given to Gentiles.' She retorted: 'Yes, but even the dogs can eat scraps that fall off the table.'

Scholars think that in Jewish culture, dogs were not pets but roamed the streets and, to feed them you threw food out of the window. Jesus used the word 'throw'. The woman, perhaps reflecting her society's different attitude to dogs, thought differently, and assumed that dogs were domestic pets fed under the table. Essentially, she disputed Jesus's understanding of who was in the family.

This is more than a story about a girl's being healed: it is about her mother's persistence in her demand, not taking no for an answer, thus opening up Jesus's ministry on earth further than, perhaps, he had envisaged. If we believe that Jesus grew in wisdom (Luke 2.52), this is not surprising. The Collect refers to Jesus's opening up a new and living way for us, and this woman played a part in opening that way to the Gentiles. We should be astounded at her sheer persistence in demanding what she wanted. She – a foreign woman – was the only person in the Gospels to get the better of Jesus, and he respected her for it.

Jesus then took a circuitous route back to Galilee, going several miles north before he went south. On the way he met a deaf man who, unlike the woman who had to act for herself, was brought to Jesus. Jesus had no hesitation in healing him, although he sought privacy for this intimate event, and we are even told about his breathing. No more talk of throwing food to dogs: here he touched the man's ears, spat (saliva was thought to be healing), and touched his tongue. Isaiah's words were fulfilled: 'Then waters shall break forth in the wilderness, and streams in the desert.' Here was God, coming to save. The thirsty ground of the woman's life, expressed in her daring retort and echoed in our petition for steadfast wills like hers, became a spring of water.

Sunday after Trinity,
Proper 19 (11–17 September)
Isaiah 50.4–9a; James 3.1–12; Mark 8.27–38

ABIDE IN GOD; SPEAK WISELY

> *God, who in generous mercy sent the Holy Spirit upon your Church in the burning fire of your love: grant that your people may be fervent in the fellowship of the gospel that, always abiding in you, they may be found steadfast in faith and active in service; through Jesus Christ our Lord. Amen.*
>
> Collect for the Fifteenth Sunday after Trinity

The power of speech has been recognized from ancient times, and rhetoric was an early and distinguished art. These readings are about speech.

Isaiah recognized the power of the tongue of the teacher when used for good, and, significantly, linked this with the hearing of the teacher whose ear is attuned to listen to, and heart inclined to obey God. We do not always make that link if we assume that the priority of a teacher is to speak and impart knowledge rather than to listen and to live well. Perhaps mindful of the demands on the teacher and the consequences of faithful listening, speaking, and acting, James counsels against aspiration to become a teacher in the Christian community. He wrote in the context of the rabbi's having an honoured place in Jewish culture, and his warning echoes Jesus's accusations of the Pharisees and Scribes for failing to live up to their own teaching. To be a teacher is to accept demands on our way of living that may never be seen by others. James provided his own sermon illustrations, but, if we want contemporary ones, there are the dangers of emailing or tweeting before we think. Instant reactions can be regretted; we are called to reflective living.

This is the mid-point of Mark's Gospel. Thus far, questions of Jesus's identity have recurred as people have tried to make sense of him. Now Jesus asks direct questions culminating, unavoidably, in: 'Who do you say that I am?' The disciples could not prevaricate: they had seen and heard enough to draw conclusions; to put their thoughts into words, and articulate what they had seen, heard, and believed. Were their hearts, like Isaiah's, inclined to God? Peter's answer is the hinge on which Mark's Gospel turns. Like a seesaw, what has been going up now starts to come down. As soon as Peter uttered the word 'Messiah', Jesus began to redefine Messiahship by putting 'suffering and death' in the same sentence with it, something that Peter proved he could not yet do. Instead, his response was in character with his passionate, rugged love for Jesus which wanted to shield him from suffering.

Jesus recognized a resurgence of demonic activity, even at this great moment of Peter's confession. From the beginning of Mark's Gospel (1.24–25), demons were quicker than the disciples to recognize Jesus, and were persistently creedally correct in their words. That was not enough, however. It is one thing to say that Jesus is the Holy One of God; it is another to live by that faith. For the demons, recognizing Jesus led them to fear (Mark 4.9–12). Now Peter's passion led his tongue to run away with him, potentially diverting Jesus from God's way. Perhaps James had him in mind when writing as he did in the epistle.

For Isaiah, the outcome of listening to God with his heart, not just his ear, was empowerment to endure abuse and insult, being shielded from disgrace by God's protection. That is what Peter needed. This week, we pray about the burning fire of God's love – asking to abide in Christ, to be fervent in the fellowship of the gospel, steadfast in faith, and active in service. Peter's fervour was there, but his steadfastness of faith was, as yet, shaky. He was in danger of not abiding in Christ, and, unlike Isaiah, not trusting that God would not let him be disgraced.

Looking forward, although Peter's faith did falter under severe pressure (Mark 14.66–72) so that, in Isaiah's words, he turned backwards, that disaster was not the end; he had the courage to turn around and keep going. Mark records that Jesus knew his friend's love well enough to send a special message to him after his resurrection (Mark 16.6), and in Luke and John, Jesus had private post-resurrection encounters with Peter. Perhaps only then did Peter realize that following Jesus meant taking up the cross without shame. The outcome was that Peter gained the tongue of a teacher, and spoke boldly of Jesus's suffering, death, and resurrection (Acts 2.36), and led the Church towards world-changing insights (Acts 11.1–18). Our prayer for that same fervency and steadfastness in service in our day is essentially to be people who abide in God, and speak wisely, even under pressure.

Sunday after Trinity,

Proper 20 (18–24 September)

Jeremiah 11.18–20; James 3.13–4.3, 7–8a; Mark 9.30–37

PRAYER BORN OF LONELINESS

> *O Lord, we beseech you mercifully to hear the prayers of your people who call upon you; and grant that they may both perceive and know what things they ought to do, and also may have grace and power faithfully to fulfil them; through Jesus Christ our Lord. Amen.*

Collect for the Sixteenth Sunday after Trinity

The journey through Galilee that Mark describes sounds a fiercely lonely one for Jesus. It was about 30 miles, and took a couple of days. Jesus was avoiding crowds, so that he could focus on getting the disciples to understand his Messiahship, which they had so recently acclaimed, before Peter had tried to silence him on its implications. It can be easier to talk about hard things when walking side by side rather than sitting looking at each other, but the disciples could not comprehend what Jesus said, and, sadly, were afraid to ask. Sometimes, it is easier not to ask questions than risk hearing answers that we fear.

Anyone who has felt unheard by someone to whom they looked for support in distress will have an insight into how isolated Jesus must have felt. He needed his closest friends to listen, receive what he had to say and keep company with him. But, like Job's comforters, they could not cope. There was no succour for him, only an intensification of the loneliness. Worse, not only were the disciples not listening to Jesus: they were having side conversations, indeed arguments, to which he was not privy, as they walked in twos and threes along the road. While he spoke of his coming suffering, death, and resurrection, in ironic and terrible contrast, they were arguing about who was the greatest. Perhaps they were trading experiences: 'I was the first to follow Jesus,' 'I healed a sick person when we went on mission,' 'Yes, but I saw Jesus transfigured.'

So, once in the house from which there was no escape, he challenged them. He sat down, thereby increasing the gravitas of the moment, as he assumed the position of a rabbi when teaching, and, having failed to get them to understand his words, resorted to a visual aid, and took a child, perhaps one of the disciples' children, and placed him or her centre stage. In a culture where children were insignificant, Jesus's action and teaching that he and, more astonishingly, God came to the disciples through children was barely imaginable.

On 14 August, the Church remembers Maximilian Kolbe, the Polish priest killed in Auschwitz, after ten prisoners were chosen randomly to die in revenge for what was wrongly thought to be an escape. One man cried: 'My wife, my children! I will never see them again,' and immediately Kolbe stepped forward to take his place, saying: 'I am a priest; he has a wife and children.' In the starvation cell, he celebrated mass daily, and, two weeks later, when his companions had died, and the cell was needed for more condemned prisoners, he was given a lethal injection.

The prisoner whom he had saved returned home at the end of the war, and was reunited with his wife, but, tragically, his sons had been killed. Every 14 August for five decades, he returned to Auschwitz to honour Kolbe. He said that he felt remorse for effectively signing Kolbe's death warrant, but came to realize that a man like Kolbe could not have done otherwise, and, as a priest, wanted to help the men condemned to starve to death to maintain hope.

One year on 14 August I focused the prayers at evensong around his story, and afterwards, a visitor reflected on Kolbe's continuing influence. He exemplified James's exhortation to show by our good lives that our works are done with gentleness born of wisdom, even when, like Jeremiah, he was led as a gentle lamb to the slaughter. Kolbe's instinctive reaction to value that prisoner's unknown wife and children was the fruit of a lifetime of perceiving and knowing what he ought to do. By embodying Jesus's teaching, he publicly reversed the 'values' of the Nazis. A memorial tablet by the cell bears continuing witness to his action.

The playwright Christopher Fry said, 'No man is free who will not dare to pursue the questions of his own loneliness. It is through them that he lives.' Jesus and Kolbe had to go on alone, without the support of their closest friends. In the Collect, we predicate our prayer on the assurance that God hears our prayer, including the prayer of our loneliness, and will enable us to embody the wisdom from above in our lives, so that we, like Kolbe, are full of good fruits.

Sunday after Trinity,
Proper 21 (25 September–1 October)
Numbers 11.4–6, 10–16, 24–29; James 5.13–50;
Mark 9.38–50

MOVING IN MYSTERIOUS WAYS

Almighty God, you have made us for yourself, and our hearts are restless till they find their rest in you: pour your love into our hearts and draw us to yourself, and so bring us at last to your heavenly city, where we shall see you face to face; through Jesus Christ our Lord. Amen.

Collect for the Seventeenth Sunday after Trinity

'Who is one of us?' was a troubling question for the Early Church, and perhaps the apostles remembered the incident in the Gospel reading when deciding whether the Holy Spirit could have been given to Gentile as well as Jewish Christians (Acts 11.1–18). Neither Moses nor Jesus stopped someone who was not 'following us' from emulating his actions if it extended God's blessing, despite the discomfort to people who wanted clear boundaries between insiders and outsiders.

Like it or not, among the people he was leading to freedom Moses had a rabble, or, more politely, 'a mixed crowd' (Exodus 12.38). Problematically, their selective memory of Egypt focused on cucumbers and garlic rather than slavery and oppression. Their complaints about the monotonous diet escalated, and set everyone wailing. If we read aloud Moses's torrent of complaint, we get the full impact of his exasperation with them, and with God who had landed him in this mess. Borrowing St Augustine's words in the Collect, Moses's heart was restless, and needed to find its rest in God.

God's response was not instant food to satisfy the people's craving, but shared responsibility to help Moses carry the burden. As long as Moses was worn down by the people's complaints, he could not rest in God. It was a higher priority to sort out the leader than to sort out the people. Quails would follow, and gluttony would be the death of people (Numbers 11.18–20, 31–34), but the answer to Moses's prayer came in the form of 70 elders who experienced, just once, something of God's spirit. It is not clear how they relieved the pressure on Moses or why two remained in the camp yet shared the blessing, only that this was God's answer to Moses's need. Perhaps they were the able men chosen a year earlier to help Moses judge disputes (Exodus 18.13–26), who needed to be reminded of this role? Perhaps Moses was not good at sharing leadership, and this demonstration of God's power was God's reminder that he was not alone? We do not know. Like the manna that bemused the people and yet fed them, God made unlikely provision in order to draw Moses close.

Jesus was not averse to using figures of speech to grab attention. So, graphically, he announced that it was better to cut off a limb than miss out on life, even though, under the law's holiness code (Leviticus 21.16–21), any physical imperfection disqualified a priest from presenting an offering; so to cut off a limb was to put oneself outside the cultic system. Jesus's new teaching was disturbing; people who had previously been excluded were now 'one of us'.

Like others, I marvelled at the Paralympics when they were in London. Literally, rather than metaphorically, being limbless need not be a bar to full participation in life. How things have changed from my time in town-planning in the 1970s when, trying to improve access to buildings, we had to plead – usually unsuccessfully – for the goodwill of developers to make a small change to the design to remove a step or provide a handrail. Years of negotiation and advising the Government followed in order to change the legislation to require access provision. For me, this often discouraging work, which sometimes felt like a journey through the wilderness, was motivated by God's purposes to deliver people from oppression and to give life in its fullness. Using the language of the Gospel, if being minus a foot, eye, or hand was no bar to entering the Kingdom of God, then I could try to stop its being a bar to entering a building. The Paralympics demonstrate that the past is now a foreign country; that early work has paid off. But with the excitement over, we have to ensure there is no regression – no going back to oppression.

We never know how God can use us to liberate others. I never dreamed of an accessible Olympic stadium when trying to negotiate access to a corner shop. We are not told what the 70 thought when they were charged with sharing Moses's responsibilities – probably unenthusiastic, given the rabble – or how the elders in the epistle felt when asked to pray for the sick for the first time. However discouraging the situation and however mundane the task, in Christ we are all called to be agents of God's liberating love in our daily lives and work.

Sunday after Trinity,
Proper 22 (2–8 October)
Genesis 2.18–24; Hebrews 1.1–4, 2.5–12; Mark 10.2–16

HARDEN NOT YOUR HEARTS

Almighty and everlasting God, increase in us your gift of faith that, forsaking what lies behind and reaching out to that which is before, we may run the way of your commandments and win the crown of everlasting joy; through Jesus Christ our Lord. Amen.

Collect for the Eighteenth Sunday after Trinity

The picture that is painted in Genesis is glorious. God's answer to man's loneliness (the first thing to be declared 'not good' after a litany of everything being good or very good) was a riotous burst of creativity. The way the story is told invites us to imagine much laughter and reciprocal delight as God created and man named things. Maybe, as this oral story was passed on through the generations, it was embellished with more and more exotic creatures and names, being pared back to basics when written down. Finally, there was woman. In a leap typical of Hebrew thought, the story was used to explain why husband and wife become one flesh. In this bigger story of God's creativity and new life, a man leaves the security of his known relationship with his parents, and clings to his wife, moving with her into an unknown future.

Marriage is always an adventure; that is why vows are made, because they provide the safe boundaries within which married life can be created. Couples who marry in Durham Cathedral stand in a place where, through the centuries, people have made their vows. Sometimes, I remind them and their guests that the Benedictine vows that the monks made as the framework for their new monastic life – stability, obedience, and conversion of life – are equally applicable as the framework for married life. Is it too much to say that they are implied in Genesis? Conversion of life is in the leaving, stability in the clinging, and there is mutual obedience, since all this is in the sight of God.

By the time of Jesus, the original understanding of the relationship between husband and wife was hedged about with legislation on divorce. When challenged on this (and we should remember that Jesus was responding to a test from the Pharisees designed to trip him up, not an appeal for pastoral guidance), Jesus immediately shifted the focus back from divorce to marriage, reiterated the original vision, and told them to make sure that they were not the cause of its being undermined. He did not directly answer the question about the legality of divorce, but threw it back at his hearers with a brief commentary on why divorce had been instituted.

Jesus located the reason for the failure of the original understanding of marriage in people's hardness of heart, something that God abhors time and again in the biblical story because it is so destructive of God's relationship with his people. Thus, harking back to disastrous events recorded in Exodus 17.7, in Psalm 95 we hear God's plea: 'Harden not your hearts, as at Meribah, as on the day at Massah in the wilderness when your ancestors tested me and put me to the proof, though they had seen my works.'

Hardness of heart is the polar opposite of creativity: it precludes growth or newness, and spells death to growth in relationships. In Benedictine terms, it leaves no room for conversion of life, while stability degenerates into stagnation, and obedience stagnates into ungracious compliance. Hardness of heart is not unconnected to this week's prayer to be able to forsake what is behind us and reach out to what is before us. The Collect borrows Benedict's insight, in the Prologue to his Rule, that as we progress in this way of life and of faith, we shall run in the path of God's commandments, our hearts overflowing with the inexpressible delights of love.

This overjoyed running in the path of God's commandments may sound strange to people who do not understand that God's commandments lead to life in all its fullness. The delight comes as we run, not only when we have completed the journey and won the crown of joy. Life lived in the way of God's commandments is to be enjoyed.

Hebrews describes Jesus as the pioneer of our salvation, who shared our humanity and suffering. We are encouraged to run with perseverance, looking to Jesus, the pioneer and perfecter of our faith (12.1–2). He ran the path of God's commandments and, in an astonishing phrase, learned obedience through what he suffered (5.8). There was no hardness of heart there, and, when we too run in God's paths, he is the one leading the way, to whom we reach out in faith.

Sunday after Trinity,
Proper 23 (9–15 October)
Amos 5.6–7, 10–15; Hebrews 4.12–16; Mark 10.17–31

HARD WORDS ABOUT CORRUPTION

O God, forasmuch as without you we are not able to please you; mercifully grant that your Holy Spirit may in all things direct and rule our hearts; through Jesus Christ our Lord. Amen.

Collect for the Nineteenth Sunday after Trinity

Two strong imperatives resound from the readings: 'seek' and 'go'. Discipleship is about seeking God and taking action, which, given our waywardness, throws us into the petition of the Collect for the Holy Spirit to direct and rule our hearts.

Jesus set out 'on a journey', which was Mark's way of referring to his journey to suffering and death. Immediately, his path crossed with a man who was seeking, and who asked Jesus a big question. Jesus gave him a big answer, which cut through the fluff to the heart of discipleship for an earnest, faithful Jew. The temptation to make it easy for this man, whom Jesus instinctively loved and might have wanted with him in these last difficult days, could have been considerable.

Jesus focused on the commandments about behaviour with others. Rather than condemn what the man had, Jesus pointed out and offered what he lacked – freedom from the hold that money had over him. Our problem is the love of money, not money itself (1 Timothy 6.10; Hebrews 13.5). Tantalizingly, we never know how the man responded in the long run: in his shock, he went away, grieving at the implications, but discipleship is a process, and being shocked may be a necessary stage on the journey.

Interestingly, Jesus inserted 'do not defraud' into what was otherwise an extract from the Ten Commandments. Defrauding people is condemned in Leviticus 6.2 and 19.13, and reading around those verses sheds piercing light on the practical implications, then and now. The peasant Amos was given a hard message for wealthy and corrupt people in his day. His words looked ahead to the fall of Israel, connecting it with the nation's unjust living, which rendered the life of the poor intolerable. Today's Psalm (22.1–15) vividly expresses the resulting suffering. From the king down (1 Kings 21, with Deuteronomy 19.4), people defrauded and exploited the poor.

We can say glibly that, as a nation or as individuals, we do not defraud people by moving boundary markers or taking excessive levies of produce (grain in an agricultural economy, but many other things for us today). But what about tax avoidance: when does that become tax-evasion by individuals on our tax returns, or by corporations that can afford large numbers of staff dedicated to finding loopholes? What about the way we make our neighbours' lives difficult through the way we live and relate to them? What is lawful might not equate with what is ethical. Jesus called the man to go beyond keeping the law into doing good.

The report on the Hillsborough Stadium disaster, recently published when I wrote this, forces us to hear Amos's words afresh: 'Ah, you who turn justice to wormwood and bring righteousness to the ground. They hate the one who reproves in the gate [where justice was dispensed] and they abhor the one who speaks the truth.' South Yorkshire police may have something to answer for, as may those involved in banking scandals, but, like the man who met Jesus, we may be shocked if we dare to examine how we, too, can defraud others. This is difficult territory; so no wonder the disciples were perplexed. Jesus reassured Peter that, in God's economy, complex equations did add up, but perhaps not as expected: they had to subtract and divide, then add and multiply; to give away in order to receive.

The Collect and epistle remind us that we cannot do this without the Holy Spirit's direction and rule of our hearts: the living and active word of God must pierce our lives to lay bare before God, as Jesus laid bare for the man, the thoughts and intentions of the heart. Mercifully, when facing what is exposed, we have a great high priest to whom we can turn for grace to help in our need. The readings point us to eternal life's being rooted in life now, not beginning at death. Jesus and Amos made connections with the way we live. The hard words of judgement on corruption in its many manifestations sit alongside the hope that God's graciousness will abound if we seek the Lord and live; if we go to take action.

This applies to us as individuals, and also to us as nations that tolerate corporate misdemeanour and corruption. Christian Aid's campaign against tax avoidance is one place to start, along with a ruthless audit of our own lives, and attention to how we vote for police commissioners.

Sunday after Trinity,
Proper 24 (16–22 October)
Isaiah 53.4–12; Hebrews 5.1–10; Mark 10.35–45

THE DISCIPLES' BLUNDER REDEEMED

God, the giver of life, whose Holy Spirit wells up within your Church: by the Spirit's gifts equip us to live the gospel of Christ and make us eager to do your will, that we may share with the whole creation the joys of eternal life; through Jesus Christ our Lord. Amen.

Collect for the Twentieth Sunday after Trinity

Mark never spares the disciples' blushes. Whereas the other Gospel-writers tend to soft-pedal when describing their failures and muddles, Mark has no such sensitivities. This week's Gospel reading jars with the other two readings, which speak of the suffering of God's servant, and with this whole middle section of Mark's Gospel (8.27–10.45) which began with Jesus's first prediction of his suffering and ends with his emphasis that his way involves being a servant, indeed a slave, of all people.

This middle section see-saws constantly between Jesus's words about suffering, service, and welcoming him in a child, and the disciples' arguments about greatness, and their blundering attempts to exclude someone who acted as Jesus did. The juxtaposition is painfully uncomfortable. Jesus had tried to settle the debate about greatness by putting a child in front of the disciples as their example (Mark 9.33–37); James and John's request, however, shows that the debate was still going on behind his back. The lectionary omits Jesus's third description of his coming death and the response of amazement and fear that it elicited; once again, the disciples failed to support Jesus as he faced impending suffering.

Matthew's version of the story has James and John's mother asking about seats in glory on their behalf, but in Mark these 'sons of thunder' (3.17) ask for themselves, thereby indicating how well Jesus knew them when giving them that nickname. They pushed their luck, wanting a guaranteed answer before they revealed the question, and can hardly have been surprised when Jesus recast the question, and the others were furious with them. In answering James and John, Jesus reversed all the norms of greatness. The same thing happens in the passage from Isaiah, part of a Servant Song, which we hear in a different context from its usual one on Good Friday. Justice is perverted, and the innocent servant suffers and is cut off from the land of the living. Far from the throne in glory that the brothers want, his grave is with the wicked. Worse, it appears that God is complicit in this. But then comes the great reversal: the righteous one will make many righteous, and be allotted a portion with the great. Why? Because he poured himself out to death, and made intercession for the transgressors.

Hebrews picks up this theme with another unimaginable turnaround. Jesus offered loud cries and tears to the one who could save him from death, and he was heard. Yet the recipients of the letter knew that he died. Could both be true? Then comes the answering paradox: he learned obedience through what he suffered. We know that is very hard as everything in us rebels against suffering, especially unjust suffering.

Jesus became the source of eternal salvation for all who obey him – that obedience word again – being designated by God a high priest for ever, thus taking the thought back to the beginning of the reading. We obey the one who learned obedience.

A little phrase at the beginning of the epistle helps to link all this together: 'He is able to deal gently with the ignorant and wayward.' Unlike wilful sin, the Bible treats ignorance and waywardness with mercy. Jesus's response to the disciples suggests that he recognized, probably wearily, that they were still ignorant rather than rebellious or disobedient. His deconstruction of the only models of leadership they knew was too radical and too new. This theme of ignorance's being met kindly underlies the post-communion prayer for the twentieth Sunday after Trinity:

> God our Father, whose Son, the light unfailing, has come from heaven to deliver the world from the darkness of ignorance: let these holy mysteries open the eyes of our understanding that we may know the way of life, and walk in it without stumbling.

Put alongside the vivid imagery of the Collect, as the Holy Spirit wells up within the Church, the fact that Mark paints a severe picture of James, John, and the other disciples becomes a consolation. Despite their and our ignorance and waywardness, the Holy Spirit's welling up in our midst can turn our ignorance into eagerness to do God's will, and to share the joys of eternal life – the very thing that James and John learned that they could not monopolize.

Sunday after Trinity,
Proper 25 (23–29 October)
Jeremiah 31.7–9; Hebrews 7.23–28; Mark 10.46–52

THE NOISE OF HEAVEN AND EARTH

> *Grant, we beseech you, merciful Lord, to your faithful people pardon and peace, that they may be cleansed from all their sins and serve you with a quiet mind; through Jesus Christ our Lord. Amen.*

> *Blessed Lord, who caused all holy Scriptures to be written for our learning: help us to hear them, to read, mark, learn and inwardly digest them that, through patience, and the comfort of your holy word, we may embrace and for ever hold fast the hope of everlasting life, which you have given us in our Saviour Jesus Christ. Amen.*
>
> Collect for the Last Sunday after Trinity

There is lots of noise in this week's readings. In Jeremiah there is singing and shouting and weeping and in Mark there is so much shouting that the people around Jesus found it all too much and tried to silence Bartimaeus who, instead of being dissuaded, simply upped the volume. God's saving works call for jubilation not polite silence.

The picture in Jeremiah of the people of God shouting among the nations is, in many ways, more like something from Second Isaiah than the often morose Jeremiah. The words follow immediately from the promise of God's unfailing love for a people who have survived sword and exile. Those weary and bruised people are encouraged to imagine themselves with tambourines and merry dances, as farmers who stay in one place long enough to enjoy the harvest and, ultimately, as pilgrims fulfilling their dream of again going to Jerusalem. It would be hard for anyone who had seen Jerusalem destroyed by the Babylonians, probably just before Jeremiah spoke these words, to envisage shouting and singing for joy. The acknowledgement that they will come with weeping and consolations recognizes this difficult leap of faith and is a compassionate response by God to the trauma of his people. It reminds us that tears are an acceptable offering to God as so many sad memories have to be assimilated into this new situation of deliverance.

The reason given for this deliverance is simply that God has become father to his people. This is all of God's gracious goodness and the reach is world-wide – God will bring people from the farthest parts of the known world (we know that some were in Babylon, far away to the east, and some in Egypt to the south), and God will bring not just those who can walk unaided but those who need help all the way, including some who need to stop en route to give birth.

The reference to the blind being brought to salvation links us to the story in Mark's Gospel of blind Bartimaeus. This story is a bridging point in Mark's narrative. In previous encounters while Jesus was on his way to Jerusalem he had sought privacy for, and silence rather than publicity after, his miracles. There is no sign of such reticence this time. Instead, after he had healed Bartimaeus, who is named and thus appears to have been known to the Early Church, Jesus does not restrain him. Bartimaeus joins the group with Jesus and it is hard to imagine him not talking 19 to the dozen about what had happened to him. Why this change in approach to proclaiming who Jesus is and what he has done? Perhaps because Mark is making a link with the next event he records, the entry into Jerusalem, which is full of hullabaloo as people shout their hosannas and, like Bartimaeus, name Jesus as the Son of David, the one bringing in the kingdom. So this healing at the end of his journey to Jerusalem, where Jesus knows he will suffer and die, is also the opening paragraph of the rest of the story as events hurtle towards their tragic climax.

Jesus's question to Bartimaeus is a telling one. Surely it was obvious what Bartimaeus wanted: he was blind, he was yelling for mercy from someone to whom he ascribed a description applicable to God's Messiah, 'Son of David'. What more did Jesus need to know? But Jesus asked and, in doing so, put his disciples James and John on the spot since they had just badly bungled the answer to the same question (Mark 10.36). Whereas they displayed raw ambition for reward, Jesus elicited from Bartimaeus an answer about both his immediate physical need and his spiritual yearning. Bartimaeus acted on this yearning in his immediate following of Jesus on the way, a word Mark uses elsewhere to indicate Jesus's way of the cross, thus making another link to the looming events in Jerusalem. Bartimaeus had already displayed spiritual insight: told it was Jesus of Nazareth walking past, he ignored this naming of Jesus in human terms and instead named him in Messianic terms. Then, like the first disciples by the Sea of Galilee (Mark 1.16–20) in response to the call of Jesus he left his possessions – his cloak – and followed Jesus.

Mercy often sounds a calm and gentle word and concept. Sometimes the only appropriate response is noisy celebration.

All Saints' Day

Wisdom 3.1–9 or Isaiah 25.6–9; Revelation 21.1–6a;
John 11.32–44

SAFE IN THE HAND OF GOD

*Almighty God, you have knit together your elect in one communion and
fellowship in the mystical body of your Son Christ our Lord: grant us grace
so to follow your blessed saints in all virtuous and godly living that we may
come to those inexpressible joys that you have prepared for those who truly
love you; through Jesus Christ our Lord. Amen.*

The readings on All Saints' Day point us to a deep, underlying confidence in
God that is not deflected by hardship and sustains people through whatever life
throws at them. Wisdom assures us that 'the souls of the righteous are in the hand
of God'. That is the sort of confidence which enabled the psalmist to pray, 'Into
your hand I commit my spirit; you have redeemed me, O Lord, faithful God.'
'My soul clings to you; your right hand upholds me' (Psalms 31.5, 63.8). What
safer place could there be?

However, that does not mean the saints were or are immune to troubles;
indeed Wisdom says foolish people thought the death of saints to be a disaster
and punishment by God. Saints knew the taunt, 'If there is a God, why doesn't
he save you?' But the fools were wrong: saints were not being punished but
tested. God tried them in the same way that gold is tried and refined of impurity
in a furnace. In so doing, God found them worthy of himself: they were like pure
gold. Being tested and purified does not mean we are not safe in God's hands.

Isaiah envisages a day when the Lord will wipe tears from all faces and take
away the disgrace of his people. That presupposes the Lord's people experience
situations which make them weep or humiliate them. Revelation picks up this
theme when, amid the vision of the new heaven and the new earth, we hear
the extraordinary truth that God's home is among mortals, that God himself
will wipe away every tear, that death, mourning and crying will be no more.
Until then there are indeed tears, for we live in a world where there is pain and
suffering. This is the world into which God came to share our human experience.
The encounter between Jesus and Mary after Lazarus's death may appear to be
an unusual reading for All Saints' Day yet it touches the depth of human grief
as even our Lord shed tears that needed to be wiped. Through the tears he led
Mary and Martha into the experience of God's bringing life out of death, the
experience to which saints through the ages have borne witness.

Our vocation as Christians includes making tangible in the world what
we claim is present among us: that the home of God is among mortals. Saints

are people who, knowing these are trustworthy words, can risk going to places where there are tears and humiliation proclaiming by their presence the presence of God to bring life and transformation. So when Mother Teresa first went to India she gambled everything on the call to go to the slums, risking that she would die of the diseases alongside the street people, that she would be raped or robbed, that her life would make no difference whatsoever, that she might miss a far more 'productive' vocation elsewhere. I once heard Joan Chittister, who led her Benedictine religious community into deep engagement with the poverty and fear in its Pennsylvanian neighbourhood, say that we should take our smallness lightly but take our presence seriously. Saints do that in everyday ways. God's presence shines through the smallness of mums at school gates, housebound people who pray for those they watch go past, businessmen who act ethically.

In the twelfth century, William of St Thierry said that the love of truth drives us from the human world to God and the truth of love sends us from God back to the human world. It is two-way traffic because we live in the now and the not yet of God's Kingdom, sustained by the visions of Revelation and of Isaiah, held in the hand of God, serving our Lord who wept with a friend in her grief. Saints are like people with bifocal vision, seeing heaven on earth, and as a result their lives are fortified by the hope of sharing the worship in heaven while they shed glimpses of heavenly glory around them on earth. They become increasingly transparent: people can see God through them. So we pray to follow their examples of godly and virtuous living.

Fourth Sunday before Advent

Deuteronomy 6.1–9; Hebrews 9.11–14; Mark 12.28–34

LOVE – WITH HEART, SOUL, MIND, AND STRENGTH

Almighty and eternal God, you have kindled the flame of love in the hearts of the saints: grant to us the same faith and power of love, that, as we rejoice in their triumphs, we may be sustained by their example and fellowship; through Jesus Christ our Lord. Amen.

The film *Of Gods and Men* tells the true story of a small group of Trappist monks in Tibhirine, Algeria. We see them living and working alongside their Muslim neighbours, and the elderly Brother Luc providing medical care. The Algerian Civil War intervenes in their lives; there are tense moments when the monastic compound is invaded by extremist militia on Christmas Eve, and the monks bravely refuse to give in to demands to hand over their medical supplies because they are needed by the local people. Ultimately, in March 1996, in a night raid, seven Brothers are kidnapped, and the film ends with their trudging, with their captors, through the snow. Their beheaded bodies were eventually found.

The film is a powerful portrayal of the faithful love of God and neighbour. The struggles are shown honestly and sensitively: we see the monks discussing the hard question whether to stay or to leave while there is time: what do their Benedictine vows of stability, obedience, and conversion of life look like, when they are faced with life and death?

Watching the film again recently, I was struck afresh by the portrayal of the monks' persistent recourse to the chapel for prayer in the midst of life. As we say at the Benedictine Weeks in Durham Cathedral, prayer is not the holy bit that interrupts the rest of life: life is an integrated whole, in which our love of God is expressed in times of focused prayer, in our work, our relaxation, and our sleep. Twice in this week's readings we hear the commandment: 'You shall love the Lord your God with all your heart, with all your soul, and with all your might.' Jesus adds the exhortation to love God: 'with all your mind'.

How do we love God with our mind? When I began to study theology, the lecturer exhorted us to pursue the intellectual love of God. Later, when I trained people for ordination, I remember encouraging new students not to fear the effect of theological study on their faith. If (as we do) we worship the God revealed in scripture, whose ways with the world are so wonderful, surely study – not just of theology – is an appropriate response and a way to know God more closely and lovingly? All study can be theological, and expand our world, not contract it.

November is a time when the Church does much remembering. We remember all the saints and all the faithful departed (All Souls); as a nation, we remember 5 November and the deliverance of our seventeenth-century forebears – a deliverance for them as momentous as any deliverance in the wars that we will recall on Remembrance Sunday. The Collect this week reminds us of the saints whom we remember: those faithful, passionate, sometimes awkward people who loved God with all their hearts, souls, minds, and strength. We pray to have the same faith and power of love; to be sustained by their example and fellowship. They were just as varied a bunch of people as we are today, loving God in millions of different ways, and setting us millions of examples to follow.

Jesus's response to the scribe who asked him about the first commandment was very different from his response to other people who questioned him during that tense final week of his life. This man must have caught Jesus's attention, because, far from being abrasive with him, he gave him a full answer, and noted the wisdom of his reply. I like to think that Jesus's response to the monks of Tibhirine would be the same, seeing in their faithful daily service a true example of loving God with one's heart, soul, mind, and strength, and loving one's neighbour as oneself. Perhaps this helps to explain Jesus's slightly enigmatic, indeed, shocking final words to the scribe: 'You are not far from the Kingdom of God.' He recognized a kindred Jew genuinely pursuing and loving God.

Mark began his Gospel with Jesus's proclaiming that the Kingdom of God had come near; now, near the end, a faithful Jew was close to the radical experience of the Kingdom of God that Jesus had brought, just as those monks brought the presence of God's Kingdom amid the violence of civil war.

Third Sunday before Advent,
Remembrance Sunday
Jonah 3.1–5, 10; Hebrews 9.24–28; Mark 1.14–20

ALLOW FOR GOD'S DISRUPTION

Almighty Father, whose will is to restore all things in your beloved Son, the King of all: govern the hearts and minds of those in authority, and bring the families of the nations, divided and torn apart by the ravages of sin, to be subject to his just and gentle rule; who is alive and reigns with you, in the unity of the Holy Spirit, one God, now and for ever. Amen.

Today's readings make no special concessions to Remembrance Sunday, which is appropriate, because war makes no special concessions to our lives. We have to make theological sense of the unlikely juxtapositions. We hear about people called to follow God. Simon, Andrew, James, and John responded almost instantly, leaving Zebedee to watch his labour force in the family business get up and leave him to it. Those four men were setting off on a life-changing adventure that would end with their cruel deaths.

On the other hand, Jonah, in the rollicking story that bears his name (and which it is worth reading in its entirety), responded completely differently. We hear him set off when called, but there is a very different back story, which a map elucidates. When God had previously sent him to Nineveh, Jonah had set off in the opposite direction entirely – going west to Spain (Tarshish), instead of east to Assyria. He could hardly have been more disobedient if he had tried. A fierce storm at sea and a brief encounter with the inside of a large fish did the trick. So, when God called again, off he went – this time in the right direction. He complained furiously, however, when God showed mercy to the city as a result of his preaching. Most people would be thrilled that their preaching had such an instant effect (even the animals repented!); but not Jonah. He would have prayed through gritted teeth the petition in the Collect about divided nations' being subject to God's just and gentle rule.

What were those men thinking, as they set out on these new directions in life under God? They had dreams that they submitted, more or less readily, to a new direction from God. What did men and women in the armed services think when war forced new directions on their lives? We remember them before God with readings about people whose lives were turned upside down. We might ask ourselves afresh how we would respond, were our lives similarly disrupted. Would we dare to be as ready as Peter, Andrew, James, and John to respond, or, like Jonah, be the ultimate reluctant conscript? This involves our control of our destinies, as well as more domestic questions about the effect on our families.

On Remembrance Sunday, we remember that the call to serve in war is a hard call, to which some respond with their lives. However wrong the injustice that war is intended to put right, the suffering of war remains antithetical to the fullness of life that God offers his world in love, and to God's just and gentle rule offered to all the families of the nations. At the end of the Remembrance Day service in Durham Cathedral, the congregation is challenged to a commitment to serve God in God's world today. This hymn, written when an awards ceremony and service for people training for ordination fell on Remembrance Day, is a reminder that not all injustices can be solved by war, and that all of us are called to catch the vision of the world as it might be under God's just and gentle rule. We are called to emulate the readiness of the disciples to serve God, wherever there are people whose lives are diminished by suffering and sin.

Once we had dreams, dreams of a new beginning,
When we had fought the war to end all war,
A world of peace, where people live in freedom,
A world where justice reigns for evermore.
And yet, and yet, each year as we remember
We know too well how subtly dreams can fade.

In this our world where peace is often fragile,
Where war and hatred grip, where children die,
Too easily our hearts are dulled to suffering,
Our ears are deafened to the hopeless cry;
We fail to grasp the call to be peace-makers,
We act in fear and let the vision fade.

Still we need dreams: O God, make us your dreamers,
Inflame our passion for a world made whole,
A world where love extends to all a welcome,
Where justice, like a powerful stream, will roll.
Come, Prince of Peace, our fading hope rekindle,
'Your kingdom come' we pray, let peace be made.
Copyright © 2000 Rosalind Brown. Tune: Finlandia

Second Sunday before Advent

Daniel 12.1–3; Hebrews 10.11–14 [15–18], 19–25;
Mark 13.1–8

NOT MADE WITH HANDS

Heavenly Father, whose blessed Son was revealed to destroy the works of the devil and to make us the children of God and heirs of eternal life: grant that we, having this hope, may purify ourselves even as he is pure; that when he shall appear in power and great glory we may be made like him in his eternal and glorious kingdom; where he is alive and reigns with you, in the unity of the Holy Spirit, one God, now and for ever. Amen.

In what or in whom do we trust? The pre-Advent readings nudge us nearer and nearer to its sobering themes of coming judgement and salvation. Daniel's sombre vision of anguish and deliverance, possibly recorded during the violent Maccabean period, encapsulates this. Amid alarm, there is hope of vindication.

The Collect, too, steers our thoughts resolutely towards cataclysmic events preceding the coming of God's Kingdom, to which Mark's Gospel has pointed from its opening verses. A natural response is to seek security.

As Jesus left the Temple, someone commented about its large stones and expansive buildings. We sense awe and approval; for Herod's Temple was indeed big and beautiful, representing God's presence among the people. Jesus did not condemn its scale, but simply stated that it would be demolished – something as unthinkable as predicting the destruction of the Twin Towers. The disciples wanted to know more, but Jesus neither explained nor answered their questions. Instead, he warned them not to be led astray by others, or to despair at alarming events. His agenda was different: essentially, whatever happened, they should continue to live by Peter's recognition of him as Messiah (Mark 8.29).

Buildings such as the Temple carry meaning. Once, when in Romania, I visited the world's second-largest building, the People's Palace in Bucharest. Its massive bulk looms oppressively over the city, speaking in stone not of God, but of tyranny. The homes of 40,000 people, hospitals, schools, churches, the national archive, a stadium, and a monastery were destroyed to satisfy Ceausescu's megalomania; 20,000 people, including conscripts and prisoners, laboured on it. Although disturbingly beautiful inside, thanks to the diversion of the life-blood of the Romanian economy, and of raw materials and craftsmanship to its construction, it is eerily empty and grotesque in its hubris. Knowing that I would be writing this column, as I walked around the tiny (but enormous) part open to the public, I pondered Jesus's seeming non sequitur about large buildings and not being led astray towards false messiahs. After the revolution in Romania in 1989, demolition was indeed proposed, but, ironically, proved too costly. Instead, the palace remains as a monstrous postscript to a toppled dictator who built it to enforce his cult of personality.

Large buildings face us with theological questions such as those about where we should place our trust. The Temple was destroyed. On the other hand, legend (and it is only legend) in Durham firmly affirms that St Cuthbert raised a mist to save Durham Cathedral from Nazi bombing, a story that makes the question 'What about Coventry Cathedral?' difficult to answer. Mercifully, with God's grace, the people of Coventry were not led astray when their cathedral was blitzed.

The Temple, where God's glory dwelt (Isaiah 6.1–4), was the very meeting-place of God and humanity, the focus of their identity as God's people. But now, as Jesus's interaction with the Temple mounted to its climax, he, the Messiah whom the Temple's religion looked towards, was present opposite it. Having looked around it, cleansed it in a way that symbolized the end of its sacrificial functions (Mark 11.15–16), condemned it as a den of robbers, sat 'opposite' its treasury boxes watching people put in large sums of money to maintain its large buildings (Mark 12.41), now Jesus sat 'opposite' it on the Mount of Olives, from where he had first entered Jerusalem a few days earlier. Jesus confronted the Temple geographically and in his fulfilment of all it represented. The references to posture are significant: in the Temple, the priest stood (Hebrews 10.11) to make repeated offerings; both inside (Mark 12.41) and outside (Mark 13.3), Jesus sat, a sign of work complete. All that remained was for its curtain, demarcating the Holy of Holies, to be shredded at the moment of his death (Mark 15.38).

At the end of the church year, we hear how Jesus opened a new and living way through his flesh for us to enter the sanctuary at the heart of the Temple. This is where Mark's Gospel has been leading us all year; it is the foundation of our hope as we look towards another Advent. As the disciples were charged, let us not be led astray, but hold fast the confession of our hope without wavering.

Christ the King,
Sunday next before Advent
Daniel 7.9–10, 13–14; Revelation 1.4b–8; John 18.33–37

HIS POWER AND HIS LOVE

> *Eternal God, whose Son Jesus Christ ascended to the throne of heaven that*
> *he might rule over all things as Lord and King: keep the whole Church in*
> *the unity of the Spirit and in the bond of peace, and bring the whole created*
> *order to worship at his feet; who is alive and reigns with you in the unity of*
> *the Holy Spirit, one God now and for ever. Amen.*

Faced with the growing brutality of Mussolini's Fascism, and wanting to
emphasize Christ's non-violent kingship and rule, in 1925 Pope Pius XI
designated the last Sunday in October as Christ the King Sunday. Since 1970, it
has been kept on the last Sunday of the church year. Daniel, too, had lived under
a series of ruthless leaders, including Nebuchadnezzar, whose despotism was
legendary (2 Kings 25.6–12; Daniel 3; Judith 6.2–4), making Daniel's vision
of God's rule as subversive as Revelation's assertion that Jesus Christ is the
firstborn of the dead, ruler of the kings of earth, who has made us a Kingdom,
serving his God and Father.

Jesus Christ's kingship is paradoxical. Despite Revelation's paean of praise,
his CV is not that of a conventional king. Having begun his earthly ministry with
the expansive vision of God's Kingdom as sheer gift, 'the kingdom of heaven
has come near, repent and believe the good news', his preaching and teaching,
his engagement with people in need, his compassion for the suffering and the
confused, and his challenge to the powers that be, wherever he saw corruption
in religion or in society – all these modelled a very different kingship from
Nebuchadnezzar's.

Mark has tantalized us throughout the past year with the question who
Jesus is. The disciples have failed time and again to grasp it, leaving a Roman
centurion to recognize Jesus, in his ghastly death, as the Son of God (Mark
15.39). In contrast, John's portrayal of Jesus makes him more overt about his
identity, despite averting an attempt to make him an earthly king (John 6.15).
Given that he will ascend to the throne of heaven, it is ironic to hear Pilate trying
to narrow Jesus's kingship to his being King of the Jews, and then being faced
with his own question: is Jesus a king?

The Gospels tell us that Jesus's is the kingship of service, of having the
attitude of a slave (Philippians 2.5–11). We pray regularly: 'Your kingdom come
on earth as it is in heaven,' predicating our prayer on the fact that, through the
incarnation, God's Kingdom is all about this world. Following him, we can

expect to find ourselves serving as he did, to become part of the answer to our prayer that the whole created order will be brought to worship at his feet.

In 1912, Canon Henry Scott Holland, who was all too familiar with London slums, said that the more you believed in the incarnation, the more you cared about drains. The kingship of Christ has profound and permanent implications for the way we live, how we spend our money and our time, our career choices, our voluntary work, the way we relate to people, and the way we worship.

Describing a Congolese gynaecologist who had recently survived a murder attempt, *The Guardian* (26 October 2012) reported:

> Who is Dr Denis Mukwege? He is the main street of hope for thousands in eastern Congo. He has stayed in a war-zone for 14 years and practised medicine with bare medical resources and witnessed the unbearable enacted on the vaginas and bodies of women day after day. He has invented surgery to meet the acts of cruelty and has helped repair 30,000 rape victims ... He has done this and has been the head pastor at his church and a teacher and a fundraiser and a mentor of hundreds of doctors and the head of the Panzi foundation which is responsible for opening justice centres. Everything he does, he does with dignity, kindness and composure.

This is a man who understands better than most of us the implications of the kingship of Christ.

The nineteenth-century statesman Thomas Erskine said that all religion was grace, and all ethics was gratitude. So, if on Sunday we sing, as many will, 'O worship the King, All glorious above; O gratefully sing His power and his love,' our response to Christ the King will be to express that gratitude in our ethical living, whether this is to do with drains or career choices, our use of our finances, or the way we vote. To acknowledge that Christ is King is to make a religious commitment that has profound and permanent implications for the way we live our lives gratefully in this world.

Year C

Advent Sunday

Jeremiah 33.14–16; 1 Thessalonians 3.9–13;
Luke 21.25–36

SONG OF JOYFUL EXPECTATION

> *Almighty God, give us grace to cast away the works of darkness and to put*
> *on the armour of light, now in the time of this mortal life, in which your Son*
> *Jesus Christ came to us in great humility; that on the last day, when he shall*
> *come again in his glorious majesty to judge the living and the dead, we may*
> *rise to the life immortal; through him who is alive and reigns with you, in*
> *the unity of the Holy Spirit, one God, now and for ever. Amen.*

The readings for Advent this year sound a more joyous note than last year, when
we began Advent by crying to God to rend the heavens and come among us. This
year, the tone is set by the opening words from Jeremiah: 'The days are surely
coming when I will fulfil the promise I made …' The initiative lies with God,
and salvation and safety are promised when God acts. The joyful theme is picked
up by Paul, writing to the new Christians at Thessalonica: 'How can we thank
God enough for you in return for all the joy that we feel before our God because
of you?' Even amid the more sombre Gospel words from Jesus, there is still the
encouragement to raise our heads because our redemption is drawing near.

Each year we add our voices to the great Advent hymn, which has
resounded down the centuries, swelling its volume as it echoes from generation
to generation: 'O come! O come! Emmanuel!' Its confident expectant prayer
is both petition and praise. As we join this song of the saints whom we have
remembered in recent weeks and whose audacious hope sustained them, we dare
to hope that our God is coming to save us, that joy is God's agenda for his
people: 'Rejoice! Rejoice! Emmanuel shall come to thee, O Israel.'

'Do you hear the people sing?' ask those who manned the barricades in the
musical *Les Misérables*. At first barely audibly, but building up to a climax, they
sing about the life that is about to start when tomorrow comes. It is a rousing
song, and the atmosphere at the end is electric. So it should be, if people are to
be infected by the vision of God's salvation when we sing the song of God's
tomorrow coming. Our Advent song is a song of joyful expectation, in the face
of aching and yearning, as the world gives voice to its weariness, its suffering, its
shattered dreams. Taking our cue from Jeremiah, who spoke his words of hope
to a weary and disconsolate people, the world's minor harmonies are part of the
Advent song; the Church's task is to incorporate the pleas of people who, for
whatever reason, cannot pray for themselves our hope-filled, 'O come!'

We sing to God, who fulfils his promises, and will one day judge the living and the dead. In words that are worth pondering, as we listen to the news from places such as Syria, Israel, and Palestine, Jürgen Moltmann writes that God's creative justice was originally the hope of victims of injustice and violence, bringing them liberty, health and new life. They await a judgement that is based not on works, but on their sufferings. He argues that, later, foreign influences turned this saving deliverer of victims into a universal criminal judge of good and evil, who no longer enquires about the victims. So a victim-orientated expectation of saving justice became a perpetrator-orientated moral judgement based on retribution (Moltmann, 2010).

Our God is surely coming to save, bringing justice and righteousness. In Advent, we live in the light of that promise, which is why we are exhorted to prayerful holiness. The Collect indicates that this involves casting away the works of darkness and putting on the armour of light. Although undergirded and sustained by joy, such living is not always easy: Jesus warned his disciples to be on their guard, not weighed down with unhealthy lifestyles, but alert, praying for strength; while Paul prayed that his new Christians would, with God's grace, abound in love, be strengthened in holiness, and be blameless before God at the coming of the Lord Jesus.

At the beginning of Advent, we hear afresh of our sure and certain hope of God's coming, a hope shared with saints through the ages. Advent challenges us to active godliness, as we sing of that hope.

> Then cleansed be every Christian breast,
> And furnished for so great a guest!
> Yea, let us each our hearts prepare
> For Christ to come and enter there.
> *Charles Coffin*

Second Sunday of Advent

Baruch 5.1–9 or Malachi 3.1–4; Philippians 1.3–11;
Luke 3.1–6

DATING AN URGENT MESSAGE FROM THE ALMIGHTY

O Lord, raise up, we pray, your power and come among us, and with great might succour us; that whereas, through our sins and wickedness we are grievously hindered in running the race that is set before us, your bountiful grace and mercy may speedily help and deliver us; through Jesus Christ your Son our Lord, to whom with you and the Holy Spirit be honour and glory, now and for ever. Amen.

'In the eighteenth year of the reign of Elizabeth II, during the premiership of Harold Wilson, when Roy Jenkins was Home Secretary and Michael Ramsey was Archbishop of Canterbury, the word of God came to Billy Graham at Wembley Stadium.' That is roughly today's equivalent of how Luke began his Gospel. It gives those of us who remember that time an idea of the time lapse between John's preaching and when Luke wrote. The point is not so much the detailed date but: 'Pay attention! I am telling you about something that happened in living memory. A herald came with an urgent message from God.'

Advent is a season of challenging prayers and vivid visual imagery that startles us with God's answers. Luke quotes Isaiah's vision of the earthworks needed to build a road across a wilderness, reconfiguring the landscape shovelful by shovelful. Malachi has equally dramatic ideas of what God's coming means: God is in the precious-metals business, refining and purifying gold and silver by putting it through the fire to reveal its pure state; God is a consuming fire. In another stunning image, God is a washerwoman armed with fuller's soap – not soft, perfumed soap, but abrasive laundry soap that scrubs and scours. When Jesus was transfigured, Mark borrowed Malachi's image to describe Jesus's clothes becoming dazzling white, such as no fuller on earth, no washerwoman, could bleach them.

The disciples had a glimpse, in Jesus, of the sheer purity that is the benchmark for all humans created in God's image. That holiness is what God made us to share. God challenges us to be what we were created to be, and, in Advent, these flamboyant images of fire, scrubbing, and highway-engineering describe what it is like to prepare to experience the salvation of God.

Advent tells us we can expect God to probe all aspects of our lives and to clean us up; that the way we live now, individually and as Church and nation, will come under God's righteous judgement, when he answers our prayer for succour and deliverance. God's purpose is always to restore the original beauty that has been lost by sin; so there is no contradiction with Baruch's more tender description of the battered city of Jerusalem taking off her garment of sorrow and putting on the beauty of the glory of God. All this and more is the saving work of God.

Malachi, whose name means 'my messenger', condemned the laxity and corruption of the leaders of his day, and, in the continuation of the Luke reading, John calls the people who heard him a 'brood of vipers'. If they were around today, they would have much to choose from when speaking uncompromising judgement. To take but one topical example, that of financial institutions, they would ask not just about bankers, but about how you and I use our money.

Do we spend more on Christmas cards and gifts for our friends than on the poor and needy? If so, perhaps we need to ask how that relates to bankers' bonuses. Are we just giving bonuses to people who already have so much? It is good to give gifts to our family and friends, because friendship is a wonderful gift to celebrate and strengthen. But we can give to others at the same time through fairly traded, environmentally friendly, or hand-made presents.

We might add up what we spend on Christmas, and make an appropriate donation to charities on top, so that the people who have no one to give them a gift can receive a gift from us. That is a tiny part of what it means to prepare for God's coming among us.

Advent is a call to wake up and respond to God's initiative. So, in 2012, the 'In the sixty-first year of the reign of Elizabeth the Second, when David Cameron is Prime Minister and Theresa May is Home Secretary and during the last days of the archiepiscopate of Rowan Williams, the word of God comes to us:

Hark! a herald voice is calling:
Christ is nigh, it seems to say;
Cast away the dreams of darkness,
O ye children of the day!'
Latin, translated E. Caswall

Third Sunday of Advent
Zephaniah 3.14–20; Philippians 4.4–7; Luke 3.7–18

RENEWED IN THE LORD'S LOVE

O Lord Jesus Christ, who at your first coming sent your messenger to prepare the way before you: grant that the ministers and stewards of your mysteries may likewise so prepare and make ready your way by turning the hearts of the disobedient to the wisdom of the just, that at your second coming to judge the world we may be found an acceptable people in your sight; for you are alive and reign with the Father in the unity of the Holy Spirit, one God, now and for ever. Amen.

Usually we are better at complaining than at rejoicing. So, this Advent, it helps to hear, time and again, the exhortation to rejoice. Building on the joy of previous weeks, this week we hear: 'Sing aloud, O daughter Zion; shout, O Israel! Rejoice and exult with all your heart, O daughter Jerusalem!' Why? Because the Lord's judgement has been taken away: God is in your midst. 'Rejoice in the Lord always; again I will say rejoice.' Why? Because the Lord is near.

Paul wrote from one prison (Philippians 1.8, 12–14) to Christians in a city where he and Silas had once spent time in another prison and had kept the other prisoners awake at midnight with their praying and singing (Acts 16.25–34). His then-jailer was probably one of the recipients of this letter, and so knew from that tumultuous night-time experience how this deliberate attitude of praise was central to Paul's way of life. Paul, writing to a church that was facing internal conflict (Philippians 4.2) and external pressures to go back on the faith (3.2, 17–19) was not naïve in what he said, but centred his confidence on his simple but profound trust that 'the Lord is near'. Earlier, Zephaniah sang to people who were facing immense national problems and a young king who was turning them back to God (2 Kings 22–23). His message? The Lord was in their midst, and active to save the lame and outcast; to turn shame into praise.

The wonderful truth of Advent hope is that our outward circumstances are not the measure of our joy, but the crucible of our joy, and of the peace that passes understanding for anyone unaccustomed to God's ways. God's joy is incarnational joy, not disembodied optimism.

Against this background, John the Baptist's words hit like icy water. 'You brood of vipers' is no way to endear yourself to anyone, and positively foolhardy when facing a potentially hostile crowd. 'Who warned you to flee from the wrath to come?' challenged them to face God's judgement, to turn to God for the purifying of gold and the robust fulling of cloth of which Malachi spoke last week.

John wanted to see fruit in the people's lives. Claiming Abraham's ancestry

252   YEAR C

and doing nothing about it was not good enough, because Abraham bore fruit in his life. He was a faithful man, who acted when God spoke and trusted when God seemed to dally. When people asked: 'What must we do to be saved?' John's reply was immensely practical: do what you can, in your particular circumstances, to care for, rather than exploit, your neighbours. Soldiers, do not take advantage of your power, and be content with your pay; tax-collectors, be scrupulously honest in your dealings (it was expected that they would take their own cut on top of what was owed to the state); ordinary people who live above the breadline, share your resources with people in poverty. His hearers, thus challenged, might not have shared Luke's view of these exhortations as 'proclaiming the good news', unless they also grasped that 'The Lord is near, rejoicing over you, renewing you in his love.'

What should we do? That question is a starting point for our response in Advent. In committing ourselves to hold together the eschatological and the ethical, praise and rejoicing mark Christians out as people of hope and joy – neither so heavenly minded that we are no earthly good, nor so absorbed in life on earth that we fail to notice the signs of God's coming. Bede said that Hild, Abbess of Whitby, devoted her earthly life to the service of heaven, thus modelling a truly joyful way of life. If it is good news that we should reform our lives and live generously, caring for others, knowing that God is in the midst of us, and if we are not to worry about anything, but to make our requests known to God in prayer with thanksgiving – then rejoicing might just break out among us. That would be a radical Christian witness in the world today.

Fourth Sunday of Advent

Micah 5.2–5a; Hebrews 10.5–10; Luke 1.39–45 [46–55]

THE CELEBRATIONS BEGIN

God our redeemer, who prepared the Blessed Virgin Mary to be the mother of your Son: grant that, as she looked for his coming as our saviour, so we may be ready to greet him when he comes again as our judge; who is alive and reigns with you, in the unity of the Holy Spirit, one God, now and for ever. Amen.

Elizabeth appears to have a bit-part in Mary's story, but what happens if we put her centre-stage?

This descendant of Aaron the priest had an impeccable past, but no future, because she had no child. Childlessness was the woman's fault: 'they had no children because Elizabeth was barren' (Luke 1.7); and, worse, her husband was a priest; so her childlessness called his piety into doubt, since sons were a sign of God's blessing. Every time he came home from a circumcision, every time there was a family gathering, the grief must have been there, the tears welling up in secret. Nevertheless, Luke emphasizes their blameless living and righteousness before God. Their lives were a perpetual paradox, because they had done everything that God commanded, and yet God had not blessed them in the way all faithful Jews expected. Instead, Elizabeth's dreams had been chipped away, month by month, as she felt her blood flow, until hope was gone.

But then something happened. An angel appeared, and told Zechariah: 'Your prayer has been heard. Elizabeth will have a son' (Luke 1.13). When had that elderly couple last prayed that prayer? Realistically, it was years ago, and God had indeed heard, yet had chosen not to answer until now. So pregnant Elizabeth hid herself, with telling words: 'This is what the Lord has done for me when he looked favourably on me and took away the disgrace I have endured among my people' (Luke 1.25). We can hear the years of silent suffering and shame that she had borne.

Six months later, on Mary's unexpected arrival and news, her baby kicked off the celebrations, and Elizabeth broke her seclusion with a loud cry of praise. The neighbours heard! She, long disgraced for not being pregnant, strengthened Mary, newly disgraced for being pregnant and facing the possibility of Joseph's rejection, her father's wrath, perhaps stoning.

Elizabeth became a prophet filled with the Holy Spirit, telling Mary that her child was indeed the Lord. That may have been the assurance that Mary desperately needed that she had not dreamed it all. Elizabeth, who had experienced blessing from God in the conception of her child, was open to an excess of blessing, as the mother of her Lord came to her. Were her words

'Blessed is she who believed there would be a fulfilment of what was spoken to her by the Lord' spoken to Mary, or to herself? Was there a chuckle in her voice, a delighted realization that, after all these years, God had kept his word?

When John was born, 'her neighbours and relatives heard that the Lord had shown his great mercy to her, and they rejoiced with her' (Luke 1.58). Was mercy the unexpected, deeper gift of God, after those years of tenacious, faithful living, in the face of silence? Indeed, what does it mean to receive the great mercy of God? Perhaps it was Elizabeth who taught Mary that 'God's mercy is for those who fear him from generation to generation.'

As Advent draws to a close, we pray for readiness to greet our Saviour when he comes. Elizabeth was open to receiving God's mercy, after years of dashed hopes. Sometimes, as a survival mechanism, we are so defended against disillusionment ('better not to ask than ask and be disappointed') that God has to prise or even wrench us open to his great mercy. Perhaps, in these last days of Advent, it is time to revisit, prayerfully, what we dare not voice or have given up praying for, and to risk that God will come with mercy, making a road in our wilderness, in the wilderness of our neighbourhood, and of our nation.

Faithful Elizabeth,
long have you waited for this sign.

Now is your time of mercy –
your time! –
no longer sharer of another's joy.

Can you receive – in awe, yet without fear –
not just this child,
but mercy, in your hidden depths,
and in that place of faithful, steady love
let mercy purge and heal your pain,
risk the disarming of the strength
that kept you faithful through the years?
Then, beloved and vulnerable,
embrace the lover of your soul.

Mercy, Elizabeth, mercy for you.
Not just a son, but joy, great joy.

Copyright © 1991 Rosalind Brown

Christmas Day
Isaiah 62.6–end; Titus 3.4–7; Luke 2.[1–7] 8–20

THE GOODNESS AND LOVING KINDNESS OF GOD HAS APPEARED

Almighty God, you have given us your only-begotten Son to take our name upon him and as at this time to be born of a pure virgin: grant that we, who have been born again and made your children by adoption and grace, may daily be renewed by your Holy Spirit; through Jesus Christ our Lord. Amen.

Luke's birth narratives have a cast of ordinary people coping with occasional extraordinary events. God had sent messages to Mary and Joseph through an angel and a dream; a baby was conceived, and then there was silence. They got on with doing what a peasant couple expecting a baby did until, with bad timing, the emperor's census forced a 90-mile trip to Bethlehem. It would be tempting to wonder whether something was amiss; whether God could have fixed better arrangements for the birth. But no: silence.

At Christmas, we rush too easily from the spare account of Jesus's birth, without divine glamour, to the angels' appearing. Mary and Joseph did not see those angels; they were left holding a newborn baby in a stable. God had been disturbingly active in their lives a while ago, but, in the mess and pain of birth away from home, God apparently was keeping quiet.

God did send an angel eventually – but not to Mary and Joseph. Instead, on a hillside, God disturbed the night watch of a group of shepherds who were not particularly looking out for God. Their responsibilities in the fields, 24 hours a day, prevented their participation in Jewish worship and made them religious outcasts. It was to this unlikely assembly, minding their sheep and minding their own business, that God's angel appeared one dark night. Luke reports their understandable fear, their decision to abandon their sheep (risking their livelihood), and their hasty trip to Bethlehem, where they found the baby and told his parents their bizarre story.

This band of breathless shepherds became God's messengers to Mary and Joseph, for whom their arrival was unexpected but probably a comfort, since it assured them that God had not abandoned them after all. They, in turn, could reassure the shepherds – who would not expect them to believe weird stories of a sky full of angels – that they were not hallucinating, but were the first to hear that God really had sent a saviour.

That was the only miraculous part of the actual birth of Jesus: otherwise, Mary and Joseph, plus any extended family with them, were on their own, dealing with a natural birth away from their own home. Perhaps through the shepherds they discovered, as we can today, that God's silence is not God's absence. Luke records that Mary treasured these words, and pondered them in her heart. Years later, she might have drawn strength from them, as she faced the seeming silence of God at Calvary.

What was the effect on the shepherds? Today's readings tell of the goodness and loving kindness of God our Saviour's appearing; of the Lord's proclaiming to the ends of the earth that salvation comes; that God's holy people are sought out, not forsaken. This is what the shepherds experienced that stunning night, and they returned, glorifying and praising God.

One medieval artist envisaged their dancing. I have a picture on an old Christmas card from a Book of Hours, showing a group of stolid medieval peasant shepherds, concentrating intensely as they solemnly attempt a circle dance. It is a dancing disaster waiting to happen: some appear to have two left feet, and one is going in the opposite direction while still holding his neighbours' hands. They have dropped their crooks on the ground because something has caused them to venture into this new territory of dancing. The clue lies with one shepherd who is outside the circle, on the right, pointing upwards – no doubt it was at the angels. Even hardened shepherds can dance when joy breaks out, when a saviour is born.

We never know how God's messengers may come to us, or what unlikely things God's messengers – for that is what angels are – may cause us to do. We know that Mary treasured the shepherds' words in her heart, and maybe, just maybe, the shepherds really did learn to dance. The Christmas Collect prays for us to be daily renewed by the Holy Spirit. Expect an unexpected answer as joy breaks out: the goodness and loving kindness of God has appeared.

First Sunday of Christmas
1 Samuel 2.18–20, 26; Colossians 3.12–17; Luke 2.41–52

GOD SHARES THE LIFE OF OUR HUMANITY

> *Almighty God, who wonderfully created us in your own image and yet more wonderfully restored us through your Son Jesus Christ; grant that, as he came to share in our humanity, so we may share the life of his divinity; who is alive and reigns with you, in the unity of the Holy Spirit, one God, now and for ever. Amen.*

A few days on, and normal life is partly restored. The sales are in full swing, public transport is restarting, offices reopening. Meanwhile, in our readings, several years have passed. Luke gives a brief but telling glance at the way Jesus was raised: piously, for not all Jewish women were like Mary who made the annual arduous trek to Jerusalem for the Passover, since only men were required to go and many of them did not. Now we meet Jesus nearing the age (13) of recognition as an adult, one who could be counted among the ten men needed for there to be a synagogue and who could recite the Torah, the law.

Theologically, in drawing parallels with Samuel and telling of his growth in wisdom and esteem as he stood on the cusp of manhood, Luke stresses Jesus's humanity. He illustrates this with a story of Jesus exploring his identity, testing his boundaries. This maturing boy, not entirely obedient to his parents, went missing. The description of the large caravan of people, walking in smaller groups, tells us how people travelled for safety and of the trusting sense of wider community in which Jesus was raised. It also suggests that Mary and Joseph had not been on their own in Bethlehem, but had extended family with them. Come nightfall, there was panic; back in Jerusalem the fact that Mary, not Joseph, told Jesus off gives a glimpse of a strong, no-nonsense, mother.

How did Jesus respond? At one level it was with typical adolescent insouciance. Why on earth were they bothered? At another level it indicates that something had clicked for him in a new way in Jerusalem; he was growing into awareness that God was his Father. In Judaism God was not normally addressed as 'Father', yet Jesus called God his Father and taught his disciples to do so. We do not know how Jesus came to know this relationship, and heresies have been built from speculation; Luke simply mentions his remarkably astute questioning and understanding, contrasting it with his parents' lack of understanding. Then Jesus got up and went with his parents to Nazareth and was obedient to them. Whatever being the Son of God meant, he expressed that in obedience to his parents and, ultimately, learned obedience through what he suffered (Hebrews 5.8).

Lest we forget, as normal life resumes, the Collect takes us into the glorious mysteries of what God has done in Jesus Christ: first creating then restoring us in the image of God, sharing our humanity so we may share the life of his divinity. God's salvation is so much more than paying off any debt arising from our sin or meeting the demands of the law. It restores humanity to what was originally intended, communion with God. Salvation is about life in its fullness, sharing God's life as he has shared ours in Jesus Christ.

There are consequences to this wonder, and the readings bring us back to earth. God's chosen ones, holy and beloved, are to live transformed lives, clothing themselves with love (was it love that enabled the 12-year-old, newly independent Jesus, who had discovered the intellectual and theological thrills of Jerusalem, to be obedient to his parents in the backwater of Nazareth?) and doing everything with thanksgiving to God in the name of Jesus.

Mary had already treasured what the shepherds had told her in her heart; now she added to that treasure store this more difficult experience of her son's growing away from the family and yet being obedient to them. Years later Jesus said, 'Where your treasure is, there your heart will be also' (12.34), and maybe he learned that, in part, from Mary.

Mary's experience reminds us that it is in the normality of life that we add to the treasures in our heart and live in the light of them. One practical suggestion for the new year is to buy a book in which to record what you wish to treasure in your heart – pictures, words, stories, photos, memories – and, like Mary, like Jesus, to live obediently in ordinary life where such treasures are created. Books like that used to be called Commonplace Books with good reason.

Second Sunday of Christmas
See Year A

Epiphany
See Year A

The Baptism of Christ,
First Sunday of Epiphany
Isaiah 43.1–7; Acts 8.14–17; Luke 3.15–17, 21–22

'YOU ARE MY SON, THE BELOVED'

> *Eternal Father, who at the baptism of Jesus revealed him to be your Son, anointing him with the Holy Spirit: grant to us, who are born again by water and the Spirit, that we may be faithful to our calling as your adopted children; through Jesus Christ our Lord. Amen.*

On the day when we remember the baptism of Christ, it is slightly surprising that the Gospel does not dwell on it – indeed, it mentions it almost in passing. Although John had spoken to the crowds with vivid words about how it would be when the Messiah came, he did not identify Jesus publicly, and it seems that Jesus simply took his place in the queue and John baptized him without fuss. Perhaps Luke felt no need to describe John's response to Jesus because the birth narratives that preface his Gospel describe the unborn John leaping in his mother's womb when Mary arrived, pregnant with Jesus. What is more important for Luke is that, after he was baptized, Jesus was praying.

Prayer is one of Luke's favourite themes, and his only story from Jesus's childhood has him dallying in the Temple, the ultimate place of prayer. So it is no surprise that his account of Jesus's adult life begins with his praying. It was then, only then, that heaven opened, and the divine voice affirmed that Jesus was God's beloved Son, as his baptism led him into ever closer relationship with his Father. Baptism leads us, too, into ever closer relationship with God. We never know what will happen once we are baptized, except that we have been made part of God's family; that God loves us with abandon. 'Do not fear. I have called you by name, you are mine. When you pass through the waters I will be with you. Do not fear; for I am with you.'

The first baby I baptized died ten minutes later. As part of my training for ordination, I was the overnight chaplain at a large hospital in the United States and was called to the neo-natal intensive-care unit where a month-old, premature twin was dying. Reaching into his incubator, I baptized him. Then, ever so gently, the nurses unplugged the numerous wires and tubes, wiped his face, and dressed him in a white gown and a white blanket. He was given to his parents who held him for the first time and took him to a side room. There they cuddled him until he died. I was struck at the time by the unconscious engagement with the symbolism of baptism: washed, dressed in white clothes, embraced and held by his family. I was also aware that the Church was added to that night; he was our baptized brother in Christ, going before us into our Father's presence.

That was a Saturday night. On my way home, the next morning, I went to church. Three healthy babies were baptized, and, as their parents and godparents promised to bring them up in the faith, I found myself thinking that they were being baptized for life, whereas my tiny baby had been baptized for death. It was all one and the same in God's sight, because there is one baptism in the name of Jesus Christ our Lord, who was himself baptized, identifying fully with our humanity, and then was faithful to his calling as the beloved Son of God. All that matters is: 'You are precious in my sight, and honoured, and I love you'; 'You are my Son, the Beloved; with you I am well pleased.'

Perhaps Luke passes over the details of Jesus's baptism because, for him, what was important was what came next in Jesus's life, and how Jesus prepared himself for it. Prayer is the natural expression of the relationship forged in baptism: we are adopted as God's beloved sons and daughters. In a family where people are loved, they communicate; they renew and strengthen their relationships constantly; they delight in each other's company, and support and challenge each other. Relationships without communication wither, and prayer is essentially an expression of God's relationship with us, and ours with God.

Sometimes, I pray for the baby's twin sister and the three babies baptized that Sunday, wondering how it has played out in their lives. Every baptism sets an adventure in motion. So, this Sunday, as more people are baptized, the Church prays that all of us, young or old, will be faithful to our calling as God's adopted children. If we follow Jesus's example, that should include nurturing the newly baptized in prayer, which George Herbert (in his poem, 'Prayer, I') describes so wonderfully as 'the Church's banquet'.

Second Sunday of Epiphany
Isaiah 62.1–5; 1 Corinthians 12.1–11; John 2.1–11

MIRACLE OF THE VILLAGE

> *Almighty God, whose Son revealed in signs and miracles the wonder of your saving presence: renew your people with your heavenly grace, and in all our weakness sustain us by your mighty power; through Jesus Christ our Lord. Amen.*

God's glory is revealed! 'The heavens are telling the glory of God' sang the psalmist (Psalm 19.1); 'the whole earth is full of [God's] glory' said the seraphs whom Isaiah saw (Isaiah 6.3). In a theological prologue, John summarizes his whole Gospel: 'The Word became flesh and dwelt among us, and we have seen his glory, the glory as of a father's only son, full of grace and truth' (John 1.14).

Isaiah tells of God's irresistible urge to scoop his people into this extravagant revelation of divine glory. Writing when political upheavals foreshadowed freedom from the Babylonian exile, his excitement was barely contained: kings would see the glory, as God vindicated this tiny, exiled nation; worn-down exiles would be a crown of beauty in God's hand, a royal diadem; their ravaged homeland would be called 'Married', 'My Delight is in Her'. The details are historical; the enduring message is that God's glory is revealed when God acts among his people.

Paul echoed Isaiah's message when trying to order worship in an immature and irrepressible church: God pours out his blessing with abandon, and reveals his glory among his people, who are open to the Holy Spirit working among them. The initiative is entirely God's, and even the exasperating Corinthians see, and themselves reveal, God's glory in Jesus Christ, the head of the Church.

Against this background of overt revelation of God's glory, the Gospel is stunningly muted. John picked up Isaiah's imagery of marriage's heralding the dawning of the Messianic age that comes in Jesus Christ, but the context was not Isaiah's international stage. Instead, events at a nondescript village wedding constituted the first sign through which Jesus revealed his glory, and few people noticed what happened, let alone saw any glory. The servants knew where the wine came from; the steward knew it tasted good, but not its origin; and the bridegroom seemed blissfully ignorant of everything. Mary and the disciples knew and believed in Jesus, but that was it. It all happened in a backwater. If this was Jesus's glory revealed, the 'wonder of his saving presence', as the Collect puts it, we have to revise our concepts of what it means for heavenly glory to be revealed. Jesus's glory revealed on earth was modest and unassertive. It was a costly glory; Michael Ramsey identified it with Jesus's utter self-giving to the Father, which breaks the power of human, sinful glory.

The crucial thing at Cana was not that everyone was wowed by something spectacular, but that the disciples believed in Jesus. The seven signs that John recorded teased and disturbed people enough to raise questions. However, for glory to be revealed, signs needed to be met by faith. Thus, near the end of his life, Jesus said to Martha: 'Did I not tell you that if you believed, you would see the glory of God?' St Augustine sums it up in his sermon 613: 'The presence of his glory walks among us, if love finds room.' For those at Cana with eyes to see and hearts open to love, the revelation of Jesus's glory was life-changing. It can be the same for us when God's glory is disclosed in the everydayness of life – and suddenly our world is charged with the grandeur of God.

When I lead pilgrimages in Durham Cathedral, we stop at the crossing, the heart of the intersecting architectural cross, to look up at the tower and be dwarfed by its design and beauty. Inevitably, people gasp in wonder. Once, Ruth Etchells, the former Principal of St John's College, was present, and said softly: 'When you are here, your fingertips are resting on glory; you are living on the edge of eternity.'

Our fingertips rest on glory: we are in the Epiphany season of glory revealed in Jesus Christ. Rarely is this glory revealed blindingly, as at the transfiguration; but it is there for the seeing, when suddenly we glimpse, as though through a crack in the ordinary into heaven, a miraculous foretaste of the fuller revelation of glory to come (John 17.24). Then our world is charged with glory, and Cana's simple marriage-feast takes on a messianic meaning, as God rejoices over us as a bridegroom with a bride. Dare we believe that we will see the glory of God where we live and work? Can love find room?

Third Sunday of Epiphany

Nehemiah 8.1–3, 5–6, 8–10; 1 Corinthians 12.12–31a;
Luke 4.14–21

WALKING AT GOD'S SIDE

God our creator, who in the beginning commanded the light to shine out of darkness: we pray that the light of the glorious gospel of Christ may dispel the darkness of ignorance and unbelief, shine into the hearts of all your people, and reveal the knowledge of your glory in the face of Jesus Christ our Lord. Amen.

In the Early Church, sin was primarily sin against the community, and the goal of penance was reconciliation to the community. As time passed, sin became less a public and more an individual matter. We live with the tension between these two understandings, and scandals that are coming to light highlight forcefully that there are public implications of the ways in which we live privately. On the whole, the world finds it more comfortable if the Church sticks to sin as private morality, but it is discovering that religious leaders have significant contributions to make in the face of current public ethical crises. The readings face us with these communal implications.

Ezra read the law to the returned exiles who, just a few days earlier (Ezra 6.15, 8.2), had completed the city walls. They lived more securely, but not righteously. The manifestation of this was that they oppressed their kin, charging them interest on loans (Nehemiah 5.3–11; Deuteronomy 23.19). The Corinthians were keen on some spiritual gifts, but seemingly not on striving (a strong verb) for gifts such as 'forms of assistance' (1 Corinthians 12.28) to aid the weaker and poorer members of the body (11.18–22). Jesus began his public ministry – in Luke by teaching, in contrast to Mark's beginning with miracles – by defining his ministry in Isaiah's words of healing, wholeness, and liberation for needy people.

The response of Ezra's hearers was penitence: they wept. That was a start, but Nehemiah wanted more of them than this; they had to learn not just to be sorry, but to live righteously, to be holy in their daily lives. At that moment, this meant worshipping God with joy and ensuring that the poor, whom they had previously exploited, had food and wine with which to join the celebration. This was to be a radical, Scrooge-like conversion.

The Corinthians struggled, as we might in their shoes, to grasp the full implications of the grace that had grasped them. Jesus's hearers were excited initially by his preaching, but, oddly, the Gospel omits the opposition once Jesus had spelt out the consequences. What really riled his former neighbours was his claim that God's track-record of favouring the Jewish people was not as pure as they liked to think: through two of their leading prophets, God acted outside religious boundaries to care for people they despised and knew as Gentiles (Luke 4.24–29).

In the sixth century, Gregory the Great described the joys of the contemplative vision of God, but also the constant need for the active life, with its discipline and service expressed in meeting the needs of the poor and caring for one's family. Put another way, Jon Sobrino defines spirituality as 'Kinship with God, it is walking at God's side. It is being and working in history as God is and works. It is our "yes" to Jesus's basic demand ..."You must be made perfect as your heavenly Father is perfect."' (Sobrino, 1990). As a liberation theologian, Sobrino argues that the means by which we know God, who is unfathomable Mystery, is the practice of right and justice towards the poor, with a goal of liberation. Jesus did this: when John's disciples asked whether he was the one sent from God, Luke has him returning to this theme of the blind seeing and the poor having good news preached to them (Luke 7.20–22). This is what revealed his identity.

Ultimately, public and private spirituality and morality are two sides of one coin: the way we live expresses and shapes who we are. Like Ezra's returned exiles, who were understandably focused on their security, and like the Corinthians, who were fascinated by the signs and wonders of their new faith but less keen on its ethical implications, we, too, can miss encountering God through the poor in our midst. This makes the petition in the Collect so important. We ask God, who caused light to shine out of darkness – an act that scientific discoveries make more wonderful almost by the day – to shine the gospel in our hearts, dispelling our (not someone else's) ignorance and unbelief, and revealing the knowledge of God's glory in the face of Jesus Christ. We, together with the world that is watching the Church, may be surprised by how God answers.

Fourth Sunday of Epiphany

Ezekiel 43.27–44.4; 1 Corinthians 13.1–13; Luke 2.22–40

HANDED OVER

God our creator, who in the beginning commanded the light to shine out of darkness: we pray that the light of the glorious gospel of Christ may dispel the darkness of ignorance and unbelief, shine into the hearts of all your people, and reveal the knowledge of your glory in the face of Jesus Christ our Lord. Amen.

Paul writes to the Corinthians of handing over his body so that he may boast, saying that without love that is worthless. Jesus spoke of his father having handed over all things to him (Matthew 11.27), which in turn enabled him to face being handed over to his enemies. So, he was handed over to the chief priests and Scribes who condemned him to death (Matthew 20.18), handed over to the Gentiles to be mocked, insulted and spat upon (Luke 18.32), handed over to be crucified (Matthew 26.2) and the third day to rise again (Luke 24.7). Paul described this in theological terms as Jesus being handed over to death for our trespasses and raised for our justification (Romans 4.25). There is a passivity about being handed over that is startling when we consider the consequences. It has to be born of utter trust in God's good purposes and the ultimate victory over evil; otherwise it is at best foolhardy, at worst, dangerous.

Being handed over started for Jesus as a baby. Mary and Joseph took him to the Temple to present him to the Lord, for he, in a tradition that went back to the Passover in Egypt, as the firstborn male was holy to the Lord. When Mary and Joseph entered the temple, Simeon, a complete stranger, took Jesus in his arms and they let go of their precious firstborn child; in effect they handed him over.

Simeon praised God and spoke of his own coming death as the fulfilment of God's promise to him, just as Jesus's eventual death would be the fulfilment of God's promise to his people. Simeon handed himself over to death.

How did Simeon know this about the baby who looked like any other 40-day-old Jewish baby? We are not told but there are hints. Simeon was righteous and devout, looking forward to the consolation of Israel – consolation that would come with the Messiah – and the Spirit rested on him. He was guided by the Spirit and responsive to the Spirit, coming into the temple from Jerusalem as soon as the Spirit nudged him. His life-time of fidelity enabled him to recognize the prompt.

Then there was Anna who, unlike Simeon, is described as a prophet. This was unusual at a time when there were no recognized prophets. Equally, it is unusual that she is named as being of the tribe of Asher since few people in the New Testament have their tribal lineage noted; specifically Jesus (Hebrews

7.14), Paul (Philippians 3.15) and Barnabas (Acts 4.36). Her commitment to worship, fasting and prayer emphasize her devotion born of decades of practice. Unusually, given that she is described as a prophet, her words are not recorded in direct speech but, since she spoke to all who were looking for the redemption of Jerusalem, maybe she had more to say than Luke could record!

The temple was an utterly holy place. Centuries earlier, when there was no temple because it had been destroyed by enemies, Ezekiel was overwhelmed by a vision of the holiness of God's glory revealed in his temple. Jesus's arrival as a baby in the rebuilt temple was not an overt manifestation of holiness, except to two elderly people. Sometimes godly elderly people are most adept at discerning the glory of God because they have had years of unsung, faithful practice through the routine of daily life.

So there is a strange and holy meeting of a young couple come to fulfil their religious duty, an old man who is something of a mystic and an old lady who hangs around the temple. All belong in the one story. That is the gift of buildings like the temple and churches; they are prayed-in enough for there to be room for all who come, and they can bring together the most unlikely people. Do we come to places of worship expecting the unexpected? As we look at the person next to us, especially if we have never talked to them, do we expect that maybe God could shine the gospel into our hearts through them, just as Mary and Joseph did for Simeon and Anna, and they in turn did for Mary and Joseph?

Sunday before Lent,
Proper 1 (3–9 February)
Isaiah 6.1–8 [9–13]; 1 Corinthians 15.1–11; Luke 5.1–11

LEAVING EVERYTHING TO FOLLOW JESUS

Almighty God, by whose grace alone we are accepted and called to your service: strengthen us by your Holy Spirit and make us worthy of our calling; through Jesus Christ our Lord. Amen.

Collect for the Fifth Sunday before Lent

Isaiah's vision is clearly dated to the year King Uzziah died, about 742 BC, when an era of national prosperity ended abruptly. Uzziah, a strong king, had reigned for 40 years and had secured the nation economically and militarily. Now, with an inexperienced leader, the country faced invasion by the powerful and brutal Assyrians. Fear was an understandable reaction. The fear was like being in Syria or other countries today where violent militia threaten; it was like losing your life savings and your job as world financial markets lurch from crisis to crisis. In that year of fear and catastrophe, Isaiah had a vision of God's glory. It filled him with dread because, realizing God's holiness, he knew his own sinfulness and was almost paralysed into inaction. Given the prevailing belief that no one could see God and live, Isaiah was sure he was doomed. Not only was his nation facing disaster, he was 'lost'.

But God did not abandon Isaiah. He did not ignore the sin of the world, which is still vented through the injustice, corruption, violence and suffering that fill the news and grieve God beyond anything we can imagine. God did not say 'Sin does not really matter, so ignore the brutality of armies on the rampage and the suffering inflicted on people by corrupt rulers.' Instead, God acted, and in a vision an angel seared Isaiah's unclean lips with burning coals, thereby blotting out Isaiah's own sin, purging it with the fire associated with the holy presence of God.

God dealt with one man and then began to change the world through him. So God asked the question, 'Whom shall I send, and who will go for us?' And Isaiah, who only minutes ago was calling himself lost, had the courage to say, 'Here am I, send me.' He was immediately sent to proclaim God's word to the people, thus enabling them to respond to God's call in the midst of their fear. We can expect God to answer us too, perhaps in ways we do not dream of: that is the power of an encounter with God to which we refer when praying to be strengthened with the Holy Spirit and made worthy of our calling.

Ultimately, God answered his own question 'Whom shall I send?' by being born among us as a human being. The incarnation is the measure of God's love and concern for our world. So, in due course, like Isaiah, Peter caught a glimpse of God's holiness revealed in Jesus and, like Isaiah before him, responded with awareness of his sinfulness in Jesus's presence, saying 'Go away from me.' In the epistle, Paul's reference to the appearance to James, brother of our Lord, glosses over what was said to this leader of the Early Church who had, perhaps understandably, once found it hard to believe that his own older brother was the Son of God. Then Paul alludes to his own experience of being suddenly and devastatingly aware of his own sinfulness in rejecting the lordship of Jesus Christ. That event led to Paul's conversion and a lifetime of demanding apostleship, often with great hardship.

In these people's lives, the revelation of God's presence led to acceptance of their sinfulness yet their call by God to proclaim good news to often unreceptive people. It was not easy for Isaiah to live the answer to his prayer in the years ahead as his nation faced the Assyrians. Yet he was willing to respond to God's unexpected revelation of his holiness, to overcome his fears for his own well-being and his nation's future. That changed things decisively. Our willingness to respond to God, whose compassion for our world is undimmed and who is always calling us to allow our worship to lead us into service in the world, may have similar effects that reverberate way beyond our immediate circumstances. Dare we, like Isaiah, like Peter, believe and respond to God's call?

Kenneth Leech wrote that Christianity goes disastrously wrong when Jesus is worshipped but not followed (Leech, 1994) The new year is a good time to be honest in our commitment to follow Jesus Christ. The grace of God to which the Collect refers is truly astounding and is expressed in the call of unlikely, sinful people who are assured of the strengthening of the Holy Spirit that, day by day, makes us worthy of our calling.

'They left everything and followed him.'

Sunday before Lent,

Proper 2 (10–16 February)

Jeremiah 17.5–10; 1 Corinthians 15.15–20; Luke 6.17–26

BLESSED ARE THOSE WHO TRUST IN THE LORD

O God, you know us to be set in the midst of so many and great dangers,
that by reason of the frailty of our nature we cannot always stand upright:
grant to us such strength and protection as may support us in all dangers
and carry us through all temptations; through Jesus Christ our Lord. Amen.

Collect for the Fourth Sunday before Lent

'Blessed are those who trust in the Lord,' says Jeremiah. Those are wonderful words if we read them out of context. But reading the rest of Jeremiah might make us wonder whether there was any blessing on offer. His story covers about a 40-year period, culminating with the fall of Jerusalem amid a bloodbath, after which most of the survivors were force marched to exile in Babylon and Jeremiah was left behind with the poorest of the poor who immediately turned their backs on God and started looking to Egypt for help.

The chapters around this reading swing from pole to pole; one minute God promises to restore Israel, the next God tells Jeremiah to stop praying for the people because there is no way God will listen to them, adding that even if Moses were to pray for them God would still send them to destruction. No wonder Jeremiah swung to and fro from praise to prayer to lament.

So in their original context the words 'Blessed are those who trust in the Lord' were words of stern challenge from God, not the pious thoughts of someone thinking nice thoughts of comfort and joy. Amid all the disaster and threat of disaster, 'trust' was the key word. Would Jeremiah or anyone trust in the Lord? If they dared to do so, the promised blessing sounds very like that of which the psalmist sang in Psalm 1.

The crucial question was in whom and in what the people trusted. The temptation was apparently to trust in 'mere mortals', a course of action which might look appealing under the circumstances where mere Babylonian mortals had the power to wreak devastating destruction and mere Egyptian mortals at least formed an army, thus appearing to be a better hope than God whose mortal army had been massacred. Yet, this choice would bring a curse beyond any curse they knew at the time. Yet the alternative, 'Blessed are those who trust in the Lord,' looked hopeless.

Jeremiah himself never lost faith in God, although in the midst of his searing doubts he had vigorous and forthright fellowship with God. Later in chapter 17 we hear his own response of stubborn trust, 'Save me and I shall be saved, for you are my praise. I have not run away from being a shepherd in your service. Do not become a terror to me; you are my refuge in the day of disaster.' Only a man who made that response could then ask the same of his people.

Amid the chaos of a great multitude of people pressing to touch him and be healed Jesus gave his disciples a perverse litany of blessing and woe. On the face of it he and his disciples were rich, full, laughing at Jesus's success, spoken well of by hundreds of people. But that situation was dangerous for their souls and so again it was a matter of where they put their trust. Was it in the healing power that was going out of him or in God, the source of that healing, the God who would sustain him and them through the coming times of suffering and death? Jesus contrasted people who know that they do not have everything and thus look to God for strength with people who have more than enough and thus have no room left for God to nourish or challenge them.

The Collect is totally realistic about the dangers we are in because of our frailty. It turns us to God for strength and protection in all dangers and temptations, including the temptation to put our trust in mere mortals. The readings challenge us about how we live with uncertainty and vulnerability. They ask us about the space carved out in our hearts which only God can fill. Can we live with vulnerable, needy, hungry, weeping hearts that have space for God's blessing? People around the world have to do so in appalling circumstances and they need the support of people who, like Jeremiah, know and have proved God's faithfulness. Are we among them?

If we believe that God raised Jesus Christ from the dead, then we can dare to live in the shadow of the cross, amid the suffering of the world and with missing answers.

Sunday before Lent,
Proper 3 (17–23 February)

Genesis 45.3–11, 15; 1 Corinthians 15.35–38, 42–50;
Luke 6.27–38

LOVING THE UNLOVELY

> *Almighty God, who alone can bring order to the unruly wills and passions*
> *of sinful humanity: give your people grace so to love what you command*
> *and to desire what you promise, that, among the many changes of this*
> *world, our hearts may surely there be fixed where true joys are to be found;*
> *through Jesus Christ our Lord. Amen.*
>
> Collect for the Third Sunday before Lent

This week the Gospel gives us principles to live by as God's people and Genesis tells us, in story form, about the implications of doing so. Jesus's command, 'Love your enemies, do good to those who hate you,' is one thing, forgiving your brothers who intended to murder you but instead sold you into slavery is another. Joseph's remarkable forbearance with his brothers suggests he had used the times when they were travelling to and from Egypt to think about his choices for action. If they returned but he chose not to forgive them they would be none the wiser but he would miss the chance for reconciliation. If they did not return he would lose the opportunity to forgive them and would live his life regretting the opportunity to see his father. Their return put him on the spot, forcing him to decide whether to forgive and do good to them.

It was not only Joseph who had to learn by gritty determination to love his enemies and do good to them. His at first unsuspecting and then appalled brothers had to learn to live with the reality that Joseph was both alive and had absolute power over them. Discomforting memories of past wrong, which maybe had haunted them when their father mourned for Joseph throughout his life, were now back to confront them. Joseph was alive, their sinful action was staring them in the face. There was no escape.

The story is told very vividly. Only at the very end did his brothers talk to him; until then Joseph made all the running until their dismay was gradually overcome by his reassurances. A few chapters later, after Jacob's death, they were still not confident of the depth of Joseph's forgiveness. They were probably right to be dubious about him given their past actions towards him and his more recent trickery and power-play as he sent them to and from Egypt, imprisoned Simeon and planted incriminating evidence among their belongings. There was much to be owned and forgiven on both sides. Reconciliation after so many cruel actions was hard work.

The turning point in the story, when everything changed, was Joseph's disclosure. It reconfigured his brothers' relationship with him and challenged their understanding of God. Joseph, using Jesus's phrase, did not judge his brothers. He did test them, as he had been tested over the years. That hard experience led to his insistence, perhaps born of years of dawning insight as his life unfolded through good and ill, that God had sent him ahead of his brothers and that good was coming out of his past terrible suffering. Those ideas were so hard for his brothers to assimilate that they were slow to respond and he had to kiss and weep with them before they would speak.

There are parallels with the disciples' reaction when Jesus appeared to them. They too held back and Jesus had to tell them to come close and see his hands and his feet. Like Joseph, Jesus said, 'See, it is I myself,' and the disciples' response was disbelieving joy and wondering (Luke 24.36–42). In both cases, life was suddenly turned upside down; everything people knew and had predicated their lives on required radical rethinking. If they would trust, then new life was coming out of death.

Jesus's words are hard. He said he was speaking 'to you that listen'. This message was not for the half-hearted or inattentive. In biblical thought to hear is to act, otherwise people have not truly listened and heard. Disciples are those who have listened and thus have acted. Jesus was calling them to swim upstream and gave four examples of what it means to be merciful and not to defend one's rights, not least because the slap on the 'other' cheek would, of necessity, be with the back of the hand and thus a gross insult.

So the petition in the Collect is apposite for both readings – there were a lot of unruly wills and passions around in that room in the Egyptian palace, as there are when people are insulted or abused in the way Jesus describes. The good news is that it is possible to live this way by the grace and strength of the Holy Spirit. Our part is to ensure our hearts are surely fixed where true joys are to be found.

Second Sunday before Lent

Genesis 2.4b–9, 15–end; Revelation 4; Luke 8.22–25

CREATED IN GOD'S IMAGE

Almighty God, you have created the heavens and the earth and made us in your own image: teach us to discern your hand in all your works and your likeness in all your children; through Jesus Christ your Son our Lord, who with you and the Holy Spirit reigns supreme over all things, now and for ever. Amen.

When this was written in 2013 scientists, using new equipment, were expecting to discover 700,000 new galaxies that year. The first few days of 2013 yielded seven new comets, and 461 potential new planets. We should remember that these are only new to us: our insight, not their existence, has changed. We are in Job's shoes on his whirlwind tour behind the scenes of creation when God asked: 'Where were you when I made all this?' (Job 38.4)

The reading from Revelation describes heaven's worship of God as creator; Genesis brings us down to earth, and reminds us that, as we humans discover and name things that God has made, we are simply following the first man's example. Theologically, Genesis tells us that the only thing not good in God's creation was man's aloneness. So God made a helper, and the outcome was delight. In the alternative story in Genesis 1, the theological refrain 'God saw that it was good' yielded to its all becoming 'very good' when humans were created.

If Genesis expresses God's primal creative interaction with the world in story form, the Gospel records how God incarnate interacted with that same world. Creation in some way knew its maker and responded to Jesus's presence and authority; a storm was stilled, water bore his weight, food fed more people than it should. Matthew may have been expressing the same theological thought when he described the earthquakes at Jesus's death and resurrection (Matthew 27.51, 28.2). By stilling the storm, Jesus demonstrated his authority over creation, and brought order into the chaos of his disciples' fear. Although apparently a rebuke, his words suggest that he expected more of them than fear: he expected to see God's likeness in his children, and assumed that, despite their distress, they were capable of having faith to face a violent storm.

Sometimes, God, who has made us in his image, has more confidence in us than we have in ourselves, and the Collects for the two Sundays before Lent express our willingness to be stretched. So this week we pray to be taught to discern God's hand in all his works, and his likeness in all his children; next week, for grace to perceive his Son's glory, that we may be strengthened to suffer with him.

It is easier to see God's hand in the glorious parts of creation than to face the crueller elements of life on this planet. We are rightly awed at the thought of spotting 700,000 more galaxies, and rejoice at all the good that humans do. Far harder is when we hear of people who traffic, enslave, rape, and murder other people, often women and children, to satisfy lust or because those people have desired to seek education. Apart from the horrific cruelty, and the denial that every person bears God's likeness, the isolation that this enforces physically or psychologically is as wrong as that of the man in Genesis, which God redressed.

Lest we slip into pointing the finger at other nations and cultures, or even at people, we should expect to be challenged as the Holy Spirit, answering our prayer, helps us to discern differently in our own situations. We may see more deeply. As an example, Etty Hillesum knew about people failing to see God's likeness in her, simply because she was a Jew living under the Nazis. While her understanding of human sinfulness grew, her faith in God awakened and blossomed, and she could relish beauty and goodness. She was able to smile at a 'pitiful' Gestapo officer who bullied her, and described trying to look even the worst crimes straight in the eye, to discover the small, naked human being amid the monstrous wreckage caused by people's senseless deeds.

'I sank to my knees with the words that preside over human life: "And God made man after his likeness." That passage spent a difficult morning with me' (Woodhouse, 2009). Then, amid the suffering, her unflagging caring brought hope to people who were losing their dignity during the transit to death, even when she was making that journey herself. Unlike the disciples, Hillesum reminds us that we can have faith in God even when we are afraid. In this Epiphany season of revelation and insight, we pray to dare to look this world straight in the eye, expecting to discern God's hand and presence. If what we see is wrong, God's example is always to bring good.

Sunday next before Lent

Exodus 34.29–35; 2 Corinthians 3.12–4.2;
Luke 9.28–36 [37–43a]

HIS ANOINTED FACE

Almighty Father, whose Son was revealed in majesty before he suffered death upon the cross: give us grace to perceive his glory, that we may be strengthened to suffer with him and be changed into his likeness, from glory to glory; who is alive and reigns with you, in the unity of the Holy Spirit, one God, now and for ever. Amen.

The readings this week are very sensory. There is much of significance for those with eyes to see, and not just on mountains where God's glory is revealed.

Luke adds significant details to Matthew and Mark's accounts of Jesus's transfiguration. Typically, given his interest in prayer, Luke says that Jesus went up the mountain to pray. This looks forward to Jesus's praying in the Garden of Gethsemane and wanting his disciples with him. Only Luke records Jesus's telling them to pray as well as to be there. Luke alone places this event on the 'eighth day', a possible resurrection allusion, given that only Luke tells us that Moses and Elijah spoke with Jesus about his departure (his 'exodus', a word brimming with salvific connections) to be accomplished at Jerusalem. Usually we speak of 'making' our departure; so this choice of 'accomplished' suggests something momentous: Jesus's departure is to be undertaken, not just to happen; it is his exodus. Those are words to take into Lent and Holy Week, when we ponder the mystery of the Passion.

When Moses came down the mountain, his face continued to shine. The people's fear caused him to veil his face to shield them from God's reflected glory. In contrast, although Luke describes Jesus's face as 'changed' on the mountain, it did not cause the disciples to fear (the cloud did that), or evoke any response when he came down, unveiled. Instead, they were thrust back into the mêlée of life, as a crowd surged around Jesus, and a distressed father begged for healing for his probably epileptic son. Luke, alone of the Gospel-writers, records the father's plea, and he uses a telling phrase: 'Look at my son; he is my only child.' 'Look at my son': very similar words to those another Father spoke of his only Son, first at his baptism, and again so recently on the mountain: 'This is my Son, my Chosen: listen to him.'

An only, beloved Son was implored to look at another only, beloved son. What was he to see? Not the overt glory of God, which the disciples saw in him on the mountain, but through and beyond the suffering, to someone who, as we were reminded last week, bore the likeness of God. Jesus shared our humanity;

in this father's son he was therefore looking at his own humanity, defaced. In *Saving Face* (a documentary shown on Channel 4 early in 2013), a surgeon, Dr Mohammad Jawad, who volunteers his skills to restore the faces of Pakistani women who have been victims of acid attacks, said: 'I am seeing my own face, because I am part of the society which has this disease. And I am doing my bit, but there is only so much I can do. Come, join the party.'

What do we see when we look at someone asking for mercy? Perhaps we should recognize our own disfigurement, and, through our active response, join the life-transforming party. Jesus acted and healed the son. Again, Luke uses a revealing phrase: Jesus 'gave him back to his father', in effect saying: 'Father, look at your son; look at what I have done for him.' Similarly, in the hymn by a nineteenth-century Regius Professor at Oxford, William Bright, we ask our Father to look at his Son, and then at us, in the light of what Christ has done for us:

> Look, Father, look on his anointed face,
> And only look on us as found in him;
> Look not on our misusings of thy grace,
> Our prayer so languid, and our faith so dim:
> For lo! between our sins and their reward
> We set the Passion of thy Son our Lord.

When the Lord makes his face to shine upon us and is gracious to us (Numbers 6.25), there is no telling how his glory will be revealed. As Paul reminds us, we have such a hope of seeing the glory of God as though reflected in a mirror, and are being transformed into the same image. So, until we see face to face, we will perceive God's glory in places where transformation is in progress.

We pray in the Collect for grace to perceive the Son's glory. Essentially, we are praying to be surprised by God's extraordinary grace in action.

Ash Wednesday
See Year A

First Sunday of Lent

Deuteronomy 26.1–11; Romans 10.8b–13; Luke 4.1–13

WHERE HAVE YOU COME FROM?

> *Almighty God, whose Son Jesus Christ fasted forty days in the wilderness, and was tempted as we are, yet without sin: give us grace to discipline ourselves in obedience to your Spirit; and, as you know our weakness, so may we know your power to save; through Jesus Christ our Lord. Amen.*

When preparing people for confirmation, I suggest that they keep a journal to record this important journey and to begin by reflecting on the two questions that the angel asked Hagar in the wilderness: 'Where have you come from, and where are you going?' (Genesis 16.8). These questions confront us with the truth about ourselves: I recommend them as we begin our observance of Lent.

Where have you come from? The people in Deuteronomy had experienced God's deliverance from slavery, and the gift of a new land; now they were to bring their offerings as an expression of their relationship with their saving God. Their history went back before slavery, to a nomadic existence: they were people of promise, who had grown from a single family; aliens who became a nation; people whose cry to God in their hardship was answered.

Where have you come from? Paul wrote to Christians who had been separated by racial origins, Jew and Greek. They were people who had learned that their backgrounds were not defining when it came to their relationship with God, and thus with each other. 'There is no distinction; the same Lord is Lord of all and is generous to all who call on him.'

Where have you come from? 'If you are the Son of God …' The devil's approach to Jesus was cunning, an attempt to get him to do the work of undermining his own vocation by doubting where he came from. Sometimes, it only takes a challenge to our sense of identity and our whole world crumbles. People who inflict mental abuse on others know too well the power of words to harm, and the power of implanted doubt.

Where have you come from? Luke has been careful to tell us. At Jesus's baptism, the voice from heaven declared: 'You are my Son, the beloved.' Luke followed this immediately with a list of Jesus's ancestry, going back not just to Abraham, as in Matthew's genealogy, but beyond that to Adam, the son of God.

Then Luke describes Jesus, full of the Holy Spirit who descended on him at his baptism, being led by that Spirit into the wilderness, where the first thing the devil did was to try to call that sonship into doubt. If the devil could undermine Jesus's awareness of where he had come from, then the rest was easy. So Jesus's robust answers went behind the particular temptations to the underlying question of vocation.

Where are you going? The people whom Moses addressed were learning to live with the fruits of God's generosity – delivered by signs and wonders, fed with abundant milk and honey. They were no longer to be wanderers, honey being the product of a settled existence, but people with land and identity, who celebrated with all the bounty that God had given, living as people who knew themselves to be the recipients of sheer gift from God.

Where are you going? In multicultural Corinth, they were going to experience God's salvation in Jesus Christ and know God's generosity to all people, regardless of racial or religious background.

Where are you going? To live as the Son of God in a broken world, and, ultimately, to save that world. At the end of the temptations, Luke omits Matthew's and Mark's reference to angels' waiting on Jesus, and instead reports that when the devil had finished every test (there were far more than the three we know about), he departed from Jesus until an opportune time.

When was that opportune time for the devil? It was in Gethsemane, when Jesus told the disciples to pray not to come into the time of trial. Where was Jesus going? To suffering and death, to resurrection and ascension, and, through that, to bring salvation to the world.

God knows our weakness, and is powerful to save us. Our readings encourage us to know ourselves as recipients of God's extraordinary generosity, which made a people of promise out of slaves; one people out of divided Jews and Greeks; people who follow the one who knows our weakness, and longs that we should know his power to save.

So, this Lent, where have you come from? Where are you going?

Second Sunday of Lent

Genesis 15.1–12, 17–18; Philippians 3.17–4.1;
Luke 13.31–35

LOOK, LOOK UP AT THE SKIES

*Almighty God, you show to those who are in error the light of your truth,
that they may return to the way of righteousness: grant to all those who are
admitted into the fellowship of Christ's religion, that they may reject those
things that are contrary to their profession, and follow all such things as
are agreeable to the same; through our Lord Jesus Christ. Amen.*

Look at the stars! Look, look up at the skies!
O look at all the fire-folk sitting in the air!
The bright boroughs, the circle-citadels there!

An entry in Gerard Manley Hopkins's journal for 1874 records the event behind
his poem 'The Starlight Night', of which these are the opening lines. 'As we
drove home the stars came out thick: I leant back to look at them and my heart
opening more than usual praised our Lord to and in whom all that beauty comes
home.' His reflections on the starlit sky prompt him to muse that the world is
to be purchased or received as a prize with prayer, patience, alms, and vows;
further, all this is but the barn (a hint of Bethlehem) within which is Christ.

Years ago, when I was staying at a retreat centre in the Rocky Mountains,
I looked out of the window one night, and saw the sky crammed with stars as I
have never seen before or since. I went outside and stood in awe. Unlike Abram,
I cannot remember where my thought led me, but I echoed the psalmist: 'The
heavens are telling the glory of God and the firmament proclaims his handiwork.
Day to day pours forth speech and night to night declares knowledge' (Psalm
19.1).

Paul wrote that creation can reveal things of God (Romans 1.20), and
Christian tradition has long recognized that, alongside the inspired revelation of
scripture, the book of nature, or general revelation of God, is available to anyone
who gives it time and attention. So Abram was led outside his tent to look.
Unlike most people gazing at a beautiful sunset, he was not left to interpret what
he saw in the book of nature. Instead, God challenged him to count the stars, and
to believe that his descendants would outnumber them. Their surprisingly direct
conversation is the author's way of indicating that somehow people understood
what God was saying to them.

In fact, this is the first time Abram has spoken to God: until now, when
God spoke, Abram complied, apparently silently. But now there is an outburst:
years have passed, Abram has done all he has been asked, but God's promise of
fathering a great nation (Genesis 12.2) remains unfulfilled. So, when God again

promises a reward, Abram complains that God's promises are hollow unless he has a child. It is a bold way to begin conversation with God. It sets the tone for the rest of the Hebrew Bible where human fellowship with God can be vigorous and God does not seem to mind a robust exchange, preferring it to people's grumbling to each other.

The primitive ritual with animals and birds sounds strange to us; dividing them in two indicates that both God and Abram were responsible partners in this God-initiated covenant, while the smoking pot appears to be a sign of God's presence in fire. That is a manifestation which recurs in the biblical story, ultimately at Pentecost. For Abram, reading the book of nature led to encounter and covenant with a holy God.

This ancient story comes from a very different culture, but its message crosses the centuries, and surfaces in the other readings: like Abram, the Philippian church was to stand firm, imitating Paul's example; like Abram, Jesus persevered in faith, refusing the escape offered by friendly Pharisees. Centuries later still, what can we take from this for our Lenten journey of faith? There is an implicit challenge to remain steadfastly faithful, not to let significant experiences (our starlit nights) pass unexamined, but to weigh them in the light of a prayerful, disciplined life. Abram's vision emerged from years of prayer and obedience. It took Hopkins three years to turn his starlit-night experience into a poem, during which time his reflections were shaped by daily worship in the monastery.

It is when the secure foundation is in place that we can respond faithfully to the unexpected; a well-founded life with God enables us to discern, and, as the Collect puts it, follow what is agreeable to our profession. This Lent, has there been time to stand firm in the Lord, and, with heart open to God, to look at the heavens with imaginative wonder?

Third Sunday of Lent

Isaiah 55.1–9; 1 Corinthians 10.1–13; Luke 13.1–9

WELCOME, DEAR FEAST OF LENT

Almighty God, whose most dear Son went not up to joy but first he suffered pain, and entered not into glory before he was crucified: mercifully grant that we, walking in the way of the cross, may find it none other than the way of life and peace; through Jesus Christ our Lord. Amen.

Thanks to an enthusiastic member of the Matins congregation, some of us at Durham Cathedral have vines growing in our gardens. Benefiting from his oversight, which included preventing our cropping it in its first three years, mine produced a cluster of grapes in its fourth year, but the dreadful weather ensured that they did not ripen. The parable rang a bell.

Leviticus 19.23–25 gave a theological rationale for the prohibition on eating fruit during the first three years of a tree's life. In the fourth year, all the produce was to be dedicated to rejoicing in the Lord, and not until the fifth year could the landowner claim his crop. In the parable, the gardener was right to tell the landowner to wait another year before looking for any fruit for himself, because he was demanding what was not his and missing the God-given opportunity to offer the fruit for rejoicing in the Lord. The harvest should lead him closer to joy in God, but he wanted the food without the relationship that, in terms of horticultural collaboration, was expressed in Genesis 1.29; 2.5, 8.

This, however, was no human landowner. In biblical thinking, when vineyards are mentioned, God is the landowner and the vineyard is his people (Isaiah 5); so this story is about God's relationship with his unyielding people. By looking forward to the fourth year, when fruit was for joyful celebration of their relationship with God, God the vineyard-owner was looking forward to rejoicing with his people. When this proved unlikely, frustration and anger led him to plan to destroy his planting, but – as at other times in the Old Testament (for example, Exodus 32.7–14) – he was persuaded towards restraint, and, by digging and adding manure, to permit one last effort to produce a crop. Thus this becomes a parable of God's mercy towards wayward people who neither bear fruit nor offer the due sacrifice.

This parable follows a discussion about whether people who die violently deserve that fate more than survivors. Jesus, not the crowd, had launched out on that subject, after hearing about violence at a time of sacrifice. At least that sacrifice was being offered, but, still, Jesus's message was harsh: rather than debate who figures where on the scale of sinfulness, everyone should take stock of their need to repent, and thus avoid perishing. He wanted the fruit of faith to be shown in everyone's lives, so that God could celebrate with them.

Isaiah resounds with the shouts of market traders drawing attention to their produce. Among them, God calls out like a hawker and yearns for the people to share his good food and drink. It is freely available to all, without money and without price. Still some people refuse the free gift, preferring to waste time, money, and effort on what does not satisfy. Isaiah's challenge is to know and avoid what does not satisfy us. This might be a significant subject to examine during Lent, taking stock of how we live in an over-consumerized society, asking whether we devote resources to non-essentials that leave a disappointed taste in the mouth, and whether we need to learn afresh the concept of 'enough'.

George Herbert began his poem 'Lent' with the thoughtful words 'Welcome, dear feast of Lent', and concluded it:

Yet, Lord, instruct us to improve our fast
By starving sin and taking such repast
As may our faults control:
That ev'ry man may revel at his door,
Not in his parlour; banqueting the poor,
And among those his soul.

Isaiah's assertion that God had not forgotten his covenant was the basis of his call to his hearers to seek the Lord, to return to him, and to keep their side of the covenant, so that it could be fulfilled. It is God's generous faithfulness that should prompt our repentance. Lent may be a time to examine whether and why we have found ourselves doubting God's goodness over the past year.

Perhaps we should be banqueting our soul alongside the poor. In the middle of Lent, being confronted with God's mercy invites a two-fold response: to receive and rejoice in God's good gifts; and to examine our lives and repent of our sin. One without the other is incomplete.

Fourth Sunday of Lent

Joshua 5.9–12; 2 Corinthians 5.16–21;
Luke 15.1–3, 11b–32

GOD'S RADICAL FORGIVENESS

Merciful Lord, absolve your people from their offences, that through your bountiful goodness we may all be delivered from the chains of those sins which by our frailty we have committed; grant this, heavenly Father, for Jesus Christ's sake, our blessed Lord and Saviour. Amen.

As a child, given a Sunday-school stamp of Jesus's parable of the Prodigal Son, I thought it told me: 'However disobedient you are, God will welcome you back if you say sorry.' The parable, however, does not stop at verse 24 with the celebratory feast. The elder brother's part in the story makes it all far less straightforward.

While training for ordination, I took a course in which we studied, learned, and performed passages from the Bible. This was one of them, and people's varied interpretations brought out nuances in the text. It is a masterpiece of story-telling, begging to be read aloud, so that the motives and tones of voice of the strong characters can be explored. So much is hinted at in so few words.

It begins and ends with conversations about property, possessions, and gifts. There are themes of famine and feasting. Two quite long journeys are summarized in one sentence each. The son's time in the distant country is told as narrative, unlike the direct speech at home. The power of the story lies in the fact that it is a situation that anyone can imagine, because it is about tensions in family life – sibling rivalry and inheritance. There is a younger son, who wheedles or demands, who truly repents or does a convincing performance to get round his father and get his own way; a soft-hearted father, who is slightly dotty and at the mercy of manipulation, or, knowing his son's need to rebel, very astute and in control of things; an older brother who is boringly conformist, a model of filial duty, deeply bitter, or discovering his anger for the first time. We may know all these people.

There is an outrageous, even offensive, element that says something more radical about the father's love and forgiveness than we realize. Apart from the son's unthinkable demand to have his inheritance early – in that culture, he was treating his father as dead – we cannot underestimate verses 15–16. The thought of eating pig-swill is revolting, but we miss the horror for people for whom pigs were unclean: the son was desperate. It helps us to understand the older brother, who may indeed be self-righteous, but may also be a faithful and observant son, trying to honour his father and keep the commandments. Mixed with his anger could be puzzlement, even distress, that his father was prepared to overlook his brother's sins – he named prostitutes, but pigs were too awful to contemplate. So was his complaint to his father spoken with anger, distress, or confusion?

Luke places this parable after two others about God's searching for sinners; but, unlike them, it comes with the sting in its tail, when the older brother confronts his father. While there are people in church who identify with the younger brother and have not yet comprehended the father's profligate welcome, many may be more like the elder brother. They are unhesitatingly faithful and yet unaware of the riches that are theirs for the enjoyment, or, until something triggers it, of their own disappointment, even bitterness, that their fidelity has never been celebrated. Although this is not the theme of the parable, perhaps it is time for families and churches to celebrate faithful devotion that has been taken for granted.

In addition to this Lukan context, in Lent we hear this story filtered through our prayer in the Collect, that we be absolved from our offences, and delivered from the chains of our sins by our heavenly Father's bountiful goodness. We are asking to be put in the place of both sons, not just the younger one. As we see the father's open-handed love, which was always looking and yearning for his wayward son's return, we might ponder how we respond when the self-centred behaviour of people whom we love challenges us, like the father, to risk bountiful goodness.

The person who is missing from the story is the mother, an interesting thought when we hear it on Mothering Sunday. I wonder how she coped with her turbulent male household. What comes to mind is Isaiah's poignant image of God as mother: 'Can a woman forget her nursing-child, or show no compassion for the child of her womb? Even these may forget, yet I will not forget you' (Isaiah 49.15). In that light, we can pray the Collect with confidence.

Fifth Sunday of Lent
Isaiah 43.16–21; Philippians 3.4b–14; John 12.1–8

ANOINTED FOR A TOMB

Most merciful God, who by the death and resurrection of your Son Jesus Christ delivered and saved the world: grant that by faith in him who suffered on the cross we may triumph in the power of his victory; through Jesus Christ our Lord. Amen.

The brother and sisters, Lazarus, Martha, and Mary, radiated hospitality. They offered their home and their hearts to Jesus and included his numerous friends. John records that Jesus loved them. Theirs was a home where Jesus felt comfortable, where he could put his feet up and relax. When facing danger or demanding situations, we need somewhere safe among friends, and it is telling that Jesus chose to stay with them during the gruelling last week of his life.

In the Gospel vignette, Jesus was their guest of honour at a thank-you dinner, after he had turned their family life around by raising Lazarus from the dead. In the relaxed atmosphere, Mary suddenly jolted everyone to attention. Her action was like breaking a very large bottle of Chanel No 5 in a small space: the fragrance would be overpowering. It was immensely valuable, about a year's wages for the average person. If, as is possible, it was part of her dowry, she was offering Jesus her love and her life's commitment in sheer grateful extravagance. Shockingly, she anointed his feet. Anointing his head would have symbolically anointed him as prophet, priest, or king, but, by anointing his feet, she likened him to a corpse, since the anointing of a dead body began with the feet.

John makes the link linguistically by using the same word, 'pound', when describing the burial spices that Nicodemus gave after Jesus's death. Mary's action carried a disturbing mixed message, which Jesus understood, of lavish gratitude and impending death.

This was an incredibly tender and intimate moment in a family home. A respectable woman let down her hair only in front of her husband or when mourning. Mary's willingness to be vulnerable to Jesus broke the barriers of convention in the way that unmarried men and women related to each other, and freed Jesus to be vulnerable in return. He had seen her hair at Lazarus's tomb; now he saw it again, foreshadowing his own death, in the midst of a celebration of Lazarus's restored life.

Sometimes, we have to hold in tension the paradox that life and death are not mutually exclusive. The funeral liturgy reminds us that 'In the midst of life we are in death'. This is true every Sunday, when congregations reconstitute themselves as assemblies of people experiencing life and death: one person's celebration of an engagement or the birth of a grandchild is part of the same offering as another person's bereavement or redundancy. The Church invites us to bring the textured fabric of our lives to God, without denying any part of them, to make one offering. Thus, over the centuries, Durham Cathedral has contained more joy and more sorrow, more fear and more hope, than most other buildings. It is a prayed-in place, a safe place that keeps itself as a place of hospitality for all, without charge, aiming to welcome people as if Christ. The same can be true, however small the village or inner-city church.

This integrity of joy and sorrow, hope and doubt, is also built into the fabric of the liturgical year. When my father died one Lent, I wondered whether I would feel any Easter joy. When Easter came, I experienced the paradox that, as I brought my sadness to the Church's celebration of Christ's resurrection, it was given back to me as a new, deeper joy: joy in a minor key, but a strange and poignant joy none the less. That is the wonder of Christian worship: it holds together the grief and the glory, the tears and the triumph, in one offering to God, and makes of it something beyond our imagining.

Just as Mary shifted the focus, so, on Passion Sunday, our gaze is refocused as the liturgy turns us from the disciplined observance of Lent to become conscious of the growing overshadowing of Calvary. The cross comes more sharply into view. We turn to face it for ourselves, but we also turn as a community that will tread the pilgrimage of the next two weeks together, bringing our joy and sorrow, our hopes and fears, to make one offering to God. 'In the midst of life we are in death.' Yes, but: 'Praise to you, Lord Jesus: dying you destroyed our death, rising you restored our life: Lord Jesus, come in glory.'

Palm Sunday

Liturgy of the Passion: Isaiah 50.4–9a; Philippians 2.5–11;
Luke 22.14–23

THE LORD RIDES ON TO DIE

> *Almighty and everlasting God, who in your tender love towards the human*
> *race sent your Son our Saviour Jesus Christ to take upon him our flesh and*
> *to suffer death upon the cross: grant that we may follow the example of*
> *his patience and humility, and also be made partakers of his resurrection;*
> *through Jesus Christ our Lord. Amen.*

On Palm Sunday, we hear the Passion narrative in its entirety. Luke's version
bears some distinctive hallmarks, not least his interest in the place of women
and of prayer. He alone tells us of the women of Jerusalem who wept for Jesus,
just as Jesus wept for Jerusalem, and that Jesus prayed for Peter, and, when Peter
denied Jesus, turned and looked at him. Whatever was in that gaze? He may
have expected Peter's failure, but we cannot guess the pain of betrayal by his
staunchest friend.

At the end of the wilderness temptations, Luke told us that the devil departed
until an opportune time. Now he was back with the same temptation, in a more
acute guise, accompanied by the torture of crucifixion. 'If you are the son of God
…' became: 'If he is the Messiah …', 'If you are the King of the Jews …'

'If you are the King of the Jews …': Luke reports the words of the crucified
criminals, and Jesus's astounding statement: 'Today you will be with me in
paradise.' 'Paradise', rarely used in the New Testament, comes from the Old
Persian word for an enclosed space. It hints at the undoing of Adam and Eve's
expulsion from the garden. Astoundingly, Jesus expected to be in paradise with a
criminal 'today'. Luke has built up the momentum by the use of 'today': 'Today
this scripture has been fulfilled in your hearing' (Luke 4.21); 'I must stay at your
house today' (Luke 19.5); 'Today salvation has come to this house' (Luke 19.9).
The time is right: this is God's time.

Amid the cruelly familiar story, Luke re-orders the rending of the veil of the
Temple that separated the high priest, representing sinful humans, from God's
holy presence. Mark and Matthew place this after the death of Jesus, harking
back to the Old Testament teaching that humans could not look on the face of
God and live. With the death of Jesus, the requirement of the law was met,
the veil of separation in the Temple was obsolete, and God shredded it. That
explanation will not work for Luke, who places the rending immediately before
Jesus's death, as a sign of the heavens' being opened to clear the way. At Jesus's
baptism, Jesus, fully identified with the human condition, was praying when

the heavens were opened, and the Holy Spirit descended; now, when he was fully obedient to the point of death, the Temple veil was torn in two, revealing the glory of God in the Holy of Holies. In a similar vein, Luke reports that just before the first Christian martyr Stephen died, the heavens opened, and Stephen saw the glory of God. For Luke, theologically, God's great love clears the way before humans tread it.

So, with the ripping of the Temple veil, the barrier that it represented was permanently breached by God, who opened the way for Jesus, fully human, and thus identified with human sinfulness, to enter his presence. No wonder Jesus could cry with confidence: 'Father, into your hands I commend my spirit,' as he entrusted himself to the Father, who had affirmed at his baptism that this was his son. His was no whimpering death: having twice in the Passion narrative called God 'Father', he cried out loudly to his Father. For Luke, this intimate relationship persisted until the end. 'If you are the Son of God ...'. Yes! is the resounding answer.

Luke's ordering of events makes sense, given his Gospel's emphasis on the Father's unbounded love which removes all barriers between him and his son. Thus we can recall the father of the Prodigal, who, in his resolute love that withstood all the shame that his son brought on him, was looking out for his son, and took all the initiative in welcoming him home. That is a wonderful theological framework for our observance of another Holy Week.

> Ride on! ride on in majesty!
> Thy last and fiercest strife is nigh;
> The Father, on his sapphire throne,
> Expects his own anointed Son.
>
> Ride on, ride on in majesty!
> To thee we lift hosannas high;
> For thou the immortal Father's Son
> The crown hast gained: thy work is done!
> *Verse 1: Henry Milman Verse 2: Copyright © Michael Sadgrove.*
> *Used by permission.*

Maundy Thursday
See Year A

Good Friday

Isaiah 52.13–end of 53; Psalm 22; Hebrews 10.16–25;
John 18.1–end of 19

IT IS ALL ONE SALVATION STORY

> *Almighty Father, look with mercy on this your family for which our Lord Jesus Christ was content to be betrayed and given up into the hands of sinners and to suffer death upon the cross; who is alive and glorified with you and the Holy Spirit, one God, now and for ever. Amen.*

'She gave birth to her firstborn son and wrapped him in a piece of cloth and laid him in a manger.' 'They took his tunic … Standing near the cross of Jesus [was] his mother … When Jesus saw his mother and the disciples whom he loved standing beside her, he said to his mother, 'Woman, here is your son' … 'There was a new tomb and they laid him there.'

In a year when we are reading Luke's Gospel, and especially in years when the Annunciation falls in Holy Week, Mary's presence at the cross recalls the birth narratives that preface Luke's Gospel. It is all one salvation story. Twice, Luke told us that Mary treasured words and experiences from Jesus's childhood in her heart, and surely some of those memories must have flooded back in the morass of emotions as she stood at the cross. So much was contradictory, the horror of the cross seemingly inverting, if not undoing, the events of his birth. Thus John Donne wrote (in 'Upon the Annunciation and Passion falling upon one day. 1608'): 'Gabriel gives Christ to her, he her to John'; her tender act of clothing Jesus was callously reversed, and, once again, he was laid in something borrowed.

At the foot of the cross, Mary stood her ground, physically and spiritually, only later being rejoined by the disciples who had abandoned Jesus. It was at the cross that her true mettle, which Gabriel's words had looked forward to, was revealed; that she had found favour with God.

Simeon's disturbing words, spoken specifically to Mary when she and Joseph presented the baby Jesus with such joy and hope in the Temple – 'This child is destined for the falling and rising of many in Israel … and a sword will pierce your own soul, too' – had probably troubled her over the years, as she pondered their meaning; now, they were horribly fulfilled.

> Mary, do you remember that
> one day a sword would pierce your soul?
> And in your darkest nightmare did
> you dream that this would be the end?
> The son you once held in your arms
> is held now by a cross of wood;

the face you once gazed on in love
appears disfigured, crowned with thorns.
The shepherds now are far away
and in their place a shouting mob;
no silent, breathless, timeless awe,
no angel hosts with glorious songs,
no priceless gifts from eastern lands,
but anger, and the stench of death:
the only gift a borrowed tomb,
the only sound a cry of pain.
And is there glory in this cross?
Can you, who sang Magnificat,
rejoiced in God who came to save,
still sing that song, see in this cross
amidst the shame, a Saviour come,
a sign of grace, a means of life?
Mary, once you waited, wept and
bore the pain to bear your son;
now as you stand and wait and weep,
you bear not only pain but shame.
So, is there life amidst this death?
And can you glory in this cross;
mingle your tears with hope
because you know the paradox
that God, your Saviour, first must die?

Good Friday remains a day for unhurried reflection on the Passion of our Lord – something that John Donne did on horseback 400 years ago. In 'Good Friday, 1613. Riding Westward', he contemplated the crucifixion, with its earthquake and darkened sky:

Yet dare I almost be glad, I do not see
That spectacle of too much weight for me.
Who sees Gods face, that is self-life, must die;
What a death were it then to see God die?
It made his own lieutenant Nature shrink,
It made His footstool crack, and the sun wink.

'That spectacle of too much weight for me.' Good Friday offers us the stern mercy of time to survey the wondrous cross, praying that God will look with mercy on us, the family for whom our Lord was content to suffer death.

This Good Friday, amid the horror of our Lord's suffering, as we hear the continuing, daily litany of the world's suffering, Mary exemplifies the epistle's exhortation: 'Let us hold fast to the confession of our hope without wavering, for he who has promised is faithful.'

Easter Day

Acts 10.34–43; 1 Corinthians 15.19–26; Luke 24.1–12

UNIMAGINABLE GOOD NEWS

Lord of all life and power, who through the mighty resurrection of your Son overcame the old order of sin and death to make all things new in him: grant that we, being dead to sin and alive to you in Jesus Christ, may reign with him in glory; to whom with you and the Holy Spirit be praise and honour, glory and might, now and in all eternity. Amen.

Some of the most powerful words in the Bible are questions; questions that, if we ask them of ourselves, may take us to new depths in our knowledge of ourselves and of God.

'Why do you look for the living among the dead?' is an ironic question. On the face of it, it was a silly question, because the women were seeking not the living among the dead, but the dead among the dead. Nevertheless, Easter is a time to be faced with supremely silly questions and situations, as we navigate the unknown territory of resurrection.

For the people who had been around Jesus in Jerusalem, life was beyond belief that first Easter Day: an enormous stone rolled from a tomb; a missing body with its grave-clothes in a neat pile; men in dazzling white appearing with ridiculous messages; women instructed to bear witness to what they had seen (something they could never do in a court, having been considered gullible, unreliable witnesses ever since Eve was deceived by the serpent); men expected to believe an idle tale told by women. And that was only the beginning.

The cast of human characters in the Gospel is familiar. The named women who went to the tomb knew Jesus well; they had (shockingly in their culture) travelled with him, and provided for him financially (Luke 8.1–3). Peter was probably his closest friend. The women were perplexed and terrified – no resurrection joy for them as yet – but at least had the presence of mind to find the others, and to report what they had seen.

Peter was curious enough to go to the tomb and look but, at that early dawn stage, did not move on from amazement. So he looked, just as Jesus had looked at him when he denied Jesus. This time, he saw not Jesus's eyes, but his absence. Was this his turning back, his repentance, of which Jesus had spoken as the prelude to strengthening the others (Luke 22.32)? Certainly, later that day, Jesus appeared to him privately (Luke 24.34) and, within weeks, Peter was at the centre of the proclamation of the gospel (Acts 1.15, 2.14). Not only was Jesus changed by resurrection: Peter became a transformed man.

We rush to Easter joy, and rightly sing 'Alleluia' with joyful hearts. Distanced from events, and knowing the end of the story, we have had time to take it all in. But, on that first early morning, nothing had prepared the women and the disciples for what they experienced, so their first reactions of fear, doubt, and perplexity are completely understandable. At dawn, all they knew was bad news – the body was missing, and their first thoughts were far from resurrection. Even when Jesus appeared to them, in stories that we shall hear in the coming days, it was not immediately good news, because they took time to make the mental leap that resurrection required.

They had seen their friend die the most horrible death; they were in shock – today we might call it post-traumatic stress – and resurrection was not in their vocabulary. So the empty tomb was not gospel, in its sense of 'good news'. To become good news, along with the emptiness there also had to be encounter with its former occupant. Their imaginations needed to be burst open by resurrection, but that was still to come. As e.e. cummings put it when he wrote (in 'I thank you God for most this amazing') of 'Unimaginable You': all this was indeed unimaginable.

> They came, as dawn was breaking,
> to finalize their loss,
> absorb death's grim, stark meaning,
> the horror of the cross.
> They came, and angels told them
> 'Recall the words he said.
> You seek the one now living,
> why look among the dead?'
>
> We dream of resurrection
> yet when it comes we cling
> to things known and familiar,
> the boundaries they bring.
> And we, who are not ready
> to let our grieving go,
> reject the angels' story,
> hold to the loss we know.
>
> You interrupt our mourning,
> an untrod path you pave;
> for you bring resurrection
> while we still seek the grave.
> Our lives are wrenched wide open,
> the wounds we nursed exposed;
> and, like a phrase of music,
> our death to life transposed.
> *Copyright © 1995 Rosalind Brown*

Second Sunday of Easter

Exodus 14.10–end, 15.20–21; Acts 5.27–32;
Revelation 1.4–8; John 20.19–31

DOUBT AND FAITH INTERACT

*Almighty Father, you have given your only Son to die for our sins and to
rise again for our justification: grant us so to put away the leaven of malice
and wickedness that we may always serve you in pureness of living and
truth; through the merits of your Son Jesus Christ our Lord. Amen.*

Thomas has had a raw deal from history: defining him as 'Doubting Thomas'
seems unfair if we look at his story more closely.

For whatever reason, Thomas missed Jesus's first resurrection appearance
to the group in the locked room. No doubt this caused him enormous regret, even
remorse. He could do nothing about it, however; he could not make Jesus appear
again. He had to wait. In this context, John's almost casual remark: 'A week later
… Jesus came and stood among them' is important. A whole week had passed;
it was now the day of resurrection again. There had been seven days of nothing
happening. What had Thomas done during that time?

The remarkable thing is that Thomas was still with the others. Far from
doubting the testimony of the other disciples, he appears to have believed them,
and stuck around. This does not come across if we see his words – 'Unless I see
the mark of the nails in his hand and put my finger in the mark of the nails in
his side, I will not believe' – as a statement that he had no faith that Jesus had
risen from the dead. His faith was keeping him, someone for whom seeing was
believing (after all, he was a twin, and was perhaps used to mistaken identities),
with the others, waiting for what happened next.

Luke (23.41) records other disciples as 'disbelieving for joy and still
wondering', after they were invited to touch Jesus's wounds. Even after touching,
which Thomas had not yet done, it was too much for some of them to take in.
Having seen Jesus die horribly, they found it hard to make sense of seeing him
alive again. I wonder whether we do Thomas something of an injustice, and
misunderstand how he spoke the words. He was looking for no more than the
others had experienced, and his tone of voice could have been one of amazed
delight: 'I'll be able to take this in properly only when I see it for myself.' Until
then, he, like some of the others, was disbelieving for joy, and still wondering.

So, instead of sulking because he was left out, Thomas committed himself
to staying with the disciples, until faith yielded to sight. It turned out to take
a week, but he stuck it out. This fits with the rock-solid commitment that he
had displayed when Jesus was about to walk into danger by going to Lazarus's
tomb, and Thomas said: 'Let us go also, that we may die with him' (John 11.16).

That level of allegiance and faith would not be abandoned easily, especially if people he trusted were reporting that Jesus had appeared to them, alive. In modern parlance, he needed time to get his head round all this, and until then, he was willing to be carried by their testimony. We should not underestimate his loyalty and devotion. He was steadfast in his commitment to Jesus and the other disciples for that whole week of testing silence.

When Jesus did appear to him, with the same offer made to the others the previous week, his exclamation 'My Lord and my God' was the most sure, instantaneous response of any of the people to whom Jesus revealed himself. It suggests that he had pondered the implications of what the others told him. So convinced was he, tradition tells us, that he travelled to southern India to proclaim the resurrection; and the Mar Thoma Churches there bear his name.

The Gospels are not afraid to let doubt sit alongside the resurrection appearances, just as many of the psalms let faith and doubt interact in curative, prayerful tension. Even at Jesus's final appearance to the disciples, they worshipped him, but 'some doubted' (Matthew 28.16).

Much pastoral work is a response to the apparent silence of God, and we can learn from Jesus's example to resist the impulse to rush people towards the cast-iron certainty that dishonours faithful questions. Thomas sets us an example of Easter alleluias that embrace doubt.

Faced with another startling victory snatched out of the jaws of death, Miriam and the women sang, in possibly the oldest text in the Bible: 'Sing to the Lord, for he has triumphed gloriously.' Thomas would echo that, doubts and all.

Third Sunday of Easter

Zephaniah 3.14–20; Acts 9.1–6 [7–20]; John 21.1–19

RESTORATION BY A CHARCOAL FIRE

Almighty Father, who in your great mercy gladdened the disciples with the sight of the risen Lord: give us such knowledge of his presence with us, that we may be strengthened and sustained by his risen life and serve you continually in righteousness and truth; through Jesus Christ our Lord. Amen.

Since John tells us (John 20.30) that Jesus did many unrecorded signs in the presence of his disciples, it raises the question why he chose to record these in particular. His Gospel is structured around a succession of signs, beginning at the wedding in Cana and culminating with the raising of Lazarus. Those before Jesus's death all involved miracles, and, since John considers the resurrection appearances to be signs, we can treat the miraculous catch of fish and breakfast on the beach as a sign. To what is it pointing?

It is easy to think of the period between Jesus's resurrection and his ascension as all excitement and miraculous appearances. It was not. There was the week-long separation between Jesus's first and second appearances, no doubt heart-wrenching for Thomas, and perplexing for everyone. It seems that Peter gave up waiting for Jesus to appear, and went back to normal routine: hence 'I'm going fishing.'

It was a disaster. Most people lived on income earned the previous day; so for experienced fishermen to work all night and catch nothing was both embarrassing and meant that their families went hungry. The disciples did not recognize Jesus on the beach until, at last, one of them understood the sign of the enormous catch, and recognized Jesus as being behind it. Peter's impetuous dive into the water was totally in character with the portrait of him in the Gospels: a man who loved Jesus deeply, despite his one devastating failure, which made this reunion all the more urgent. It is not hard to imagine the reaction of the other fishermen, who were left to do the arduous work with the heavy catch, while he swam ashore excitedly.

They counted the fish, probably in amazement, quantifying the miracle. Numbers often have symbolic significance in the Bible: three, seven, 12, and 40 are examples. But 153 has no particular symbolic significance (although it has subsequently attracted various theories), and we should treat this as a sign of resurrection plenteousness, expressed in the routine of daily life. Further, apart from the potentially net-breaking scale of the catch, what was remarkable was that these were large fish. This was no mediocre provision; the fish would sell well, and the disciples' families would feast tonight. Jesus had done it again: as with the wine at Cana and the food for the 5000, there was more than enough.

Breakfast followed, for which, as at the Passover meal, Jesus had made all the preparations. In fact, he had made them meticulously because, for Peter, there was to be a new beginning. John is careful to specify that a charcoal fire was involved. Our sense of smell evokes long-forgotten memories, and this smell would bring back for Peter the vivid, painful memories of betraying Jesus by a charcoal fire. Jesus intended to take the sting out of those memories, so that they did not paralyse him for life.

The Gospel is about new beginnings, and he dealt with Peter's three denials by providing opportunities for three affirmations of love. Their use of the word 'love' is more nuanced than in English, alternating between 'love' and something closer to our 'care for', but its heart was Jesus's offer of a new beginning to his hot-headed, loyal friend. He undid the power of Peter's memory of failure, taking him back past his betrayal to his memories of Jesus's command to love and to his prayer for them to be protected (John 14–17). In that context, Jesus called Peter to share his responsibility as the good shepherd (John 10) by feeding his sheep.

John ends his Gospel as he began, with Jesus's call to 'follow me' (John 1.43, 21.19). Since the Venerable Bede is buried in Durham Cathedral, we were delighted when, soon after his election, Pope Francis quoted Bede's homily on St Matthew's Gospel: 'Jesus saw the tax-collector, and, by having mercy, chose him as an Apostle, saying to him "Follow me."'

Peter's encounter with Jesus was essentially an act of mercy, a sign of the power of the resurrection to open up new beginnings. The Collect describes the disciples as gladdened by the sight of the risen Lord, before praying that we may be strengthened and sustained by his risen life to serve continually. In praying this prayer, we may find something similarly powerful and merciful happening in our lives, too.

Fourth Sunday of Easter

Genesis 7.1–5, 11–18, 8.6–18, 9.8–13; Acts 9.36–43;
Revelation 7.9–17; John 10.22–30

IT TAKES COURAGE TO FOLLOW

Almighty God, whose Son Jesus Christ is the resurrection and the life: raise
us, who trust in him, from the death of sin to the life of righteousness, that
we may seek those things which are above, where he reigns with you in the
unity of the Holy Spirit, one God, now and for ever. Amen.

One of the joys of hearing three readings on a Sunday and praying a Collect
is that the readings and prayers interpret each other, sometimes in unexpected
ways. Children tend to hear the Noah story on its own as a vivid tale that grabs
their attention because of all the animals, while a few weeks before I first wrote
this column a full cathedral at Durham enjoyed seeing and hearing the story sung
in a wonderful performance of Benjamin Britten's *Noye's Fludde.*

Each year, my baptism and confirmation group look at the story of Noah
and the flood in the context of God's saving actions, as recounted in the overall
biblical story, and, in particular, of its baptismal imagery for Christians. Today,
however, we hear it alongside a very different story –that of Jesus's being quizzed
by antagonistic people, and of his reply, which refers to sheep hearing his voice
and following him.

Jesus had been speaking about being the good shepherd, in the same
breath as he spoke of thieves, bandits, and wolves. He faced the animosity of
the religious leaders of his day, and his disciples could be forgiven for feeling
uncomfortable. Perhaps they were tempted to slip away quietly. The opposition
had ganged up and surrounded Jesus in the Temple – a malicious and threatening
mob, which, in the very next verse, took up stones ('again', John tells us) to
attack him.

In this situation, Jesus was a model to the disciples of how their shepherd
was not afraid to face danger, and would not abandon his calling in order to
protect himself. He embodied the commitment of a good shepherd who does
not run away; no one would snatch them out of his hand or, indeed, from God's
hand. Jesus, the Lamb of God, the Lamb at the centre of the throne in the vision
of heaven in Revelation, was their shepherd.

What does the story of Noah look like if we let it rub up against
Jesus's words and example? When God created the world, he saw that it
was very good; now (Genesis 6.11) he saw that it was corrupt and filled
with violence. God, who had made such a glorious world, now considered
the unthinkable idea of destroying it. Noah alone was righteous; so, as a

corollary to the destruction of the world, Noah needed rescuing, like a sheep in danger. The question was: would Noah hear God's voice and follow?

In Benjamin Britten's *Noye's Fludde*, it is Mrs Noah who refuses to listen. She mocks the idea of going into the ark because she is having too much of a good time with her friends – an early version of a girls' night out. The Bible, however, remains tantalizingly silent about how God and Noah debated the crazy proposition that he should build a large ark in the middle of dry ground and then goad the animals into it. It is easy to imagine the neighbours mocking as they watch him devote all his time and resources to this seemingly daft construction project. His reputation would be in tatters, and no attempt at explanation would be taken seriously.

Behind a good story with much dramatic potential, exploited by Britten, lies a more serious point, especially in the context of today's Psalm (Psalm 23) and Gospel reading. Sometimes, the call of God comes to us when we are living in a context that is hostile to this call, that mocks and laughs. Hearing and following in that situation takes courage.

Besides these two readings, we hear how Peter raised Dorcas. There is an interesting little detail in the way the story is told. Peter put all the weeping people outside, and turned to the body, saying: 'Tabitha, get up.' It seems that Peter was following Jesus's example when he raised Jairus's daughter from the dead. Jesus put all the weeping people outside, and took the girl by the hand, and said: 'Little girl, get up.' Also on that occasion, the people had laughed at Jesus (Mark 5.40). Had Peter learned to ignore the mocking, to hear Jesus's voice and follow him, just as Jesus told people that his sheep would do?

Fifth Sunday of Easter

Baruch 3.9–15, 32–4.4 or Genesis 22.1–18; Acts 11.1–18; Revelation 21.1–6; John 13.31–35

THE JOY OF ALL CREATION

Almighty God, who through your only-begotten Son Jesus Christ have overcome death and opened to us the gate of everlasting life: grant that, as by your grace going before us you put into our minds good desires, so by your continual help we may bring them to good effect; through Jesus Christ our risen Lord. Amen.

Sometimes, we forget that not only Christians are joyful: creation sings God's praise. Poets such as Gerard Manley Hopkins and e.e. cummings relish this, as did the psalmist: 'Let the heavens be glad, and let the earth rejoice; let the sea roar, and all that fills it' (Psalm 96.11).

I love Baruch's arresting depiction of this gladness: 'The stars shone in their watches and were glad; he called them and they said, "Here we are!" They shone with gladness for him who made them. This is our God; no other can be compared to him.' Job (Job 38.7) encountered a noisily jubilant creation: the morning stars sang together, and all the heavenly beings shouted for joy. Jesus expected that if the people who shouted as he rode into Jerusalem were forcibly silenced, the stones would cry out instead (Luke 19.40).

Creation is ecstatic, beside itself with joy in God's presence. The root of 'ecstatic' lies in being led out of stasis, of standing or stopping. It is not merely an emotion; at its heart is decisive action like that of Jesus, who, for the joy set before him, endured the cross. Sometimes, God has to unsettle us into ecstasy, to get us moving from what holds us in stoppage or inactivity.

A few weeks ago, we heard of Abraham's being taken to look at the stars to learn that his descendants would outnumber them. He named his son Isaac, which means 'laughter', unwittingly echoing the gladness of the stars. Now, in the troubling story of the binding of Isaac, the focus shifts from promise to the seemingly perverse command of God to offer his son, his laughter, in sacrifice. It was appallingly unsettling.

Then there is Peter, coming to terms with the extraordinary mercy of God. Had he been a hymn-writer, he might have expressed it in Faber's words: 'There's a wideness in God's mercy like the wideness of the sea,' as he discovered that the Holy Spirit was given to people whom he believed to be beyond the pale. Two weeks ago, we heard Jesus's searing, repeated question to him: 'Do you love me?' Nothing mattered more. Only once he knew Peter's answer could Jesus entrust his followers to Peter's care. Now, when the hitherto unimagined implications of the resurrection unsettled Peter's dubious fellow apostles, Peter's love and commitment to these unexpected recipients of God's mercy silenced the Church into wonder.

As we hear in the Gospel, love is commanded; it does not always come naturally, albeit it is a response to being loved with inconceivable love. Love involves a response of commitment. So St Benedict instructed his monks to prefer nothing whatever to Christ, and sharpened this in the vows of stability, obedience, and conversion of life. Together they provide for a sure foundation for Christian joy and faithfulness.

In their separate ways, Abraham and Peter were learning that love is expressed not just in emotion, but in stable, obedient, and ecstatic lives, even when life is perplexing. Meanwhile, in the Revelation to St John, the source of all this obedient joy is revealed, as we glimpse the worship of the one who makes all things new, who gives water as a gift from the spring of the water of life.

Ecstatic love is the response to God's love, which has been poured into our hearts. Baruch writes of wisdom: 'Turn ... and walk towards the shining of her light.' On Good Friday in Durham Cathedral, we sang of God's loving wisdom and wise love, expressed in Jesus Christ, the second Adam. Turning to Christ is our vocation this Easter. Two days later we had the joy of hearing people, some converting from other faiths, affirm that they turned to Christ as they were baptized and confirmed at dawn on Easter Day, and of hearing from them afterwards of the wonder and happiness of their new life.

In this Easter season, we respond with joy to our risen Lord, who calls us to love one another, and gives the water of life. He gives us, too, the stars shining with gladness for the God who made them, calling eagerly, 'Here we are!': they set us an example of love, as does Abraham, who responds with gritty commitment, and Peter with his trusting loyalty.

Sixth Sunday of Easter

Ezekiel 37.1–14; Acts 16.9–15; Revelation 21.10, 22–22.5;
John 14.23–29 or John 5.1–9

GOD BRINGS LIFE TO DUST AND DRY BONES

*God our redeemer, you have delivered us from the power of darkness and
brought us into the kingdom of your Son: grant that, as by his death he has
recalled us to life, so by his continual presence in us he may raise us to
eternal joy; through Jesus Christ our Lord. Amen.*

It is wise to pay attention to the questions in the Bible, which often cut to the
heart of things. This week there are two: 'Can these bones live?' and 'Do you
want to be made well?' Both ask whether God can bring new, transforming life
in a deadlocked situation.

Ezekiel hedged his bets. By shifting the focus back to God, the answer
had to be 'yes' because God had once breathed life into dust so that it became
a living being (Genesis 2.7). This time, God involved Ezekiel in the life-giving
project, telling him to prophesy to dry bones. These were only later identified as
those of the house of Israel, as God had previously instructed him to prophesy
to the mountains of Israel (Ezekiel 36.1). Both people and land needed new life
(Ezekiel 36.17). This happened for the sake of God's holy name, not for that of
the people (Ezekiel 36.22), but the outcome was that both land and people could
flourish.

So, can these bones live? Yes, because God is holy, and brings life even to
dust and bones.

Jesus's question was disconcertingly out of the blue to a lonely man who
had been an invalid for 38 years, begging for charity, and never able to get into
the water when it was disturbed (the belief apparently being that the first person
in would be healed). Jesus's seemingly naïve question was not just about being
made well, but about being ready to begin a new life, in place of resignation to
sad hopelessness. The man, who was quite reasonably unable to conceive of
any other way of life, gave a practical reason for not expecting to be made well.
So Jesus took the initiative – for reasons unknown to us, except that he was the
life-giver – cut through the evasion, and, in a symbolic sense, brought the man
into the Sabbath rest of God. In doing so, in the words of the Collect, he called
the man to life, and chose to face the ensuing controversy about healing on the
Sabbath rather than waiting another day.

Like the man who had lived with disappointment for 38 years, Paul had
been disappointed. Forbidden by the Holy Spirit to preach in Asia, he diverted
to Phrygia and Galatia, was stopped from going to Bithynia, and so went to

Troas via Mysia. Plotted on a map, it is clear that his plans to go east or north were thwarted into a journey north-west, ending up on the Aegean coast, where he was ideally placed to respond to a visionary call to Macedonia, across the Aegean. Surely this was the reason for all this disappointment?

Once there, however, instead of the man in his vision he met an independent businesswoman from Thyatira, a manufacturing city ironically close to where Paul had just come from, across the Aegean. Lydia, a wealthy dealer in purple cloth, dyed with madder-root found near Thyatira, was not a Jew, but was interested enough to join women gathered by the river, a traditional gathering place for Jews where there was no synagogue. Paul went there, and, on another Sabbath, she responded to his message, being baptized with her household.

The Collect holds these readings together, reminding us that God recalls us to life, and raises us to eternal joy. Can these bones live? Do you want to be made well? Like the man whom Jesus met, we can have eminently realistic reasons for not expecting new life, but, mercifully, God is not constrained by our lack of faith. Like Ezekiel, even if we are dubious, remembering God's past deliverance helps us to trust that God is still our redeemer. Indeed, Ezekiel's confidence seemed to grow as he saw God's acting in response to his prophesying.

Lydia had no such qualms, and, after baptism, her instinct was hospitality. Perhaps that gift for making people welcome was instrumental in the foundation of the Philippian church, which was particularly dear to Paul's heart. She might also have been involved in the church in Thyatira, which is commended for its life-enhancing love and service (Revelation 2.19). Hospitality is a good foundation for mission.

God has recalled us to life, the life-giving consequences of which may never cease to amaze us.

Ascension Day
See Year A

Seventh Sunday of Easter

Ezekiel 36.24–28; Acts 16.16–34;
Revelation 22.12–14, 16–17, 20–21; John 17.20–26

A RESPONSE OF GLORIOUS HOPE

> *O God the King of glory, you have exalted your only Son Jesus Christ with*
> *great triumph to your kingdom in heaven: we beseech you, leave us not*
> *comfortless, but send your Holy Spirit to strengthen us and exalt us to the*
> *place where our Saviour Christ is gone before, who is alive and reigns with*
> *you, in the unity of the Holy Spirit, one God, now and for ever. Amen.*

Ascension Day sets the theological context for this week's readings. Jesus, a
forerunner on our behalf, has entered heaven (Hebrews 6.20), taking with him
human nature. This has profound implications for us, and Bishop Wordsworth's
Ascension hymn is unrivalled:

> Thou hast raised our human nature
> In the clouds to God's right hand;
> Mighty Lord, in thine Ascension
> We by faith behold our own.

A consequence of this is expressed when, at the Eucharist, the president exhorts
everyone: 'Lift up your hearts'; and the confident response is 'We lift them to
the Lord.' Because we are in Christ, our hearts belong in heaven with the Lord. A
rarely sung verse of the same hymn by Bishop Wordworth expresses this:

> Raise us up from earth to Heaven,
> Give us wings of faith and love,
> Gales of holy aspirations
> Wafting us to realms above;
> That, with hearts and minds uplifted,
> We with Christ our Lord may dwell,
> Where he sits enthroned in glory
> In his heavenly citadel.

Although without sin, Jesus bore the consequences of sin, as a result of which his
human body was wounded. He took those scars into heaven. Because there is a
place in heaven for his wounds, through the ascension, there is a place in heaven
for our wounds. Another hymn, by Matthew Bridges, expresses this:

> Crown him the Lord of love!
> Behold his hands and side,
> Rich wounds, yet visible above
> In beauty glorified.

What are the down-to-earth outworkings of this? The story from Acts began in the pitch black of a prison, possibly a dungeon, where Paul and Silas were incarcerated. They had been wounded from being flogged and fixed in stocks. They were not complaining about it but keeping the other prisoners awake, as they prayed and sang hymns to God. Whatever happened to their bodies, their hearts were in heaven.

A violent earthquake followed, which, while terrifying, would not in itself unlock chains. Something strange was going on, as the rest of the story explains. The jailer's response to these extraordinary events, and the astonishing behaviour of Paul and Silas, was belief in Jesus. He washed their wounds, and took them home for a meal. Did he see that the battered Paul and Silas were – as Jesus said – loved by God, as Jesus was loved? Given Paul's later fond letter to the Philippian church, the jailer became someone dear to Paul's heart. It all began here in the prison, as hearts were transformed. This was something that Ezekiel looked forward to, when speaking of God's promise of a new heart and new spirit, which are responsive to God's call and open to God's way of life.

There is a great deal of washing in this week's readings: water for cleansing, for healing, for entry into the city of God. The baptismal imagery is strong, which is appropriate in the Easter season. Christian initiation is into Christ, not just into a Christian lifestyle or beliefs; we are made one with Christ, and in him with his Father. The foundation for this is Jesus's prayer that, as the Father is in him and he is in the Father, all who believe in him will be one in God.

'Love' is Jesus's repeated way of speaking of divine relationships. We are called to live into and out of the richness of God's love within the Trinity, which cannot help but overflow and embrace all of God's creation. Ascensiontide is the theologically logical culmination of the creation of the world and the incarnation of the Son of God.

The petition in the Collect – that the Holy Spirit will strengthen us and exalt us to the place where our Saviour Christ is gone before – is not mere presumption, but our faithful, joyful response to Jesus's high priestly prayer that 'those also, whom you have given me, may be with me where I am, to see my glory'.

This is our glorious hope. Before then, we may find ourselves washing the wounds of some unexpected future companions, people with whom we break bread.

Pentecost

Acts 2.1–21; Genesis 11.1–9; Romans 8.14–17;
John 14.8–27

THE SPIRIT BANISHES FEAR AND SPREADS BLESSING

> *God, who as at this time taught the hearts of your faithful people by sending*
> *to them the light of your Holy Spirit: grant us by the same Spirit to have a*
> *right judgement in all things and evermore to rejoice in his holy comfort;*
> *through the merits of Christ Jesus our Saviour. Amen.*

The Babel story vividly concludes the primeval myths in chapters 1–11 of
Genesis. Other cultures had similar stories, including a Sumerian myth about a
tower, and a Greek myth about the confusion of languages. What distinguished
the Genesis story from the others was its distinctive theology which provided a
theological explanation for the different languages that the people encountered
when they pushed back their geographical boundaries.

After the flood, God instructed Noah's descendants to multiply and spread
across the world, which they duly did. They came to a plain, and discovered how
to make bricks. Their fear of being scattered drives the story, and so they built
a city with the bricks in order to stay in one place. In doing this, they resisted
God's purposes for them to fill the earth (Genesis 9.1, 10.18, 32). Then they
added a tower, intending its top to be in the heavens.

In their cosmology, God lived not in but beyond the heavens, which were
merely the vault over creation. So puny was the tower that God had to come
down from his home to see it. Having done so, God joined in the action and the
thrice-repeated phrase 'Come, let us …' shapes the story as the people made
bricks, built a city, and God confused their language. It seems that God did
not judge them for their hubris in building upward to the heavens. Instead,
God's judgement was that they were not spreading outwards across the earth as
intended. So God faced them with what they dreaded (something that Job also
experienced and described in Job 3.25) and scattered them over the face of the
earth, confusing their language in the process. Thus God went full-cycle, back
to his original purposes when humans and animals were first told to fill the earth
and care for it so that all could flourish (Genesis 1.22, 28). The story completes
the cycle of stories of the beginning.

The Genesis story of people who did not listen to each other, or hear with
understanding, foreshadows all human history that is controlled by the fear of
people whom we do not understand: I wrote this as a Korean crisis was in the
news, a clash of international cultures that do not understand each other.

At Pentecost, however, all that changed. The disciples, who had been hiding for fear of the Jews, were out on the streets, proclaiming the gospel. People from many nations were amazed that, despite the language barrier which confused the people in Genesis, they understood about the powerful deeds of God which Peter proclaimed. Having heard and understood, they were converted.

Acts gives us vignettes of how these new Christians spread out across the earth, proclaiming the gospel. Visitors to Jerusalem took the gospel back home with them; persecution drove others out; and soon there were Christians in Samaria, Ethiopia, Damascus, Lydda, Sharon, Joppa, Cyprus, Phoenicia, and Antioch, and, with Paul's conversion, Europe and parts of Asia. At Pentecost, the Holy Spirit achieved what the fear lying behind building the city and tower had prevented: the spread of God's blessing across God's world. God's impulse is always for mission and blessing. The post-exilic people had not always grasped their prophets' message that they were blessed by God in order to be a blessing to the whole world. No wonder that Peter quoted the prophets: Pentecost expresses God's perpetual yearning for humans to share his world-wide mission, and it emboldened the disciples to live with diversity without fear, because God is love, and lovingly reconciles humanity.

Last week, we heard about our sharing the life of God because we are in Christ. This week, we understand more of the consequences. Jesus told his confused disciples about his gift of peace that is not as the world gives. So, whereas Babel was about people controlled by fear, Paul could write to the Romans about not falling back into fear, but receiving a spirit of adoption. Babel and Pentecost remind us that God asks us to take risks to face our fears, so that God's world may be blessed and cared for, as God intends. The Early Church had its struggles with this (Acts 10–11), as have we today, but our confidence lies in Jesus's promise that the Spirit of truth, who empowered the early disciples, is with us for ever.

Trinity Sunday
Proverbs 8.1–4, 22–31; Romans 5.1–5; John 16.12–15

THE 'CATHOLICK' FAITH IS THIS

Almighty and everlasting God, you have given us your servants grace, by the confession of a true faith, to acknowledge the glory of the eternal Trinity and in the power of the divine majesty to worship the Unity: keep us steadfast in this faith, that we may evermore be defended from all adversities; through Jesus Christ our Lord. Amen.

If you go up a narrow, wooded lane, off a B-road in Northumberland, you find a tiny stone church, which was built in 1107. Nothing prepares you for what you see inside on an overcast day, when the dark nave is effectively invisible, and your eyes are drawn to the beautifully lit, tiny apse. 'Holy, Holy, Holy, Lord God of Hosts' is inscribed above the gold altar frontal, below a starry ceiling. Old Bewick Church is a window into the Trinity, because the only appropriate response is to worship, to join the angels' cry: 'Holy, holy, holy.'

Sadly, many preachers dread Trinity Sunday, feeling (rightly) unequal to the task of explaining the Trinity. But the Trinity is not a concept to be explained intellectually: the Holy Trinity is God to be worshipped. The worshipping approach to Trinity Sunday yields something far richer and more wonderful than attempts at explanation using inadequate illustrations.

Gospel readings in recent weeks have emphasized abiding in Christ and thus, in him, our relationship with God the Father and God the Holy Spirit. The Orthodox Churches emphasize this through their understanding of the divinization of humanity in Christ, who has taken his humanity into the life of the Godhead. Through abiding in Christ, humanity shares the life of God, not becoming God, but being drawn into the life that the Son shares with the Father and the Holy Spirit. The Greek word is *perichoresis*, and one way to understand it is through the language of the dance of God, as Father, Son, and Holy Spirit respond to one another in love. In Christ, we are bidden to join the dance: in George Herbert's famous words, 'Love bade me welcome.'

This invitation to participation is a lovely frame for reflection on Trinity Sunday's readings. Jesus's words about the life of God into which his disciples were being drawn continue with his assurance that his departure from them was but the doorway to a new beginning. The Holy Spirit would guide them and glorify Jesus to them. In Proverbs, Wisdom calls us wherever she can waylay us – on mountains, roadsides, by city gates, by the entrance to the Temple – calling us to find her, and thus find life and favour from the Lord. Paul reiterates that it is through Jesus Christ that we have access to the grace in which we stand, and can boast of our hope of sharing the glory of God, experiencing (sometimes through suffering) that God's love is poured into our hearts through the Holy Spirit that has been given to us.

Our worship of God as Trinity flows from who God is, and it is enabled by the joyful miracle of our relationship with God through Jesus Christ. We call God 'Father' only because Jesus called him 'Father'. Always, always, Trinity is about the life and love of God, and the invitation, indeed bidding, to participate.

Today's Collect is strong on doctrine, as the Church needs to be, because within that frame of orthodox belief we are liberated to worship. In the fourth century, faced with the Arian heresy, which denied the divinity of Christ and thus that there are three Persons in one God, the Church not only developed its Creeds, but concluded its prayers and hymns with a Trinitarian ascription. In the century after that, the Athanasian Creed expounded the doctrine of the Trinity more fully, while retaining a realm of mystery in its language, as it tried to give voice to wonders beyond human comprehension: 'And the Catholick faith is this: that we worship one God in Trinity, and Trinity in Unity; Neither confounding the Persons: nor dividing the Substance.' The salient word is 'worship', and no wonder this creed ends with the Gloria.

If Pentecost is about language's transcending human constraints to proclaim the wonders of God, Trinity is about the limits of language to express our worship. The Collect uses language of glory and majesty to call us to worship, and Old Bewick Church proclaims 'Holy, holy, holy' as the adoring response. So, on Trinity Sunday, hymns such as Reginald Heber's 'Holy, holy, holy' and John Mason's 'How shall I sing that Majesty?' express our response, when language surrenders to transcendence. We are called to be 'lost in wonder, love and praise'.

Sunday after Trinity,
Proper 4 (29 May–4 June)
1 Kings 8.22–23, 41–43; Galatians 1.1–12; Luke 7.1–10

PREDICATED ON GOD'S MERCY

O God, the strength of all those who put their trust in you, mercifully accept our prayers and, because through the weakness of our mortal nature we can do no good thing without you, grant us the help of your grace, that in the keeping of your commandments we may please you both in will and deed; through Jesus Christ our Lord. Amen.

Collect for the First Sunday after Trinity

We begin our post-Trinity reading of Luke's Gospel with the story of the centurion, a Roman soldier in charge of 100 men, who maintained the sometimes uneasy peace in Israel through policing rather than military duty. The Roman occupation was deeply unpopular resulting in regular uprisings and what we would call terrorist attacks by individuals and groups.

Jesus had two disciples – Simon the Zealot and Judas Iscariot – whose names suggest links with Jewish freedom-fighters. He also had Matthew, formerly a Roman tax-collector and collaborator. The centurion's request could not help but provoke tension among the disciples.

There are parallels with the world today: a military leader on peace-keeping work in a volatile country far from home. In this harsh world, the centurion was an unusually kind man. Not only did he care about his slave's well-being, but he had the enthusiastic support of the local Jewish leaders who said that he was worthy, loved the Jewish people, and had built a synagogue for them. In today's jargon, he had won their hearts and minds. In the political context of the day, it was extraordinary.

Everything about the centurion's actions was topsy-turvy. We might expect a story about a slave's being sent to secure healing for the centurion's friend; instead, the centurion sent Jewish elders and then his friends to secure healing for his slave. He treated both the slave and Jesus with immense respect. He knew his authority and maintained discipline – he spoke, and people acted – yet he recognized the limits of his authority, and, powerful man that he was, acknowledged his need, and turned to an itinerant preacher with a reputation for healing. Having done that, he did not presume anything and so did not command Jesus, his social inferior, but tried to avoid inconveniencing him.

Unlike Matthew, Luke does not actually record Jesus's healing of the slave, or even his sending back of the messengers; having been amazed at the centurion's faith, Jesus's part in the story is no longer recorded. The friends simply returned, and found the slave healed. This suggests a link between authority and faith: the centurion and his friends trusted the right use of authority as expressed in kind action.

Worthiness is central to all this week's readings. The Jewish elders (not always an easily satisfied group) said that the centurion was worthy to have Jesus heal his slave, while he described himself as not worthy to have Jesus come to his house. Solomon acknowledged that there was no God like the Lord, who could be approached only because he kept covenant and steadfast love with his people, including foreigners such as the centurion. Paul described his commission as God-given, having no human origin, and his message as given by revelation – neither, therefore, earned by his worthiness. The Collect underlines this in acknowledging the weakness of our mortal nature, which means that we can do no good thing without God.

Related to the question of worthiness is the question of presumption. The centurion's 'I did not presume to come to you' surely inspired the beautiful prayer in the Book of Common Prayer: 'We do not presume to come to this thy Table, O merciful Lord, trusting in our own righteousness ... We are not worthy so much as to gather up the crumbs under thy Table.' Faced with this truth, we might despair, were it not for two 'buts': 'but [we trust] in thy manifold and great mercies'; 'But thou art the same Lord, whose property is always to have mercy.' This echoes the way in which Solomon dared to predicate his prayer on the steadfast love of God, and thus his articulation of the theological underpinning of the centurion's later trusting and humble use of his own authority.

What do we presume: is it the manifold mercy of God? What do lives predicated on the mercy of God look like today for each of us, whether on peace-keeping duty in Afghanistan, or in the way we trust God to act for good in a gruelling family or work situation? The Collect's double emphasis on our intent and our action reminds us that, having trusted God's mercy, we please God through our response in both will and deed. The readings show how this might work out.

Sunday after Trinity,
Proper 5 (5–11 June)
1 Kings 17.17–24; Galatians 1.11–24; Luke 7.11–17

COMPASSION AND TRANSFORMATION

Lord, you have taught us that all our doings without love are nothing worth: send your Holy Spirit and pour into our hearts that most excellent gift of love, the true bond of peace and of all virtues, without which whoever lives is counted dead before you. Grant this for your only Son Jesus Christ's sake. Amen.

Collect for the Second Sunday after Trinity

Luke makes women far more visible than was normal in his culture, where they counted for little. More than 25 times, Luke pairs stories of men and women, showing them in similar circumstances, beginning with the angel who appeared to Zechariah, and then to Mary. So he pairs the story of the centurion's slave with the widow's son. Radically, what Jesus did for a man, he did for a woman; what he taught about a man, he taught about a woman.

Luke models his telling of this story on that of Elijah and the widow. Two young men had died, both the only sons of widowed mothers. A situation tragic in any setting, this was devastating in the cultures of their day, since the death of an only son condemned a widowed mother to poverty and privation. Miraculously, however, both stories culminate with 'He gave him back to his mother.' Incidentally, Shumen and Nain may have been in similar locations.

In the Old Testament, the context was a severe famine in which the three people were surviving only thanks to God's miraculous provision. In the Gospel, Jesus turned up just as a funeral procession was leaving town. Motivated purely by compassion for the widow's plight, he interrupted the mourning, made himself ritually unclean by touching the bier, and told the young man to get up. As far as we know, Jesus was a complete stranger who had not introduced himself or offered his condolences; he simply brought the dead man back to life. Imagine this happening at a funeral today and we understand why fear gripped the people and word spread fast.

These two stories embody God's compassion for people in need, particularly vulnerable people. They ask us to explore what it means to embody God's compassion for the world even when, as in Elijah's case, our own survival is precarious, or, in Jesus's case, we sacrifice our religious good standing for the sake of a social nobody.

Serendipitously, given that the epistle is a course reading and not specially chosen, the lectionary places these two stories alongside the story of another young man whose life was transformed instantaneously, this time through a

YEAR C

revelation that overturned his whole way of life. Paul had seen it as his religious duty to persecute Christians, not flinching even when watching Stephen, the first martyr, being stoned to death. While Acts records what happened to Stephen, what we have in the epistle is Paul's admission to its part in his own history, and his theological understanding of the extraordinary events. He ascribed it all to God's grace which called him to proclaim the gospel among the Gentiles, the very people whom he had once despised in his fanatical religion.

The people who observed these three events responded in similar ways, realizing that God was at work in the unlikely context of their own situations. So the woman recognized Elijah as a man of God; the people around Jesus recognized that a prophet had arisen among them; the churches that heard about Paul glorified God that he was proclaiming the faith that he had tried to destroy.

This has to raise questions about our response when we see signs of God at work in the familiarity of our lives. These stories challenge us to allow space for the possibility that God will act, and will breathe new life into situations that seem hopeless. They remind us that God up-ends situations and ways of life that feel immutable.

The famine was cruel and long, and (maps show us) Elijah had previously walked more than 100 miles through countryside devastated by it, enough to sap anyone's faith. Yet God not only provided food: he restored life.

The widow faced the brutal loneliness of being on her own in a culture where family was vital for support, when suddenly Jesus acted as her son to provide for her – in this case, by restoring her own son.

The Church faced persecution and death from Saul, but God broke in audaciously and commissioned him to proclaim the very gospel he had once despised.

These stories remind us that God delights in acting with unprovoked compassion, bringing life in situations locked into death, startling us with unlikely recipients of his mercy.

Sunday after Trinity,
Proper 6 (12–18 June)
2 Samuel 11.26–12.10; Galatians 2.15–end; Luke 7.36–8.3

SIMON'S BREACH OF ETIQUETTE

Almighty God, you have broken the tyranny of sin and have sent the Spirit of your Son into our hearts, whereby we call you Father: give us grace to dedicate our freedom to your service, that we and all creation may be brought to the glorious liberty of the children of God; through Jesus Christ our Lord. Amen.

Collect for the Third Sunday after Trinity

The Gospel is more about Simon the Pharisee than about the woman. In contrast to the centurion two weeks ago, who did not consider himself worthy to have Jesus as his guest, Simon invited Jesus to his home only to humiliate him outrageously. The offence is lost in cultural translation. Simon disregarded all the normal courtesies when receiving a guest. Luke records the gruesome details: he did not kiss Jesus in greeting, have his feet washed, or put olive oil on his hands. It is like not speaking to your guest or taking his overcoat, but expecting him to sit down to dinner still wearing it. Jesus was blatantly insulted, and everyone would have noticed.

To understand what happened next, we need to know that people could watch a dinner party. An unnamed woman emerged into the limelight, a shocking place for any woman in that culture. Luke describes her as a sinner, which could mean many things including simply that she had married a Gentile. Whatever the reason for her being an outcast, it seems that she came to anoint Jesus, knowing that he befriended and ate with sinners. Observing Simon's insulting behaviour, the pain of which she would have felt from her own experience, she wept because Jesus was humiliated, and did what Simon should have done. She washed Jesus's feet using the only available resources – her tears and her hair – and then anointed them. That was extraordinary because while feet were washed when someone entered a house, they were never anointed on their own. Probably she intended to anoint his head and hands, but could not reach them, since he was reclining, and so she anointed his feet instead, after washing them.

This woman broke all the social codes of the time. It was taboo for a woman to touch a man in public, and her body language, standing over a reclining man, was scandalous. A respectable woman never uncovered her hair in public: it was considered sexually provocative. If she did, her husband, who first saw her hair on their wedding night, was expected to divorce her.

This helps to explain Paul's strictures to the Corinthians on this subject. Middle Eastern cultures retain this approach, and Kenneth Bailey, in his fascinating book *Jesus through Middle Eastern Eyes*, quotes a recent Iranian Prime Minister: 'Women's hair exudes vibrations that arouse, mislead and corrupt men'(Bailey, 2008).

The men present would expect Jesus to be outraged, and to throw her out. Instead, Jesus accepted it all without comment, breaking the silence only when his host was thoroughly discomforted. Then, instead of addressing the woman, as people expected, he laid into his host and placed responsibility for the serious breach of etiquette with him. Worse, Jesus drew Simon's attention to her ('Do you see this woman?') and commended her, instead of his host. Jesus was being as offensive as Simon and the woman had been. The air would have been electric.

After this unforgettable episode, Luke describes the group of women travelling with Jesus. Perhaps she was among them. Even though social customs are more relaxed now, Bailey writes that, in conservative Middle Eastern societies today, women may stay overnight only with relatives, whereas these women stayed with Jesus and the male disciples in strange villages.

Jesus broke new ground for women, being more concerned to include them in his life than to conform to society's expectations. In turn, women provided for him, offering their resources to meet his needs. It is remarkable that Luke is prepared to admit this in writing. In the words of the Collect, Jesus's attitude to them gave them grace to dedicate their freedom to God's service.

Paul wrote to the Galatians: 'I have been crucified with Christ; it is no longer I who live but Christ who lives in me.'

As Christians, the offering of all that we have is at the heart of life and worship. Our example is the woman who poured out her ointment and any remaining scraps of her reputation in love for Jesus. Her actions had blatant overtones: she was making an ultimate pledge of loyalty to Jesus, letting him feel her touch, her tears, her kiss. Her response to grace was gratitude; our response can be no less.

Sunday after Trinity,
Proper 7 (19–25 June)
Isaiah 65.1–9; Galatians 3.23–29; Luke 8.26–39

LEAVING THE DARK SIDE

O God, the protector of all who trust in you, without whom nothing is strong, nothing is holy: increase and multiply upon us your mercy; that with you as our ruler and guide we may so pass through things temporal that we lose not our hold on things eternal; grant this, heavenly Father, for our Lord Jesus Christ's sake. Amen.

Collect for the Fourth Sunday after Trinity

We should not lose sight of the context of the Gospel reading: it is the same basic story as the previous one when Jesus stilled a storm on the lake. Both resulted in calm, and people were afraid as a result of what they experienced. What Jesus did for his disciples, he promptly did for a man who was, in that culture, unclean in every way. Although this is Luke's only example of Jesus's going deliberately into Gentile territory, it looks forward to his story in Acts (16.16–24) of Paul's healing of a Gentile girl who was possessed by demons.

Entering the culture helps us to understand this unsettling story. Disturbing behaviour, whatever medical cause we understand today, was ascribed to demons and thus was opposed to God. The abyss was either the home of demons, or the place of their ultimate judgement. Water symbolizes chaos and disorder. We see this in the stories of creation, where God brings order to the waters, and the flood. It was believed that demons could not survive in water, hence Jesus's reference to demons' wandering in waterless places (Luke 11.24). Houses in some parts of the world are still painted blue (representing water) for protection from evil. To know people's name was to have authority over them, hence the significance in the Bible of who gives names.

Put all that together, and the story emphasizes Jesus's complete authority over powers opposed to God. Having tried unsuccessfully to heal the man, he demanded to know the demon's name, thus claiming authority. The demons named themselves as multiple, legion; recognized his power; and pleaded not to be sent to judgement in the abyss, but into the pigs. Jesus, for whom, as a faithful Jew, pigs were unclean, gave permission. Perhaps as a result of general pandemonium, they plunged to their own destruction in the water. At this point, the disciples should have recalled their recent experience of the chaotic power of water and of Jesus's authority over it.

The baptismal imagery is strong: we are saved through water, which is both essential for life, and, as in this story, a cause of death. Baptismal candidates are asked if they reject the devil and all rebellion against God (exemplified in this story by the demons), and are then plunged under water or have it poured on them.

A visitor to Durham Cathedral once told me of her shock, indeed anger, on being told by a parish priest that, at her grandchild's baptism, the parents and godparents would have to renounce the devil and evil. She was surprised when I explained that this has been part of the baptismal liturgy since the early days of the Church. With the murders of little April Jones and Drummer Lee Rigby in the news as I wrote this, we cannot pretend that there is no evil in the world today. It is antithetical to all that the Christian faith proclaims about the good news of God's Kingdom, and Christians have to make choices: we cannot be on two sides at once. Baptism is a significant and demanding choice.

Alongside the story of the healing of a Gentile outcast, it is significant that we hear Paul's describing those who are baptized as being clothed with Christ, and therefore there being no distinction in Christ between Jew and Greek (or Gentile). Conversion involves putting off the old way of life, and clothing ourselves with the new self (Ephesians 4.22–24). The Early Church clothed the newly baptized in new white garments. At the end of this story, the man was to be found sitting at the feet of Jesus, 'clothed and in his right mind'. Jesus had again calmed a storm, and the man was clothed, healed, and saved.

By sitting at Jesus's feet, the place of a disciple of a rabbi, the man recognized Jesus's authority and became his disciple. Like the demons, he 'begged' Jesus, but, whereas they begged to escape Jesus, this man begged to be with him. Paradoxically, Jesus granted their request, but turned down his and, instead, sent him home where his transformation would raise questions to which he had a life-changing answer. Jesus sends the most unlikely people on mission, sending this man even before he sent the Twelve.

Sunday after Trinity,

Proper 8 (26 June–2 July)

1 Kings 19.5–16, 19–21; Galatians 5.1, 13–25;
Luke 9.51–62

PLOUGH AND EASY YOKE

> *Almighty and everlasting God, by whose Spirit the whole body of the
> Church is governed and sanctified: hear our prayer which we offer for
> all your faithful people, that in their vocation and ministry they may serve
> you in holiness and truth to the glory of your name; through our Lord and
> Saviour Jesus Christ. Amen.*

Collect for the Fifth Sunday after Trinity

The readings this week are about steadfast discipleship. 'Stand firm,' Paul says.
'Follow me,' says Jesus, spelling out what that meant for people with good
religious reasons to delay – to bury one's father was a sacred duty.

Twice, we are told that Jesus had 'set his face' to go to Jerusalem. When
that phrase occurred recently in an Old Testament reading at evensong, someone
commented afterwards on the strong element of willed determination. We were
in Durham Cathedral, a place with a tradition of willed commitment, where,
for centuries, people have followed Benedict's example of discipleship that is
stable, obedient, and open to conversion of life. That takes staying power.

There are two linked images for discipleship in the readings. Today,
ploughing as a metaphor for discipleship has rather lost its power. In those days,
it was arduous work, demanding undivided attention as you pressed down hard
on the plough and constantly watched where you were going behind the animal.
If you looked back, your course wobbled, and the loss of pressure did not dig up
the earth.

Then there was the yoke. Two animals yoked together had no option but
to stay together, come what may. Paul told his readers not to be yoked again to
slavery, while Jesus (Matthew 11.29) offered people his well-fitting yoke which
meant going wherever he went, walking at the same pace. As Paul put it: 'Since
we live by the Spirit, let us keep in step with the Spirit' (Galatians 5.25, NIV).

This willed commitment caused Jesus and his disciples to be rebuffed,
angering James and John who forgot Jesus's instruction to shake the dust off
their feet when they were not welcomed (Luke 9.5) and instead wanted to call
down fire in revenge. Jesus, however, simply moved on.

Elijah was prone to call down fire on people when he was in trouble (1
Kings 18.37–38; 2 Kings 1.10, 12). Today, however, we find him in a tangle of

despairing commitment, running away and wanting to die. But he was yoked to God, who would not let him lash out, sulk, or get lost. So, having stabilized him by feeding him (thus setting us a wise example), God asked a deceptively simple, penetrating question, which cut to the chase: 'What are you doing here, Elijah?' It is one that we should ask ourselves from time to time.

What was Elijah doing there? By travelling to Mount Horeb, he appeared to be trying to recreate the scene with Moses on the same mountain (Exodus 19.16–19). But he was not Moses. Moses's experience could not sustain him, and God was not in the earthquake, wind, and fire – all places where Moses had encountered God. Instead, God launched Elijah into new territory, forcing him out of hiding by coming in disarming silence. Then there was the same penetrating question: 'What are you doing here, Elijah?'

Elijah gave the same answer, perhaps in more muted tones, as he protested his solitary faithfulness. In his desolation, he had lost the bigger picture and overlooked the hundreds of other faithful people. Sometimes, God has to draw our attention to and help us appreciate the most unlikely companions. Elijah was sent back over territory that would trigger memories of God's previous care for him. It was time to buckle down again to ploughing; time – in Paul's words – to stand firm; time – in Jesus's words – to follow without looking back. Faithfulness, not fireworks, was needed. So Elijah found Elisha, who, unlike the man whom Jesus had met who wanted to delay commitment until his father died, promptly burned the yoke of his old commitment, kissed his parents, and followed immediately.

This week's Collect focuses on all God's faithful people. Although our specific vocations and ministries differ, we have in common our baptismal commitment to turn to Christ, and submit to him as Lord. This brings with it the call to stand firm, following God faithfully in holiness and truth, not turning back when the going gets tough. 'If we live by the Spirit, let us keep in step with the Spirit.'

So, a question for each of us, as we pray the Collect this week: 'What am I doing here?'

Sunday after Trinity,
Proper 9 (3–9 July)
Isaiah 66.10–14; Galatians 6.[1–6] 7–16;
Luke 10.1–11, 16–20

ON THE ROAD FOR JESUS

Merciful God, you have prepared for those who love you such good things as pass our understanding: pour into our hearts such love toward you that we, loving you in all things and above all things, may obtain your promises, which exceed all that we can desire; through Jesus Christ our Lord. Amen.

Collect for the Sixth Sunday after Trinity

What is left unsaid in the Gospel reading is as significant as what is said. We know that Jesus appointed 70 people to go in pairs to the places that he intended to visit on the familiar pilgrim-route from Galilee to Jerusalem – a journey he had made many times since his childhood. This time, however, having set his face to go to Jerusalem, he made careful plans and sent people ahead of him, like John the Baptist, to prepare the way.

What we do not know is who these people were. In Luke 6, after a night in prayer, Jesus chose the Twelve from his larger group of disciples. It seems that the choice was not obvious and he considered others when praying. Jesus was surrounded by a larger group of male and female disciples and, after the ascension, Peter referred to people who had accompanied the Twelve all the time that the Lord was with them. These faithful people had allowed their lives to be disrupted by the Kingdom of God's coming among them. Despite any disappointment they might have felt about not having been chosen as part of Jesus's inner circle, especially when they saw the actions of some of those who had been chosen, they had stuck with Jesus.

Now it was their opportunity as Jesus chose some of them for a special task. Their number suggests a symbolic link to the 70 elders of Israel (Exodus 24.1). We should not forget that there were still more who were not so chosen. Most staunch discipleship is not lived in the limelight but is embodied by the multitude of people who never hit the headlines yet are always there, ready to respond when a new call comes.

As come it did to these 70. They were sent with the same basic instructions as the Twelve had previously been sent: to go from place to place, healing the sick, casting out demons (although not a specific instruction, they later reported that they had done this), and proclaiming the Kingdom of God. They were to expand the reach of Jesus's ministry substantially. This meant staying where they were welcomed and moving on when they were rejected. Shaking the dust off their feet was not a literal action, but a saying like our 'Wash your hands of it.' In addition to any implied judgement, by shaking themselves free they left unencumbered by the baggage of bad memories gnawing away at their hearts. It was primarily about how they went forward, not whom they left behind.

Where they were welcomed they were to eat what was offered, however meagre, plentiful, or unappetizing, and to respond to the needs that they met. They were not to move to another house where the hospitality looked better, but to stay where they had been first welcomed. Underlying this is a sense of receiving and being content with what is enough, even if not ideal – a concept of which our consumer society has lost sight.

Jesus sent his disciples without purse, bag, or sandals, rendering them completely vulnerable to the hospitality of others. If it was not forthcoming they had no resources to fall back on, and it could be risky to move on, especially at dusk. So Paul, who knew too well from his travels about exposure to the dangers of inhospitality, reminded his former hosts in Galatia that those who were taught the word must share in all good things with their teacher, a theme that he also wrote about to the Romans (Romans 15.27).

This mutual sharing of what people have – the good news of the Kingdom of God's coming near, the material resources necessary for daily life – sounds a wonderful concept, but it depends on faithfulness by all concerned. According to Jesus, the initial risk is to be taken by those whom he sends, who are to go with openness to others who have not yet heard their message. Barbara Kingsolver's brilliant novel *The Poisonwood Bible* exposes how difficult this can be (Kingsolver, 1998).

Rather than a story to be glossed over as one that we have already heard in a slightly different form in the previous chapter of Luke's Gospel, the commitment of these unnamed disciples is something to celebrate. The outcome for all, Jesus included, was joy.

Sunday after Trinity,
Proper 10 (10–16 July)
Deuteronomy 30.9–14; Colossians 1.1–14; Luke 10.25–37

THE SEAT OF THE WILL

> *Lord of all power and might, the author and giver of all good things: graft in our hearts the love of your name, increase in us true religion, nourish us with all goodness, and of your great mercy keep us in the same; through Jesus Christ our Lord. Amen.*
>
> Collect for the Seventh Sunday after Trinity

Jesus met the lawyer on his own ground. When asked what he must do to inherit eternal life, Jesus pointed to his area of expertise, the law. He did not have to look elsewhere, or learn new things, to find the answer to his yearning. In the words of Deuteronomy, the word was not unreachable, but in his mouth and his heart for him to observe. That accessibility is extraordinarily comforting, and yet also challenging, because it removes any excuses, for him and for us, about not knowing how to express our love for God.

Thomas Troeger, the poet and hymn-writer, writing in *The Preacher* in April 2013, has some wise insights on the summary of the law which Jesus commended:

> If we love God with all our heart, but not with all our mind, then feeling runs untested and unchecked by reason's light, and we will not grow up into the full stature of Christ. Or if we love God with all our mind, but not with all our heart, then our thought becomes entirely calculating, lacking tenderness and grace, and we will not grow into the full stature of Christ. Or if we love God with all our soul, but not with all our strength, then we will fail to embody our faith in acts of compassion, and we will not grow up into the full stature of Christ. If we love God with all our strength, but not with all our soul, then our lives become spiritually vacuous, and we will not grow up into the full stature of Christ. By way of contrast, when we give all of us to all of God, then faith becomes a process of allowing our varied ways of knowing to correct and balance each other so that we are no longer 'divided creatures'. Instead we become whole people, able to help heal the fracture epistemologies that divide our world into conflicted camps.

Troeger puts his finger on the integrity of love for God. Flowing from a holistic way of being, it entails openness to honour and develop our hearts, minds, souls, and strengths. Equally important, as the lawyer said, the law binds loving God to loving our neighbour as we love ourselves. The Colossian Christians had grasped this: their 'faith in Christ Jesus and love ... for all the saints' fell naturally into one sentence.

At the end of the parable, Jesus reframed the lawyer's question, 'Who is my neighbour?' to the subtly but significantly different 'Who was a neighbour to the man?' He made it personal, because there cannot be disembodied or inactive love. Snoopy's much quoted observation, in Schultz's 'Peanuts' cartoon, 'I love mankind; it's people I can't stand,' expresses humorously the real challenge involved. Jews and Samaritans were estranged, and yet a lawyer should have known the law's command to love not just his neighbour but the alien as himself (Leviticus 19.34). The depth of his discomfort is evidenced by his inability to bring himself to say 'the Samaritan', resorting instead to describing actions impersonally. It was challenging stuff, once Jesus had put flesh on the bones.

In Hebrew thought, the heart is the seat of the will; so loving God with all our heart means steadfastly directing our resolve towards God. This is a richer and deeper understanding of love than most popular culture allows. This week's Collect prays for love of God's name to be grafted in our hearts. This is another way of expressing the prayer in Colossians that the Christians will be 'filled with the knowledge of God's will and lead lives worthy of the Lord, bearing fruit in every good work as you grow in the knowledge of God'. Love takes shape in action. Once the Christians at Colossae 'truly comprehended the grace of God', the gospel began to bear fruit among them.

The petition in the Collect is wisely comprehensive, predicating our prayer for help to grow in the knowledge and love of God on the fact that God is the author and giver of all good things. The readings remind us that 'The Lord will again take delight in prospering you,' and that, in the process, we may encounter strange neighbours who are our path to loving God. This is a deceptively challenging Collect to pray.

Sunday after Trinity,
Proper 11 (17–23 July)
Genesis 18.1–10a; Colossians 1.15–28; Luke 10.38–42

A WELCOME AND A MEAL

Almighty Lord and everlasting God, we beseech you to direct, sanctify and govern both our hearts and bodies in the ways of your laws and the works of your commandments; that through your most mighty protection, both here and ever, we may be preserved in body and soul; through our Lord and Saviour Jesus Christ. Amen.

Collect for the Eigth Sunday after Trinity

Two vivid stories focus us on hospitality, which was a *sine qua non* in biblical times. Without it, people would die, especially in locations such as Abraham's, seeking shade from the heat of the day. Like the father of the prodigal son, he ran to greet his guests, then provided water for refreshment. From the quantities mentioned, his 'little bread' was, in fact, a large meal that took time to prepare from scratch. This was warm hospitality, offered readily to strangers. Martha and Mary similarly welcomed Jesus into their home. As he had taught his disciples to do (Luke 9.4, 10.5–7), Jesus accepted the hospitality gladly, and their home became a place of shelter for him; he grew to love them, and eventually chose their home as refuge during the terrible last week of his life.

Theologically, Colossians tells us, we are recipients of the ultimate hospitality from God who 'was pleased to reconcile to himself all things … making peace through the blood of the cross'. Thus reconciled to God and one another, we pray to be kept in the ways of God's law and the works of God's commandments; essentially to live and act appropriately as Christians who have ourselves been made welcome by God.

Benedict, in his Rule (chapters 53 and 66), offers timeless wisdom, which sheds light on these stories. He assumed the presence of guests in monasteries, which, like Abraham, sheltered unexpected travellers. Knowing the importance of the way guests are welcomed, he specified the qualities of the person who opened the door.

The role of the Porter, a title still used at Durham Cathedral for the gatekeeper, derives from the French *porte*, 'door'. An older person with the wisdom not to wander off was always at the gate, like Abraham at his tent entrance, to welcome anyone who knocked with 'the gentleness that comes from the reverence of God', and 'the warmth of love'. The first words were to be 'Thanks be to God' for this opportunity to greet Christ present in the tired stranger. Guests were then announced (how important it is to be known by name), and greeted by the abbot and community 'with all the courtesy of love'. A kindly and appropriate welcome at our church doors is too important to be left to chance. Benedict knew that it requires skill to make a visitor feel welcome, neither ignoring nor overwhelming them.

Both Bible stories allude to the time-consuming cooking involved in welcoming a guest. Benedict prescribed a separate guest kitchen, so that food could be prepared at all hours without disrupting monastery life. It was more important to feed a guest than for the abbot to fast: hospitality can be part of keeping a holy Lent. Two monks were on kitchen duty but, at busy times, additional helpers were provided, 'so the monks can prepare the food without grumbling'. Grumbling about lack of kitchen help was Martha's problem.

The guest might not hear the grumbling, although Martha made sure Jesus did. While the finished meal would taste the same, grumbling corroded the heart of the grumbler, and diminished his or her capacity to welcome. Esther de Waal sums it up: 'It is only because I carry a heart of silence that I can welcome the guest' (de Waal, 2006). Jesus, like Benedict, wanted the practical side of hospitality to be life-giving for all, including Martha as host.

These biblical stories focus on the welcome and the meal. They tell us that 'The question is not whether what we have is sufficient for the situation or not. The question is simply whether or not we have anything to give. That's what hospitality is about. Not abundance and not totality. Just sharing, real sharing' (Chittister, 1992).

Hospitality opens up our hearts. How we welcome people is how we welcome God.

O God who walked Emmaus Road and joined in Cana's feast,
at times you slip into our lives when we expect you least;
surprising God, your acts reveal
what your appearance may conceal.

O God of hospitality, still welcoming us all,
you also come through those in need, the inconvenient call;
O God, let all our acts reveal
the welcome that from you we feel.
Copyright © 1995 Rosalind Brown

Sunday after Trinity,

Proper 12 (24–30 July)

Genesis 18.20–32; Colossians 2.6–15 [16–19];
Luke 11.1–13

FAMILIAR BUT STILL HOLY

Almighty God, who sent your Holy Spirit to be the life and light of your Church: open our hearts to the riches of your grace, that we may bring forth the fruit of the Spirit in love and joy and peace; through Jesus Christ our Lord. Amen.

Collect for the Ninth Sunday after Trinity

Abraham's bold approach to the Lord reflects bargaining between nomads; it may jar with us, but the Lord seems untroubled and joins in with gusto. Jesus's parable has similar bluntness, especially since the request for bread required the householder to get up and make it from scratch, not just to hand over loaves. The word 'persistence' could equally be 'shamelessness'. These were big, daring demands.

The context of this audacity is stories about hospitality given and received. Further, Abraham was the recipient of promise. We are in the realm of welcome and generosity, of relationships of trust and love, knocking at an open door. The Collect expresses this in terms of the riches of God's grace.

The relationship that allows this freedom in prayer emerges from Jesus's teaching his disciples to call his Father our Father. Brian Wren, a hymn-writer who has expanded our language for God in faithful, evocative ways, has written: 'Jesus taught his disciples to pray "Our Father", not to make them idolize a word, but to help them focus a relationship' (Wren, 1989). This was unbelievably revolutionary. The Old Testament rarely referred to God as Father, even then usually as simile or metaphor rather than direct address. All that changed with the incarnation when God was revealed as the 'Father of our Lord Jesus Christ' (Ephesians 1.3), and Jesus taught us to call his Father 'Our Father'. We do this only through his invitation.

Radically, Jesus dared to abandon special religious language when addressing God. He spoke Aramaic in daily life, but when Jews prayed, they spoke Hebrew. Now Jesus used, and taught the disciples to use, 'Abba', the Aramaic familial name. This intimacy was lost when Latin became the language of the Church; only at the Reformation was the wonder of speaking to God in the vernacular reclaimed. It is hard to imagine the shock of hearing English used in public prayer for the first time. It was more than a change of language: it was theological transformation, even revolution. Suddenly God spoke our language. Neither linguistic skill nor an intermediary was needed.

Praying in everyday language is the natural consequence of the incarnation. Other implications of Jesus's use of the Aramaic in calling God 'Abba' are that the vernacular Greek, rather than Hebrew, was used in the New Testament writings. It also paved the way for the faithful work of Bible translators through the ages.

God is also holy. 'Abba' was similarly used with great reverence to address a person of rank or a teacher. Familiarity must never breed contempt. By following 'Father' with 'hallowed [or holy] be your name', we recognize this further meaning of 'Abba' and its consequences for us. For God's name to be hallowed, we must become holy ourselves, since 'You shall be holy; for I the Lord your God am holy' (Leviticus 19.2).

Then we couple a prayer for forgiveness with a commitment to forgive those indebted to us, effectively offering ourselves for growth in holiness. In praying as Jesus taught us, we ask our Father to help us grow in family likeness. Finally, the petition not to be brought to the time of trial is essentially an expression of deep, confident trust that God will not let us be lost or tried beyond our ability to bear it.

The Collect summarizes all this as 'bringing forth the fruit of the Spirit in love and joy and peace'. Like the Colossians, we live our lives in Christ, rooted and built up in him. This means not limiting our expression of our faith to rigid adherence to law about food and drink, festivals, and Sabbaths, or their contemporary counterparts that divide the Church. Instead, in the words of Jesus's parable, we open our hearts to receive our Father's gift of the Holy Spirit, who will work in us to make our Father's name holy in our lives.

We pray to a God rich in grace and come to our Father with the boldness born of confidence in a mutual relationship that makes daring requests possible. We pray for open hearts to the riches of God's grace. So, of course, God may return the compliment, and make bold requests of us.

Sunday after Trinity,
Proper 13 (31 July–6 August)
Ecclesiastes 1.2, 12–14, 2.18–23; Colossians 3.1–11;
Luke 12.13–21

A SEVERE MERCY SHOWN

Let your merciful ears, O Lord, be open to the prayers of your humble
servants; and that they may obtain their petitions make them to ask such
things as shall please you; through Jesus Christ our Lord. Amen.
Collect for the Tenth Sunday after Trinity

The idea, in the Collect, of the Lord's having merciful ears is a rich one to ponder. What kind of ears do we think God listens with? What other ears do people listen with? What kind of ears do we listen with?

The prayer is predicated on mercy. The man who approached Jesus did not obtain his petition but Jesus's response was the result of more merciful listening than he expected, or perhaps wanted.

Israelite inheritance practices were designed to keep family land holdings as viable units. Land, therefore, normally passed undivided to all the heirs. It appears that this father died without leaving instructions about the inheritance, and one son wanted to split it into independent units. This rare approach was permitted only if the older brother agreed, indicating that this man was a younger brother who was frustrated by his older sibling's desire to keep the land, and thus the family, together. Jesus's merciful ears heard undertones of a rift in family relationships. By quoting what sounds like a wisdom saying about being on our guard against all kinds of greed, Jesus went to the unspoken heart of the issue. In refusing the man's request, he exposed some hidden motives, and refused to collude with greed that could destroy a family's relationships for generations to come. It was not the answer that the man craved: in the words of a 1970s book title, it was 'a severe mercy'; but it was mercy, none the less, because unchecked greed was in danger of destroying the family and preventing his being 'rich toward God'.

The parable showed that Jesus grasped the potential of this situation to engender loneliness. In the culture of the day, no decision like this was made without hours of discussion with family, friends, and neighbours. In contrast, this man 'thought to himself' about what to do. He was cut off from other people, entirely self-sufficient and isolated. At creation, God had said: 'It is not good for man to be alone.' Yet, by his wilfully independent actions, this man was pursuing separation that was contrary to God's good purposes. So God called him a fool, putting him on a par with the fool who says in his heart, 'There is no God' (Psalm

53.1). This headstrong pursuit of self-sufficiency was essentially God-denying, as he planned to eat, drink, and be merry for many years rather than recognize that his life and death were in God's hands.

Luke sets this story soon after the parable of the Good Samaritan who used his wealth for others, and the petition in the Lord's Prayer about trusting God for our daily bread. With this juxtaposition, he set up a stark contrast with the selfish attitude of the man in the parable who planned to use his wealth to make himself impregnable.

It is a shame that the Gospel reading stops where it does, because, tellingly, Jesus follows this condemnation of the man's plans to build larger barns to store his food with commendation of birds, who do not have barns, but trust God to feed them daily. The disciples of Jesus were to learn from the example of the birds, and to know themselves even more cared for than they. The birds in my garden live with implicit trust that my primary purpose in life is to keep them fed and watered; when I fill the feeders, they tweet the good news of food so that others can share it too, while a robin clearly thinks that I dig the garden solely to provide him with worms.

Living with trust like that, directed towards God, leads disciples (then and now) to a radically trusting way of life which does not attempt to secure the future solely through reliance on amassed possessions. Possessions gratefully received and stewarded need not stand in the way of our relationship with God, or indeed with other people; but there is always that danger. This difference in the foundational trust in our lives is about being free to live vulnerably and trustingly, and thus to be rich towards God. These two men needed to be released from the grip of their possessions and their greed. So the merciful answer to their prayer was to refuse it in the hope they might learn to ask what is pleasing to God.

The Lord has merciful ears.

Sunday after Trinity,
Proper 14 (7–13 August)
Genesis 15.1–6; Hebrews 11.1–3, 8–16; Luke 12.32–40

WALKING SURE-FOOTEDLY

O God, you declare your almighty power most chiefly in showing mercy and pity: mercifully grant to us such a measure of your grace, that we, running the way of your commandments, may receive your gracious promises, and be made partakers of your heavenly treasure; through Jesus Christ our Lord. Amen.

Collect for the Eleventh Sunday after Trinity

Walking around the extensive grounds of a National Trust property a few years ago, I discovered that the signage expected everyone to walk anticlockwise. By chance, I had set off clockwise. So, while there were always signs at junctions, none showed me which way to go. Instead, they all pointed back the way I had come, telling me that I was on a recognized road but leaving me to make my own decisions.

Although I was walking, the Collect (drawing on St Benedict as well as the psalmist) envisages our running on the way of God's commandments, sure-footed even when the route is not marked out inch by inch.

God has made us for more than following directional arrows. In Robert Bolt's play, *A Man for All Seasons*, Thomas More says: 'God made … man … to serve him wittily, in the tangle of his mind.' We are not called to robotic compliance, but to intelligent, feisty discipleship, and the Bible paints a sometimes messy picture of the outcome. Faithful living is dynamic, a constantly evolving relationship with God.

'Faith is the assurance of things hoped for, the conviction of things not seen. By faith Abram … set out, not knowing where he was going.' He had no directional arrows. Having left settled city life, at God's call, to become a nomad, childless Abram believed God's promise that his own son would be his heir. Despite many further childless years, he kept going, sometimes having vigorous words with God about his doubts. This was faith. It was not merely the spiritual equivalent of following directional arrows.

Hebrews tells of people who died in faith without receiving God's promises, seeing and greeting them only from a distance. We, too, walk by faith, not by sight. Faith is a relationship, not an abstract construct. We strengthen our faith as we set our lives in the context of the Bible's overarching story. This gives us the confidence to live by faith that God's Kingdom is indeed coming. As Jesus put it: 'Do not be afraid, it is your Father's good pleasure to give you the Kingdom.' We are invited to live in an expansive, generous faith environment.

YEAR C

Faith is a response to an invitation to adventure. It is not mind-over-matter blind faith, or (to quote the White Queen in *Through the Looking Glass*) believing 'six impossible things before breakfast'. Neither does living by faith involve sitting around waiting for a vision or step-by-step instructions to emerge from heaven. It is our active, informed, and loyal response to the bigger story of God's ways with the world. We nurture it each time we recognize signs of God's activity, the signs confirming that we are on the right path; and we express it, as the Gospel describes, by being dressed for action, waiting to respond and do our duty even at inconvenient times.

Twice in this week's readings we hear: 'Do not be afraid.' If we are to nurture our faith so that we can go on in the face of fear, we are helped by having a good store of faith-engendering memories like those recounted to the recipients of the epistle. It may help to hear from older people, who often have remarkable faith in God, because they have more history to draw on to remind them of God's past faithfulness. It is never too soon, or too late, to start laying down memories of God's power shown in God's mercy and pity towards us.

This approach to faith applies whether we face life in general, specific decisions, or entrenched difficulties such as ill-health, family problems, unemployment, or bereavement. Living faithfully requires tenacity, and sometimes is as unglamorous as doing whatever the next thing in front of us is, keeping on keeping on, doing the best we can in the circumstances. Jesus commended the servants who retained their alertness when doing their boringly repetitive duty. Amazingly, he then turned the tables. Outrageously, the servants who were faithful ended up as the master's guests at the celebration.

We all have to start somewhere; even Abraham, the man held up to us as a model of faith, had to set out afresh each morning, and he walked – as far as National Trust signage went – in a clockwise direction. We are called to nothing less.

Sunday after Trinity,
Proper 15 (14–20 August)
Jeremiah 23.23–29; Hebrews 11.29–12.2; Luke 12.49–56

SEEK TRUE PEACE, NOT CALM

> *Almighty and everlasting God, you are always more ready to hear than we to pray and to give more than either we desire or deserve: pour down upon us the abundance of your mercy, forgiving us those things of which our conscience is afraid and giving us those good things which we are not worthy to ask but through the merits and mediation of Jesus Christ our Lord. Amen.*
>
> Collect for the Twelfth Sunday after Trinity

It is tempting to rush to the familiar words at the end of the epistle, without thinking what lies behind them: 'Let us lay aside ... run with perseverance ... looking to Jesus who, for the joy that was set before him, endured the cross, disregarding its shame, and has taken his seat at the right hand of God.' Perhaps disconcertingly, in the Gospel, Jesus describes this joy as a severe stress for as long as he lived with the tension of waiting for God's time, for his baptism of death.

The people mentioned in the epistle shared the stress of keeping faith before God's promise was fulfilled. Remarkable faith was not rewarded instantly with blessing. So, while some, by faith, were delivered in extraordinary circumstances, others, also by faith, were tortured, imprisoned, and stoned to death. It is hard to reconcile being mocked, destitute, or sawn in two with the blessings promised in the Old Testament when God's people were faithful. We cannot measure faith by outcomes that are expressed in terms of human success.

There are also paradoxes inherent in the Gospel reading. Jesus said that he came to bring division, and he has certainly done that over the centuries. Beginning with his siblings (John 7.5), families were set against each other, as they responded to him (Luke 21.16). Jesus insisted uncompromisingly on the cost of discipleship – that people must love him more than their family (Luke 14.26). Yet this seems the exact opposite of John the Baptist's mission to reconcile families (Luke 1.17) and Jesus's own expansion of the definition of his family (Luke 8.21). Just as perplexingly, on the face of it, Jesus spoke of bringing fire and division to the earth, not peace. Yet, beginning with the angels' message, Luke's Gospel is pervaded by messages of peace, and ends with the resurrected Jesus's speaking peace to his terrified disciples (Luke 24.36–37).

Jesus had rebuked James and John for wanting to call down fire on a Samaritan village that rejected him because he was going to Jerusalem (Luke

9.52–54). Now he refers to bringing fire to the earth himself. His fire could be that which destroys all that does not bear good fruit (Luke 3.9, 17), or the eschatological fire of judgement accompanying the revealing of the Son of Man (Luke 17.28–30). Jeremiah, too, refers to fire in the hand of the Lord. His words were directed at false prophets, who encouraged evildoers and led the people astray by tacking 'says the Lord' on to their own words. Jeremiah knew, like Isaiah (Isaiah 13.6), that the Lord brings destruction of all that is evil. Whereas James and John were avenging the snub of inhospitality, Jesus brought fire to purify and to cleanse.

So how should we interpret today's readings? Jesus was speaking to his disciples, not to the crowds. This week's readings are best understood in the context of living by faith in a world that is beloved of God, and yet tragically far from the righteousness of the Kingdom of God. Despite the cruelty referred to in Hebrews, despite the corruption of Jeremiah's contemporaries, the world is the location of the incarnation of the one who brings fire to purify. The angels' song of peace on earth among those with whom God is well pleased does not preclude judgement where this is necessary. As we listen to the world news, and the relentless stories of cruelty and injustice, this should be a comforting spur to prayer.

While biblical commentators understand the fire Jesus referred to as purifying all that is ungodly, God also sent Pentecostal tongues like fire (Acts 2.3), when the Holy Spirit was poured out on the disciples. This takes us back to Hebrews, because the peace that Jesus brought to his disciples was a product of this fire. They then readily and bravely gave their lives for the gospel, looking to Jesus, the pioneer and perfecter of their faith.

The readings this week challenge us with seeking true peace, shalom, wholeness, and not just a convenient, insipid calm. Zechariah spoke prophetically of God's acting to guide our feet into the way of peace (Luke 1.79). Mercifully, God's peace gets to the heart of all that is wrong in our wayward world.

Sunday after Trinity,

Proper 16 (21–27 August)

Isaiah 58.9b–end; Hebrews 12.18–29; Luke 13.10–17

WORSHIPPING A HOLY GOD

Almighty God, who called your Church to bear witness that you were in Christ reconciling the world to yourself: help us to proclaim the good news of your love, that all who hear it may be drawn to you; through him who was lifted up on the cross, and reigns with you in the unity of the Holy Spirit, one God, now and for ever. Amen.

Collect for the Thirteenth Sunday after Trinity

These readings share a common concern about what is acceptable worship. In Hebrews, the holiness of God requires that we offer worship with reverence and awe, but there is no discussion, at least this week, of what that means. That question is raised most sharply in the Gospel reading, where the ruler of the synagogue has clear ideas about what constitutes acceptable keeping of the Sabbath and challenges Jesus head on for not conforming to his expectations. This was after Jesus had dared to heal a crippled woman. Isaiah has much to say about this, too, although in less specific terms than Luke's case study.

Luke's description of the woman, especially the phrase 'quite unable', suggests that she was known to the people present. The objection was not that Jesus healed her, but to the day on which he did it. While a midwife could work on the Sabbath to bring new life, rabbis taught that the Sabbath should not be desecrated for anything that could be done the day before or after. Seen from that perspective, after 18 years, there was a perfectly logical argument that one more day made no big difference. But logical arguments are not satisfactory when they diminish a person made in God's image.

There is no suggestion that the woman asked to be healed. Nevertheless, the leader of the synagogue blames her; so Jesus retorts by calling her 'a daughter of Abraham', a very rare phrase, matched only by his description of Zacchaeus as a 'son of Abraham' (Luke 19.9). These people, overlooked in their need by others, are members of God's family. Seeing this, the crowd rejoices in Jesus's mighty deeds, a phrase also used to describe deliverance from slavery and other great acts (Deuteronomy 10.21; Exodus 34.10). God's mightiest deed of deliverance and new life was the resurrection, and Christians soon transferred corporate worship from the Sabbath day of rest to the day of resurrection, the first day of the week, which they called the eighth day, the beginning of the new creation.

The Sabbath, when God is described, anthropomorphically, as both resting and being refreshed after creating a very good world (Exodus 31.17), became a day of rest and refreshment for God's people too, including slaves (Deuteronomy 5.12–14). So, when Jesus, the bearer of life in all its fullness, is confronted with suffering that enslaved a woman, preventing her from experiencing Sabbath refreshment and leaving her parched, he understands God's good purposes for the world to be thwarted.

Seeing it from God's and the woman's point of view, for Jesus, worshipping God acceptably means healing her immediately, in order to avoid what Isaiah called 'trampling the Sabbath'. So often, people plead that they have done 'nothing wrong', but Isaiah wants the more positive 'doing good'. His commendation of the people restoring streets to dwell in would be a powerful image to exiles living with painful memories of the streets of their beloved Jerusalem being razed to the ground some years earlier.

Jesus sets an example of worship in action which issues seamlessly from God's justice. That holding together of theological conviction and action is expressed by Benjamin Whichcote's quaint but prescient prayer, in the seventeenth century, to 'make it the work and business of our lives to reconcile the temper of our spirits to the rule of righteousness, and to incorporate the principles of our religion into the complexions of our minds, that what we attribute to God, as his moral excellencies and perfection, we may propose to ourselves as matter of practice and imitation'.

Hebrews reminds us that we worship a holy God who is a consuming fire. We pray regularly 'hallowed be your name', and Isaiah and Jesus give us down-to-earth examples of what it means to worship this holy God.

Acceptable worship does not need a grand gesture, and, significantly, Luke follows this story with the parables of the mustard seed and the yeast – both small, powerful, rising agents that effect great change. We might keep that accessible, grass-roots focus in mind, as we pray this week: 'Help us to proclaim the good news of your love, that all who hear it may be drawn to you.'

Sunday after Trinity,
Proper 17 (28 August–3 September)
Ecclesiasticus 10.12–18 or Proverbs 25.6–7;
Hebrews 13.1–8, 15–16; Luke 14.7–14

THE VIEW FROM A PRISON CELL

Almighty God, whose only Son has opened for us a new and living way into your presence: give us pure hearts and steadfast wills to worship you in spirit and in truth; through Jesus Christ our Lord. Amen.

Collect for the Fourteenth Sunday after Trinity

This week's readings begin by sounding a little like Miss Manners' book of etiquette, but they have a distinct sting in the tail. Luke asks us to imagine a banquet with no seating plan. Where people sat was dictated by their estimation of themselves in relation to the other people present, and, tantalizingly, Luke does not say where Jesus was seated. His parable would be heard differently by those coming from the lowest place rather than from the place of honour.

By referring to a wedding banquet, Jesus was alluding to the Kingdom of God, which alerts us that some unexpected distinguished guests have been invited. Exploring this, R. S. Thomas's poem 'The Kingdom' vividly describes 'festivals in which the poor man is king'.

Like last week's story, this happened on a Sabbath. The fact that Jesus was invited to a Pharisee's house for the Sabbath, a day when meals were essentially family occasions, and that he had recently been warned by some Pharisees about Herod's violent intentions towards him (Luke 13.31), sheds light on Jesus's recognition in pharisaic society. Certainly, Luke paints Pharisees in a kinder light than do the other Gospel-writers, and this host was not just a Pharisee, but a leader of the Pharisees. There were, however, underlying tensions, and Luke tells us that 'they were watching Jesus closely'. Jesus adopted a trusted rabbinic method of teaching by illustrating a scriptural saying with a memorable story. Essentially, Proverbs and the first half of the Gospel say the same thing about how to behave when invited to a banquet, except that Jesus brought Proverbs' principles from the royal court down to earth with plain good sense about avoiding humiliation.

With the bit between his teeth, Jesus then turned on his host, and made a bold criticism of his guest list. We can imagine heads turning as a shocked silence descended, and, were we to read on, we would hear one of the guests breaking it with a pious statement. That simply gave Jesus a platform for another parable about people who refused hospitality before he again commended his socially bizarre guest list. This comprised the poor, the crippled, the lame, and the blind, none of whom could repay the hospitality they experienced – as he himself could not, since he was travelling to Jerusalem. It appears that his message was not heard because, soon after this incident, one of the criticisms that the Pharisees made of Jesus (Luke 15.2), was his astonishing choice of dining companions, which included tax-collectors and sinners – the religious scum of the earth at the time.

The recipients of the letter to the Hebrews were instructed to show hospitality to strangers, and to remember those in prison as though in prison with them. Durham has three jails and once, when the Dean and I were in a Victorian cell-block in Durham Prison where there are excellent views (through barbed wire) of the cathedral, prisoners kept inviting us: 'Come and see the view from my cell.' The story goes that, at the cathedral's behest, as a humanitarian gesture the Victorian prison was designed with cathedral views rather than blank walls. Whether or not this is true, the prisoners certainly see and remember the cathedral and we remember them in our prayers, and through various contacts, including the choir men's singing evensong in their chapel.

Even without going into prison, offering hospitality is something we can all do. Years ago, when I moved to a new area and, on my first Sunday there, attended the local church, I was invited to lunch with a family. Rarely in all the years I lived there did I eat Sunday lunch on my own, because hospitality was a way of life in that church. Not surprisingly, it was a growing congregation.

Recently, a distressed family arrived at Durham Cathedral after evensong; on receiving tragic news, they had dropped everything to drive 15 miles to the cathedral. It was a very hot day and they had been in the garden. The father apologized for not being properly dressed for a cathedral so I reassured him that his presence was more important than his clothing. We prayed and lit candles. It was a small gesture, but it restored some peace for them, and his tearful thanks were profuse. He called me an angel. But perhaps he was an angel for me.

In our churches, we have a banquet to offer people in need, and God appears to have no seating plan for his extraordinary guest list.

Sunday after Trinity,
Proper 18 (4–10 September)
Deuteronomy 30.15–20; Philemon 1–21; Luke 14.25–33

A QUESTION OF PRIORITIES

God, who in generous mercy sent the Holy Spirit upon your Church in the burning fire of your love: grant that your people may be fervent in the fellowship of the gospel that, always abiding in you, they may be found steadfast in faith and active in service; through Jesus Christ our Lord. Amen.

Collect for the Fifteenth Sunday after Trinity

Our prayer in the Collect to be fervent in the fellowship of the gospel raises the question of with whom we are to be in fellowship. The answer in the epistle is rather startling to people in a society with slavery as one of its building blocks. A slave owner was to be fervent in the fellowship of the gospel with one of his runaway slaves, who might also have defrauded him.

There are two cultural changes to bear in mind as we hear these readings. Slavery in the Graeco-Roman world differed from that in nineteenth-century America, or, indeed, in parts of the world today, where people are still enslaved in evil conditions. Slavery, first-century style, while not something that we would want to condone, was in some ways closer to medieval serfdom, with its duties and relentless hard work, than it was to kidnap and cruelty. Slaves could own property and, for some, especially those with important masters, it was a way to make progress in the world.

Second, the idea of hating someone meant 'love less than' rather than 'positively loathe', except where overt sin was involved. Thus the Bible records that the patriarchs had favourite wives, and uses the stark language of loving and hating (Genesis 29.30, 33) in a way that we would not. The cruelty of the choice in the film *Sophie's Choice* was that, on arriving at Auschwitz, Sophie had to choose which of her two children would be murdered, and which sent to a labour camp. She loved both, and had protected both until then, but was suddenly forced, in biblical language, to love one and hate the other. That dreadful moment puts the question of priorities into sharp focus. Applied to Jesus's words, we begin to understand him as speaking not about the depth of our love for our families, but about our priorities when a choice has to be made between them and God. This can occur in the context of life choices – for example, the decision to serve God overseas, or to stay near to the family. Either answer may be right, depending on the circumstances, but it is then that we feel the full impact of our baptismal vows.

Jesus spoke to large crowds in generalities, albeit it hard generalities: 'Whoever does not hate father and mother, wife and children ... cannot be my disciple.' Paul, on the other hand, spoke to one man in specifics: 'I am appealing to you for my only child ... have him back no longer as a slave but as a beloved brother.' God's generous mercy has transformed relationships, and we live in the context of the generosity that has given the Holy Spirit to make us fervent, steadfast disciples who are active in service.

What does Paul want of Philemon? Onesimus, Philemon's slave, had run away, possibly having stolen something from Philemon, and somehow ended up with Paul under whom he had been converted. Paul was sending him back to face his master, not just as runaway slave, but as brother and Paul's messenger. Being uncertain about how Philemon would receive him, Paul wrote this letter, with its appeal for generous mercy. In a pun on his name ('Onesimus' meant 'useful'), Paul described him as once useless to Philemon – perhaps he was a hopeless slave – but now useful to both Philemon and Paul.

Hearing this reading alongside the Gospel, we see Paul acting in accordance with it. He had become a loving father to Onesimus, but, loving God still more, was prepared to let him go. His subtle appeal was for Philemon to let his love for God similarly trump his claim on his slave, and to return him to Paul. Whether or not Philemon took the hint, Paul asked him to receive Onesimus as if he were Paul, which echoes Jesus's teaching that whoever welcomed a child in his name welcomed him (Mark 9.37). It also recalls last week's reminder that by entertaining strangers, some have entertained angels without knowing it. Philemon might have received far more than he expected by welcoming Onesimus back.

Deuteronomy commands us to give priority to our hearts' orientation towards God, and then live out the consequences: to love, walk, observe, live, and be blessed. This poignant and personal letter gives us an insight into the personal cost of doing so.

Sunday after Trinity,

Proper 19 (11–17 September)

Exodus 32.7–14; 1 Timothy 1.12–17; Luke 15.1–10

CHRIST'S UTMOST PATIENCE

O Lord, we beseech you mercifully to hear the prayers of your people who call upon you; and grant that they may both perceive and know what things they ought to do, and also may have grace and power faithfully to fulfil them; through Jesus Christ our Lord. Amen.

Collect for the Sixteenth Sunday after Trinity

We encounter humanity in all its perversity in all this week's readings – quick to abandon God's way, stiff-necked, foolish, blaspheming, persecuting, violent, ignorant, sinful, grumbling.

What response does this litany of waywardness evoke from God? It is two-fold. In the Gospel, Jesus did not disagree with the Pharisees and Scribes about the sinfulness of humanity; he differed only in his response to it. Yes, people were sinful but, whereas the Pharisees grumbled that Jesus ate with sinners, he rejoiced with the angels over even one sinner who repented. We see the same two-fold response in the Old Testament: on the one hand, the people were sinful, and God's wrath 'burned hot'; on the other hand, God withdrew his judgement when Moses pleaded with him.

Similarly, Paul knew himself to be a sinner, but a sinner who had received mercy and grace. He had been judged faithful and made an example of the utmost patience of Jesus Christ, in turning him from violence and blasphemy to become an example to others.

Paul's phrase, 'the utmost patience' of Jesus Christ, can act as a frame for the Gospel's stories. It takes patience to eat a meal with someone, especially in Middle Eastern culture where meals cooked from scratch were long, drawn-out affairs, occasions for much conversation. Similarly, it takes patience to turn a house upside down, looking for a small coin.

Tax-collectors and sinners were 'coming near to listen to Jesus', to the dismay of the Scribes and Pharisees. Luke is often specific about whom Jesus is addressing; in this case, the complainers not the crowds. Jesus praised two people as examples of patience in action, patience in searching until what was lost was found before further time was devoted to rejoicing at the outcome. Sometimes, we forget to rejoice so I was delighted when, recently, someone came to find me to ask me to give thanks to God for a good outcome to a very difficult situation he had been patiently plodding through.

The psalmist rejoiced to call God his shepherd, yet, by Jesus's time, shepherds were social outcasts because their duties kept them from proper religious observance. So, provocatively, Jesus compared religious leaders to shepherds, challenging them to give priority over their religious duties to searching out just one of God's lost sheep. Piling on the agony, he followed that parable about an outcast man with a parable about a woman, another inferior person in society, holding her up to the Pharisees and Scribes as an example of diligence. The shock value of God's being described as a woman searching for something lost cannot be overestimated. The woman's coin was probably part of her marriage dowry. In the Old Testament, God's relationship with his people was expressed as marriage, and the coin in the parable thus represented something lost in that relationship with God. The coins could be drachmae and one coin probably equalled the value of one sheep, thus linking the two stories and exemplifying Luke's habit of balancing a story about a man with one about a woman.

Jesus was patient with the tax-collectors and sinners, seeing their potential to repent and change. Moses persisted patiently in imploring God to have mercy on the wayward people. Paul's life was transformed by the patience of Christ towards him, which overturned a career dedicated to persecuting Christians, and made an apostle of him. Few of us, in the shoes of the early Christians, would have been able to see Saul, the zealous persecutor, as a potential candidate for grace. Ananias, when told to go to Saul, rightly feared him and his reputation (Acts 9.13). So he needed further encouragement from God to imagine that the patience of Jesus Christ had opened an entirely new future for Saul, and thus for the Church.

We pray this week to perceive and know what things we ought to do, and to have grace and power faithfully to fulfil them. In all the stories we hear this week, someone had to take patient action, action that was inspired by a greater vision of what sinful humanity can become in God's gracious hands. It is one thing to know what we ought to do; it is another to do it. As Hamlet said: 'Ay, there's the rub.'

Sunday after Trinity,
Proper 20 (18–24 September)
Amos 8.4–7; 1 Timothy 2.1–7; Luke 16.1–13

SHREWD RATHER THAN HONEST

Almighty God, you have made us for yourself, and our hearts are restless till they find their rest in you: pour your love into our hearts and draw us to yourself, and so bring us at last to your heavenly city where we shall see you face to face; through Jesus Christ our Lord. Amen.

Collect for the Seventeenth Sunday after Trinity

Amos is forthright about justice in business dealings. Since Magna Carta introduced national standards for weights and measures we have taken these for granted, but in Amos's day there was no benchmark or redress against fraudulent measures. Only God heard the cry of the poor (Job 34.28) and Amos declared that God never forgot abuses that brought them to ruin.

Even though Deuteronomy (23.19–20) forbade charging interest, by Jesus's time there was endless scope for working round that prohibition and business interest rates of 50 per cent were normal. Knowing this, Jesus has a story of huge volumes of goods and money: this was a massive enterprise. The level of trust in the manager had been enormous.

Human nature does not change, and the readings remind us that, although more sophisticated in manifestation, banking scandals today are but part of a dishonourable history of the misuse of other people's money and the manipulation of facts and figures to secure financial advantage at other people's expense. Like the prodigal son in Luke's previous chapter, this manager was squandering someone else's property. Jesus is clear that the money was owed to his master: it was not simply unauthorized commission to line the manager's pockets.

When called to account, the manager's priority was to ensure that he would have friends after his 'banking collapse'. His action in rewriting the legal documents, to reduce what was owed, was a wily way of achieving his stated ends, although far from an honest way of serving his master, who commended him for his shrewdness, not his honesty. We can imagine the master shaking his head in dumbfounded amazement at this latest twist to the tale, as he realized he had been out-manoeuvred, yet again, by his manager.

When commending this approach to making friends, Jesus was undoubtedly speaking ironically, which we miss because we cannot hear the tone of voice that he used. We also lose something significant in translation, because whereas the manager wanted to ensure that he would be received into people's 'homes', Jesus used a different word the second time, and spoke of his being received into people's eternal 'tents'. That is an oxymoron: there is nothing eternal about tents and Jesus's hearers would have picked up the mockery: the steward wanted earthly security, but Jesus said, in effect: 'Go ahead and do what he did; join the company of rogues and share their eternal insecurity.'

Another, subtler, reading of Jesus's comment to the disciples, to whom this parable was directed, looks forward to the ensuing parable about the rich man and Lazarus (Luke 16.19–31). In this reading, Jesus was challenging his disciples to use their money to ensure that the poor, like Lazarus, will receive them into their eternal home with God.

If the parable is surprising, so, too, are Jesus's next words. Instead of saying, as we might expect: 'If you have not been faithful with what belongs to you, who will entrust you with what belongs to other people?', Jesus reversed it and placed the onus on our proving our reliability with what belongs to other people before we are given what is our own. Perhaps the key lies in the fact that we are held accountable for our stewardship of what belongs to others, whereas what we do with our own possessions does not normally involve such answerability to other people; so any deceit or selfishness can go unchecked. We have to have our own internal moral standards, which we learn by being held responsible for our actions.

Jesus was overheard and ridiculed by Pharisees, whom Luke describes as 'lovers of money' (Luke 16.14). Attempts to unpick corrupt systems and live ethically, uncontrolled by money, frequently bring scorn. In his comment at the end of the parable, Jesus brings it down to what masters us. On another occasion, Jesus said: 'Where your treasure is, there your heart will be also' (Matthew 6.21). So this week we pray, wisely, to get the foundation right: for God's love to be poured into our hearts. We predicate our prayer on St Augustine's confession: 'Our hearts are restless till they find their rest in thee.' Hearts at rest in God should be less likely to be trying to find ways to seek security by exploiting others.

Sunday after Trinity,
Proper 21 (25 September–1 October)
Amos 6.1a, 4–7; 1 Timothy 6.6–19; Luke 16.19–31

GODLY CONTENTMENT AND JUST LIVING

> *Almighty and everlasting God, increase in us your gift of faith that,*
> *forsaking what lies behind and reaching out to that which is before, we may*
> *run the way of your commandments and win the crown of everlasting joy;*
> *through Jesus Christ our Lord. Amen.*
>
> Collect for the Eighteenth Sunday after Trinity

Godliness combined with contentment is a potent concept and aspiration. The rich man in the parable had contentment without godliness, as did the people Amos condemned. Both then and now, contentment without awareness of God's call to lead a holy life leads too easily to complacency about the unjust distribution of wealth and resources which is so tragically evident in the world.

The description and condemnation of the people in Amos's sights is vivid and crosses the centuries. These are loungers and layabouts, chasing all the sensuous experiences on offer in their day, oblivious to awful need around them. If they do notice the poor in their midst, at the gate, they push them to one side (Amos 5.12). In the immediately preceding verses God rejected their worship and cried out for justice to roll down like waters and righteousness like an everflowing stream. If they did not respond, the consequence was to be enforced end to their revelry and exile.

The rich man's sin was similarly one of omitting to do justice for the poor who gathered at his gate. The word used to describe his gate implies an impressive edifice, no doubt leading to an equally impressive house. Today's equivalent might be a high wall and security gate. Jesus does not say that the man had mistreated Lazarus, he had just ignored him. However, he had noticed him enough to know his name. Startlingly, even when being tormented, he did not recognize Lazarus as a person so much as someone at his beck and call. Instead, he instructed Abraham to send Lazarus as messenger to his equally contented and complacent brothers. Even when suffering terribly, he failed to grasp any sense of responsibility to Lazarus.

In the passage before this parable, which we read last week, Jesus was teaching about the proper use of earthly possessions, using the stark parable about a dishonest manager who nevertheless acted shrewdly to secure his own well-being. The debtors also benefited even though this was not the motivation of the steward. So, in this week's parable, the rich man is shown as far less shrewd that the steward because he had not even had the sense to use enlightened self-interest to give Lazarus the crumbs from his table, thus securing his own eternal well-being.

The antidote to all this lies in the epistle. First we need a realistic assessment of where any wealth that we have comes from and what lasting benefit it can bring us: we brought nothing into the world and we can take nothing out. As we hear every Ash Wednesday, when the ashes are imposed on our forehead where the cross was placed at baptism, 'Remember you are dust and to dust you will return.' When we have that mind-set, our relationship to money and to riches can take its proper form and we can be content with food and clothing we have.

The language of the first part of the epistle is quite passive: people fall into temptation, are trapped by desires, plunged into ruin and wander (an aimless, unfocused action) from the faith. In contrast, Timothy, as a man of God, was to be far more intentional and active: he was to shun all this, to pursue righteousness, to fight the good fight of faith, to take hold of eternal life, to keep the commandment. Faithful discipleship is not for the passive or the complacent whose contentment is devoid of godliness. Therein lies ruin for them and distress for others.

But all is not lost. Those who are rich can still turn and set their hopes not on their uncertain riches but on God, they can do good, they can be rich in good works and share with generosity. Then they will, unlike the rich man in the parable, store up the treasure of a good foundation for the future: they can rebuild their lives and take hold of the life that really is life. It is with the promise implicit in that exhortation that the Church prays, 'increase in us your gift of faith that, forsaking what lies behind and reaching out to that which is before, we may run the way of your commandments and win the crown of everlasting joy'.

Sunday after Trinity,
Proper 22 (2–8 October)
Habakkuk 1.1–4, 2.1–4; 2 Timothy 1.1–14; Luke 17.5–10

WAITING FOR GOD'S ANSWER

O God, forasmuch as without you we are not able to please you; mercifully grant that your Holy Spirit may in all things direct and rule our hearts; through Jesus Christ our Lord. Amen.

Collect for the Nineteenth Sunday after Trinity

The Gospel acts as a frame for this week's readings. In asking Jesus to increase their faith, the apostles actually asked for their faith to be tested and stretched. Jesus put them in the place of slaves and, discussing with them how a faithful slave should live, returned to a previous hyperbolic illustration (Luke 13.18–19). Naming, probably deliberately and for effect, a tree with deep extensive roots, Jesus described faith as being like a mustard seed's uprooting that tree and planting it in the sea. It was preposterous, but servants should never be startled at what their master can do through them. Their job is to be full of faith, ready to serve at all times, and trusting God for the outcome.

Habakkuk's dilemma illustrates this in practice. Living in Jerusalem around 600 BC was like living in Poland in the 1930s, watching Hitler rearm Germany. Jerusalem, under the control of Egypt, watched Babylon prepare to invade. Seeing the enemy's violence and the suffering of nations that fell into its power, Habakkuk trusted God enough to dare to ask very hard questions about international life. He wanted God to see what he saw, and to hear his urgent cry of 'Violence!' Habakkuk would understand today's cries from Syria and other places of violence.

In response, God told him that he was not seeing the whole picture. He needed to look differently, to 'look' at the proud, to understand what he saw. It is so easy not to look properly, especially in international life where world leaders can compound problems through a quick glance and panicked action. We should pray for them to look wisely and deeply. These eight verses contain 18 words about sight, sound, and waiting: 'look', watch', 'stand', 'vision', 'cry', 'station', 'answer'. God was not acting as Habakkuk thought he should. His religious training told him that God was too pure and holy to look on evil (Habakkuk 1.13), but it seemed that God not only looked on the treacherous; God was silent, perhaps powerless, when justice was perverted and the wicked swallowed the righteous.

Having protested, Habakkuk was brave enough to be a faithful servant, standing on his rampart watch-post, watching for God's answer. Jerusalem's watchmen spent lonely hours staring into empty space, alert for the slightest sign indicating the presence of friend or enemy, and shouting a warning when they saw something wrong. Lives depended on the watchman.

In due course, God answered with a command to create, in effect, an early advertising hoarding: 'Write the vision on tablets, so that even someone running can read it.' Everything turned on the fact that there was still a vision for the appointed time. God might seem inactive or powerless in the face of treachery and wickedness, but the vision was certain and true. Habakkuk was not told its precise content, only that it spoke of the end and he was to wait patiently. The timing was God's.

In practice, the Babylonians captured Jerusalem, taking the people into exile. It was years before they returned to their land. But God assured Habakkuk that he was not powerless; that the apparent success of the enemy could not thwart the vision for the appointed time. Other prophets even understood that the enemy could be part of God's purpose.

So often, people ask God for something, and, faced with troubles, almost immediately pronounce the prayer unanswered. Habakkuk dared to express his doubts and fears, and, despite his impatient question, waited patiently for God's timing. Had Habakkuk not asked his questions or waited for answers, he would never have heard God's somewhat indirect answer, asking him to interpret what he saw. It did not make the situation right, as Habakkuk defined right, but it assured him that God was not offended by Habakkuk's honesty, and was active in ways as yet not understood.

The epistle expresses this same basic concept slightly differently, seeing suffering as a consequence of God's calling to proclaim the gospel, reliant on God's power. Holding, with the Holy Spirit's indwelling help, to the revelation given and to the faith passed on, we are to guard the good treasure entrusted to us. Habakkuk knew that this takes staying power; the Gospel that it takes willingness to serve faithfully and entrust the outcome to our master, to God. No wonder we pray for the Holy Spirit to direct and rule our hearts: the temptation is to give up too quickly.

Sunday after Trinity,
Proper 23 (9–15 October)
2 Kings 5.1–3, 7–15c; 2 Timothy 2.8–15; Luke 17.11–19

NEED OVERCOMES DECISIONS

> *God, the giver of life, whose Holy Spirit wells up within your Church: by the Spirit's gifts equip us to live the gospel of Christ and make us eager to do your will, that we may share with the whole creation the joys of eternal life; through Jesus Christ our Lord. Amen.*
>
> Collect for the Twentieth Sunday after Trinity

It is always wise to pay attention to the questions in the Bible. We have a few this week: 'Why have you torn your clothes?', 'Surely our rivers are better than all Israel's put together?', 'Why would you do something difficult if God asked, but not something as simple as going to wash?', 'Ten people were healed; where are the other nine?', 'Do only foreigners return to give thanks to God?'

If we probe, behind these questions lie some politically charged situations. Aram was making border raids on Israel, and the King of Israel read the King of Aram's letter as a deliberate provocation, perhaps setting up a diplomatic incident. In the Gospel, Jesus was in the territory between Samaria and Galilee, a route normally avoided by faithful Jews who shunned the Samaritans, considering them apostate. It does not take much stretch of the imagination to identify these very familiar enmities and fears in the world today. In such situations, questions help to get to the bottom of things.

In both stories, human need overcame political and religious divisions. By recording that one leper was a Samaritan, Luke implies that some of the others were not. Yet their common predicament, of being cast out of their respective societies for fear of contagion, had overcome centuries of antagonism to create an unlikely community in this geographically in-between territory.

Community that is based entirely on need is not always healthy, but it is often a starting point for God's extraordinary grace to be evident. This is evident in some churches in inner cities or economically deprived areas, where vibrant, faithful Christian communities emerge as testimony to God's reconciling power.

In these stories, the action is driven by people with no reputation. The little slave-girl spoke out to her mistress with disarmingly simple faith. Perhaps unaware of the politics, she knew enough of her faith heritage to trust the prophet to help her master. Later, other brave servants dared to interrupt their master's rage, calm him down, and point out the irrationality of his fury.

Elijah cut Naaman down to size. Having sent an instruction to come to his house, he then blatantly ignored him, despite the cavalcade of chariots which doubtless drew astonished crowds. Unawed, he sent another messenger with a humiliating instruction. Transpose the story to Afghanistan or Syria, and we see how degrading it was for an army commander to wash himself in an enemy river at the command of a local person. Sometimes, it is much easier to be seen to be doing something to earn our reward: to be the recipient of sheer grace can be extraordinarily disarming and hard, especially if we have a reputation to maintain in front of others. Naaman had to become desperate enough to be open to sheer gift.

The author of the epistle was chained like a criminal for the sake of the gospel; yet he kept proclaiming it. The lepers were ostracized; yet they shouted at Jesus from a distance, and one fell at his feet. They seized the moment. This is unlike other encounters with people who wanted healing. Jesus did not touch the lepers, or even speak words of healing: he simply sent them to the priests to be pronounced clean and reintegrated into society. Like Naaman, there was just an instruction to act in faith that healing would follow obedience.

The Collect leads us in prayer that the Holy Spirit who wells up within the Church will equip us to live the gospel and make us eager to do God's will. We pray for God's uncontainable life to burst out as it did in the little girl, who could not contain herself because she knew what the prophet could do, and as it did in the lepers who yelled at Jesus. We pray to be pushed into action, even in daunting situations.

Faithful action may be very simple: say what we know, calm a situation down, notice what is happening, stop to say thank you to God. The outcome may be out of all proportion. This week, it is the outcasts of society who challenge us to be full of faith and the Holy Spirit's life. Then the whole of creation, including people against whom we have built societal or international barriers, can share the joys of eternal life.

Sunday after Trinity,
Proper 24 (16–22 October)
Genesis 32.22–31; 2 Timothy 3.14–4.5; Luke 18.1–8

WRESTLING FOR A BLESSING

Grant, we beseech you, merciful Lord, to your faithful people pardon and peace, that they may be cleansed from all their sins and serve you with a quiet mind; through Jesus Christ our Lord. Amen.

Collect for the Twenty-First Sunday after Trinity

When someone will not take no for an answer, a friend says: 'What don't you understand, the N or the O?' I can imagine the judge shouting something similar to the woman in Jesus's parable.

Unlike some parables, Jesus spelled out the meaning of this one before he told it. Having recently told the disciples not to be distracted by false signs of the coming of the Son of Man, he told this parable to encourage them to pray always and not lose heart. How we live while we wait for God to act is at the centre of this. We know, for example, that the Thessalonian Christians needed to be reminded by Paul to get on with normal life while waiting (1 Thessalonians 5).

To emphasize his point, Jesus made the protagonist a widow, the classic example of vulnerability in his society. Worse, this widow was being harassed by an opponent. Women did not go to court because their menfolk did that for them. So the fact that this widow had to go herself to face not merely a judge, but an unjust judge who cared nothing for anyone and answered to no one, tells us that she was totally alone. With the odds stacked against her, desperation drove her on. She has many equivalents today, not least poor people around the world who take on opponents such as corrupt sweatshop-owners or multinationals which are deforesting the Amazon basin.

Jesus had already taught about persistence, using the example of a man pestering his neighbour (Luke 11.5–13). Now it was a woman's turn, and he may have had words from Ecclesiasticus 35.14–18 in mind. There, a widow persisted in pressing her case, with tears running down her cheeks. Her judge was not unjust: it was the Lord, who does not show partiality, even to the poor, and yet listens to the one who is wronged. This time, however, Jesus described a worse situation with a very powerful outcome, because Jesus's judge did not listen. Jesus's language built the tension: 'pray always ... not lose heart ... kept coming to him ... keeps bothering me ... wear me out by continually coming ... cry to God day and night ... delay long in helping ... quickly grant justice'. The climax is that God will grant justice quickly to those who persist, crying to God day and night and not giving up. At the end of this parable, Jesus returned to the heart of his concern, asking the pointed question: 'When the Son of Man comes, will he find faith on earth?'

Hearing this parable alongside Jacob and the mystery man wrestling obstinately, neither willing to give up, exemplifies the prayerful persistence that Jesus had in mind. Neither man would desist until the stranger changed the rules of engagement, striking Jacob rather than wrestling with him. Still Jacob refused to yield, and demanded a blessing. The exchange about names was about control. To know someone's name, or to give someone a name, was to have some power over him or her: in the creation story, God gave humans authority over the animals by inviting Adam to name them. When Jacob told the man his name ('supplanter') and received a new name ('one who strives with God' or 'God strives'), he conceded his power to his opponent. Then, when Jacob asked his opponent's name (this time saying 'please', which suggests some nascent humility), the man dodged the request and reinforced his mastery over Jacob by blessing him. Finally, Jacob got the message: he had seen God and lived, and yet he limped as a permanent, sobering reminder of the struggle with God.

The epistle is also about persistence: 'Proclaim the message; be persistent whether the time is favourable or unfavourable,' and have 'utmost patience in teaching'. Timothy was to endure suffering, and his persistence in his vocation was not rewarded immediately with unalloyed bliss.

Putting all this together, we are challenged to be faithful, and to persist when things are against us or there is no immediate answer to our prayer. If an unjust judge can be worn down by someone who will not take 'no' for an answer, how much more will God, who yearns to grant justice, answer? This may not be in the way or the timeframe we expect; yet persistence and willingness to yield to God's power and authority will yield a blessing. That is God's nature.

Sunday after Trinity,
Proper 25 (23–29 October)
Jeremiah 14.7–10, 19–end; 2 Timothy 4.6–8, 16–18;
Luke 18.9–14

WHAT IT IS TO BE RIGHTEOUS

Blessed Lord, who caused all holy Scriptures to be written for our learning:
help us so to hear them, to read, mark, learn and inwardly digest them that,
through patience, and the comfort of your holy word, we may embrace and
for ever hold fast the hope of everlasting life, which you have given us in
our Saviour Jesus Christ. Amen.

Collect for the Last Sunday after Trinity

There was a crisis: Jeremiah's devastating words came when the nation,
threatened with destruction by a powerful enemy, faced severe drought. He
described starkly what we see so often on the news: parched and cracked ground,
empty water cisterns, dead animals (Jeremiah 14.1–6). People cried in despair,
pleading with God not to spurn them. We can hear echoes of Habakkuk, three
weeks ago, berating God for not seeing what he saw, or failing to hear his cry of
'Violence!'

Shockingly, God ignored the people, refusing to hear their pleas, seeming
to act like the unjust judge with whom the widow pleaded in last week's Gospel.
In practice, God's silence was in response to the people's persistent refusal to
hear his previous calls to them; but they crudely likened him to a lost stranger, a
confused, disoriented, powerless warrior.

In contrast to the Lord's abandonment of the citizens of Jerusalem to be
killed or exiled by the Babylonians, the author of the epistle averred boldly that,
whereas others deserted him, the Lord stood by him and gave him strength. He
likened the experience to Daniel's rescue from lions. He prefaced this testimony
to God's power by saying: 'I have finished the race, I have kept the faith' –
something that could also be said of Jeremiah, who remained faithful, despite his
people's waywardness.

We hear the Gospel in the light of these two contrasting readings. This
parable is about what it is to be righteous, the issue at the heart of Jerusalem's
dilemma. Greeks thought that to be righteous was to be civilized; Hebrews
considered that it was to be in relationship with God. Jesus had the Hebrew
concept in mind, and directed this parable at people who trusted themselves for
their righteousness.

Besides challenging us about where our trust is placed, the parable asks
us with whom we compare ourselves. Jesus offered two options and I wonder

whether he acted them out. They beg for drama: a Pharisee standing by himself, a tax-collector standing afar off; a Pharisee reminding God that he was not like other people, a tax-collector describing himself as a sinner; a Pharisee with confident stance exalting himself, a tax-collector looking down, beating his breast, pleading for mercy (literally, here, 'atonement'). Since women, not men, beat their breasts and the only other time Luke describes men doing so is in the crowds' response to the crucifixion (Luke 23.48), he is emphasizing the depth of the man's distress.

In contrast, lest there be any doubting his righteousness, the Pharisee announced to the world that he fasted twice a week (a work of supererogation, since fasting was mandatory only on the annual Day of Atonement) and gave away one tenth of his income. But then came the shock, as stunning as the Lord's refusal of the pleas of Jerusalem centuries earlier. While both men 'went up' to the Temple, only one man 'went down' justified, and it was not the Pharisee. He even lost his identity: no longer was he 'not like other men'; Jesus simply dismissed him as 'the other'. Like the people to whom Jesus directed this parable, his self-directed trust was misplaced, and he could not save himself. He justified himself, but remained unjustified in God's sight.

Barbara Kingsolver's marvellous portrayal of a self-righteous Appalachian mother-in-law humorously portrays a contemporary Pharisee given to telling others how they fail to match her virtue:

> Hester's confidence in her own rectitude was frankly unwomanly. She never doubted a thing about herself, not even her wardrobe. Hester owned cowboy boots in many colours, including a round-toed pair in lime green lizard. (Kingsolver, 2012)

Boots like that might not be our manifestation of smug conceit, but we all have ways of substituting self-righteousness for the epistle's godly source of confidence.

Today is the Last Sunday after Trinity. We end this season with salutary and sobering readings. At the same time, we pray in the Collect that we may learn through patience and the comfort of God's holy word to embrace and ever hold fast the hope of eternal life. To do this means knowing in whom our righteousness lies. That there is such hope leads us to share the epistle's exaltation: 'To God be the glory for ever and ever. Amen.'

All Saints' Day

Daniel 7.1–3, 15–18; Ephesians 1.11–23; Luke 6.20–31

ORDINARY SAINTLINESS

Almighty God, you have knit together your elect in one communion and fellowship in the mystical body of your Son Christ our Lord: grant us grace so to follow your blessed saints in all virtuous and godly living that we may come to those inexpressible joys that you have prepared for those who truly love you; through Jesus Christ our Lord. Amen.

All Saints' Day invites us to see things differently. We may not have visions, as Daniel did, which trouble us and require help before we can understand them. Instead, we see differently because we are the recipients of an inheritance that is beyond human imagining. This requires a God-given spirit of wisdom and revelation which leads us to know the God and Father of our Lord Jesus Christ who is the source of all this wonder. The emphasis in Ephesians is on knowing God and knowing the hope to which he has called us, not on knowing how every 'i' is dotted and 't' is crossed in his good purposes. Saints are people who know God and live their lives accordingly – for the praise of Christ's glory, as the epistle puts it. They are not necessarily people who understand everything but they know enough to risk living by faith in God who has raised Christ from the dead.

There are inevitable paradoxes involved because as Christians we have our sights both on heaven and earth. That is where seeing things differently comes in: at times we have to reconcile seeming opposites. God has raised Christ from the dead and seated him in the heavenly places, far above all rule and authority; he has made him head over all things for the Church which is his body, and yet Jesus himself acknowledged that same body would face hatred, reviling, defamation, hunger and situations that reduce disciples to tears.

On the face of it, the beatitudes which Jesus taught are outrageous and irrational: they simply do not make sense as a way to thrive in any society at any time. No one thinks of being hungry or weeping as a blessing, of being reviled and hated as a blessing. Whereas happiness depends on our circumstances, blessing flows from relationship with God which brings, peace, wholeness, and is not dependent on everything going well for us. In that context, to weep may indeed be a blessing because weeping can be a sign that we are not in denial but face to face with reality and thus open to receive what God and other people have to offer, without pretending we do not need it.

We pray to follow the saints in all virtuous and godly living. While a very few saints have moments of supreme faith or sacrifice for which they are remembered at the expense of all else, those moments are but the visible tip of the iceberg of day-to-day faithful, at times plodding and unglamorous, commitment to God. If we remove the halo we can see the saint. Saintly lives are forged out of the stuff of daily life and the real example of saints is not the spectacular moment but the lifetime of steady, godly days. Lest we think they are unlike us, so holy and pure, we should remember that every saint was someone's next door neighbour once and they too struggled to get up in the morning, had rain come in the roof, a baby that cried all night, a donkey that went lame. Those circumstances were the raw material of transformation.

Etty Hillesum, who eventually died at Auschwitz, was transformed from a troubled young woman into someone who, in ghastly circumstances, brought hope and comfort to fearful people around her. Her diary records the day-to-day preparation that would enable her to face the challenging time she knew was coming: 'Every day I shall put my papers in order and every day I shall say farewell. And the real farewell, when it comes, will only be a small outward confirmation of what has been accomplished within me from day to day' (Smelik: 2002).

On All Saints' Day we honour and give thanks for the example of the saints through the ages. Their encouragement to us is surely that we too will grow as Christians amid the routine, as we do the unspectacular, normal things of life. Who are the saints? Simply people who live intentionally, fully and passionately in this life, who see things differently with their eyes fixed on heaven but their feet firmly on the ground. They are people whose way of life is a reflection of the love and life of God, people who cannot help but draw others closer to God.

Fourth Sunday before Advent

Isaiah 1.10–18; 2 Thessalonians 1.1–12; Luke 19.1–10

THE LITTLE MAN IN THE TREE

Almighty and eternal God, you have kindled the flame of love in the hearts of the saints: grant to us the same faith and power of love, that, as we rejoice in their triumphs, we may be sustained by their example and fellowship; through Jesus Christ our Lord. Amen.

The contrast between the Old and New Testament readings is stark. Isaiah voices God's complaint and argument against those who trample his courts; Paul writes of God's grace and peace towards the Church. Isaiah speaks of God's hiding his eyes from the people; Paul of God's making the Christians worthy of his calling and fulfilling by his power every good resolve and work of faith. Isaiah describes God's hatred of the hollow rituals of the wayward people, while Paul boasts of the Thessalonians' steadfastness and faith.

In their different ways, both provide commentaries on the familiar story of Zacchaeus, whose way of life brought opprobrium, and who yet received grace, and promptly began faithful works. Luke gives Zacchaeus's story a particular Gospel frame: last week, we heard of a fictional tax-collector (Luke 18.9–14); now we meet a real one. Earlier, Jesus had described an outcast woman as a daughter of Abraham (Luke 13.16); and now he describes an outcast man as a son of Abraham.

Luke has recently recorded the parable of the rich man who spent his wealth on himself (Luke 16.19–31), and described Jesus's encounter with a rich ruler for whom selling his possessions and following Jesus was too demanding (Luke 18.18–25). Zacchaeus is a contrast to both men. Here is a rich man, not just any despised tax-collector, but a chief tax-collector. Unlike the rich ruler, he does not need to be told what to do with his wealth, but volunteers to give half his possessions to the poor, and to repay anyone he has defrauded – thus vastly out-giving the Pharisee who boasted ostentatiously of giving one tenth.

There is urgency in this encounter. In a culture where men neither ran in public nor climbed trees, Zacchaeus did both. Then Jesus told him to hurry up and come down because, remarkably: 'I must stay at your house today.' No reason for the imperative is given. Luke has said that Jesus was 'passing through' Jericho, not stopping, but suddenly he must spend time with Zacchaeus. In doing so Jesus, who was on his way to Passover in Jerusalem where ceremonial cleanliness was imperative, defiled himself by entering the house of a recognized sinner. This was nothing unusual for Jesus, who had been criticized for eating with tax-collectors and sinners when he ate with Levi, another tax-collector who did not let his wealth come between him and Jesus's call to follow him (Luke 5.27–31).

In Isaiah, God rejected the people's sacrifices because they 'trample his courts' with their hollow offerings; in the Gospel, Jesus not only accepted Zacchaeus's offering, he precipitated it. Unlike people who reached out to Jesus in their need before he responded to them, here the roles were reversed: had Jesus not acted, Zacchaeus, hiding in the tree, would not have responded.

We pray for God to kindle the flame of love in our hearts, so that we have the same faith and power of love as the saints. The kindling in Zacchaeus's life was Jesus's seeking and knowing acceptance of him. That kindling welcome lit a fire of transformation of Zacchaeus's way of life – just as, in the lives of the Thessalonians, God's grace kindled steadfastness and faith in the face of persecution and affliction.

Jesus acknowledged Zacchaeus's conversion: 'Today salvation has come to this house.' Zacchaeus would live the rest of his life discovering the implications of this saving encounter, beginning by doing voluntarily what John the Baptist had commanded as a sign of repentance (Luke 3.7–14).

At the start of his ministry, Jesus spoke of the Spirit's empowering him to proclaim release to captives and freedom to the oppressed. In this final story from Jesus's journey to Jerusalem, Luke records an encounter in which release and freedom were offered and accepted.

Why 'must' Jesus eat with Zacchaeus? Perhaps because forcing him out of hiding to host a dinner was the only way to enable Zacchaeus to realize that he, too, was – in Paul's words – worthy of his call. One wonders: who was the true host at this meal? George Herbert's words, from 'Love (III)', come to mind:

Love bade me welcome: yet my soul drew back,
Guilty of dust and sin …

You must sit down, says Love, and taste my meat:
So I did sit and eat.

Third Sunday before Advent,
Remembrance Sunday

Job 19.23–27a; 2 Thessalonians 2.1–5, 13–17;
Luke 20.27–38

SPEAKING DOWN THE YEARS

Almighty Father, whose will is to restore all things in your beloved Son, the King of all: govern the hearts and minds of those in authority, and bring the families of the nations, divided and torn apart by the ravages of sin, to be subject to his just and gentle rule; who is alive and reigns with you, in the unity of the Holy Spirit, one God, now and for ever. Amen.

The fictional but truth-telling story of Job is, at one level, all about words. Having recognized the force of honest words (Job 6.25), Job railed against his friends' 'windy words', which had no limit (Job 16.3). Then, in words people who are bullied online today might use, he protested, 'How long will you torment me and break me in pieces with words?' (Job 19.10). Then he echoed Habakkuk's lament from a few weeks ago that even God did not heed his words: 'Even when I cry "Violence!" I am not answered.'

It is in that desperate context that we hear Job's yearning: 'O that my words were written down! O that with an iron pen and lead they were engraved on a rock for ever!' We take it for granted that words are written, but in Job's society this was rare. Most words were spoken, and, although the oral culture was reliable as a means of transmission and remembrance, there was not the permanence or the potency of the written word. This explains the impact of Hilkiah's discovery of the written book of the law which led to Josiah's reforms (2 Kings 22), and Jehoiakim's determination to destroy the written words of Jeremiah, which challenged his rule (Jeremiah 36.20–32). It helps us to understand the depth of Job's desire to record his words for posterity.

Paul also knew the power of words. He wrote to warn the new Thessalonian Christians not to be shaken in mind, or alarmed by words or letters purporting to come from him. Knowing how words could deceive, he wanted them to stand firm and hold fast to what they had been taught by him, by word of mouth and by letter.

What words did Job want to write? If we can resist humming Handel's aria which lifts the words out of Job's context, we hear his sublime protestation in the face of total disaster and misunderstanding by his friends. His defiant hope, 'I know that my redeemer lives,' rings through the centuries as a bold affirmation of confidence in God that transcends circumstances. It made the entrusting of his bitter complaints to writing an act of robust faith.

We saw the power of the written word in Durham in summer 2013. For three months, the World Heritage Site hosted the Lindisfarne Gospels. Written on Holy Island, kept for a century at Chester-le-Street, and then at Durham Cathedral for several more centuries, the Lindisfarne Gospels were displayed and interpreted in their original North-Eastern context. Over 100,000 people came from all over the country and overseas to see the Gospels, alongside a stunning collection of similar writings, including the Durham Gospels which are still in the Cathedral's care. Seeing all those handwritten and illustrated words side by side has been a powerful testimony to the enduring word of God. Through written interpretation, pilgrimages, and talks, we reminded people what a Gospel book is, and have told the story of Christianity in the region. We prayed regularly that people coming to the exhibition would encounter the Lord of whom the words of the Lindisfarne Gospels speak. Many people told me of weeping when they saw them.

When Eadfrith wrote the Lindisfarne Gospels, and Aldred later inserted a translation into Old English so that people could understand it (long before Tyndale and others sacrificed their lives so people could have the Bible in their language), they were writing for the glory of God, but also, as it has transpired, for posterity. Like Job, the community of St Cuthbert knew the power of written words, and left us carefully written words as testimony to their faith and worship.

On Remembrance Sunday, we hear Laurence Binyon's familiar words: 'They shall grow not old, as we that are left grow old ...', and we are stirred by the evocative power of a very few well-chosen words. The war poets have left us a terrible, disturbing beauty in writing. Job has left us his written words of defiantly daring faith. Cuthbert's community has left us a breath-taking, life-giving Gospel book. In a world where we tweet and blog almost mindlessly, if we could leave only 20 or 30 words for posterity, what would they be?

Second Sunday before Advent

Malachi 4.1–2a; 2 Thessalonians 3.6–13; Luke 21.5–19

WITNESS OF THE TEMPLE

> *Heavenly Father, whose blessed Son was revealed to destroy the works of the devil and to make us the children of God and heirs of eternal life: grant that we, having this hope, may purify ourselves even as he is pure; that when he shall appear in power and great glory we may be made like him in his eternal and glorious kingdom; where he is alive and reigns with you, in the unity of the Holy Spirit, one God, now and for ever. Amen.*

Living and working at Durham Cathedral, I find it hard to envisage a situation where the building is destroyed, no stone left upon another, and all thrown down. The cathedral has stood for nearly a millennium to the glory of God. Countless visitors describe it as a prayed-in place, in which they feel (sometimes surprisingly, even involuntarily) drawn closer to God. We hear endless stories of people who did not expect to encounter God here, but do so, and leave with their lives transformed in some way. Were it to be destroyed, all that would end, and many of us would face serious questions about God's presence and power to save, as well as our vocation to serve God through the ministry and mission of the cathedral. How would we add it all up?

Herod began building his temple a few years before Jesus's birth, creating a fantastic edifice that was still being added to when Jesus was there. Although Jesus spoke before the fall of Jerusalem and its destruction in AD 70, Luke wrote about 20 years later and his readers heard his words in the light of those terrible events. They knew that something built to be impregnable lay in ruins, that the city at the heart of their relationship with God was razed to the ground.

Faced with such faith-shattering events, being reminded that Jesus looked ahead to them would help people keep faith through the confusion. These words, astonishing and bewildering at the time, were, with hindsight, words to sustain the faithful in times of trial. It was the comment on the beauty of the temple's stones and gifts dedicated to God which gave Jesus the cue to undermine any confidence in the buildings. These are hard words for people who love church buildings that have faithfully borne witness to the gospel over the centuries.

Malachi's call for reverence of God is always the appropriate response, and his judgement on the arrogant challenges any over-confidence in the works of our own hands. Buildings can be profound bearers of the gospel and the underlying question is not about buildings *per se*, but about where our trust is placed: in the splendour of the buildings, or in the God whom we worship in them?

Significantly, these hard words followed immediately from Jesus's drawing attention to a widow who offered two small copper coins to the treasury of that same temple; he commended her for giving everything, more than all the people who gave some of their spare cash put together. Her small, sacrificial giving for the temple's upkeep indicated the orientation of her heart.

Jesus's words are a challenge to be faithful to God through thick and thin, to be wise and not misled: in Malachi's words, to revere God's name in times of burning trial; in Paul's words, not to be weary in doing what is right. Then we need not fear the fallout from desolating destruction such as that which Luke's readers recalled when they heard Jesus's words read to them.

Cataclysm is not finality in God's hands: persevering faith is still needed. Jesus said that, paradoxically, troubles would provide opportunities to testify in all kinds of unlikely places for which meticulous preparation was unnecessary since they could not guess where they would find themselves. If they had radical, persevering trust in God, he would provide the needed words. This is illustrated by Paul's experiences in front of people he never expected to meet and his eloquence as the need arose: a tent-maker instructed a king (Acts 24–25; Philippians 1.12–30).

All this should influence our prayers for Christians in Egypt, Syria, Iraq, Pakistan, Nigeria, and other places of persecution where church buildings are destroyed. The contrast between the violent destruction of the temple and Jesus's reassurance that not even a hair of their heads would perish, hairs that were counted by God (Luke 12.7), is stunning. The widow knew that. Therein lies our confidence in God, and the basis for the exhortation not to be terrified when trouble strikes. As we approach Advent, this is a big challenge about our hope and our commitment.

Christ the King,
Sunday next before Advent
Jeremiah 23.1–6; Colossians 1.11–20; Luke 23.33–43

SO WHAT THAT CHRIST IS KING?

Eternal God, whose Son Jesus Christ ascended to the throne of heaven that he might rule over all things as Lord and King: keep the whole Church in the unity of the Spirit and in the bond of peace, and bring the whole created order to worship at his feet; who is alive and reigns with you in the unity of the Holy Spirit, one God now and for ever. Amen.

Collect for the Third Sunday after Trinity

Time magazine once described charitable work as Prince Charles's passion in life. It reported that he wanted to do as much as possible before becoming King, when, an aide said, 'the prison shades close' (*Time*, 2013). Soon after this article was published, a dinner-party conversation turned to the 'So what?' question in relation to academic research, and – with this column in mind – I put the themes together and asked myself: 'So what that Christ is King?'

What do the readings say about kingship? Jeremiah records that kingship derives from God, who rescues his people from being scattered like lost sheep; kingship is about wisdom, bringing justice and righteousness to the land and people, creating the security that facilitates well-being. This is, however, only part of the story. Borrowing an ancient hymn, which describes this King as the pre-existent Son of God, through whom and for whom all things in heaven and earth were created and in whom all things hold together, Colossians' royal imagery draws us from human time and space to glimpse eternal things. So what?

Christ's kingship is the source of our redemption and forgiveness of sin; in making Christ King, God has rescued us not just from darkness, but from the power of darkness, transferring us into the Kingdom of his beloved Son, establishing new relationships and authority. All that can be known of God is revealed in his Son. He who is before all things, the image of the invisible God, was born into human time and space as a human child, to a young mother in an occupied country, at a particular time in human history, and named Jesus. So what?

Our only appropriate response is wonder and surrender to the mystery of God's glory revealed in Jesus Christ, to whom every knee in heaven and earth and under the earth will bend (Philippians 2.10). A familiar hymn summarizes this succinctly: 'King of kings, yet born of Mary, as of old on earth he stood'. In the Gospel, however, kingship is more like 'the prison shades'. Few have expressed this more intensely than W. H. Vanstone, in his stunning hymn, 'Morning glory, starlit sky' where he describes no enthroned monarch but God whose aching, spent arms sustain the world.

Human sinfulness, encountering divine kingship, tried to consign it to a cruel human death, with unspeakable physical pain and mocking humiliation. Yet, just a few weeks later, Peter, who knew Jesus as a man, announced: 'God has made him both Lord and Messiah, this Jesus, whom you crucified' (Acts 2.36).

The soldiers mocking Jesus were wrong; he was far more than the King of the Jews, whom they could deride callously in his suffering. Something much vaster was at stake. Human vision is minuscule, and Jeremiah's insight that kingship in David's line brings justice, righteousness, and safety in the land was but part of the truth.

Through his Son's dying in agony, God reconciled to himself all things on earth or in heaven. This kingship is cosmic, and so we pray in the Collect that God will bring the whole created order, not just humanity, to worship at his feet. The Orthodox Church grasps these truths more readily than we do. For Vladimir Lossky, the source of Christian theology is the confession of the incarnation of the Son of God (Lossky, 1978). In Christ, transcendence became immanent. On the cross, Christ reunited the terrestrial cosmos to Paradise, and, after the resurrection, Christ's body mocks spatial limitations to unify earth and heaven. By the ascension, Christ reunites the celestial and terrestrial worlds; sitting at the right hand of the Father, he takes his humanity into the Trinity itself. These are the first-fruits of what the Orthodox Church calls cosmic deification.

So what that Christ is King? Worship, yes; but Colossians prefaces this exaltation of the cosmic consequences of divine kingship with a prayer for spiritual wisdom and insight, to enable Christians to lead lives worthy of the Lord.

If we are challenged by Jeremiah's vision that service and care of others are at the heart of ruling in righteousness – an outworking of God's kingship – then giving ourselves to charitable work may not be a bad place for both a future king and his subjects to begin.

Saints and Festivals

Stephen, Deacon and First Martyr

26 December

2 Chronicles 24.20–22 or Galatians 2.16b–20;
Acts 7.51–end; Matthew 10.17–22

MARTYRDOM AND CHRISTMAS

Gracious Father, who gave the first martyr Stephen grace to pray for those who took up stones against him: grant that in all our sufferings for the truth we may learn to love even our enemies and to seek forgiveness for those who desire our hurt, looking up to heaven to him who was crucified for us, Jesus Christ, our mediator and advocate. Amen.

Some people are surprised that the Church seems to abandon Christmas so quickly – the birth of Christ yields abruptly to sobering readings about martyrdom and Jesus' warning to his disciples of impending flogging and imprisonment. All in all it is not quite Christmas.

Stephen, a good and faithful man, was appointed deacon to care for Christian widows. Religious authorities do not martyr people for feeding elderly women, so there was more to the role of deacon and scholars suggest they had financial and teaching responsibilities. Stephen provoked opposition and was hauled before the religious authorities who saw his face was like that of an angel, a messenger of God. It sounds like a fulfilment of Jesus' promise that when disciples were arrested the Spirit of God would speak through them. In his defence, Stephen summarized the Old Testament story before suddenly turning on his listeners, accusing them of opposing God. Frenzied, they stoned him. Now, being a Christian became literally a matter of life and death. Poignantly, we hear Paul's reflections on life and death, perhaps recalling his presence at Stephen's stoning.

What has this to do with Christmas? Do we have to put our celebrations on hold and then return to them after this distraction of commemorating Stephen? The Church through the centuries has said 'No' and probably placed his day close to Christmas in order to honour the first person to die for the Saviour whose incarnation was being celebrated. Our forebears understood the radical impact the incarnation had on the world: God's coming among us brings 'Peace on the earth, goodwill to men, from heaven's all-gracious King', but is also the ultimate threat to and disruption of life as the world has known it.

St Stephen's Day stretches our grasp of the incarnation. The 'little Lord Jesus asleep on the hay' was heading for exile to escape King Herod's murderous intent; Jesus' mother was warned that her soul would be pierced because her son was set for the falling and rising of many people. In the Gospel, Jesus speaks of facing trial and death as a consequence of remaining faithful to God's radical and incredible way with the world – he was born into it in order to heal and redeem it from within its life.

Stephen was following his Lord who 'came to what was his own, and his own people did not accept him'. Like him, Stephen prayed for forgiveness for his murderers. Gazing into heaven, he saw the glory of God and Jesus standing at the right hand of God. He saw in heaven what had been revealed on earth through the incarnation: 'We have seen his glory, the glory as of a father's only son, full of grace and truth.' Like Stephen, our lives can never be the same again. The incarnation, the Christmas story, set in motion something unstoppable.

The Collect is a tough prayer. We can be tempted to abandon our commitment to Christ when we are facing opposition or when it is simply easier not to be known as a Christian. Or, perhaps because we wonder how we can keep faith in the midst of troubles since we tend to assume that, if there is a God, surely he will act to end our suffering? So we look hopelessly at circumstances and doubt our way into loss of trust. Instead of doing that, we pray to look to heaven to see Jesus, our mediator and advocate, and to draw strength from him.

Christmas, for many people, is not a time of unalloyed joy. It can be a time of loneliness, of missing people, of looking back on a year that has not gone as we hoped. Nevertheless, the message of the incarnation is undimmed. The challenge of St Stephen's Day falling a day after Christmas is that we do not settle for either glory or sorrow but hold the two together because, as St John tells us, 'The light shines in the darkness, and the darkness did not overcome it.'

In the incarnation, at the time of Stephen's death, at unexpected times in our own lives, the heavens are opened and we can see the glory of God. That is the story of Christmas and of St Stephen. It can be our story too.

John the Apostle and Evangelist

27 December

Exodus 33.7–11a; 1 John 1; John 21.19b–end

TO LOVE FOR A LIFETIME

> *Merciful Lord, cast your bright beams of light upon the Church: that, being enlightened by the teaching of your blessed apostle and evangelist Saint John, we may so walk in the light of your truth that we may at last attain to the light of everlasting life; through Jesus Christ your incarnate Son our Lord. Amen.*

In his beautiful, thought-provoking novel, *John* (Williams: 2008), Niall Williams asks, 'What would it be like to have the most profound experience of your life when you were that young, to have witnessed what he had witnessed and then be left alone in the aftermath? … What it might be to love for a lifetime.'

Whether John the apostle (was he 'the one whom Jesus loved', or not?) and John the evangelist, author of the Fourth Gospel, were the same person has provided opportunity for the spilling of much scholarly ink. Either way, today we honour the person who wrote so profoundly that the Word became flesh and dwelt among us.

John the apostle was Zebedee's son and brother, probably younger, of James who was the first of Jesus' 12 disciples to be martyred. Jesus gave them the nickname 'Sons of thunder', so for all the serenity and mystical insight we associate with John's writings, there was a fiery element to his nature. With James and Peter, he was part of Jesus' inner circle of disciples, present at some of the most private or profound moments of Jesus' life. Handling that privilege is a significant responsibility and we know today of too many intimate confidants of people in power who then betray them. Not so with John, young as he apparently was. If John was the disciple whom Jesus loved then he was the only one of the Twelve to stay with Jesus during the crucifixion and, at Jesus' behest, he subsequently cared for Mary in his home, with his mother who had also been present at the crucifixion.

John was prominent in the early Church, along with Peter. After his brother James became the first of the 12 disciples to be martyred (we should never underestimate the impact this would have had on John), Christian tradition places him in Ephesus, a city dominated by the temple dedicated to Diana, or Artemis, and a place visited by Paul on his missionary journeys. Ephesus was one of the seven churches addressed by letters in the book of Revelation, being commended for its patient endurance and resistance to evil-doers but criticized for its loss of its first love for Jesus Christ. If John the apostle is author of the three epistles that bear his name, then they were probably written from Ephesus before he was banished to the island of Patmos, which is the traditional location for the writing of Revelation.

In old age, John trained Polycarp, later Bishop of Smyrna, who passed on John's teaching and writings to future generations. Tradition indicates that John's exile on Patmos was eventually ended and he returned to Ephesus where he died at a great age, some time after AD 98, the only one of the 12 disciples not to be martyred.

What might it be to have your most profound experiences at a young age and then to love for a lifetime? In the first epistle bearing John's name he writes of seeing and touching the word of life who was with the Father. John lived his long life convinced that his early experiences were true and trustworthy, that it was not foolishness to predicate his whole life on that foundational truth. In the words of his epistle, it was to walk in the light as God is light. Moses was told that he could not see the face of God and live, yet John claimed to have done just that in Jesus Christ. If Moses who could not see God was the friend of God, how much more could John, the one who saw and touched Jesus, God in human form, be the one whom Jesus loved?

At the end of John's Gospel, after all these sublime and yet difficult experiences for a young disciple, we are told that these things are written down by someone prepared to testify to them, and they are true. A chapter earlier in the Gospel we are told that these things were written so that we might believe that Jesus is the Messiah, the Son of God, and thus might have life in his name. It is one thing to have profound experiences at a very early age, it is another to write them down and share them for the life-giving benefit of others. John did both and we pray, wisely, to walk in the light of the truth thereby revealed.

The Holy Innocents

28 December

Jeremiah 31.15–17; 1 Corinthians 1.26–29;
Matthew 2.13–18

THE HORROR FROM HEROD

> *Heavenly Father, whose children suffered at the hands of Herod,
> though they had done no wrong: by the suffering of your Son and by the
> innocence of our lives frustrate all evil designs and establish your reign
> of justice and peace; through Jesus Christ our Lord. Amen.*

How quickly joy can be disrupted. No sooner had the Magi left the house,
leaving immensely valuable and symbolic gifts, than Mary and Joseph were
themselves on the road going further and further from their home in Galilee.
'Now after they had left, an angel of the Lord appeared to Joseph in a dream
…', reports Matthew, echoing almost word for word the events of a few months
earlier (Matthew 1.20).

Mary and Joseph had good reason to be disturbed by angels: in their
experiences angels turned life upside down. After both angelic dreams Joseph
acted as soon as he woke, this time not even waiting for daybreak. The shocking
TV pictures of refugees around the world fleeing from danger with nothing more
than they can carry (Mary and Joseph had a baby to carry before anything else)
give us a glimpse of the deprivation and degradation that Jesus and his family
faced. And they did it on foot.

By getting a head start – we do not know how long it took Herod
(significantly Matthew removes his title 'king') to realize he had been tricked
– Joseph ensured their safety. Being outside Herod's jurisdiction but still part
of the Roman Empire, Egypt, once the place of oppression for God's people,
became a refuge for people fleeing from the violence Herod unleashed on his
people. There were Jewish refugee communities near modern Alexandria and
Cairo.

Egyptian Christians are proud that their country offered protection to the
infant Jesus and many Egyptian icons show the flight to Egypt. I have a modern
icon from Aswan Cathedral showing Joseph leading a wonderfully cross-eyed
donkey bearing Mary and the baby. However, we cannot assume that Mary rode
a donkey; as poor people they probably walked first from Nazareth to Bethlehem
and then to Egypt. Life was hard in violent times as it is today: few of us can
imagine what it is like to live so provisionally, to be uprooted with no warning,
whether by the action of others or because we believe God is calling us, with no

guarantee of where we are going or how long we will be there. In this instance Joseph was simply told to go until God indicated otherwise.

The journey to Egypt was long – some 260 miles, much of it through barren desert. There was a well-trodden coastal route known as 'the way of the sea', which linked Egypt with its trading partners in Mesopotamia. Mary and Joseph, joining the southern part of this route, would have linked up with a caravan group for protection against bandits. Matthew referred to the Galilean part of this route at the start of Jesus' ministry (Matthew 4.13–16, echoing Isaiah 9.1).

Although Jesus was safely out of the way, other baby boys were not and the massacre was a horrific, but not out of character, act by Herod who also killed his own wife and some of his sons, and, according to Josephus writing in the first century, ordered that when he died a member of every family was to be killed in order to ensure widespread mourning. Matthew does not shrink from reporting the horror that, given the likely population of Bethlehem at the time, probably involved about 20 baby boys, leaving 20 traumatized families. While Matthew links it to Jeremiah's description of Rachel, mother of Israel, who weeps for her children, he chooses his words carefully: in a Gospel in which Jesus is repeatedly shown as fulfilling the Lord's word through the prophets (e.g. Matthew 1.22; 5.17; 8.17), in this instance he uses the passive, 'Then was fulfilled what had been spoken', in order to avoid any suggestion that God was responsible for this cruel fulfilment.

So why does the Church observe this dreadful commemoration three days after Christmas? By denuding Christmas of tinsel, it is realistic about the world into which God sent his Son, reminding us starkly of the risk God took in the incarnation and of the role that humans are called to play in God's story. In Jeremiah, God assumed his people would be rewarded for their work and would return from exile; the Corinthians, although weak in the world's eyes, were to shame the strong of the world. Joseph shows us how: he listened and acted despite the cost. As we remember the Holy Innocents, surely we are so called today to act for good, however weak, insignificant and discomforted we feel.

The Naming and Circumcision of Jesus

1 January

Numbers 6.22–end; Galatians 4.4–7; Luke 2.15–21

YESHUA, CALLED BY A COMMON JEWISH NAME

Almighty God, whose blessed Son was circumcised in obedience to the law for our sake and given the Name that is above every name: give us grace faithfully to bear his Name, to worship him in the freedom of the Spirit, and to proclaim him as the Saviour of the world; who is alive and reigns with you, in the unity of the Holy Spirit, one God, now and for ever. Amen.

How do you name the Son of God? The answer, it seems, is with a very common name so that there is nothing to make him stand out from other Jewish boys. 'Jesus', a shortened form of 'Joshua', or 'Yeshua' in Hebrew, was a common name for pious Jews to give their sons. The meaning of names was important and Yeshua meant 'Yahweh, God, is salvation.'

Naming, in the biblical stories, is both a divine and a human activity. In the creation stories God starts by naming his creation but then, in a delightful twist to the story, waits to see what his own creation, the man, will name the animals. There's a sense of collaborative purpose in naming that continues through the Old Testament as, very occasionally, God intervenes to specify the name of a child for a particular reason.

Matthew explains that this child is named Jesus because he will save his people from their sins (1.21). This extension of the meaning of Yeshua from 'God is salvation' hints at this baby's divinity. The same applies in Luke's Gospel, although the angel's explanation to Mary is slightly different: this child will be great, the Son of the Most High, will inherit David's throne and reign over the house of Jacob for ever (1.32–33). This recalls Isaiah's words about a child being born who will inherit David's throne for ever, being called 'Wonderful, Counsellor, Mighty God, Prince of Peace' (Isaiah 9.6).

But none of that prophetic weight of meaning would be obvious to look at this child, born in a stable in a strange town, looking and crying like any other eight-day-old baby when he was circumcised, with a name that did nothing to draw attention to his future. Unlike the unfortunate sons of Isaiah who, to make a prophetic point, were named 'A remnant shall return' and 'The spoil speeds, the prey hastens' (Isaiah 7.3; 8.1, 4), Jesus would not stand out because of his name. Only Mary and Joseph knew the particular reason for it and, unlike the naming of John, no one thought it odd.

Both the Gospel and the Epistle assert that this baby was born of a woman who gave him his Jewishness, born under the law, a child of the covenant, circumcised on the eighth day. Today's observance of the naming of Jesus reminds us of Jesus' full humanity and, in his first 30 years of life, his unremarkableness as he lived and worked with his family.

We, who confess that Jesus is Lord, can find ourselves reading back into this story with the wisdom of hindsight what we know about his death, resurrection and ascension. But Luke, who has been quite free with his stories of angelic messengers in the events leading up to and at his birth, suddenly goes silent on divine interventions and instead tells us of a routine circumcision as far as the people around Mary and Joseph were concerned.

Luke is setting up the story of Jesus' ministry by telling us that although a few people had special insight into who Jesus was, most people thought he was an ordinary good Jewish boy. As the Gospel unfolds, people will have to respond to Jesus' actions and his words in order to understand that he is indeed God's salvation living among them. And those who do come to understanding and make the confession that this Jesus is the Christ, the Messiah, have the joy of calling his father, our father, 'Abba'.

The lovely reading from Numbers acts as a commentary on what it means that Jesus bears God's name. We know the words of the blessing, but the frequently overlooked final comment is important, 'So I shall put my name on the Israelites, and I will bless them.' God's name imparts God's blessing. We who bear the name of Jesus today, Jesus now revealed to be the Son of God and bearing the Messianic name 'Christ', are blessed in him. That is cause for celebration on this feast of the naming of Jesus when we begin a new calendar year of our Lord.

The Conversion of Paul

25 January

Jeremiah 1.4–10 or Galatians 1.11–16a; Acts 9.1–22;
Matthew 19.27–end

CONVERSION OF LIFE

> *Almighty God, who caused the light of the gospel to shine throughout the
> world through the preaching of your servant Saint Paul: grant that we who
> celebrate his wonderful conversion may follow him in bearing witness to
> your truth; through Jesus Christ our Lord. Amen.*

We read of three conversions that changed three lives and the course of history.
Jeremiah lived at a traumatic time of national loss of faith in God when the
Babylonians were threatening to capture Judah and take the people into exile,
events he later lived through. We can understand his reluctance to be called to
serve God. But God would not take 'No' for an answer, or allow excuses of
youth and inexperience. Instead he touched Jeremiah's lips and sent him anyway.
Jeremiah spent his life faithfully ruing that day.

Paul's conversion was literally the last thing on earth that he expected. He
was going to Damascus to arrest and imprison the Christians, not to join them.
Instead, over the course of three days he was thoroughly converted. Passionately
religious, a rising star of first-century Judaism, his commitment was not in
doubt, only the direction of it. His conversion redirected his passion and fervour
for God so that it embraced an encounter with God incarnate, Jesus Christ, and
recognition that he was, unwittingly, rebelling against God through his religious
zeal. Three days of blindness before Ananias arrived enabled him to take in
the devastating answer to his question as he fell to the ground, 'Who are you,
Lord?' He had no problem calling God 'Lord' because he was a devout religious
man. What took time to assimilate was the answer, 'I am Jesus, whom you are
persecuting.' As he wrote later to the Galatians, God revealed his Son to him so
that he could proclaim him to – of all peoples – Gentiles.

Ananias is simply introduced as a disciple in the fledgling Christian
community in Damascus. His initial conversion to Jesus Christ as Lord is not
described, only a further conversion to openness to its implications. Suddenly
the Lord asked him to go to look for the very man the Christians dreaded as a
purveyor of evil. Ananias was not told what to do, except to find Saul who had
had a vision of a man laying hands on him to restore his sight. In fact, once he was
converted from his reluctance, Ananias went further and called Saul 'brother',
words he would never have dreamed would pass his lips in the same sentence,
then introduced him to the church where he was baptized, welcomed with food –

almost certainly including the Eucharist – and offered a home. Ananias became willing to accept the inconceivable, even outrageous, consequences of what the Lord was doing.

Conversion, as expressed in baptism, is about both profession of faith and conversion of life. It matters what we believe: Paul had to profess Jesus Christ's lordship. Everything in his religious upbringing and faithful religious observance militated against that. For some people, conversion means a radical change in belief about Jesus Christ, leading to acknowledging that he is Lord.

However, belief is not enough as Ananias' conversion reminds us. Already committed to following Jesus as Lord, he needed to turn again and be open to God doing something so radical he simply could not conceive it without a direct vision from God. Belief sets us on the right path but conversion of life is, as Benedict reminds us in his Rule, a daily openness to God's mercy and grace in our lives and in the world.

Conversion is about on-going, life-changing encounters with Jesus Christ, about walking with God day by day and converting the way we live in the light of that. Conversion will go on affecting everything we do – how we spend our time and our money, how we relate to people, how we engage with politics and national life and, if we are caring for a dependent relative, how we repeat the endless daily delicate tasks involved. If we want to know where conversion affects us, asking ourselves what is the hardest thing that God could ask us to change can point us in the right direction, but God may yet surprise us from beyond our frame of reference.

We are all invited to respond to God having mercy on us, calling us to follow. What does conversion mean? It means acting in response to that call whether for the first time or the thousandth time. Conversion is our response to Jesus Christ's invitation to joy and transformation.

The Presentation of Christ in the Temple

2 February

Malachi 3.1–5; Hebrews 2.14–end; Luke 2.22–40

FOUR PEOPLE AND A BABY

> *Almighty and ever-living God, clothed in majesty, whose beloved Son was this day presented in the Temple, in substance of our flesh: grant that we may be presented to you with pure and clean hearts, by your Son Jesus Christ our Lord, who is alive and reigns with you in the unity of the Holy Spirit, one God, now and for ever. Amen.*

Just before Christmas a few years ago, the Cathedral choir had an evening off so we said Evening Prayer. Afterwards I met an Indian family who were sitting in the nave. There were three generations: grandparents, parents and an uncle, and a tiny baby just three weeks old, wrapped up warmly in a white shawl. Her mother held her out to me while her father told me they had promised to bring her to the cathedral if all went well with her birth. So here they were on this cold winter's night, thrilled to bring their first baby to the cathedral, but slightly disappointed there was no choir and music for her. Her father took his new daughter to look at the Christmas tree and I watched as he stood there for a long time, holding her up to see the lights.

In the middle of Morning Prayer next day it dawned on me that I had been part of a similar experience to that when Mary and Joseph brought their firstborn to the Temple in thanksgiving for a safe delivery and to mark the fact that the Temple was to be part of his life, a place where he belonged. For me, this encounter was an unforeseen delight. For them, it was a significant moment, planned from before the birth but with no idea how it would work out. There was that same mixture in Mary and Joseph's experience of a felicitous meeting of people with different reasons for being in the Temple.

Mary and Joseph were there to fulfil religious rituals involving the redemption of the firstborn and the purification of the mother following the rigours of childbirth, marking her re-entry into society. These did not have to be performed in the Temple but, nevertheless, Mary and Joseph had made the three-hour journey from Bethlehem.

There was Simeon, a devout man who was aware of the Holy Spirit's nudging to go to the Temple in time for Mary and Joseph's arrival. On seeing them, he recognized that this was a long-awaited moment. He took the child – undistinguishable from all other babies brought to the Temple by their parents – and praised God in the words we know as the Nunc Dimittis, accepting that the arrival of this baby signalled the ending of his life. It is as though Simeon stepped out of temporal time and had a foretaste of eternity into which he released himself. Then Simeon blessed the parents and spoke hard words to Mary about her son. Simeon's peace and Mary's disturbance have their roots in the same place.

There was someone else with yet another reason for being in the Temple. Anna, at least 84 years old, was one of those people who find a home in a sacred space and are just there. She had not come to the Temple specially; it was where she belonged and she was caught up in this little drama because she walked past when Simeon blessed Jesus' parents. Her part was to speak to others about the baby.

So we have four people and a baby, all touched by this unplanned meeting. Out of it came a song sung through the centuries and this festival, which is the hinge when we turn from Christmas towards Lent, Holy Week and the passion of this child, the light of the world. There is a bitter-sweetness about today, a poignancy as, like Mary, we take in Simeon's difficult words.

Presentation:

That time will come,
Oh yes, that time will come.
As inexorable as the convergence
of heaven and earth
once 'yes' was hanging in the air.
That time will come.

But now, another time, this time
an offering of true love
(two turtle doves) suffices
to make the one convergence clear
as salvation, raw, incarnate holiness,
is presented.

Child and sword presented and
exchanged.
And so that time will come.
© 2000 Rosalind Brown

We never know where a chance encounter will lead or how joy and sorrow will interweave. This strange meeting assures us that no gathering in God's presence is random. Just as Jesus was presented to God, we pray to be presented to God for his service. As we are open to letting events unfold we may experience chance encounters that are life-changing in ways we cannot imagine.

Joseph of Nazareth

19 March

2 Samuel 7.4–16; Romans 4.13–18; Matthew 1.18–end

FACING THE INSCRUTABILITY OF GOD

God our Father, who from the family of your servant David raised up Joseph the carpenter to be the guardian of your incarnate Son and husband of the Blessed Virgin Mary: give us grace to follow him in faithful obedience to your commands; through Jesus Christ our Lord. Amen.

Although (unlike Winnie the Pooh's friend Wol) we should not use long words where short ones will do, there is no avoiding a six-syllable one as we honour St Joseph: Joseph was up against the inscrutability of God.

We hear in Samuel how David had plans to do great things for God which God acted to restrain. He was unlike Joseph whose carpentry business appears to have been all the excitement he expected in life. Whereas David was king and a player on the then world stage, Joseph was simply from a backwater town in Galilee, off the political map. He was a righteous man, soon to be married to an equally righteous woman, yet his life was thrown into turmoil when God intervened in his life and the woman to whom he was engaged was discovered to be pregnant in an age when that meant she should be disgraced, possibly stoned to death.

Matthew tells his readers more than Joseph knew, at least initially. It would seem to be so easy for the angels, already portrayed as working overtime in the Nazareth and Bethlehem area, to have put in an appearance to Joseph and made everything clear from the beginning. It would have spared him, as well as Mary and her parents, a lot of agony. Instead, God left Joseph with the dilemma of what to do when a lifetime of fidelity to God was suddenly rewarded with seeming disaster. To make matters worse, God appeared to be silent. And Joseph had to make his own plans. How was Joseph going to risk belief in God and act faithfully?

Being a righteous man, Joseph tried to put the pieces of his jigsaw puzzle together using the template of the law of God and his own loving compassion for Mary. When we are in doubt about something it is helpful to go back over our past history and what we know of God and try to make sense of it. But we must also be prepared for the unexpected, for God to do something new. So Joseph was working with the wrong picture for his jigsaw puzzle, because God was at this very minute putting the finishing touches on a new one. God is like an artist painting a new perspective of the age-old promise of the Messiah. Hope in God cannot stand still, because – as Isaiah reminds us (Isaiah 43.19) – we hope in a God who is constantly doing a new thing.

The initial silence of God was just as demanding for Joseph as the clarity of God's words had been for David. In both situations God was testing the man: Are you going to act faithfully? Does your hope in God hold fast in the face of chaos and confusion in your life? Ambitious, faithful David, can you live with the clear word of God to hold back? Righteous, ordinary Joseph, can you live with the silence of God?

Joseph's fidelity should remind us that often the times of silence or awkward questions are the prelude to new works of God in our lives. The times when God appears to be silent are times to practise the scales of fidelity that will enable us to play the new music when God puts it in front of us. It is only people who have learned to maintain their hope during God's silences who can be trusted with hearing God's word spoken to their situation. Faced with God's apparent silence, Joseph resolved to act as faithfully as he knew how and, when God did finally speak, he acted even more faithfully. By then the sturdiness of his love of God had been proven, robustness that would be needed in the months and years to come.

So, remembering and honouring Joseph, we should pray for people who have lost hope, people around the world who live with the seeming silence of God without hope. If we are people who practise the scales of faithful hope we are called to prayer and action for people like this, to live as people of hope in a hopeless world. Very often it is the people who have been tested by God's word who can embrace without hesitation the unanticipated presence of God when he comes among us, when suddenly our night sky is torn apart by angels singing, 'Glory to God in the highest and peace to his people on earth.'

The Annunciation of our Lord to the Blessed Virgin Mary

25 March

Isaiah 7.10–14; Hebrews 10.4–10; Luke 1.26–38

RESPONDING TO GOD'S ANGEL

We beseech you, O Lord, pour your grace into our hearts, that as we have known the incarnation of your Son Jesus Christ by the message of an angel, so by his cross and passion we may be brought to the glory of his resurrection; through Jesus Christ our Lord. Amen.

Have you ever wondered how Gabriel appeared to Mary? Luke leaves the question hanging, tantalizingly unanswered. Artists have had a field day. Among my hundreds of pictures of the Annunciation there is no artistic stone left unturned. Gabriel stands, he kneels; he commands, he beseeches, he cajoles; he leans towards Mary, he pulls back from her. He is in such a hurry that he is still halfway down from the ceiling when speaking, he is composed and kneeling gracefully in front of her; he is tranquil, he is flustered; he whispers, he declaims, he shouts, he wags his finger. Mary kneels calmly and serenely as though this happens every day or she pulls back in fright. Gabriel looms over her and she is overwhelmed, she stands stolidly while Gabriel pleads. In one picture her cat has a fit, in another the cat looks on curiously. Mary scowls, she smiles knowingly, she is impassive. In one modern picture a tiny angel climbs her neck to whisper in her ear, while Andy Warhol's understated painting simply shows Gabriel's raised hand on the left of the picture and Mary's tense fingers pulling back on her prie-dieu on the right-hand side. That depiction is far from Braccesco's painting in the Louvre where Gabriel zooms in on a sort of fifteenth-century surfboard and Mary, quite reasonably, ducks as he heads straight for her head at full tilt.

Yet in the Bible most angels looked human when they appeared and Gabriel may have looked like any other person in Nazareth until he opened his mouth and spoke God's message to Mary. Only then did the enormity of this encounter become clear. From this day on both heaven and earth were changed because Mary said 'Yes' to God's astonishing proposition that God the Son should be born into this world and she would be his mother. Sometimes God's ways of doing things are way beyond anything that any sensible human could think up.

Mary's response to the angel's message is staggering. 'Here am I, the servant of the Lord. Let it be with me according to your word.' 'Here am I' echoes Isaiah, although unlike Mary he did not know what he was letting himself in for. Mary did not ask for time to think it over or talk to her parents or fiancé, as would be the cultural norm. Instead this young girl from a backwater village in a small part of the Roman Empire quite simply said 'Yes' to God and risked all the consequences. In Hebrews Christ says, 'See, God, I have come to do your will.' Maybe he learned that from Mary.

I wonder if St Benedict had Mary's response in mind when formulating his three monastic vows of stability, obedience and conversion of life. Stability – the refusal to run away when things get too hard – is there in Mary's statement 'Here am I' as she positioned herself before God, open to God's unexpected intervention in her life.

Obedience is more than doing what we are told; it is the recognition that we are not our own or totally autonomous individuals, ultimately we are God's. So Mary described herself as the servant of the Lord. As Jesus pointed out, obedience is not just saying we will do what is asked, but actually doing it. In Mary's case she was called to a lifetime of obedience by this one response, and the Collect points to the cost of that obedience: ultimately she was faced with her son's cross.

Conversion of life is expressed by Mary's prayer, 'Let it be with me according to your word.' It is openness to growth in holiness as God leads us; it is not change for change's sake but focused commitment to godly living as we follow God's lead, risking the new things that God does in and through us.

God's call to us usually comes in more subtle ways than an angel with enormous wings arriving on our doorstep, or dropping in through the ceiling, or however else we may imagine the Annunciation actually happened. Thank God for the creativity of artists who have opened up so many possibilities. We will each recognize some as more true in our experience of God than others. The more demanding question is how we respond when God does come, as come God will.

George, Martyr and Patron Saint of England

23 April

1 Maccabees 2.59–64 or Revelation 12.7–12;

2 Timothy 2.3–13; John 15.18–21

A FAITHFUL SOLDIER OF GOD

God of hosts, who so kindled the flame of love in the heart of your servant George that he bore witness to the risen Lord by his life and by his death: give us the same faith and power of love that we who rejoice in his triumphs may come to share with him the fullness of the resurrection; through Jesus Christ our Lord. Amen.

Laying aside myths about dragons, we know a little about George who was probably born in Lydda around 280 to a Greek Christian family. His father was one of Emperor Diocletian's best soldiers and the Emperor welcomed George's decision to follow the same career. He was soon promoted to become a tribune in the Imperial Guard. Then Diocletian issued an edict in February 303 ordering the arrest of all Christian soldiers in the army and requiring the rest of the army to sacrifice to the Roman gods. Bravely, George not only objected but approached the Emperor who, wanting to retain this reliable soldier, attempted unsuccessfully to buy his compliance with gifts of land, money and slaves. George refused. Left with no alternative, Diocletian ordered his execution and, following extreme torture, George was decapitated on 23 April 303. His conduct under torture led to the conversion and immediate martyrdom of the Empress and a pagan priest.

The legend of the dragon-slaying was brought back with the Crusaders. In icons, images of George saving a maiden are linked to the martyrdom of the Empress as George, through his example, which prompted her conversion, saved her from Satan's power. After the Crusades, George replaced Edward the Confessor as patron saint of England. He is also patron saint of, or honoured in, many other countries including Georgia, Malta, Cyprus, Portugal, India, Bulgaria and Macedonia, and cities including Moscow, Genova and Beirut.

The readings pick up themes from George's life. Jesus prepared his disciples for the hatred of the world. They would be persecuted because they served the One who was himself persecuted and their suffering would be because they bore the name of Jesus Christ. The crux of it is that they do not belong to the world, so the world will hate them for it.

The Epistle to Timothy, a young man called to leadership, draws on the imagery of being a good soldier – focused, committed, hardworking, law-abiding and prepared to share in suffering. To do this faithfully, Timothy is exhorted to remember Jesus Christ who was raised from the dead – death is not the ultimate victor – and the example of the author who himself is suffering hardship and imprisonment. Revelation focuses not on the characteristics of a good soldier but on the triumph of Michael and the angels in heaven against the dragon, Satan. Having defeated the dragon the praise goes not to the victorious angels but to the one they serve – God whose salvation, power and kingdom are established – and there is rejoicing at the conquest of all the martyrs who did not cling to life. A soldier serves others and seeks their glory.

There is a crucial phrase in the description in Maccabees of the way that Daniel and his three faithful companions were saved from lions and fire. The author makes the observation that from generation to generation none of those who put their trust in God will lack strength. The reading concludes, 'My children, be courageous and grow strong in the law, for by it you will gain honour.' There is no suggestion that the faithful person will automatically be safe: the promise is of strength, which we need when we feel weak, and of honour, rather than life and prosperity.

We honour George for his unflinching witness to his Lord, through horrific torture to death. He certainly had strength and, through the centuries, has been honoured. The danger is that thoughts like these trip off the tongue too easily, however true they are, and that in remembering George and hearing these readings we descend into pietistic platitudes. That is why we need the counterbalance of the exhortation to Timothy which spells out the total dedication of a soldier whose aim is to please the enlisting officer. In George's case, there came a point where he could not please the Emperor and his God, so, like a good soldier of Jesus Christ, his loyalty stopped short of obeying Diocletian's demand. For someone who loved soldiering, that cannot have been an easy decision. What sustained him? The Collect suggests it was the flame of love that God kindled in his heart, and the Epistle instructs us to 'remember Jesus Christ, raised from the dead'. George's story is one of robust faith and ordered priorities.

Mark the Evangelist

25 April

Proverbs 15.28–end or Acts 15.35–end;
Ephesians 4.7–16; Mark 13.5–13

AUTHOR OF AN URGENT STORY

Almighty God, who enlightened your holy Church through the inspired witness of your evangelist Saint Mark: grant that we, being firmly grounded in the truth of the gospel, may be faithful to its teaching both in word and deed; through Jesus Christ our Lord. Amen.

Who was Mark?

'Mark' was a common name, and one Mark was the son of a wealthy woman with a house in Jerusalem, perhaps used for the Last Supper (Acts 12.12), although scholars discount him as the young man fleeing naked after Jesus' arrest (Mark 14.51). Barnabas' cousin Mark accompanied Paul and Barnabas on a missionary journey but left them in Turkey for undisclosed reasons, and later, when Barnabas wanted to take Mark with them again, Paul disagreed and they parted company. Barnabas ('son of encouragement') then took Mark to his native Cyprus.

So it is surprising to find Mark with Paul in Asia Minor (Colossians 4.10), where he had previously abandoned Paul, and to hear him described as his fellow worker (Philemon 24). Barnabas' persistence probably brokered the reconciliation which would not be easy for either of them, so to hear that Mark was 'useful' to Paul (2 Timothy 4.11) is a testament to mutual staying-power. Similarly, given that Paul and Peter worked in separate mission fields, it is surprising to find that Peter and Mark worked closely. Probably written by one of Peter's disciples, 1 Peter calls Mark 'my son' (1 Peter 5.13) and the second-century Bishop of Hieropolis wrote:

Mark, who was Peter's interpreter, wrote down accurately though not in order, all that he recollected of what Christ had said or done. For he was not a hearer of the Lord, or a follower of his. He followed Peter, as I have said, at a later date, and Peter adapted his instruction to practical needs, without any attempt to give the Lord's words systematically. So that Mark was not wrong in writing down some things in this way from memory, for his one concern was not to omit or falsify anything that he had heard.

Although the church of Alexandria claimed Mark as its first bishop and martyr, scholars think the Gospel was written soon after Peter's death, in Rome around

AD 65. Mark's colloquial Greek is unpolished, lacks the sentence structure of literary Greek and reflects the Greek spoken by the Roman lower classes. The Gospel bears hallmarks of an eyewitness account – only Mark records that the people sat on 'green' grass at the feeding of the 5,000 or includes Jesus' Aramaic phrases, like 'Talitha cum' spoken to Jairus' daughter.

Mark's deceptively simple but very clever construction of his Gospel does not give us a biography of Jesus but simply tells us the good news of Jesus Christ, the Son of God. Proverbs tells us that good news refreshes the body, while the ear which heeds admonition will lodge among the wise, and the 'fear of the Lord is instruction in wisdom and humility goes before honour'. If Mark the evangelist is the Mark who abandoned Paul and then had to be reconciled, he knew something about humility.

Mark's is a very urgent story. He loves the word 'immediately' and strings events together with 'and' rather than the more sophisticated linking used in literary Greek. The result is a breath-taking account with events tumbling out in rapid succession. It opens as Mark drops us into an already moving story set in the wilderness, which, in the thinking of the time, was a place of chaos where demons and evil spirits held sway. We hear in this extract of Jesus in a similar place of threat just before his death, teaching his disciples. The wilderness is not a safe place – literally or figuratively – as in it people are brought face to face with the precariousness of their existence and their littleness in relation to natural forces. People in the wilderness are at the mercy of wild animals – it is no coincidence that the symbol for Mark is a lion, given to him because his Gospel is like a lion roaring with nothing delicate or pretty, just the powerful message Mark tells.

In a world where chaos and evil seem to rule so relentlessly, we pray to be faithful to Mark's inspired witness as he, like a lion, roars the good news to us from places of chaos and evil, telling us that God sends people – even his Son – into that place of bedlam in order that lives might be turned around by repentance and the good news proclaimed. Are our ears attuned to hear and proclaim hope in places of turmoil – our own or that of the wider world?

Philip and James the Apostles

1 May

Isaiah 30.15–21; Ephesians 1.3–10; John 14.1–14

TWO STEADFAST, UNSPECTACULAR DISCIPLES

Almighty Father, whom truly to know is eternal life: teach us to know your Son Jesus Christ as the way, the truth, and the life; that we may follow the steps of your holy apostles Philip and James, and walk steadfastly in the way that leads to your glory; through Jesus Christ our Lord. Amen.

Philip and James are rarely mentioned in the Bible and usually defined in reference books by who they should not be confused with: James, the son of Alphaeus, is neither James the brother of John nor James the brother of Jesus; Philip is not Philip the evangelist in Acts.

James was probably the son of a Mary who was present at the crucifixion. His nickname, 'the Lesser' ('younger' or 'shorter'), distinguished him from James the brother of John. Always being called 'the Lesser' probably did wonders to develop an inferiority complex. Someone saddled with that nickname could either simply live into it, complying with the expectations, or fight it, doing everything possible to live it down. Since James is never mentioned as doing anything special it seems he took the former route and was in the shadow of the other disciples. But he stuck with Jesus and tradition has him martyred for proclaiming the gospel, possibly in Egypt, faithful to the end.

Philip, one of the first disciples, came from Bethsaida in Galilee. His name implies Greek ancestry. He knew the Scriptures and was looking for the Messiah, telling Nathanael that Jesus was the one written about in the law and prophets. He was not put off by Jesus' unlikely Messianic lineage and, since Jesus described Philip's friend as an Israelite in whom there is no guile (John 1.47), the same description probably could be applied to Philip.

Before feeding a crowd of 5,000 people, Jesus first tested Philip by asking where they would buy enough bread (John 6.5–6). Jesus had a reason and the answer may lie in Philip's character. He answered with a mathematical calculation of how much it would cost to give a scrap to everyone. This man who knew exactly where Jesus came from, and calculated things logically, liked to have everything measured out, pigeonholed and under control, so gave the rational answer. I suspect there was little room for the unexpected in Philip's life and wonder whether Philip ever believed that when he did something with or for Jesus the result might be a miracle. Was the object lesson of the 12 baskets left over, which he had to help to collect piece by piece, lost on Philip? Was Jesus trying to encourage him to believe in miracles, to see beyond the obvious, to trust himself to be a channel of Jesus' miraculous provision for people? Philip can be the patron saint of people who find it easier to rejoice in what God is doing in and for others than to believe and risk that God will do something in, for or through them.

At the Last Supper, when Jesus had just told the disciples that no one comes to the Father except through him, Philip demanded, 'Show us the Father and we will be satisfied.' Interestingly, Philip had moved on from referring to Joseph as Jesus' father (John 1.45), so he had made some progress in faith even though he still had doubts about Jesus' heavenly father and, as usual, needed positive proof. All he wanted was to see the Father, no other excitement or miracles, just tangible proof of God and he would be happy. We can almost hear Jesus sighing as he replied, 'Have I been with you so long and still you don't believe me? If believing my words is too hard, then at least believe the evidence of my miracles.' We can be encouraged that Jesus did not give up on him even after three years of Philip's inability to take things on trust or understand the significance of the miracles.

So we celebrate two disciples who never did anything spectacular. James lived in the shadow of others and Philip seemed unable to believe, even in the face of evidence, that Jesus would do anything miraculous through him. He was probably more of a doubter than Thomas. Jesus would have known from his experience with them what Isaiah meant when saying, 'the Lord waits to be gracious to you' – Philip and James did not rush headlong into God's blessing but were steady plodders, unspectacular saints, probably without much ambition but solidly faithful to what they did know. According to the Collect, they walked steadfastly in the way that leads to glory. That example is cause for celebration.

Matthias the Apostle

14 May

Isaiah 22.15–end or 1 Corinthians 4.1–7; Acts 1.15–end;
John 15.9–17

A BRIEF MOMENT IN THE LIMELIGHT

> *Almighty God, who in the place of the traitor Judas chose your faithful*
> *servant Matthias to be of the number of the Twelve: preserve your Church*
> *from false apostles and, by the ministry of faithful pastors and teachers,*
> *keep us steadfast in your truth; through Jesus Christ our Lord. Amen.*

In Durham Cathedral there is a stunning, colourful, modern stained-glass
window by Mark Angus known as the Daily Bread window. It shows an aerial
view of six round figurative 'heads' on each side of a long table with one at the
end. It takes a while for some people to realize it is the Last Supper, while others
see it immediately. One of the 'heads' is less colourful and slightly pulled back
from the table. A cathedral guide asked a group of children who that might be
and a child replied, 'Him what grassed on Jesus'.

It could be, but I think that is too neat and tidy, so when I lead pilgrimages
I suggest that it could be any one of us; we all pull back from the demands of
discipleship at times or, at other times, may overstretch ourselves as Judas, either
disillusioned with Jesus or trying to force Jesus to reveal himself as the Messiah,
did when he betrayed Jesus. So Paul, who was very aware of the importance of
honest self-awareness, was concerned for the new Christians in Corinth who
were placing too much store on worldly power in their estimation of God's
messengers to them. The reading from Isaiah is a searing judgement on one
official whose self-aggrandisement led to his downfall and replacement by a
more faithful servant.

For Paul, trustworthiness was at the core of the calling to be an apostle.
He saw his apostleship as stewardship of the mysteries of God which, in his
case, meant a dangerous life of travelling to proclaim the gospel – not a future
he might have envisaged as a young Pharisee learning the details of the Jewish
law from the revered Rabbi Gamaliel. God never ceases to surprise us about our
vocation in life.

Matthias has a brief moment in the biblical limelight and was, no doubt,
surprised at the turn of events that led to his call to be an apostle. He knew Judas
because he had accompanied the 12 disciples from the time that John the Baptist
baptized people. Such long-standing, proven commitment which continued
despite any disappointment at not being chosen as one of the 12 disciples was
Peter's principal criterion for the replacement for Judas. Peter wanted someone

who was trustworthy. Knowing Judas, Matthias, like the others, would be very aware how easy it was to slip up in discipleship and the (perhaps once-coveted) position as one of the 12 closest to Jesus might have seemed less inviting now. In the second or third century, Clement of Alexandria wrote:

> Not that they became apostles through being chosen for some distinguished peculiarity of nature, since also Judas was chosen along with them. But they were capable of becoming apostles on being chosen by Him who foresees even ultimate issues. Matthias, accordingly, who was not chosen along with them, on showing himself worthy of becoming an apostle, is substituted for Judas.

The intriguing thing about the whole process described in Acts 1 is that we never hear of Matthias again. It begs the question whether Peter's proposal was necessary: was he simply making up the symbolic number of 12 disciples, while the Holy Spirit, moving on, was about to fill not just the 12 disciples but the entire house where people were praying with wind and flame? On the other hand, Matthias' brief moment in the limelight reminds us of the importance of fidelity out of the limelight.

We know nothing of what exactly Matthias did before or after this moment, but we do know where he was in the immediate future. Having been with Jesus for the past three years, letting his life be turned upside down by the demands of travelling with an itinerant preacher, he remained in Jerusalem with the eleven when persecution, prompted by Stephen's martyrdom, scattered the rest of the church (Acts 8.1). Jerusalem was a place of danger for Christians and Matthias expressed that same fidelity by staying there to give leadership, not least at the Council of Jerusalem a few years later (Acts 15.4–6). Christian tradition then disagrees about where he went – variously the coasts of the Caspian Sea, modern Georgia where he was stoned to death, among cannibals in Ethiopia, or that he remained in Jerusalem where he was stoned or died of old age. Whatever happened to him, his watchword is faithfulness. He never grassed on Jesus.

The Visit of the Blessed Virgin Mary to Elizabeth

31 May

Zephaniah 3.14–18; Romans 12.9–16;
Luke 1.39–49 [50–56]

FAITHFUL FOR THE LONG HAUL

> *Mighty God, by whose grace Elizabeth rejoiced with Mary and greeted her as the mother of the Lord: look with favour on your lowly servants that, with Mary, we may magnify your holy name and rejoice to acclaim her Son our Saviour, who is alive and reigns with you, in the unity of the Holy Spirit, one God, now and for ever. Amen.*

'It is a fearful thing to fall into the hands of the living God' (Hebrews 10.31) was paraphrased by a friend when he achieved one of his dreams: 'It is a fearsome thing to fall into the hands of a dream come true.' Mary and Elizabeth did both – they fell into the hands of the living God and of their dreams come true.

Jeremy Taylor, the seventeenth-century divine, wrote:

> [Mary] was full of joy, yet she was carried like a full vessel, without the violent tossings of a tempestuous passion or the wrecks of a stormy imagination: and, as the power of the Holy Ghost did descend upon her like rain into a fleece of wool, without any obstreperous noises or violences to nature, but only the extraordinariness of an exaltation ... It is not easy to imagine what a collision of joys was at this blessed meeting: two mothers of two great princes. (Taylor: 1990)

Elizabeth and her husband Zechariah were the epitome of faithful Jews, living blamelessly according to all the commandments and regulations of the Lord. But Luke adds the devastating sentence, 'They had no children, because Elizabeth was barren, and both were getting on in years.' The prevailing belief, that God blessed the righteous with sons, meant that if you did not have children it must be because you were sinful. Elizabeth later refers to the shame that she had lived with for years. Eventually God stepped in and today we recall an event when Elizabeth, having fallen into the hands of the living God and her dream come true, was six months pregnant. Mary showed up on her doorstep with her own story of a miraculous pregnancy. On hearing Mary's greeting, Elizabeth's baby jumped for joy and the two women started praising God. I wonder which of them Elizabeth was speaking about when she said, 'Blessed is she who believed there would be a fulfilment of what was spoken to her by the Lord.' Did Elizabeth treasure an unspoken assurance that God had once spoken to her of extraordinary things?

Elizabeth's question, 'Why has this happened to me?' is a question many of us have asked at one time or another. She and Zechariah are a reminder that God does not read a calendar as we do. Their prayers of a lifetime were heard, yet only now was Elizabeth reaping the full joyful consequences of God's response to years of gritty devotion in the face of humiliating childlessness. Mary's response to their meeting was to sing the Magnificat; it is unlikely she made it up on the spot, maybe it was a hymn she already knew. Sometimes when we are bursting with joy we run out of words and need to borrow from other people. In this case, the words root God's action in the lives of these two peasant women in the vaster history of God's saving works among the nations, providing a steadying yet boundless context for their experience.

We focus today on the first joyful moments of the visitation, yet Mary stayed three months. We do not know what happened then but can imagine endless talking about the strange ways of God that had precipitated these two women into unfamiliar territory – one long shamed for having been childless, the other about to be shamed and perhaps stoned to death when her pregnancy became known. They gave each other the gift of encouragement. Surely Mary needed to learn from Elizabeth's wisdom how to endure for the long haul of commitment to the God who was entrusting his son as a baby to be born and raised by her in tempestuous times. In Romans, Paul writes to Christians at the heart of the pagan Roman Empire of how to live faithfully for the long haul. It comes down to very basic, at times hard things, things that Elizabeth knew all about: love, zeal, service, blessing one's persecutors, harmonious living, noble thoughts, not seeking to avenge but to live peaceably, overcoming evil with good and – what epitomizes Elizabeth's life – rejoicing in hope.

Barnabas the Apostle

11 June

Job 29.11–16 or Galatians 2.1–10; Acts 11.19–end;
John 15.12–17

BARNABAS, THE GREAT ENCOURAGER

*Bountiful God, giver of all gifts, who poured your Spirit upon your servant
Barnabas and gave him grace to encourage others: help us, by his example,
to be generous in our judgements and unselfish in our service; through
Jesus Christ our Lord. Amen.*

Jesus commanded his disciples to love one another as he had loved them.
From what we know of Barnabas, even though he did not hear Jesus give that
instruction, he put flesh on those bones. He must have been a lovely man to meet
and work with and, as we honour him today, we can celebrate human goodness
and kindness. Barnabas shows us that it is possible to love one another as Jesus
commanded.

Acts describes Barnabas as a good man, full of the Holy Spirit and of faith.
A Greek-speaking Cypriot, he was named 'Son of Encouragement' by his fellow
Christians after he sold a field and gave the money to the church. Later, when
the church in Jerusalem, at that time largely comprising Jewish Christians, heard
rumours of large numbers of Greeks, or Gentiles, turning to the Lord and needed
someone to go to Antioch to find out what was going on, Barnabas was the man
of choice. As well as willingness to travel some 300 miles to get to Antioch (no
mean willingness, especially since he then unexpectedly stayed for over a year),
he had the skills of discernment to sort out whether or not this was truly a work
of God.

Barnabas' response to what he found is delightful in every way: when he
saw the grace of God he rejoiced and exhorted them all to remain faithful to the
Lord. He did not need to build from scratch and make his own mark, he simply
joined in with what God was already doing.

Then, in a remarkable piece of discernment about how Antioch's needs
could be met, coupled with trust in what God could do with people who had
once persecuted the church, Barnabas travelled 85 miles to Tarsus to find Saul
and take him back to Antioch. Previously, Barnabas had taken Saul, the terror
of Christians, to the church in Jerusalem and described what God had done with
him (Acts 9.27), and now he did it again. They stayed there for a year teaching.
No doubt Saul, later Paul, learned much from Barnabas. If anyone was the
midwife of Paul's missionary ministry, surely it was Barnabas.

Barnabas and Paul then went to Jerusalem with gifts from the church in Antioch to relieve the famine. Their first missionary journey took them to Barnabas' native Cyprus, before ending back in Jerusalem where the Christians recognized their call to proclaim the gospel to the Gentile world. Acts records how Barnabas had nurtured the gifts in yet another person, John Mark, but that story ended in the separation of Paul and Barnabas, because Barnabas, typically, wanted to give John Mark another opportunity after he pulled out of the first mission. At that point, Barnabas returned to his native Cyprus, perhaps fulfilling a yearning to return to his native land. Tradition says he was martyred there in AD 61.

Paul refers to the Jerusalem Christians telling him and Barnabas not to forget the poor. That was close to Barnabas' heart since he was courier for the famine relief funds sent from Antioch and had originally sold a field to provide funds. It seems that his gift of encouragement encompassed not just spiritual encouragement, important as that was and is, but material encouragement as well. In that light, it is instructive to read the words of Job defending himself against accusations that the fact he was suffering meant he must be a sinner. He recounts how he delivered the poor and the helpless orphan, how the wretched people and widows rejoiced because of him, how he clothed himself in righteousness and justice, guided the blind, supported the lame and championed the cause of the needy and the stranger.

The Collect picks up these themes from Barnabas' life in its petition that we should follow Barnabas' example and be generous in our judgements and unselfish in our service. Barnabas appears to have been able to see beneath the surface to what was really going on, whether in people or in the church as a whole. It would have been easy to avoid the tension in the room when he first took Saul to the church in Jerusalem and to have judged him as beyond the pale, to have treated John Mark's initial failure as definitive for the rest of his life, to have summed up the situation in Antioch and asked Jerusalem to send someone else to help. In every case he acted with generosity. We need sons and daughters of encouragement like him, today.

The Birth of John the Baptist

24 June

Isaiah 40.1–11; Acts 13.14b–26 or Galatians 3.23–end;
Luke 1.57–66, 80

DISCIPLESHIP IN THE WILDERNESS

> *Almighty God, by whose providence your servant John the Baptist was*
> *wonderfully born, and sent to prepare the way of your Son our Saviour by*
> *the preaching of repentance: lead us to repent according to his preaching*
> *and, after his example, constantly to speak the truth, boldly to rebuke vice,*
> *and patiently to suffer for the truth's sake; through Jesus Christ our Lord.*
> *Amen.*

Some things in life are impossible – like seeing our faces except in reflection.
Hearing people's expectations of us when we were born is another. With John's
birth, the sense of expectation and excitement is palpable across the centuries.
Odd events had set tongues wagging, now this healthy baby boy born to elderly
parents was truly a gift from God and caused great rejoicing among all the
neighbours.

Events at John's circumcision produced fear among these neighbours and
the news spread like wildfire, leading people to ask what it could all mean.
Zechariah had no doubts that his son would be the prophet of the Most High,
going before the Lord to prepare his way, fulfilling all the expectations and
yearning of the nation.

It was a good thing John could not hear all this. What a weight of expectation
on his shoulders, not just from his parents but from the whole community, and,
indeed, from God. There is a fine line between hopes that hold out opportunities
and fixed expectations that a child is forced to fulfil. We cannot have a master
plan for other people's lives: hopes and dreams certainly, supported by the help,
encouragement and freedom to become who God has made them to be. The
challenge for Zechariah and Elizabeth was to raise John to be himself so that he
could be what he was called to be for others.

God has given us the gift of each other to love, respect, enjoy and
encourage, but not to control. God is always out in front, calling us to be more
than we think possible. Dominic Gaisford (Boulding: 1982) writes of vocation
as not 'an external calling, but an internal growing up into oneself ... a constant
wakening up to God and myself, new challenges, new fears, new joys and new
relationships'. He describes being on a journey into the unknown with God,
saying that God calls us to grow up into ourselves, constantly waking up to what
God is making possible in our life. It is never too late to stop dedicating our lives

to fulfilling the unrealistic expectations of other people or to start finding out who God is calling us to be. We may be surprised where this leads.

If the people around John at his birth had high expectations, they appeared to be dashed as John's life unfolded. He lived in the wilderness and some scholars speculate that he was raised at an orphanage run by the Essene community for the children of priests, the ruins of which have been found in the desert. John emerged from the wilderness to proclaim the coming of the Messiah, gained a following of disciples whom he then encouraged to follow Jesus, and eventually was imprisoned by King Herod after he condemned him for marrying his brother's wife. While in prison he had doubts about whether Jesus was the Messiah and sent his disciples to ask Jesus, who in turn affirmed John's calling. This baby, who bore so many expectations and was so faithful, ended up with a hard life, imprisonment and eventual execution.

His parents never saw what John achieved. The Gospel reading ends, 'The child grew and became strong in spirit, and he was in the wilderness until the day he appeared publicly to Israel.' 'He became strong in spirit' is the crucial factor that enabled John to face the uncertain future. Isaiah spoke of the voice crying to exiles separated from their home by a vast wilderness: 'The voice of one crying out, in the wilderness, "Prepare the way of the Lord."' That harsh wilderness environment formed John into the man who could endure the hardships coming to him and it was in the wilderness that the Lord's way was and is prepared. Harsh circumstances in our lives can become the crucible in which our Christian character is honed and formed, we grow and become strong in spirit.

Our vocation as baptized Christians is to hear God's glad tidings even in the wilderness, to be open to God and to grow up into ourselves in God, to become more than we dream possible because God is leading and guiding us day by day. We do this through small steps in daily life. For all of us, John's call comes ringing through the ages, inviting us to respond to God's gracious love and like him to become strong in spirit.

Peter and Paul the Apostles

29 June

Zechariah 4.1–6a, 10b–end or 2 Timothy 4.6–8, 17–18;
Acts 12.1–11; Matthew 16.13–19

CAPTAINS OF THE SAINTLY BAND

> *Almighty God, whose blessed apostles Peter and Paul glorified you in their*
> *death as in their life: grant that your Church, inspired by their teaching and*
> *example, and made one by your Spirit, may ever stand firm upon the one*
> *foundation, Jesus Christ our Lord. Amen.*

I wonder what Peter and Paul would have thought in their lifetimes about ending up as saintly bedfellows in the church calendar. Maybe both would be bemused, but, I like to think in their better moments they would have laughed uproariously.

Why? They were not natural companions in life, except by the grace of God. Paul had publicly rebuked Peter at Antioch, condemning him for recanting his previous willingness to eat with Gentiles. He accused him of undermining the whole basis of Paul's ministry and leading even Barnabas astray (Galatians 2.11–13). Perhaps Peter, a fisherman and not a trained rabbi, felt humiliated. Later he, or someone writing in his name, described Paul as writing things that are hard to understand and that people twisted in meaning (2 Peter 3.16). We can imagine mutual sparks flying. We cannot choose our baptismal family.

But here we are, celebrating Peter and Paul, apostles, at the time when the Church ordains new deacons and priests for particular ministries within the Church. Petertide ordinations are a long tradition and all sorts of seemingly incompatible people are ordained. We need not limit ourselves to ordained ministry: Peter and Paul have something to say about the ministry of all the baptized people of God, however mismatched we appear.

One Sunday during the 50 days of Easter, I presided at the Eucharist at Durham Cathedral, which was a glorious and joyful affirmation of our unity in Christ expressed in different traditions: the regular international and ecumenical congregation that is Durham Cathedral worshipped alongside visiting Swedish Lutheran clergy and their bishop (now the first female archbishop) and a group of Romanian, Madagascan, Japanese and European nuns from the Roman Catholic, Anglican, Orthodox and Reformed Churches, and other overseas visitors. Someone said later that, when I gave the blessing and the deacon sent us to go and serve Christ throughout the world, we should have broken out into applause. God uses us all, with our different gifts and traditions, to proclaim the good news of the gospel wherever we are.

Underlying this godly unity of otherwise diverse people is a demanding

SAINTS AND FESTIVALS

question. We hear it in one form from Jesus when he probed Peter's commitment: 'Who do you say that I am?' Other people's answers would not do; Peter had to answer from his growing knowledge of his friend Jesus. On the other hand Paul, the scholar, rabbi and official expert on God, had to face the question turned on its head, so, his religious certainties shattered, he asked, 'Who are you, Lord?' (Acts 9.5). God has a way of disarming and confronting us according to our need: Peter, who knew a man called Jesus, came to affirm that he was God; Paul, who knew that this man could not be God, came to affirm that he was.

Zechariah, the prophet called by God at the time the people were rebuilding their lives back in Jerusalem after the exile, was also faced with the gaps in his knowledge. Asked by an angel to describe what he saw, he in turn had to ask what it all meant. We can sense the angel's bemusement as twice he had to ask, 'Do you not know?' Peter, Paul and Zechariah in their different ways had to face similar questions: 'What do you know?' 'What does it mean?'

Both Peter and Paul answered those questions, ultimately, with willingness to be imprisoned for the sake of the gospel. We hear, today, of one of Peter's escapes, but eventually he was martyred, tradition says in Rome under Nero's savage persecution of Christians in which he subjected Christians to such immense horrors and cruelties that pagan writers were appalled: Seneca wrote after one gladiatorial contest at the Coliseum in which Christians were fodder for wild animals, 'I felt as if I had been in a sewer.'

Paul, too, was imprisoned in Rome under Nero. Facing the prospect of death, Paul could say, 'I have finished the race, I have kept the faith.' Like Peter, he had not necessarily won the race in the world's eyes, but he had finished it. And so we give thanks today that they kept faith to the end and can take heart that even the most unlikely companions can serve God together.

Peter the Apostle

29 June

Ezekiel 3.22–end or 1 Peter 2.19–end; Acts 12.1–11; Matthew 16.13–19

TAPPED ON THE SIDE BY AN ANGEL

Almighty God, who inspired your apostle Saint Peter to confess Jesus as Christ and Son of the living God: build up your Church upon this rock, that in unity and peace it may proclaim one truth and follow one Lord, your Son our Saviour Christ. Amen.

There is so much that could be (indeed, has been) said about Peter but the readings narrow our focus considerably. Ezekiel and the Epistle written in Peter's name speak of being steadfast in the face of opposition, of suffering and of enduring pain, specifically of Christ's example of suffering for us, leaving us an example to follow. Were we to read on just two verses in the Gospel, we would hear Jesus speaking about his own coming great suffering to which the Epistle refers. Peter was a man who knew his share of suffering, both in his early attempts to follow Jesus faithfully, which ended in bitter remorse at betrayal, and, ultimately, in his own martyrdom, traditionally ascribed to crucifixion, possibly upside down, in Rome.

Then there is the Acts reading which tells of one of Peter's early encounters with imprisonment. Having emerged as the spokesman for the early Church, for which he was occasionally arrested and imprisoned, we find him once again in prison. This time he was bound with two chains to soldiers either side of him and four squads guarding him (since this situation lasted the duration of the Passover, this was an expensive operation for the authorities!), thus making any attempt at escape impossible: maybe the authorities remembered the perplexing incident recorded in Acts 5 when the apostles they had imprisoned one night appeared in the Temple next morning, carrying on where they left off with their teaching.

It was a time of sleepless nights, but not for Peter. He was sleeping soundly while the church gathered in a house, very much awake and praying fervently for him. Then, suddenly, in events bearing some resemblance to the Annunciation and the appearance to the shepherds, an angel interrupted proceedings, shone a light in the cell and tapped Peter on the side to wake him up. Peter's bemusement is indicated by the way the angel had to tell him what to do, but out they went miraculously. Then the angel disappeared.

If we read on, we would read the comic story of how the church could not believe the answer to its prayer and Rhoda shut the door in Peter's face when he knocked: it was easier for Peter to get out of prison than to get into the church. There are echoes here of Peter and the other disciples' response when the women told them they had seen the risen Lord – it seemed to them an idle tale. Have we ever had a dramatic answer to prayer standing on our doorstep, or been tapped on the side by an angel, or become an answer to prayer? Would we know what to do if that did happen?

Peter, for all his failings, about which the Bible is brutally honest, for all his ability to open his mouth and speak before thinking, to put his foot in things and to let fear get the better of him, was the man to whom Jesus appears to have been particularly close. This was perhaps not in the way that Jesus was close to 'the disciple whom Jesus loved' but close because here was a man whose heart was in the right place, who was passionately loyal and who would do anything for Jesus. Maybe he was what we would call a rough diamond.

So when Jesus took the disciples out of the way, on a sort of retreat, and asked them who people said he was before asking the more penetrating question, 'But who do you say that I am?', it was Simon Peter who answered without hesitation, 'You are the Messiah, the Son of the living God.' Sophisticated his thinking might not be, but his instinct and insight were correct and Jesus blessed him, using a pun to say that it was on that rock his Church would be built. Jesus immediately spoke of his suffering, as though Peter's confession cleared the way for this difficult conversation. In the light of this, it is perhaps not such a shock to find Peter in prison; so we honour him today with readings associated with suffering.

The Epistle sums it all up and puts it all in context: Peter's life and death have to be seen in relation to Jesus, his friend in life whom he came to know as his Lord and Messiah. He knew what it was to be tapped on the side by an angel and to follow where that angel of God led.

Thomas the Apostle
3 July
Habakkuk 2.1–4; Ephesians 2.19–end; John 20.24–29

NOT DOUBTING BUT DEVOTED

> *Almighty and eternal God, who, for the firmer foundation of our faith, allowed your holy apostle Thomas to doubt the resurrection of your Son till word and sight convinced him: grant to us, who have not seen, that we also may believe and so confess Christ as our Lord and our God; who is alive and reigns with you, in the unity of the Holy Spirit, one God, now and for ever. Amen.*

It was hardly a hotbed of faith that Jesus invaded when he bypassed the locked door which was the evidence of the disciples' fear that first Easter morning. Thomas was missing and, unfairly, has entered history as doubting Thomas. He simply wanted to see Jesus' hands and side, as his companions had a week earlier, so he could be sure it was Jesus. He was a twin, and if anyone is demanding about identity it is a twin.

What must it have been like for Thomas in the intervening days? Jesus stretched him by waiting a week to reappear; in the words of the Collect he allowed Thomas to doubt the resurrection. It is to Thomas' credit that he stayed around people who had his missing assurance and they stuck with him. When we are with someone who has doubts about God it is tempting to rush in with reassurance rather than let doubt run its sometimes necessary course, thus opening us up in greater depth to God's presence. Just because Thomas had not seen Jesus did not mean that Jesus was not risen, simply that Thomas had not seen him. When we doubt that God is with us or has heard our prayers, it does not mean that God is not there, just that we are not yet aware of God's presence.

Thomas had a track record of stubborn, courageous devotion to Jesus. It was he who insisted the disciples go with Jesus even to death (John 11.16) and, at the Last Supper, he voiced the question the others dared not ask, 'How can we know where you are going?' (see John 14.5).

Habakkuk, living in precarious times, also asked questions. Jerusalem, under the power of one foreign nation (Egypt), was watching as a greater power (Babylon) prepared to invade. Habakkuk knew the suffering of nations that fell into its power. He dared to ask God questions and complain that God was not listening: 'O LORD, how long shall I cry for help, and you will not listen? Or cry to you "Violence!" and you will not save?' (Habakkuk 1.2). Then he went on to complain about the lack of law enforcement and the perversion of justice. He spoke and expected God to listen.

Like Thomas, Habakkuk took the risk of daring to ask God hard and honest questions. Then he stopped speaking and listened. Like Thomas, he waited faithfully; he did not merely draw breath and expect God to jump into the brief pause to defend himself against the charges levelled against him. He really listened, saying he would be like a watchman on a city wall – perhaps he was one himself – stationed on the rampart, keeping watch to see what God would say.

How did watchmen look and listen? They spent lonely days and nights staring into empty space, alert for the slightest sign of activity that might indicate the presence of friend or enemy. They could neither fall asleep nor indulge in distractions to keep awake. The watchman's job was simply to know the scene he was looking at and to wait until someone else made a move, which he reported immediately to those who needed to hear.

In due course God moved and commanded Habakkuk to write the vision on tablets so that even someone running could read it. In an age when little was written, it was to be recorded for posterity that God was not silent in the face of injustice. Habakkuk was not told what the end would be; instead the message from God was about how the people should live while they waited. That much was within their control: they were to live faithfully and to wait patiently, even if the vision seemed to be late.

Thomas and Habakkuk waited. Thomas' faithfulness in staying put until Jesus made a move led him to believe not in Jesus – he did that already – but in Jesus' resurrection from the dead. Fired by that unshakeable belief, by AD 52 Thomas had travelled to India proclaiming the gospel. The Mar Thoma Church based in Kerala bears his name to this day. In the words of Ephesians, it is built on the foundation of the apostles. Waiting faithfully can bear extraordinary fruit.

Mary Magdalene

22 July

Song of Songs 3.1–4; 2 Corinthians 5.14–17;
John 20.1–2, 11–18

HER FRIEND, THE GARDENER

*Almighty God, whose Son restored Mary Magdalene to health of mind and
body and called her to be a witness to his resurrection: forgive our sins and
heal us by your grace, that we may serve you in the power of his risen life,
who is alive and reigns with you, in the unity of the Holy Spirit, one God,
now and for ever. Amen.*

The resurrection of Jesus Christ is an invitation to gloriously vulnerable living.
Mary Magdalene, the first to receive it, found it so unexpected that she struggled.
Three times she had used the same distressed lament, 'They have taken the Lord
out of the tomb, and we do not know where they have laid him', 'They have
taken away my Lord, and I do not know where they have laid him', 'Sir, if
you have carried him away, tell me where you have laid him'. Each was more
personal – from 'they have done it' to 'if you have done it', from 'the Lord' to
'my Lord'. Finally, she demanded to do the same thing, 'I will take him away.'
Her repeated phrase echoes the similar lament for a lost beloved in the Song of
Songs where the beloved has not been taken but has gone of his own accord: 'I
will seek him', 'I sought him', 'Have you seen him?'

Mary had seen her Lord cruelly tortured and had bought and prepared
expensive spices for the burial rites precluded by the rush to inter the body before
the Sabbath. Now all she could hope for, and she hoped for it passionately, was
to have the body and to remove it from danger. As a woman, she knew what
to do for a dead body: that was women's work because men would not make
themselves ritually unclean by touching a dead body, they let the women put up
with that. All her longing was expressed in that phrase, 'they have taken away'.
She had been violated, deprived of her responsibility to handle his broken body
and wipe his blood, the right to express her love.

Then Jesus spoke. We overhear one of the intimate moments in the Bible
without knowing how it sounded. What tone of voice did Jesus use when he said
that one word, 'Mary', and she responded, 'Teacher'? When reading in a service
it is difficult to know how to inflect those two names; it is worth reading it aloud
in private, trying different modulations of voice to hear some of the possible
depths of meaning in that world-changing exchange of two names.

In the Song the woman found her beloved, held him and would not let him
go until she brought him to her mother's house. In the Bible, this was the place

where marriages were arranged, where commitment was made. Like the lover in the Song, Mary's instinctive reaction was to cling to her beloved. Many artists portray Jesus pulling away to stop her touching him at all but it sounds more like his attempt to break free from a long embrace. Taking him away to safety was not an option; she had work to do for her teacher, a message to proclaim. So, unlike the lover in the Song, Mary did not take her beloved to the safety of her mother's house; instead he sent her to his brothers' house to risk their disbelief and with a message to expand their world. He was ascending to his Father and her Father. The world needed to hear her voice, her testimony. She obeyed and went, vulnerable to miracle.

She thought he was the gardener. Once before, God made and cared for a garden and met humans there, enjoying their company, until everything went wrong. Then Adam and Eve were banished from the garden. Cruelly, centuries of tradition had further punished women by maintaining that Eve's naivety in falling for the serpent's deceit was evidence enough that women were corruptible, incapable of understanding properly or bearing witness reliably, so their testimony was considered inadmissible in court.

Now, in another garden and by entrusting Mary to tell the men what she had seen and heard, Jesus destroyed the tradition that silenced women. At Jesus' birth, Mary was the new life-giving Eve; at his resurrection, Mary Magdalene was the new truth-telling, witness-bearing Eve, freed from Eve's remaining bonds and given back her voice. At last men listened, believed and followed her leadership in proclaiming the resurrection.

Supposing him to be the gardener ... How wrong could she be, and yet how right could she be.

James the Apostle

25 July

Jeremiah 45.1–5 or 2 Corinthians 4.7–15;
Acts 11.27—12.2; Matthew 20.20–28

FIRST TO FOLLOW, FIRST TO DIE

Merciful God, whose holy apostle Saint James, leaving his father and all that he had, was obedient to the calling of your Son Jesus Christ and followed him even to death: help us, forsaking the false attractions of the world, to be ready at all times to answer your call without delay; through Jesus Christ our Lord. Amen.

James was the first of the 12 disciples to be martyred. The Collect summarizes his life very succinctly: he left his father, forsook all he had, was obedient to the call of Jesus and followed him to a martyr's death. That is it, in a nutshell. The Gospel reading mentions none of this, but introduces us to James' mother who is portrayed as ambitious on behalf of her two sons, who are not in the least embarrassed by her asking Jesus that they may have seats of honour in his kingdom; indeed in Mark's Gospel they ask for this privilege themselves. We know that James' mother was faithful to Jesus, being present at the crucifixion (Matthew 27.56) and probably at the anointing of Jesus' body, so commitment was a family affair despite her husband's initial loss of part of his labour force.

James was one of the first to be called by Jesus in the episode by the lakeshore in Galilee. Putting the Synoptic Gospel stories together, we learn that James and his (probably younger) brother John were fishermen, working with their father who was well-enough off to employ hired men. They were in partnership with Simon and his brother Andrew and were at home in each other's houses – as was Jesus whom they appear to have known before he called them to follow him. So, when he did call, they dropped everything and went, abandoning their father in the boat.

Jesus nicknamed James and John 'Boanerges', or 'sons of thunder', obviously for well-founded reasons perhaps to do with short tempers. They were not only angry themselves, the disciples were angry with them for allowing their mother to plead for special favour for them. It is remarkable, therefore, that these were two of the three men closest to Jesus during his life, along with Peter who was prone to speak before he thought. Jesus was apparently not afraid of shouting matches among his disciples.

James went with Peter and John to the bedside of Jairus' dead little daughter, a very tender as well as sensational occasion when Jesus restored her to life in front of their eyes. These three were also his companions of choice on the mountainside at the transfiguration and on his last night in Gethsemane when, in great distress, he had to face gruesome death. At times of such intense agony we want people with us whom we can trust not to let us down. Although they fell asleep, these three men at least remained with Jesus until he was arrested. Then, in fear, they fled. It was only later that James would be strong enough to face death without flinching.

Normally we hear of James and John together in the Gospels, with James named first. However, once they had all been present at the ascension of Jesus, the prayer in the upper room and the outpouring of the Holy Spirit at Pentecost, we find Peter with John. There is hardly any mention of James by name, and he is no longer associated with the other two. Did he begin to carve out a different direction for his ministry while Peter, accompanied by John, took overt leadership?

Ironically James was first, but not first as he or his mother had intended. When Herod arrested some unnamed members of the church, James – now defined as the brother of John rather than being named first – was among them. Herod had him killed with a sword, a relatively merciful death compared to what others would later face. James' zeal had attracted attention from his enemies. For all his fiery temper and his ambitious mother, James was steadfast and did indeed drink the cup of martyrdom that Jesus drank.

Had James learned in the intervening period to be a servant, a slave, among the disciples, as Jesus taught? Maybe. While many people are ready to step forward to take up more prominent roles in an organization, including the Church, fewer are prepared to step back and out of the limelight and to let their younger siblings overtake them. Yet that appears to be what James, who once wanted to be first, achieved. In doing so, he followed Jesus even to death. It is that example the courageous Collect prays we will be ready to follow.

The Transfiguration of our Lord

6 August

Daniel 7.9–10, 13–14; 2 Peter 1.16–19; Luke 9.28–36

THE PLACE OF PRAYER

Father in heaven, whose Son Jesus Christ was wonderfully transfigured before chosen witnesses upon the holy mountain, and spoke of the exodus he would accomplish at Jerusalem: give us strength so to hear his voice and bear our cross that in the world to come we may see him as he is; who is alive and reigns with you, in the unity of the Holy Spirit, one God, now and for ever. Amen.

The Gospel of the transfiguration is read on 6 August, when the Church focuses on the revelation of the radiant heavenly glory of Christ, a feast ironically nuanced by also being Hiroshima Day with its contrasting radiance of the destructive power of the atomic bomb, and on the last Sunday before Lent, when it is the culmination of the revelation of Christ that began at Epiphany. It also occurs in the daily lectionary as part of our journeys through the Gospels. Each time we encounter it differently.

Today we hear the story alongside Daniel's apocalyptic vision of the Ancient One in glory, before whom one like a human being came and was given dominion, glory and kingship. Daniel's original purpose was to show God's working through violent political events, but the Church reads it as also pointing to Christ's glory. Then the Epistle of Peter records eyewitness testimony to seeing the glorious majesty of Jesus Christ.

As they later did in Gethsemane, the disciples dozed, but were awake enough to see Moses and Elijah. More than that, they saw the glory of God revealed in Jesus of Nazareth and heard the voice from heaven. Their lives were irretrievably altered as they comprehended that their friend truly was the Son of God. Next day came the transition into the chaos and pathetic need of human life before Jesus spoke to the disciples about his coming death. They had to learn to listen to him, not to cling to moments of glory but to put the two together somehow. The Collect hints at this in its petition to hear Christ's voice and bear his cross in the world.

Once I was invited to preach and preside at the Soweto church a few yards from where the first child was killed during the students' protest march in 1976. At the end of the three-hour service, in true African style, the congregation just kept singing. Afterwards the priest said that he does not like to stop them because, for some people, coming to church takes their mind off the situations they face when they go home. He used the phrase, 'worshipping here is like

SAINTS AND FESTIVALS

a moment of transfiguration for them and they do not want to let go of it'.

Our natural reaction is to want to hang on to profound experiences. That is probably what motivated Peter's suggestion to build booths and thus cling to the glory when Jesus was transfigured. But Jesus, Moses and Elijah were not simply enjoying the glory of the moment, they were talking about Jesus' departure, his exodus, which he was to accomplish in Jerusalem. That is a strange phrase since we normally talk of 'making' our departure or 'taking' our leave, not accomplishing it. For Jesus, though, his departure, his exodus – with all the salvific connotations associated with Moses and the exodus deliverance from Egypt – was something to accomplish, to undertake.

After the transfiguration, Jesus immediately had to face the horror of what human sin would do: betrayal, crucifixion and death, the ultimate rejection of God's faithful servant. Maybe Moses and Elijah could strengthen him not just because they represented the law and the prophets, but because both knew the pain and loneliness of fidelity to God in the face of the infidelity of the people. It is speculation, but it is also true that people who have struggled with remaining faithful to the call of God under intense pressure, people who have known God's seeming silence when yearning for a sign of his presence, are often the best companions for someone facing similar experiences.

Both Jesus' experience of the transfiguration and the Sowetan priest's comment challenge us about how worship that brings deep experience of God equips us to live in God's world. Michael Ramsey wrote of the challenge facing worshippers in places like Durham Cathedral, in which he prayed so frequently:

> Prayer with beautiful buildings and lovely music must be a prayer which speaks from the places where men and women work, or lack work, and are sad and hungry, suffer and die. To be near to the love of God is to be near, as Jesus showed, to the darkness of the world. That is the 'place of prayer'. (Ramsey: 1982)

The Blessed Virgin Mary

15 August

Isaiah 61.10–end or Revelation 11.19—12.6, 10;
Galatians 4.4–7; Luke 1.46–55

THE WOMAN WHO SAID 'YES' TO GOD

Almighty God, who looked upon the lowliness of the Blessed Virgin Mary and chose her to be the mother of your only Son: grant that we who are redeemed by his blood may share with her in the glory of your eternal kingdom; through Jesus Christ our Lord. Amen.

Browsing a catalogue of discount books I found *You Never Call! You Never Write! A History of the Jewish Mother*. I wonder if Mary complained like this to Jesus when he went off with his disciples. After all, she was a Jewish mother.

Nazareth shaped her. It was a small village off the beaten track in a rural backwater. Her extended family was pious – few families disrupted their daily life each year, as they did, to make the long journey from Galilee to Jerusalem each Passover. Later, she was exiled to Egypt before returning to Galilee. Other children were born, some named in the Gospels. Mary was the Jewish mother of quite a brood.

The Church believes that Jesus was fully divine and fully human, taking his humanity from Mary. Deny the possibility that he looked like her, had her mannerisms and spoke with her Galilean accent and we deny his humanity. By her example, she taught him of God and of human love.

The Bible's portrayal of Mary is less saccharine than ours and the danger is that we put her on a pedestal, making her unlike us. When Jesus ignored the family departure one Passover it was she, not Joseph, who told him off. Yet there was another side to Mary: she pondered and treasured things in her heart, starting with the story the shepherds told and then Jesus' impetuous 12-year-old response to her rebuke when he spoke about being in his father's house. To ponder is to muse about things, to go back to them in search of new meaning. Mary had an inner life with God that shaped the way she raised Jesus and her other children as faithful Jews. So as we honour Mary we might ask ourselves what we ponder in our hearts and how that shapes our lives.

After the Passover episode, Jesus was obedient to his parents, increasing in wisdom and in years and in divine and human favour. They raised their son well. Mary was widowed before Jesus began his public ministry and was proud of him. She expected him to solve the wine shortage at a family wedding. Perhaps, since her other children did not believe in Jesus until after the resurrection, there

SAINTS AND FESTIVALS

were family tensions, even rows. She faced her neighbours' anger when Jesus caused a storm in the village synagogue. It was not easy being his mother.

Once Mary and Jesus' siblings, questioning Jesus' sanity, tried to remove him from the crowds. His reply – that his mother and brothers were not his blood relations but those who do the will of God – embodied a call to her to become his disciple, a call Mary accepted.

Mary was present at the crucifixion. That is more than many mothers could cope with and John describes Jesus, her eldest son and thus with a duty of care to his widowed mother, entrusting her not to his siblings but to the disciple he loved. That disciple took Mary into his own home and cared for her: her family was indeed those who do the will of God. So Mary was part of the group that gathered constantly for prayer after Jesus' ascension and therefore she was part of the group who were filled with the Holy Spirit. She must have rejoiced when her other children came to believe their brother was the Son of God. One of her sons, James, even became a leader in the church.

In attempts to honour Mary, the Church has added further traditions, including her immaculate conception, perpetual virginity and assumption into heaven. In doing so, the Church has rubbed some of the human edges off Mary so that she is no longer a robust Jewish peasant woman but someone who was conceived, gave birth and died in ways that other humans do not experience. She becomes an idealized figure rather than a feisty, vivacious, down-to-earth woman who, confronted with quite extraordinary events, enthusiastically and faithfully cooperated with God.

Mary is rightly honoured by the Orthodox Church as *Theotokos*, Bearer of God or Mother of God. She is someone we should revere and emulate. The reason she is so honoured and we can follow her example is that she said 'Yes' to God, faced the consequences and took the risk of being faithful in the midst of daily life. As we remember her, the readings are rightly full of rejoicing.

Bartholomew the Apostle

24 August

Isaiah 43.8–13 or 1 Corinthians 4.9–15; Acts 5.12–16;
Luke 22.24–30

FIDELITY WITHOUT FUSS

Almighty and everlasting God, who gave to your apostle Bartholomew
grace truly to believe and to preach your word: grant that your Church may
love that word which he believed and may faithfully preach and receive the
same; through Jesus Christ our Lord. Amen.

Bartholomew is something of an enigma. We are not even sure of his name.
If he is, as is often assumed, the Nathanael of John's Gospel then, in addition
to Jesus' calling him as one of his 12 disciples, we know of his perplexity that
anything good could come out of Nazareth, that he came from Cana and thus
Jesus' first miracle was on his doorstep, and that he was one of the fishing crew
who experienced Jesus' resurrection appearance by the Sea of Galilee (John
1.46; 2.1; 21.1–8). Beyond that, we have to imagine him as one of the crowd
of disciples, a man who was faithfully present, through thick and thin, but did
nothing notable enough to be recorded in the Gospels. Yet he did remarkable
things afterwards; tradition associates him variously with mission to India,
Ethiopia and Mesopotamia before martyrdom in Armenia. It is never too late to
serve God in new ways.

The one, telling character reference we have for him is as an Israelite in
whom there was no guile or deceit (John 1.47). Few people are totally transparent
and truthful, yet that was how Jesus summed him up, only explaining himself
by an enigmatic comment about something that happened under a fig tree,
possibly an allusive reference to study of the Torah or some significant moment
of Nathanael's life.

Bartholomew was part of the dispute at the Last Supper (of all places!)
about greatness. In the sharp exchange it prompted, Jesus said the greatest sit
at table but his and the disciples' role was to be the youngest and the servant.
Thoroughly rebuked, the disciples could be forgiven for being confused when
Jesus promptly described them as not only sitting at table in his kingdom but
sitting on thrones as judges. Were they great or were they least?

The Collect, forced to be general in its description of Bartholomew, is
nevertheless penetrating as it recalls the grace given to him to truly believe and
preach God's word. That took courage, even for a man without deceit. He was,
in Isaiah's words, one of God's witnesses.

Bartholomew and the other apostles discovered that God did signs and wonders through them, causing people to set them apart, to hold them in high esteem and to turn to the Lord whom they proclaimed. Yet, read on and those same revered apostles were in prison before, irrepressible after miraculous release, they returned to their place of arrest and picked up teaching where they left off.

As Paul wrote to Christians being misled by false apostles who denigrated the true apostles, God has a strange way of using his witnesses. Read Paul's inventory of apostolic trials and tribulations too quickly and the import is lost: these people were treated as fools, hungry, thirsty, poorly clothed, beaten, homeless and exhausted. They were reviled, persecuted, slandered and treated as the dregs of the world. Who would choose to be an apostle?

But, slipped into that catalogue of oppression was something to mark them out as disciples of Jesus Christ: amid it all they blessed, endured, spoke kindly. They were among their oppressors as those who serve. That remarkable grace was expressed by their standing by Christ in his trials, their growing conformity to Christ in his suffering.

Faithfully facing such turbulence of praise and persecution without demur can only spring from a profoundly godly character. Some better-known disciples like Peter have their moments of shambles and success recorded for posterity. Bartholomew is different. He remains unremarked, subsumed in the phrase 'the Twelve' or 'the Apostles', perhaps naturally reticent, one of the steady, faithful and reliable people who stay out of the limelight but get on with things nonetheless.

There have been millions of such faithful people through the ages. Sometimes, when listening to lists of unpronounceable names in the Old Testament readings at Morning and Evening Prayer (or, worse, reading them), the temptation is to skip them, but I find myself wondering who these people were, what they were like and why they merited the recording of their names.

Whoever they may be, St Bartholomew's Day gives us an excuse to celebrate their inclusion, to celebrate Bartholomew's inclusion, and to be invited to follow their example of living without fuss but with enormous fidelity. Can it be said of us that, like Bartholomew/Nathanael, we are without deceit?

Holy Cross Day

14 September

Numbers 21.4–9; Philippians 2.6–11; John 3.13–17

TO GLORY IN THE CROSS

Almighty God, who in the passion of your blessed Son made an instrument of painful death to be for us the means of life and peace: grant us so to glory in the cross of Christ that we may gladly suffer for his sake; who is alive and reigns with you, in the unity of the Holy Spirit, one God, now and for ever. Amen.

Holy Cross Day commemorates the dedication, in 335, of the Church of the Holy Sepulchre in Jerusalem which was built over the supposed site of the crucifixion and tomb of Jesus. It can feel slightly odd, in September, to commemorate the cross on its own, shorn from Holy Week's full narrative of salvation history. Then our focus is rightly on the solemnity of the cross and the events of those dreadful hours, but now we have a different opportunity to reflect on the cross and its meaning.

Under these circumstances, we must remember that the cross referred to is not a generic cross but the cross of Jesus. Forget that, and we are in danger of glorifying cruel death; remember it, and we are commemorating the heart of the Christian gospel in which, as the Collect prays, God has made an instrument of painful death to be the means of life and peace. So, following the imagery of the reading from Numbers and Jesus' reinterpretation of it in the Gospel reading, the cross of Jesus is something to which we turn for life.

As Christians, we are shaped by and imbued with the cross. At baptism we are signed with the cross; at ordination many priests have their hands marked with the cross by the bishop; we make the sign of the cross over ourselves in prayer and are absolved from our sins with the sign of the cross. Once, when I was preaching on Good Friday in a small church in a small town in the USA, I asked the children how many crosses they could see in the church. We were all amazed when they reported over 100 (it helped that every pew end and prayer book had a cross on it!).

In early Christian art, Jesus reigns from the cross; only in the medieval period was he shown suffering on it. Hymnody and poetry apostrophized the cross, addressing it in direct speech, or (as in the *Dream of the Rood*) letting it speak to us. Thus we sing the words of Fortunatus, a seventh-century Spanish Christian:

412   SAINTS AND FESTIVALS

Faithful cross, above all other;
One and only noble tree!
None in foliage, none in blossom,
None in fruit thy peer may be:
Sweetest wood and sweetest iron,
Sweetest weight is hung on thee.

Bend thy boughs, O tree of glory,
Thy relaxing sinews bend;
For awhile the ancient rigour
That thy birth bestowed, suspend;
And the king of heavenly glory
Gently on thine arms extend.

In the light of this, it is perhaps surprising that the only direct reference to the cross in the readings on Holy Cross Day is Paul's quotation, probably from an early hymn, referring to Jesus humbling himself and becoming obedient to the point of death, even death on a cross. The cross was for Jesus not something that he sought out but something that happened to him as he humbled himself.

Sam Portaro describes a conductor who rebuked over-enthusiastic percussionists, 'One does not beat the music into the drum; one coaxes the music out of the drum.' Portaro drew a parallel:

The cross is like the music of the timpani: it is not something one puts on, but rather something that is coaxed out of us. The wearing of the cross is not an accessory to life, but rather is the embrace of life itself ... Christians bear the cross within, in the daily embrace of all that it means to be human. To be a Christian is not to take the cross upon oneself, but rather to have the fullness of life coaxed out of oneself. (Portaro: 1998)

The Collect prays that we may glory in the cross of Christ so that we may gladly suffer for his sake. That is a tough petition. At the time of first writing this, current news told of the ghastly suffering of thousands of Christians driven from their homes in northern Iraq and of a young mother who was imprisoned in the Sudan for holding to her Christian faith. Their fortitude is remarkable, as commitment, rather than hatred, is coaxed out of them through their suffering. On this Holy Cross Day, maybe our most profound response is to pray for them and for grace to follow their, and Jesus', example.

Matthew the Apostle and Evangelist

21 September

Proverbs 3.13–18; 2 Corinthians 4.1–6; Matthew 9.9–13

AN UP-ENDED LIFE

O Almighty God, whose blessed Son called Matthew the tax collector to be an apostle and evangelist: give us grace to forsake the selfish pursuit of gain and the possessive love of riches that we may follow in the way of your Son Jesus Christ, who is alive and reigns with you, in the unity of the Holy Spirit, one God, now and for ever. Amen.

In chapters 8 and 9 of Matthew's Gospel there are 13 instances when people 'came', 'followed', 'approached', were 'brought' or 'carried' to Jesus. Time after time the initiative lay with them. Only twice did Jesus take the lead – in healing Peter's mother-in-law and in calling Matthew. One has to wonder why. Did Jesus need Matthew, or see hidden potential in him, or know that Matthew was afraid of rejection and needed a challenging invitation?

Jesus was walking from his home town of Capernaum, which was near the frontier between territories controlled by Herod Agrippa and Philip. Tax collectors sat on the border collecting duty on goods in transit (plus their own substantial rake-off, which helped to make them so hated) and possibly Jesus had seen Matthew many times. The story makes it almost casual – Jesus was walking along, saw him and said 'Follow me.' As with Simon, Andrew, James and John (Matthew 4.18–22), the response was instantaneous and life-changing.

In Mark and Luke, the tax collector is called Levi; here he is Matthew, derived from 'gift of God'. Maybe whoever wrote the Gospel – scholars are divided on whether it is the same Matthew – used this name to be subtly self-referential to God's mercy in his life. Very soon life was further up-ended as this disciple became an apostle, although he never quite shook off his former identity as a tax collector (Matthew 10.1–4). Tradition tells us that, after Jesus' resurrection, he remained in Palestine before heading to Ethiopia, Persia or Parthia (now north-eastern Iran) once persecution started under Herod Agrippa. He may have been martyred.

But that is jumping ahead. What happened next? Simply a meal, which is quite typical of Jesus. The guest list comprised Matthew's companions, which provoked a predictable response from the Pharisees. Jesus' retort is more stinging than in Mark and Luke because he adds to his comments about being sent to call sinners, 'Go and learn what this means, "I desire mercy and not sacrifice."' That alludes to Proverbs (21.3), 'To do righteousness and justice is more acceptable to the Lord than sacrifice', and Hosea (6.6), 'I desire steadfast love and not sacrifice, the knowledge of God rather than burnt-offerings.'

Jesus sent the Pharisees to 'go and learn what this means'. Although teachers of the law, they needed to become disciples, to learn not about the niceties of the sacrificial system but about the practice of mercy. Before long, Jesus was again challenging them for failing to do this, this time for criticizing his disciples: 'If you had known what this means, "I desire mercy and not sacrifice", you would not have condemned the guiltless' (Matthew 12.7).

In that light, it is salutary to hear Paul, himself a Pharisee, referring to God's mercy as the catalyst for the ministry to which he was called. It took dramatic events to convert him and he invoked the creation story and God's life-giving words, 'Let light shine out of darkness', to describe what happened to him, as to Matthew, when God's light shone in his heart. In each case there was a new creation. It could happen to a Pharisee, just as it could to a tax collector.

Why did Jesus have to challenge Matthew to follow him? What stopped Matthew coming to Jesus of his own accord, like the other people in the stories surrounding his encounter with Jesus? What stops us from following Jesus? If we ask ourselves what or who is the hardest thing God could ask us to give up, we might find the answer. The Collect points us to the dangers of selfish pursuit of gain and the possessive love of riches, and Matthew learned the truth in Proverbs that wisdom's income is better than silver, gold or jewels, that in wisdom is a tree of life. For some people this is where the rubber hits the road. For others it might be something else entirely, but 'selfish pursuit' and 'possessive love' are probably at the heart of what holds us back. So, expecting God to put a finger on where the problem might lie for us, we pray for grace, like Matthew, to follow the way of Jesus Christ.

Michael and All Angels

29 September

Genesis 28.10–17 or Hebrews 1.5–end;
Revelation 12.7–12; John 1.47–end

ANGEL VOICES, EVER SINGING

> *Everlasting God, you have ordained and constituted the ministries of angels
> and mortals in a wonderful order: grant that as your holy angels always
> serve you in heaven, so, at your command, they may help and defend us on
> earth; through Jesus Christ our Lord. Amen.*

Angels glide in and out of the biblical stories and today are centre stage. Never at
our beck and call, they are at God's command and are more often messengers and
strengtheners for an uncomfortable task than the feel-good comforters of popular
culture. People in the Bible often failed to recognize an angel; sometimes they
are described as 'men', indistinguishable from anyone else. It is certainly not a
mark of deep piety to see an angel – even Balaam's ass did that. We may never
see them. I remember as a teenager hearing the missionary Helen Roseveare
describe hiding in a hut watching Congolese rebels advance with intent to rape
or kill her and her companions. Suddenly they retreated. She discovered later
that they feared the armed warriors they saw encircling her house, warriors she
and her companions never saw. Then friends wrote to say they had suddenly felt
compelled to pray for her at that very moment.

The Bible assumes an angelic army of the Lord with Michael in charge. The
picture language of Revelation describes a final conflagration where Michael and
his angelic host throw Satan and his angelic host into the lake of fire. Inevitably,
that reminds us of Coventry Cathedral where St Michael stands victorious
over Satan. However, in the Gethsemane Chapel of the same cathedral a more
disturbing image is seen through a crown of thorns: an angel holds out the cup
of suffering.

The Genesis and John readings focus not on angels but two very human,
very different, people. Jacob is one of the Bible's less pleasant characters,
despite being a key player in the story of God's salvation. He thrived on deceit
and it seems he couldn't tell the truth if he tried. Contrast him with Nathanael,
an Israelite in whom was no deceit. Jacob was running away from his family,
having deceived his father and usurped his brother's birthright. In contrast,
Nathanael was coming towards Jesus.

Jacob knew little about God; only after his dream did he recognize, 'Surely
the Lord is in this place and I did not know it.' In contrast, Nathanael realized that
God was present in Jesus who knew something very significant about him; we

SAINTS AND FESTIVALS

are not told what had happened under that fig tree. For both Jacob and Nathanael the encounter with God was life-changing.

Where do the angels come in? In both stories angels were travelling between earth and heaven. There was a ladder between earth and heaven in Jacob's story, while Jesus, anticipating his later words 'I am the way, no one comes to the Father but by me', claimed to be that bridge.

The common factor is that angels are involved in the opening of heaven to earth. This can be experienced today in those 'thin' places and times where heaven seems very present. This fits with other accounts of angelic activity. They were at the incarnation when God came among us, at Jesus' arrest and crucifixion bringing Jesus strength to face the coming trials – opening heaven to him. At the resurrection they rolled the stone away: God emptied the tomb, angels opened that emptying to human eyes. In the visions of the end times angels draw us into heavenly life and worship.

We pray in the Collect that the angels who always serve God in heaven may help and defend us here on earth. Angels are a reminder of our need of help, our dependence on God's grace. In praying as we do we are praying for God's strength, because God's angels work at God's command. It is far better to pray and to get on with life, believing that God is strengthening us, than to fret about whether or not we see an angel. The point is not so much the angels, but the God whom they and we serve.

'You will see heaven opened, and the angels of God ascending and descending upon the Son of Man.' Heaven is opened to us – what Jacob saw in a dream is now a reality in Jesus Christ. For that, and all God's provision for us through angels, we give thanks.

Angels, help us to adore him;
Ye behold him face to face;
Sun and moon, bow down before him,
Dwellers all in time and space.
Alleluia, alleluia,
Praise with us the God of grace.
(H. F. Lyte)

Luke the Evangelist

18 October

Isaiah 35.3–6 or Acts 16.6–12a; 2 Timothy 4.5–17;
Luke 10.1–9

USING OUR GOD-GIVEN GIFTS

*Almighty God, you called Luke the physician, whose praise is in the gospel,
to be an evangelist and physician of the soul: by the grace of the Spirit and
through the wholesome medicine of the gospel, give your Church the same
love and power to heal; through Jesus Christ our Lord. Amen.*

There are two ways of telling most stories. While the Epistle records 'Only Luke
is with me', Luke's version might be more like: 'Luke, a servant of Jesus Christ
and travelling companion of Paul, to Theophilus, beloved in the Lord. Having
followed Paul round Asia and Europe, been shipwrecked, thrown out of cities,
had to say goodbye to several travel companions, sometimes after they fell out
with Paul, we are in Rome where he is under house arrest and I'm running round
looking after him.'

Luke was a faithful travel companion to Paul for many years as well as
author of the Gospel of Luke and the Acts of the Apostles. He wrote those for
Theophilus, 'lover of God', possibly a particular person or perhaps a symbolic
name for a group of Christians. Luke was already a Christian when he met Paul
and his switch to the first person plural in the Acts reading suggests that at Troas
he became Paul's travel companion and eventually found himself on board
ship accompanying the now-prisoner Paul to Rome. Unlike others, who had at
various times declined to go along with Paul's plans, Luke stuck with him.

Luke is described as 'the beloved physician' (Colossians 4.14). Paul was
continually troubled by a serious physical affliction, possibly an eye complaint,
which was not healed by prayer. Who do we think dealt regularly with that
medical problem? Paul had an unfortunate habit of being stoned, lashed,
shipwrecked, mistreated by his enemies or bandits, and at times was hungry,
cold and worn out. Who patched him up and kept him on the road?

I suspect Paul was not an easy travel companion since he could fall out with
people in big ways. In Rome, Luke was the only one of several previous travel
companions to have stuck with Paul. So for Luke to make it through to the end
suggests abnormal grace and patience with Paul that others had not managed.

Who was Luke? Christian tradition tells us that he was a Gentile, born in
Antioch, who died unmarried aged 84. His writings indicate that he was well
educated, perhaps city-based. Tradition also recognizes Luke as the first person
to write icons and some icons of Luke show him sitting at an easel doing this.

SAINTS AND FESTIVALS

So we have a picture of a faithful man who was prepared to sacrifice the opportunity and gift of family life for travel to support one of the early missionaries of the church, who used his medical skills to keep that missionary going and his education to record some of the stories that would otherwise be lost to the church. He also offered the simple but demanding gift of stable friendship to a complex, volatile person, thus facilitating the spread of the gospel through much of the known world. This was at enormous personal cost, including his own grief when other close companions left. It was physically demanding: it took stamina to walk the distances involved and, when Paul was shipwrecked, Luke was shipwrecked too and faced the likelihood of drowning.

In the Gospel, Jesus, having previously sent his 12 closest disciples out on mission, sent 70 or 72 (in Jewish tradition both numbers represented all the nations of the earth, so this hints at global mission) who went in pairs. Perhaps Luke saw his own eventual vocation here as he ended up in a pair with Paul on the road doing what Jesus said: staying wherever they were offered hospitality, going to many of the nations of the known world and using his skills as a physician when they met people in need of healing.

Luke's life reminds us that Christian vocation is not so much about doing something religious as it is about finding ways to use our particular circumstances, gifts and skills in God's service wherever we are. It is about putting up with difficult people, hanging in when it would be easier to drop out, keeping going, accepting changes in the direction of life when circumstances demand it. In Luke's case it is about literally going the extra mile for God.

There is a lot behind those five words, 'Only Luke is with me.' It is the story of a lifetime given to God. We can thank God for Luke's example and set out to follow it.

Simon and Jude the Apostles

28 October

Isaiah 28.14–16; Ephesians 2.19–end; John 15.17–end

PASSION, NOT FANATICISM

Almighty God, who built your Church upon the foundation of the apostles and prophets, with Jesus Christ himself as the chief cornerstone: so join us together in unity of spirit by their doctrine, that we may be made a holy temple acceptable to you; through Jesus Christ our Lord. Amen.

Today the Church remembers two disciples defined by who they are not: not Simon Peter or Judas Iscariot. Anyone living in the shadow of someone else with their name has their own patron saints!

Perhaps unsurprisingly, we know little about them. Simon was known as 'Simon the Cananaean' or 'Simon the Zealot', possibly because he was a member of the Zealots, Jewish freedom fighters not averse to seeing off the odd Roman in a dark alley, or because he was zealous for the Jewish law but without any connotation of extremism. To avoid any confusion John describes Jude as 'Judas, not Iscariot' while Matthew and Mark use another name altogether, Thaddaeus. If he wrote the letter of Jude, then, influenced by Jewish eschatological thought, he yearned for the day of the Lord to right all wrongs. His religious zeal would be strong, perhaps verging on the fanatical, making the zealot Simon a kindred spirit.

Somewhere in history Jude became the patron saint of desperate or lost causes. It has been suggested that is because, to avoid any possible confusion with Judas Iscariot, people avoided invoking the aid of anyone called Judas until they were totally desperate, or because his epistle stresses that the Christians should persevere in difficult circumstances. History tells us that people with lost or desperate causes can be violent in their desperation but, in contrast, Jude discouraged persecuted Christians from violence, exhorting faithfulness to God (Jude 20–21).

What we do know is that Simon and Jude were with Jesus from the beginning and stuck with him faithfully without shining in the limelight for good or ill. When Jesus was being somewhat obscure the night before he died, Jude asked, 'Lord, how is it that you will reveal yourself to us and not to the world?' (John 14.22). Since both the question and questioner are remembered, it seems the others were glad he asked. If you or I were to go down in history for asking one important question, what would we want that to be?

The answer Jesus gave to Jude centred on loving him and keeping his word. After Jesus' death, what did these zealous disciples do with their passion? Unlike

420   SAINTS AND FESTIVALS

Judas Iscariot, they both made the leap from religious fanaticism to passion for the way of Jesus who suffered and died. They are associated with the proclamation of the gospel in several countries from Libya to Armenia, including Persia where both were martyred around AD 65, Simon (gruesomely) by being sawn in two. Their passion for the kingdom of God led to passionate action, and any latent Jewish nationalism was recast as passion for all nations to hear the gospel.

The question of how we direct our zeal and passion is a topical issue in the world today, most obviously in the decisions some people make to use violence to pursue their ends. But what of the violence of words which can be used destructively everywhere from politics to domestic disputes, including, to our shame, the Church? Simon and Jude's conversion to being passionate disciples rather than violent religious fanatics was testimony to the power of the gospel to transform not their passion – that was never quenched – but their pattern of living. They give us an example to emulate, of zeal directed to godly ends.

Most of us are fairly ordinary people who want to be faithful to God day by day and who have ideals and causes about which we are passionate. Our faith should be among them. In the midst of daily discipleship, what is God calling us to do with our passion? That affects decisions about our whole lives: careers, money, time. Maybe we need to rediscover our passions if they have been lost in the routine plod of daily life. If we experience the desolation Jesus described in the Gospel, or if despair or loneliness tempt us to give up as a lost cause, then the reading from Ephesians reminds us we are members of the household of God, built together spiritually into a dwelling place for God on the foundation of people like Simon and Jude, with Christ Jesus as the cornerstone. Simon and Jude would never have anticipated that future when they first followed Jesus in the shadow of better-known namesakes.

Andrew the Apostle and Patron Saint of Scotland

30 November

Isaiah 52.7–10; Romans 10.12–18; Matthew 4.18–22

THE MAN WHO MADE INTRODUCTIONS

Almighty God, who gave such grace to your apostle Saint Andrew that he readily obeyed the call of your Son Jesus Christ and brought his brother with him: call us by your holy word, and give us grace to follow you without delay and to tell the good news of your kingdom; through Jesus Christ our Lord. Amen.

If we remember Andrew for anything, surely it should be for his ability to bring other people to Jesus. He does it on three recorded occasions and we must assume that they were just some of many such introductions brokered by Andrew.

First, he brought his own brother. Although we read the Gospel account of Jesus calling Simon Peter and Andrew to follow him, from their instant response and the account in John's Gospel it appears they already knew him. The lakeside call emerged from an existing friendship, calling them to deeper commitment to him. In John's account (John 1.35–42) Andrew was already one of John the Baptist's followers. This suggests he was actively seeking more in his religious life than mere attendance at the local synagogue, Andrew was seeking deeper commitment to God. So when John pointed out Jesus as the Lamb of God, Andrew and his companion followed Jesus and effectively invited themselves to tea – asking where someone was staying indicated a desire to follow them. John is remarkably precise in saying that it was around four o'clock and they stayed with Jesus that day. Convinced that Jesus was the Messiah, Andrew promptly went to find his brother and introduced him to Jesus.

Jesus then met Philip who was from Bethsaida where Andrew lived, and the subsequent association of Andrew and Philip suggests they were friends. That led to the second introduction when, much later, some Greek people came to Philip (whose name suggests Greek ancestry) asking to see Jesus. Philip found Andrew and the two of them went to make the introductions to Jesus. Something about that encounter was significant for Jesus who immediately spoke of his death.

Andrew made another significant introduction when Jesus bemused the 12 disciples by asking them where they were going to find bread to feed the crowd of 5,000 people. Philip responded saying practically that six months' wages would not solve the problem, but Andrew produced a boy with five barley loaves and two fish. He admitted it wasn't much but at least he offered it. And the rest is history.

So Andrew was a man who made introductions to the man he had come to know as the Messiah, the answer to his religious yearnings. What else do we know about Andrew? He was one of the four men called by Jesus to leave their fishing businesses in order to follow him. In one version of the story he was mending his nets, in another he was casting them into the sea. Either way, he was a hands-on worker in the family business. The other three men, Peter, James and John, became a trio who were particularly close to Jesus; Andrew appears as the odd one out who seems to have teamed up with Philip. Only once, not long before Jesus' death when he had spoken of the destruction of the Temple, is Andrew named along with Peter, James and John as being part of a private conversation with Jesus after they asked him when this destruction would happen. Otherwise, he was prepared to be overshadowed by his brother and his friends and instead carved out his own way of discipleship.

Christian tradition indicates Andrew travelled as far as Kiev and Novgorod (in addition to Scotland, he is patron saint of Ukraine, Russia and Romania) and in the other direction to Greece where he was eventually martyred by crucifixion. His X-shaped cross (since he did not consider himself worthy of the same cross as his Lord) is probably a medieval tradition.

The lectionary readings celebrate the proclamation of the gospel throughout the world and allude to Andrew's Greek connections – his name, like that of his friend Philip, has Greek derivations. The Epistle stresses that there is no distinction between Jew and Greek, which was a radical theological thought for most of the early Church but perhaps not for Andrew. So we pray to be as ready as Andrew to follow Jesus without second thought and to proclaim the gospel. We could do that by introducing the people we know to Jesus.

Bibliography

Bailey, Kenneth, 2008, *Jesus through Middle Eastern Eyes*, London: SPCK.

St Benedict, 1980, *The Rule of St Benedict in English*, Collegeville: Liturgical Press.

Bonhoeffer, Dietrich, 1937, 2001, *The Cost of Discipleship*, London: SCM Press.

Bonhoeffer, Dietrich, 1953, *Letters and Papers from Prison*, London: SCM Press.

Boulding, Maria, 1982, *A Touch of God*, London: SPCK.

Brown, Rosalind, 2001, *How Hymns Shape our Lives*, Cambridge: Grove Books.

Bryson, Bill, 2010, *At Home*, London: Doubleday.

Bryson, Bill, 2013, *One Summer, America 1927*, London: Doubleday.

Carroll, Lewis, 1865, *Alice's Adventures in Wonderland* and *Through the Looking Glass*, London: Macmillan.

Casey, Michael, 2005, *Strangers to the City*, Brewster: Paraclete Press.

Cawley, A. C. (ed.), 1974, 1993, *Everyman and Medieval Miracle Plays*, London: J. M. Dent.

Chittister, Joan, 1991, *Wisdom Distilled from the Daily*, London: HarperCollins.

Chittister, Joan, 1992, *The Rule of Benedict*, New York: Crossroad.

de Waal, Esther, 2006, *A Life-Giving Way*, London: Continuum.

Dix, Gregory, 1945, *The Shape of the Liturgy*, London: A & C Black.

Donaldson, Stephen, 1980, *The Wounded Land*, Glasgow: William Collins.

Forrest, Jim, 1997, *Praying with Icons*, Maryknoll, NY: Orbis Books.

Forsythe, P. T., 1909, 1999 (reprint), *The Person and Place of Jesus Christ*, London: The United Reformed Church.

Herbert, George, 1991, *The Complete English Poems*, ed. John Tobin, London: Penguin.

Hillesum, Etty, 1983, *An Interrupted Life: The Diaries of Etty Hillesum*, London: Jonathan Cape.

Hopkins, Gerard Manley, 1985, *Poems and Prose*, London: Penguin.

Jamison, Christopher, 2006, *Finding Sanctuary*, London: Weidenfeld & Nicolson, Orion Books.

Kingsolver, Barbara, 1998, *The Poisonwood Bible*, London: HarperCollins.

Kingsolver, Barbara, 2012, *Flight Behaviour*, London: Faber and Faber.

Lane, Belden, 2007, *The Solace of Fierce Landscapes*, Oxford: Oxford University Press.

Leech, Kenneth, 1994, *We Preach Christ Crucified*, Boston, MA: Cowley.

Lewis, C. S., 1950, *The Lion, the Witch and the Wardrobe,* London: Puffin Books.

Lossky, Vladimir, 1957, 1991, *The Mystical Theology of the Eastern Church*, Cambridge: James Clarke.

Lossky, Vladimir, 1978, *Orthodox Theology*, Yonkers, NY: SVS Press.

Mantel, Hilary, 2012, *Bring up the Bodies*, London: Fourth Estate.

Mayne, Michael, 2006, *The Enduring Melody*, London: Darton Longman and Todd.

Moltmann, Jürgen, 1992, *History and the Triune God*, New York: Crossroad.

Moltmann, Jürgen, 2010, *Sun of Righteousness, Arise!*, London: SCM Press.

Portaro, Sam, 1998, *Brightest and Best*, Boston MA: Cowley.

Ramsey, Michael, 1936, *The Gospel and the Catholic Church*, London: Longmans Green and Co Ltd.

Ramsey, Michael, 1964, *Canterbury Essays and Addresses*, London: SPCK.

Ramsey, Michael, 1974, *Canterbury Pilgrim*, London: SPCK.

Ramsey, Michael, 1982, *Be Still and Know*, London: Collins.

Salbi, Zainab, 2011, 'No Peace without Women', in *Reflections*, New Haven: Yale Divinity School.

Smelik, Klaas A. D. (ed.), Arnold J. Pomerans (trans.), 2002, *The Letters and Diaries of Etty Hillesum 1941–1943*, Grand Rapids: Eerdmans Publishing Company.

Sobrino, Jon, 1990, *Spirituality of Liberation*, Maryknoll, NY: Orbis Books.

Taylor, Jeremy, 1990, 'Jesus Christ the Great Exemplar', in Thomas K. Carroll, *Jeremy Taylor, Selected Works*, Mahwah, NJ: Paulist Press.

Temple, William, 1940, *Readings in St John's Gospel*, London: Macmillan.

Troeger, Thomas, 2010, *Wonder Reborn*, Oxford: Oxford University Press.

Trollope, Anthony, 1868, 1982, *Phineas Finn*, Oxford: Oxford World Classics.

Ware, Kallistos, 1963, 2011, *The Orthodox Church*, London: Penguin.

Williams, Niall, 2008, *John*, London: Bloomsbury.

Woodhouse, Patrick, 2009, *Etty Hillesum: A Life Transformed*, London: Continuum.

Wren, Brian, 1989, *What Language Shall I Borrow?*, New York: Crossroad.

Index of Bible References

Genesis

1.1–5	142
1.3–4	27
1.22	307
1.29	283
1.31	60
1.1—2.3	32
2.4b–9	275
2.5	283
2.7	303
2.15–17	38
2.15–end	275
2.18–24	229
3.8–15	194
3.9	34
3.17–19	32, 89
4.10–12	32
4.24	104
6.3	60
6.11	299
7	60
7.1–5	299
7.1–15	180
7.11–18	299
8	283
8.1–19	62
8.20–22	160
8.20—9.17	64
9.1	307
9.7	160
9.8–17	160
10.18	307
11.1–9	307
12.1–4a	40
12.2	282
12.3	96
12.3	26

14.17–20	146
15.1–6	331
15.1–12	281
15.17–18	281
16.8	94, 279
17.1–7	162
18.1–10a	325
18.18	26
18.20–32	327
22.1–18	182, 301
22.18	26
28.10–17	416
29.30	339
32 307	
32.22–31	351
45.3–11	273
50.15–21	104

Exodus

12.1–4	50
12.5–10	50
12.11–14	50
12.38	227
14.10–31	56
14.10–end	295
16.2–4	211
16.9–15	211
17.1–4	79
17.1–7	42
17.7	230
18.13–26	227
19.2–8a	78
19.16–19	74, 320
20.1–17	164
20.8–11	192
24.1	321
24.12–end	34

24.16	15
25.8	15
31.17	335
32.7–10	64
32.7–14	283, 341
33.7–11a	368
33.18–23	15
34.10	335
34.29–35	277
40.34–35	15

Leviticus

6.2	231
19.1–2	30, 116
19.2	328
19.9–18	30
19.13	231
19.15–18	116
19.23–25	283
19.34	324
21.5	29
21.13	26
21.16–21	228
21.17–23	29

Numbers

6.22–end	372
11.1	70
11.4–6	227
11.10–16	227
11.18–20	227
11.24–29	227
11.24–30	70
11.31–34	227
18.19	26
20.11	74
21.4–9	166, 412

INDEX OF BIBLE REFERENCES

INDEX OF BIBLE REFERENCES   433

INDEX OF BIBLE REFERENCES